A

COLLECTION

OF ALL THE

TREATIES

OF

*PEACE, ALLIANCE AND COMMERCE*

BETWEEN

GREAT BRITAIN

*AND OTHER POWERS*

BY

CHARLES JENKINSON

*First Earl of Liverpool*

IN THREE VOLUMES

VOLUME II

1713 - 1748

[1785]

REPRINTS OF ECONOMIC CLASSICS

AUGUSTUS M. KELLEY · PUBLISHERS

*NEW YORK 1969*

First Edition 1784

Reprinted 1785

( London: *Printed for* J. Debrett, *Opposite Burlington House,*
*Piccadilly,* 1785 )


Reprinted 1969 by

AUGUSTUS M. KELLEY · PUBLISHERS

NEW YORK NEW YORK 10010


SBN 678 00486 2


LIBRARY OF CONGRESS CATALOGUE CARD NUMBER

69-16554


PRINTED IN THE UNITED STATES OF AMERICA
*by* SENTRY PRESS, NEW YORK, N. Y. 10019

A

# COLLECTION

OF ALL THE

# TREATIES

O F

## Peace, Alliance, and Commerce,

BETWEEN

# GREAT-BRITAIN

AND

# OTHER POWERS,

From the Treaty figned at MUNSTER in 1648, to the
Treaties figned at PARIS in 1783.

To which is prefixed,

# A DISCOURSE

ON THE

Conduct of the Government of GREAT-BRITAIN in
refpect to Neutral Nations,

By the Right Hon. CHARLES JENKINSON.

In THREE VOLUMES.

## VOL. II.

From 1713, to 1748.

LONDON:

PRINTED FOR J. DEBRETT, OPPOSITE BURLINGTON
HOUSE, PICCADILLY.

MD,CC,LXXXV.

# C O N T E N T S.
## SECOND VOLUME.

A

# COLLECTION

O F

# TREATIES.

*Treaty of Peace and Friendſhip between the moſt ſerene and moſt potent Princeſs Anne, by the grace of God, Queen of Great Britain, France, and Ireland, and the moſt ſerene and the moſt potent Prince Lewis XIV. the moſt Chriſtian King, concluded at Utrecht the $\frac{3}{11}$ day of $\frac{March}{April}$ 1713. Reprinted from the copy publiſhed by the Queen's ſpecial command.*

I. THAT there be an univerſal perpetual peace, and a true and ſincere friendſhip, between the moſt ſerene and moſt potent Princeſs Anne, Queen of Great Britain, and the moſt ſerene and moſt potent Prince Lewis XIV. the moſt Chriſtian King, and their heirs and ſucceſſors, as alſo the kingdoms, ſtates, and ſubjects of both, as well without as within Europe; and that the ſame be ſo ſincerely and inviolably preſerved and cultivated, that the one do promote the intereſt, honour and advantage of the other, and that a faithful neighbourhood on all ſides, and a ſecure cultivation of peace and friendſhip, do daily flouriſh again and encreaſe.

II. That all enmities, hoſtilities, diſcords, and wars, between the ſaid Queen of Great Britain, and the ſaid moſt Chriſtian King, and their ſubjects, do ceaſe and be aboliſhed, ſo that on both ſides they do wholly refrain and deſiſt from all plundering, depredation, harmdoing, injuries, and annoyance whatſoever, as well by land, as by ſea and freſh water, in all parts of the world, and chiefly through all tracts, dominions, and places, of what kind ſoever, of the kingdoms, countries, and territories of either ſide.

III. All

III. All offences, injuries, harms, and damages, which the aforesaid Queen of Great Britain, and her subjects, or the aforesaid most Christian King, and his subjects, have suffered, the one from the other, during this war, shall be buried in oblivion, so that neither on account, or under pretence thereof, or of any other thing, shall either hereafter, or the subjects of either, do, or give, cause, or suffer to be done or given to the other, any hostility, enmity, molestation or hindrance, by themselves or by others, secretly or openly, directly or indirectly, under colour of right, or by way of fact.

IV. Furthermore, for adding a greater strength to the peace which is restored, and to the faithful friendship which is never to be violated, and for cutting off all occasions of distrust, which might at any time arise from the established right and order of the hereditary succession to the crown of Great Britain, and the limitation thereof by the laws of Great Britain, (made and enacted in the reigns of the late King William III. of glorious memory, and of the present Queen) to the issue of the abovesaid Queen, and in default thereof, to the most serene Princess Sophia, dowager of Brunswick-Hanover, and her heirs, in the Protestant line of Hanover. That therefore the said succession may remain safe and secure, the most Christian King sincerely and solemnly acknowledges the abovesaid limitation of the succession to the kingdom of Great Britain, and on the faith and word of a king, on the pledge of his own and his successors honour, he does declare and engage, that he accepts and approves the same, and that his heirs and successors do and shall accept and approve the same for ever. And under the same obligation of the word and honour of a king, the most Christian King promises, that no one besides the Queen herself, and her successors, according to the series of the said limitation, shall ever by him, or by his heirs or successors, be acknowledged, or reputed to be King or Queen of Great Britain. And for adding more ample credit to the said acknowledgment and promises the most Christian King does engage, that whereas the person who, in the life-time of the late King James II.

did

did take upon him the title of Prince of Wales, and fince his deceafe, that of King of Great Britain, is lately gone, of his own accord, out of the Kingdom of France, to refide in fome other place, he the aforefaid moft Chriftian King, his heirs and fucceffors, will take all poffible care, that he fhall not at any time hereafter, or under any pretence whatfoever, return into the kingodm of France, or any the dominion's thereof.

Moreover, the moft Chriftian King promifes, as well in his own name, as in that of his heirs and fucceffors, that they will at no time whatever difturb, or give any moleftation to the Queen of Great Britain, her heirs and fucceffors, defcended from the aforefaid Proteftant line, who poffefs the crown of Great Britain, and the dominions belonging thereunto. Neither will the aforefaid moft Chriftian King, or any one of his heirs, give at any time any aid, fuccour, favour, or council, directly or indirectly, by land or by fea, in money, arms, ammunition, warlike provifion, fhips, foldiers, feamen, or any other way, to any perfon or perfons, whofoever they be, who for any caufe, or under any pretext whatfoever, fhould hereafter endeavour to oppofe the faid fucceffion, either by open war, or by fomenting feditions, and forming confpiracies againft fuch Prince or Princes who are in poffeffion of the throne of Great Britain, by virtue of the act of parliament aforementioned, or againft the Prince or Princefs, to whom the fucceffion of the crown of Great Britain fhall be open, according to the faid acts of parliament.

VI. Whereas the moft deftructive flame of war, which is to be extinguifhed by this peace, arofe chiefly from thence, that the fecurity and liberties of Europe could by no means bear the union of the kingdoms of France and Spain under one and the fame king; and whereas it has at lenghth been brought to pafs, by the affiftance of the divine power, upon the moft earneft inftances of her facred royal Majefty of Great Britain, and with the confent both of the moft Chriftian, and of the Catholic King, that this evil fhould in all times to come be obviated, by means of renunciations drawn in the moft moſt effectual form, and executed in the moſt ſolemn manner, the tenor whereof is as follows:

*Letters Patents by the King, which admit the renunciation of the King of Spain to the crown of France, and thoſe of M. the Duke of Berry, and of M. the Duke of Orleans, to the crown of Spain.*

LEWIS, by the grace of God, King of France and Navarre, to all people preſent, and to come, greeting. During the various revolutions of a war, wherein we have fought only to maintain the juſtice of the rights of the King, our moſt dear and moſt beloved grandſon, to the monarchy of Spain, we have never ceaſed to deſire peace. The greateſt ſucceſſes did not at all dazzle us, and the contrary events, which the hand of God made uſe of to try us, rather than to deſtroy us, did not give birth to that deſire in us, but found it there. But the time marked out by divine Providence for the repoſe of Europe was not yet come; the diſtant fear of ſeeing one day our crown, and that of Spain, upon the head of one and the ſame prince, did always make an equal impreſſion on the powers, which were united againſt us; and this fear, which had been the principal cauſe of the war, ſeemed alſo to lay an inſuperable obſtacle in the way to peace. At laſt, after many fruitleſs negociations, God being moved with the ſufferings and groans of ſo many people, was pleaſed to open a ſurer way to come at ſo difficult a peace. But the ſame alarms ſtill ſubſiſting, the firſt and principal condition, which was propoſed to us by our moſt dear and moſt beloved ſiſter the Queen of Great Britain, as the eſſential and neceſſary foundation of treating, was, that the King of Spain, our ſaid brother and grandſon, keeping the monarchy of Spain and of the Indies, ſhould renounce for himſelf, and his deſcendants for ever, the rights which his birth might at any time give him and them to our crown; that on the other hand, our moſt dear and moſt beloved grandſon the Duke of Berry, and our moſt dear and moſt beloved nephew the Duke of Orleans, ſhould likewiſe renounce for themſelves, and for their deſcendants male and female for ever, their rights to the monarchy of

Spain

Spain and the Indies. Our faid fifter caufed it to be reprefented unto us, that without a formal and pofitive affurance upon this point, which alone could be the bond of peace, Europe would never be at reft; all the powers which fhare the fame, being equally perfuaded, that it was for their general intereft, and for their common fecurity, to continue a war, whereof no one could forefee the end, rather than be expofed to behold the fame Prince become one day mafter of two monarchies, fo powerful as thofe of France and Spain. But as this princefs,(whofe indefatigable zeal for re-eftablifhing the general tranquility,we cannot fufficiently praife)was fenfible of all the reluctancy we had to confent, that one of our children fo worthy to inherit the fucceffion of our forefathers, fhould neceffarily be excluded from it, if the misfortunes wherewith it has pleafed God to afflict us in our family, fhould moreover take from us, in the perfon of the Dauphin, our moft dear and moft beloved great grandfon, the only remainder of thofe princes which our kingdom has fo juftly lamented with us; fhe entered into our pain, and after having jointly fought out gentler means of fecuring the peace, we agreed with our faid fifter to propofe to the king of Spain other dominions, inferior indeed to thofe which he poffeffes, yet the value thereof would fo much the more increafe under his reign, in as much as in that cafe he would preferve his rights, and annex to our crown a part of the faid dominions, if he came one time or other to fucceed us. We employed therefore the ftrongeft reafons to perfuade him to accept this altetnative. We gave him to underftand, that the duty of his birth was the firft which he ought to confult; that he owed himfelf to his houfe, and to his country, before he was obliged to Spain; that if he were wanting to his firft engagements, he would perhaps one day in vain regret his having abandoned thofe rights, which he would be no more able to maintain. We added to thefe reafons, the perfonal motives of friendfhip, and of tender love which we thought likely to move him; the pleafure we fhould have in feeing him from time to time near us, and in paffing fome part of our days with him, which we might promife ourfelves from the neighbourhood

of

of the dominions that were offered him, the fatisfaction of inftructing him ourfelves concerning the ftate of our affairs, and of relying upon him for the future; fo that, if God fhould preferve to us the Dauphin, we could give our kingdom, in the perfon of the King our brother, and grandfon, a regent inftructed in the art of government; and that if this child, fo precious to us and to our fub-jects, were alfo taken from us, we fhould at leaft have the confolation of leaving to our people a virtuous King, fit to govern them, and who would likewife annex to our crown very confiderable dominions. Our inftances reite-rated with all the force, and with all the tender affection neceffary to perfuade a fon, who fo juftly deferves thofe efforts, which we made for preferving him to France, produced nothing but reiterated refufals on his part, ever to abandon fuch brave and faithful fubjects, whofe zeal for him had been diftinguifhed in thofe conjunctures, when his throne feemed to be the moft fhaken. So that perfifting with an invincible firmnefs in his firft refolu-tion, afferting likewife, that it was more glorious, and more advantageous for our houfe, and for our kingdom, than that which we preffed him to take, he declared in the meeting of the ftates of the kingdom of Spain, affem-bled at Madrid for that purpofe, that for obtaining a general peace, and fecuring the tranquillity of Europe by a balance of power, he of his own proper motion, of his own free will, and without any conftraint, renounced for himfelf, his heirs and fucceffors, for ever and ever, all pretenfions, rights and titles, which he, or any of his defcendants, have at prefent, or may have at any time to come whatfoever, to the fucceffion of our crown; that he held for ever excluded therefrom himfelf, his children, heirs, and defcendants, for ever; that he confented for himfelf and for them, that now, as well as then, his right and that of his defcendants, fhould pafs over and be transferred to him among the Princes, whom the law of fucceffion, and the order of birth calls, or fhall call to inherit our crown in default of our faid brother and grandfon the King of Spain, and of his defcendants, as it is more amply fpecified in the act of renunciation, ap-proved by the ftates of his kingdom; and confequently he

he declared, that he defifted particularly from the right
which hath been added to that of his birth, by our letters patents of the month of December, 1700, whereby
we declared, that it was our will, that the King of Spain
and his defcendants fhould always preferve the rights of
their birth and original, in the fame manner as if they
refided actually in our kingdom; and from the regiftry
which was made of our faid letters patents, both in our
court of Parliament, and in our chamber of Accounts at
Paris. We are fenfible, as King, and as father, how
much it were to be defired, that the general peace could
have been concluded without a renunciation, which
makes fo great a change in our royal houfe, and in the
ancient order of fucceeding to our crown; but we are
yet more fenfible, how much it is our duty to fecure
fpeedily to our fubjects a peace which is fo neceffary for
them. We fhall never forget the efforts which they
made for us during the long continuance of a war, which
we could not have fupported, if their zeal had not been
much more extenfive than their power. The welfare of
a people fo faithful, is to us a fupreme law, which ought
to be preferred to any other confideration. It is to this
law that we this day facrifice the right of a grandfon who
is fo dear to us; and by the price which the general peace
will coft our tender love, we fhall at leaft have the comfort
of fhewing our fubjects, that even at the expence of our
blood, they will always keep the firft place in our heart.

For thefe caufes, and other important confiderations
us thereunto moving, after having feen in our council
the faid act of renunciation of the King of Spain, our
faid brother and grandfon, of the fifth of November laft,
as alfo the acts of renunciation, which our faid grandfon
the Duke of Berry, and our faid nephew the Duke of Orleans, made reciprocally of their rights to the crown of
Spain, as well for themfelves as for their defcendants, male
and female, in confequence of the renunciation of our faid
brother and grandfon the King of Spain, the whole hereunto annexed, with a copy collated of the faid letters patents of the month of December, 1700, under the counter-
feal of our chancery, of our fpecial grace, full power, and
royal authority, we have declared, decreed, and ordained,
and

and by thefe prefents figned with our hand, we do declare,
decree, and ordain, we will, and it is our pleafure, that the
faid act of renunciation of our faid brother and grandfon
the King of Spain, and thofe of our faid grandfon the Duke
of Berry, and o? our faid nephew the Duke of Orleans,
which we have admitted, and do admit, be regiftered in all
our courts of Parliament, and chambers of our Accounts
in our kingdom, and other places where it fhall be neceffary, in order to their being executed according to their
form and tenor. And confequently we will and intend,
that our faid letters patents of the month of December,
1700, be and remain null, and as if they had never
been made, that they be brought back to us, and that in
the margin of the regifters of our faid court of Parliament, and of our faid chamber of Accounts, where the en-
rolment of the faid letters patents is, the extract of thefe
prefents be placed and inferted, the better to fignify our
intention, as to the revocation and nullity of the faid
letters. We will, that in conformity to the faid act of renunciation of our faid brother and grandfon the King of
Spain, he be from henceforth looked upon and confidered as excluded from our fucceffion, that his heirs, fucceffors, and defcendants, be likewife excluded for ever, and
looked upon as incapable of enjoying the fame. We underftand, that in failure of them, all rights to our faid
crown, and fucceffion to our dominions, which might at
any time whatfoever belong and appertain to them, be and
remain transferred to our moft dear, and moft beloved
grandfon the Duke of Berry, and to his children, and
defcendants, being males, born in lawful marriage ; and
fucceffively in failure of them, to thofe of the Princes of
our royal houfe and their defcendants, who in right of
their birth, or by the order eftablifhed fince the foundation of our monarchy, ought to fucceed to our crown.
And fo we command our beloved and trufty counfellors, the Members of our court of Parliament at Paris,
that they do caufe thefe prefents, together with the acts of
renunciation made by our faid brother and grandfon the
King of Spain, by our faid grandfon the Duke of Berry,
and by our faid nephew the Duke of Orleans, to be read,
publifhed, and regiftered, and the contents thereof to be
kept,

kept, obferved, and executed, according to their form and tenor, fully, peaceably, and perpetually ceafing and caufing to ceafe, all moleftations and hindrances, notwithftanding any laws, ftatutes, ufages, cuftoms, decrees, regulations, and other matters contrary thereunto; whereto, and to the derogations of the derogations therein contained, we have derogated, and do derogate by thefe prefents, for this purpofe only, and without being brought into precedent. For fuch is our pleafure.

And to the end that this may be a matter firm and lafting for ever, we have caufed our feal to be affixed to thefe prefents. Given at Verfailles, in the month of March, in the year of our Lord 1713, and of our reign the 70th. Signed *Lewis*, and underneath by the King, *Phelypeaux*. *Vifa, Phelypeaux.* And fealed with the great feal on green wax, with ftrings of red and green filk.

Read and publifhed, the court being affembled, and regiftered among the rolls of the court, the King's Attorney-general being heard, and moving for the fame, to the end that they may be executed according to their form and tenor, in purfuance of, and in conformity to the acts of this day. At Paris, in Parliament, the 15th of March, 1713. Signed *DONGOIS.*

## THE KING.

WHEREAS, on the fifth of November in this prefent year, 1712, before Don Manuel of Vadillo and Velafco, my Secretary of State, and chief notary of the kingdoms of Caftile and Leon, and witneffes, I delivered, fwore to, and figned a public inftrument of the tenor following, which is word for word as here enfues:

Don Philip, by the grace of God, King of Caftile, Leon, Arragon, the Two Sicilies, Jerufalem, Navarre, Granada, Toledo, Valentia, Galicia, Majorca, Seville, Sardinia, Corduba, Corfica, Murcia, Jaen, the Algarves, Algezira, Gibraltar, the Canary Iflands, the Eaft and Weft-Indies, the Iflands and Terra Firma of the Ocean, Archduke of Auftria, Duke of Burgundy, Brabant, and Milan, Count of Habfpurg, Flanders, Tirol, and Barcelona, Lord of Bifcay and Molina, &c. By the account and information of this inftrument and writing of renunciation and relinquifhment,

quifhment, and that it may remain for a perpetual re-
membrance, I do declare and make known to Kings,
Princes, potentates, commonwealths, communities, and particular perfons, which now are, and fhall be in future ages:
that it being one of the principal pofitions of the treaties
of peace, depending between the crowns of Spain, and of
France, with that of England, for the rendering it firm and
lafting, and proceeding to a general one, on a maxim of
fecuring for ever the univerfal good and quiet of Europe,
by an equal weight of power, fo that many being united
in one, the balance of the equality defired might not turn
to the advantage of one, and the danger and hazard of the
reft; it was propofed, and infifted on by England, and it
was agreed to on my part, and on that of the King my
grandfather, that for avoiding at any time whatever the
union of this monarchy with that of France, and the
poffibility that it might happen in any cafe, reciprocal renunciations fhould be made by me, and for all my defcendants, to the poffibility of fucceeding to the monarchy of
France, and on the part of thofe Princes, and of all their
race, prefent and to come, to that of fucceeding to this
monarchy; by forming a proper project of abdication of
all rights which might be claimed by the two royal houfes
of this, and of that monarchy, as to their fucceeding mutually to each other; by feparating, by the legal means of
my renunciation, my branch from the royal ftem of France,
and all the branches of France from the ftem of the blood-
royal of Spain; by taking care, at the fame time, in purfuance of the fundamental and perpetual maxim of the balance of power in Europe, which perfuades and juftifies
the avoiding, in all cafes imaginable, the union of the monarchy of France with that of Spain, that the inconvenience fhould likewife be provided againft, left, in default
of my iffue, the cafe fhould happen that this monarchy
fhould devolve again to the houfe of Auftria, whofe dominions and dependencies, even without the union of the
empire, would make it formidable; a motive which at
other times made it juftifiable to feparate the hereditary
dominions of the houfe of Auftria from the body of the
Spanifh monarchy; it being agreed and fettled to this end
by England with me, and with the King my grandfather,

that

that in failure of me, and of my iffue, the Duke of Savoy, and his fons, and defcendants, being males, born in conftant lawful marriage, are to enter upon the fucceffion of this monarchy; and, in default of his male line, the Prince Armadeo, of Carignan, and his fons, and defcendants, being males, born in conftant lawful marriage; and, in default of his line, Prince Thomas, brother of the Prince of Carignan, his fons, and defcendants, being males, born in conftant lawful marriage, who, as defcendants of the Infanta Donna Catherina, daughter of Philip II. and being exprefsly called, have a clear and known right, fuppofing the friendfhip and perpetual alliance, which the Duke of Savoy, and his defcendants, are to folicit and obtain from this crown; it being to be believed, that by this perpetual and never-ceafing hope, the needle of the balance may remain invariable, and all the powers, wearied with the toil and uncertainty of battles, may be amicably kept in an equal poife; it not remaining in the difpofal of any of the parties to alter this federal equilibrium, by way of any contract of renunciation, or retroceffion, fince the fame reafon which induced its being admitted, demonftrates its permanency, a fundamental conftitution being formed, which may fettle, by an unalterable law, the fucceffion of what is to come. In confequence of what is above faid, and for the love I bear to the Spaniards, and from the knowledge I have of what I owe to them, and the repeated experience of their fidelity, and for making a return to Divine Providence, by this refignation to its deftiny, for the great benefit of having placed and maintained me on the throne, among fuch illuftrious and well-deferving vaffals, I have determined to abdicate, for myfelf, and all my defcendants, the right of fucceeding to the crown of France, defiring not to depart from living and dying with my beloved and faithful Spaniards; leaving to all my defcendants, the infeparable bond of their fidelity and love. And to the end that this refolution may have its due effect, and that the matter may ceafe, which has been looked upon as one of the principal motives of the war which has hitherto afflicted Europe, of my own motion, free, fpontaneous, and unconftrained will, I Don Philip, by the grace of God, King of Caftile, Leon,

Leon, Arragon, the Two Sicilies, Jerusalem, Navarre, Granada, Toledo, Valencia, Galicia, Majorca, Seville, Sardinia, Corduba, Corsica, Murcia, Jaen, the Algarves, Algezira, Gibraltar, the Canary Islands, the East and West-Indies, the Islands and Terra Firma of the Ocean, Archduke of Austria, Duke of Burgundy, Brabant, and Milan, Count of Habspurg, Flanders, Tirol, and Barcelona, Lord of Biscay and Molina, &c. do by this present instrument, for myself, for my heirs and successors, renounce, quit, and relinquish, for ever and ever, all pretensions, rights, and titles, which I have, or any descendant of mine hath at present, or may have at any time to come, to the succession of the crown of France; and I declare, and hold myself for ever excluded and separated, me, and my sons, heirs, and descendants for ever, excluded and disabled absolutely, and without limitation, difference, and distinction of persons, degrees, sexes, and times, from the act and right of succeeding to the crown of France. And I will and consent, for myself, and my said descendants, that now, as well as then, it may be taken to be passed over, and transferred to him, who by mine and their being excluded, disabled, and incapacitated, shall be found next and immediate in degree to the King, by whose death it shall become vacant; and the succession to the said crown of France is at any time, and in any case to be settled on, and given to him, to have and to hold the same as true and lawful successor, in the same manner, as if I, and my descendants, had not been born or been in the world; since for such are we to be held and esteemed, because in my person, and in that of my descendants, there is no consideration to be had, or foundation to be made of active or passive representation, beginning, or continuation of lineage effective, or contentive of substance, blood, or quality; nor can the descent, or computation of degrees of those persons, be derived from the most Christian King, my lord and grandfather, nor from the Dauphin my father, nor from the glorious Kings their progenitors; nor by any other means can they come into the succession, nor take possession of the degree of proximity, and exclude from it the person, who, as is abovesaid, shall be found next in degree. I

will

will and confent for myfelf, and for my defcendants, that from this time, as well as then, this right be looked upon and confidered as paffed over, and transferred to the Duke of Berry my brother, and to his fons and defcendants, being males, born in conftant lawful marriage; and in default of his male iffue, to the Duke of Orleans my uncle, and to his fons and defcendants, being males, born in conftant lawful marriage; and in default of his iffue, to the Duke of Bourbon my coufin, and to his fons, and defcendants, beidg males, born in conftant lawful marriage; and in like manner fucceffively to all the Princes of the Blood of France, their fons, and defcendants, being males, for ever and ever, according to the place and order in which they fhall be called to the crown by right of their birth; and confequently to that perfon among the faid Princes, who (I and all my faid defcendants being, as is above-faid, excluded, difabled, and incapacitated) fhall be found the neareft in immediate degree after that King, by whofe death the vacancy of the crown of France fhall happen, and to whom the fucceffion ought to belong at any time, and in any cafe whatfoever, that he may poffefs the fame as true and lawful fucceffor, in the fame manner as if I, and my defcendants, had not been born. And for the greater ftrength of this act of abdication of all the rights and titles, which appertained to me, and to all my fons and defcendants, of fucceeding to the aforefaid crown of France, I depart from, and relinquifh efpecially that which might moreover accrue to the rights of birth from the letters patants, or inftrument, whereby the King my grandfather preferved and referved to me, and enabled me to enjoy the right of fucceffion to the crown of France, which inftrument was difpatched at Verfailles in the month of December, in the year 1700, and paffed, and approved, and regiftered by the Parliament. I will that it cannot ferve me for a foundation to the purpofes therein provided for, and I reject and renounce it, and hold it for null, void, and of no force, and for cancelled, and as if no fuch inftrument had ever been executed. I promife and oblige myfelf, on the faith of a King's word, that as much as fhall relate to my part, and that of my fons and defcendants, which are and fhall be, I will take care of the obfervation

and

and accomplishment of this writing, without permitting or consenting that any thing be done contrary thereunto, directly or indirectly, in the whole, or in part; and I relinquish and depart from all and all manner of remedies, known or unknown, ordinary or extraordinary, and which by common right, or special privilege might belong to us, to me, and to my sons and descendants, to reclaim, mention, or alledge against what is abovesaid; and I renounce them all, and especially that of evident prejudice, enormous, and most enormous, which may be reckoned to have happened in this relinquishment and renunciation of the right of being able, at any time, to succeed to the crown aforementioned. I will that none of the said remedies, nor others, of whatsoever name, use, importance, and quality they may be, do avail us, or can avail us. And if in fact, or under any colour we should endeavour to seize the said kingdom by force of arms, by making, or moving war, offensive or defensive, from this time for ever, that is to be held, judged, and declared, for an unlawful, unjust, and wrongfully-undertaken war, and for violence, invasion, and usurpation, done against reason and conscience; and on the contrary, that is to be judged and esteemed a just, lawful, and allowed war, which shall be made, or moved in behalf of him, who by the exclusion of me, and of my said sons and descendants, ought to succeed to the said crown of France, to whom the subjects and natives thereof are to apply themselves, and to obey him, to take and perform the oath and homage of fealty, and to serve him as their lawful King and Lord. And the relinquishment and renunciation, for me, and my said sons and descendants, is to be firm, stable, valid, and irrevocable perpetually, for ever and ever. And I declare and promise, that I have not made, neither will I make any protestation, or reclaiming, in public, or in secret, to the contrary, which may hinder, or diminish the force of what is contained in this writing; and that if I should make it, although it be sworn to, it is not to be valid, neither can it have any force; and for the greater strength and security of what is contained in this renunciation, and of what is said and promised on my part therein, I give

again

again the pledge of my faith, and royal word, and I fwear folemnly by the gofpels contained in this miffal, upon which I lay my right hand, that I will obferve, maintain, and accomplifh this act and inftrument of renunciation, as well for myfelf as for all my fucceffors, heirs, and defcendants, in all the claufes therein contained, according to the moft natural, literal, and plain fenfe and conftruction; and that I have not fought, neither will I feek any difpenfation from this oath; and if it fhall be fought for by any particular perfon, or fhall be granted *motu proprio*, I will not ufe it, nor take any advantage of it. Nay, in fuch cafe as that it fhould be granted me, I make another the like oath, that there may always be and remain one oath above and beyond all difpenfations which may be granted me. And I deliver this writing before the prefent fecretary, notary of this my kingdom, and I have figned it, and commanded it to be fealed with my royal feal; there being provided, and called as witneffes, the Cardinal Don Francifco de Judice, inquifitor general, and Archbifhop of Montreal, one of my council of ftate; Don Jofeph Fernandez, of Velafco and Tobar, conftable of Caftile, Duke of Frias, gentleman of my chamber, my high fteward of my houfhold, great cup-bearer, and great huntfman; Don Juan Claros Alphonfo Perez de Gufman el Bueno, Duke of Medinf Sidonia, Knight of the order of the Holy Ghoft, my great mafter of horfe, gentleman of my chamber, and one of my council of ftate; Don Francifco Andres de Benavides, Count of Santiftevan, one of my council of ftate, and high fteward to the Queen; Don Carlos Homodei Laco de la Vega, Marquis of Almonacir, and Count of Cafa Palma, gentleman of my chamber, one of my council of ftate, and great mafter of the horfe to the Queen; Don Reftayno Cantelmo, Duke of Popoli, knight of the order of the Holy Ghoft, gentleman of my chamber, and captain of my Italian life-guards; Don Fernando of Aragon and Moncada, Duke of Montalto, Marquis of los Velez, commander of the Silla and Benaful in the order of Monteffa, gentleman of my chamber and one of my council of ftate; Don Antonio Sebaftian de Toledo, Marquis of Manfera, gentleman of my chamber, one of my council of ftate, and prefident of that of Italy; Don

Juan

Juan Domingo, of Haro and Guzman, great commander in the order of St. James, one of my council of ſtate; Don Joachim Ponce de Leon, Duke of Arcos, gentleman of my chamber, great commander in the order of Calatrava, one of my council of ſtate; Don Domingo de Giudice, Duke of Giovenazzo, one of my council of ſtate; Don Manuel Coloma, Marquis of Canales, gentleman of my chamber, one of my council of ſtate; and captain general of the artillery of Spain; Don Joſeph de Solis, Duke of Montellano, one of my council of ſtate; Don Rodrigo Manuel Manrique de Lara, Count of Frigiliana, gentleman of my chamber, one of my council of ſtate, and preſident of that of the Indies; Don Iſidora de la Cueva, Marquis of Bedmar, knight of the order of the Holy Ghoſt, gentleman of my chamber, one of my council of ſtate, preſident of that of the orders, and firſt miniſter of war; Don Franciſco Ronquillo Briceno, Count of Gramedo, Governor of my council of Caſtille; Don Lorenzo Armangual, biſhop of Gironda, one of my council, and chamber of Caſtille, and governor of that of the revenues; Don Carlos de Borja and Centellas, patriarch of the Indies, one of my council of the orders, my chaplain and great almoner, and vicar-general of my armies; Don Martin de Guzman, Marquis of Montealegre, gentleman of my chamber, and captain of my guard of halberdiers; Don Pedro de Toledo Sarmiento, Count of Gondomar, one of my council, and chamber of Caſtille; Don Franciſco Rodrigues de Mendaroſqueta, commiſſary general of the Cruzada; and Don Melchior de Avellaneda, Marquis of Valdecanas, one of my council of war, and director general of the infantry of Spain.

*I THE KING.*

NOW in regard to the federal conventions, whereof mention is made in the ſaid inſtrument here inſerted, and to the end it may appear authentically to all the parties where it appertains, and who may pretend to make uſe of the contents thereof; and for all the effects which may take place in right, and which may be derived from the delivery hereof, under the clauſes, conditions, and ſuppoſitions therein contained, I have commanded theſe
preſents

prefents to be made out, figned with my hand, and fealed with the feal of my royal arms, and counterfigned by my underwritten fecretary of ftate, and chief notary of thefe my kingdoms, at Buen Retiro, the feventh of November, 1712.

(L. S.) *I THE KING,*
*Manuel de Vadillo y Velafco.*

Read and publifhed, the court being affembled, and regiftered in the rolls of the court, the King's advocate general being heard, and moving for the fame, to the end that it may be executed according to the form and tenor thereof, in purfuance of, and in conformity to the acts of this day: at Paris in parliament, the 15th of March, 1713.
*Signed* *DONGOIS.*

CHARLES, fon of France, Duke of Berry, Alenfon, and Angoulefme, Vifcount of Vernon, Andely, and Gifors, Lord of the chantellenies of Coignac and Merpins; to all kings, princes, commonwealths, communities, and to all other bodies, and private perfons, prefent and to come, be it known. All the powers of Europe finding themfelves almoft ruined on account of the prefent wars, which have carried defolation to the frontiers, and into many other parts of the richeft monarchies, and other dominions, it has been agreed in the conferences and treaties, of peace, which are negotiating with Great Britain, to eftablifh an equilibrium, and political boundaries between the kingdoms, whereof the interefts have been, and are ftill the fad occafion of a bloody difpute; and to hold it for a fundamental maxim in order to preferve this peace, that provifion ought to be made, that the forces of thefe kingdoms may not become formidable, nor be able to caufe any jealoufy, which, it has been thought cannot be fettled more folidly, than by hindering them from extending themfelves, and by keeping a certain proportion, to the end that the weaker being united together, may defend themfelves againft the more powerful, and fupport themfelves refpectively againft their equals.

For this purpofe the King, our moft honored Lord and grandfather, and the King of Spain, our moft dear brother, have agreed and concluded with the Queen of Great Britain,

Britain, that reciprocal renunciations fhall be made by all
the princes, both prefent and to come, of the crown of
France, and of that of Spain, of all rights, which may
appertain to each of them, to the fucceffion of the one,
or of the other kingdom, by eftablifhing an habitual right
to the fucceffion to the crown of Spain, in that line which
fhall be made capable thereof, and declared immediate
after that of King Philip V. our brother, by the eftates of
Spain, who were to affemble for this purpofe ; by making
an immoveable balance to maintain the equilibrium, which
is intended to be placed in Europe, and by going on to
particularize all the cafes of union which are forefeen, to
ferve as an example for all fuch as may happen. It has
likewife been agreed and concluded between the King, our
moft honored Lord and grandfather, King Philip V. our
brother, and the Queen of Great Britain, that the faid
King Philip fhall renounce for himfelf, and for all his defcendants, the hopes of fucceeding to the crown of France ;
that on our fide we fhall renounce in like manner for us,
and for our defcendants, the crown of Spain ; that the
Duke of Orleans, our moft dear uncle, fhall do the fame
thing ; fo that all the lines of France and of Spain, refpectively and relatively, fhall be excluded for ever, and
by all kind of ways, from all the right, which the lines of
France might have to the crown of Spain, and the lines
of Spain to the crown of France ; and laftly, that care
fhall be taken, that under pretence of the faid renunciations, or under any other pretence whatfoever, the houfe
of Auftria may not make ufe of the pretenfions, which it
might have to the fucceffion of the monarchy of Spain ;
forafmuch as by uniting this monarchy to the hereditary
countries and dominions of that houfe, it would become
formidable, even without the union of the empire, to the
other powers, which are between both, and which would
find themfelves as it were furrounded ; which would de-
ftroy the equality, that is eftablifhing at prefent, to fecure
and ftrengthen more perfectly the peace of Chriftendom,
and to take away all manner of jealoufy from the powers
of the North, and of the Weft, which is the end that is
propofed by this political equilibrium, by removing and
excluding all thefe branches, and calling to the crown of

Spain,

Spain, in default of the lines of King Philip V. our brother, and of all his children and defcendants, the houfe of the Duke of Savoy, which defcends from the infanta Catherina, daughter of Philip II. it having been confidered, that in making the faid houfe of Savoy fucceed immediately in this manner, this equality and balance between the three powers, may be fixed as it were in its centre, without which it would be impoffible to extinguifh the flame of war, which has been kindled, and is capable of deftroying every thing.

Being willing therefore to concur, by our relinquifhment, and by the abdication of all our rights, for us, our fucceffors and defcendants, to the eftablifhing of the univerfal repofe, and the fecuring the peace of Europe, becaufe, we believe, that this method is the fureft, and moft effectual, in the terrible circumftances of this conjuncture, we have refolved to renounce the hopes of fucceeding to the crown of Spain, and all the rights thereunto, which belong to us, and may belong to us, under any title, and by any means whatfoever. And to the end that this refolution may have its full effect, and alfo by reafon that King Philip V. our brother, did on his part, the 5th of this prefent month of November, make his renunciation of the crown of France, we of our meer, free, and frank will, and without being moved thereunto by any refpectful awe, or by any other regard, except thofe abovementioned, to declare, and hold ourfelves from this prefent, we, our children, and defcendants, excluded and difabled abfolutely for ever, without limitation or diftinction of perfons, degrees, or fexes, from every act, and from all right of fucceeding to the crown of Spain. We will, and confent for us, our faid children and defcendants, that from this time, and for ever, we and they, in confequence of thefe prefents, be held to be excluded and difabled, in like manner as all the other defcendants of the houfe of Auftria, who, as it has been faid and fuppofed, ought alfo to be excluded, in whatever degree we may be, both the one and the other ; and if the fucceffion falls to us, our line, that of all our defcendants, and all the others of the houfe of Auftria, as it has been faid, ought to be feparated and excluded therefrom. That for this reafon the

kingdom

kingdom of Spain be accounted as devolved, and transferred to him, to whom in fuch cafe the fucceffion ought to
devolve and be transferred, at any time whatfoever, fo that
we do take and hold him for true and lawful fucceffor, becaufe for the fame reafons and motives, and in confequence of thefe prefents, neither we, nor our defcendants,
ought any more to be confidered as having any foundation of reprefentation active or paffive, or making any
continuation of line effective, or contentive of fubftance,
blood, or quality, or likewife to derive any right from our
defcent, or to reckon our degrees from the perfons of
the Queen Maria Therefa of Auftria, our moft honored
lady and grandmother of the Queen Anne of Auftria, our
moft honored Lady and great-grandmother, or of the glorious
kings their anceftors ; on the contrary, we ratify the claufes
of their wills, and the renunciations made by the faid ladies,
our grandmother and great-grandmother, we renounce likewife the right, which may belong to us, and to our children and defcendants, by virtue of the will of King Charles
II. which, notwithftanding what is abovementioned, calls
us to the fucceffion of the crown of Spain, in cafe of failure of the line of Philip V. We therefore relinquifh this
right, and renounce the fame, for us, our children and
defcendants ; we promife and engage, for us, our faid
children and defcendants, to employ ourfelves with all our
might, in caufing this prefent act to be fulfilled, without
allowing, or fuffering that the fame be violated directly or
indirectly, in the whole, or in part ; and we relinquifh all
means, ordinary or extraordinary, which by common
right, or by any fpecial privilege might belong to us, our
children and defcendants ; which means we likewife renounce abfolutely, and particularly, that of evident, enormous, and moft enormous prejudice, which may be found
in the faid renunciation of the fucceffion to the crown of
Spain. And we will that none of the faid means may, or
can have any effect, and that if, under this pretext, or any
other colour, we fhould poffefs ourfelves of the faid kingdom by force of arms, the war which we fhould make, or
ftir up, be deemed unjuft, unlawful, and unduly undertaken. And on the contrary, that the war, which he fhould
make upon us, who by virtue of this renunciation fhould
have

have right to fucceed to the crown of Spain, be deemed juft and allowable. And that all the fubjects and people of Spain, do acknowledge him, obey him, defend him, do him homage, and fwear fealty to him, as to their king and lawful lord.

And for the greater fecurity of all that we fay and promife for ourfelves, and in the name of our children and defcendants, we fwear folemnly on the Gofpels contained in this miffal, upon which we lay our right hand, that we will keep, maintain, and fulfil the fame in all and every part thereof : that we will never afk to be relieved from the fame, and if any one do afk it for us, or if it be granted us *motu proprio*, we will not make ufe, or take advantage of it. But rather, in cafe it fhould be granted us, we over and above make this other oath, and this fhall fubfift and remain for ever, whatever difpenfations may be granted us. We fwear and promife likewife, that we have not made, neither will we make, in public, or in fecret, any proteftation, or reclamation to the contrary, which may hinder what is contained in thefe prefents, or leffen the force thereof ; and if we fhould make any, whatever oaths they may be accompanied with, they fhall not have any force or virtue, or produce any effect.

In witnefs whereof, and to render thefe prefents authentic, they have been paffed before mafters Alexander le Fevre, and Anthony le Moyne, counfellors to the King, Notaries, Minute-keepers to his Majefty, and Seal-keepers in the Chatelet of Paris, hereunder written, who have wholly delivered this prefent act ; and for caufing thefe prefents to be publifhed and regiftered, wherever it fhall be neceffary, my Lord the Duke of Berry has conftituted the bearers of thefe difpatches, by duplicates thereof, his general and fpecial Attornies to whom my faid Lord has, by thefe faid prefents, given fpecial power and authority in that behalf. At Marly, the 24th day of November, 1712, before noon, and has figned the prefent duplicate, and another, and minute thereof remaining in the hands of the faid Le Moyne, notary.

Signed,                                        C H A R L E S.

*Le Fevre, Le Moyne.*

PHILIP, grandson of France, Duke of Orleans, Valois, Chartres, and Nemours ; to all kings, princes, commonwealths, potentates, communities, and to all persons, as well present as to come, we make known by these presents ; that the fear of the union of the crowns of France and Spain, having been the principal motive of the present war, and the other powers of Europe having always apprehended, left these two crowns should come upon one head, it has been laid down as the foundation of the peace, which is treated of at present, and which it is hoped may be cemented more and more, for the repose of such a number of countries, which have sacrificed themselves, as so many victims, to oppose the dangers, wherewith they thought themselves threatened, that it was necessary to establish a kind of equality and equilibrium between the princes, who were in dispute, and to separate for ever, in an irrevocable manner, the rights which they pretend to have, and which they defended, sword in hand, with a reciprocal slaughter on each side.

That with intent to establish this equality, the Queen of Great Britain proposed, and upon her instances, it has been agreed by the King, our most honored Lord and uncle, and by the Catholic King, our most dear nephew, that for avoiding at any time whatsoever the union of the crowns of France and Spain, reciprocal renunciations should be made, that is to say, by the Catholic King Philip V. our nephew, for himself and for all his descendants, of the succession to the crown of France ; as also by the Duke of Berry, our most dear nephew, and by us, for ourselves, and for all our descendants, of the crown of Spain ; on condition likewise, that neither the house of Austria, nor any of the descendants thereof, shall be able to succeed to the crown of Spain, because this house itself, without the union of the empire, would become formidable, if it should add a new power to its ancient dominions ; and consequently this equilibrium, which is designed to be established for the good of the princes and states of Europe, would cease. Now it is certain, that without this equilibrium, either the states suffer from the weight of their own greatness, or envy engages their neighbours to make alliances to attack them, and to reduce them to such

a point,

a point, that thefe great powers may infpire lefs fear, and may not afpire to an univerfal monarchy.

For attaining the end which is propofed, and by reafon that his Catholic Majefty has on his part made his renunciation, the 5th of this prefent month, we confent that, in failure of Philip V. our nephew, and of his defcendants, the crown of Spain do pafs over to the houfe of the Duke of Savoy, whofe rights are clear and known, inafmuch as he defcends from the infanta Catherina, daughter of Philip II. and as he is called by the other kings his fucceffors ; fo that his right to the fucceffion of Spain, is indifputable.

And we defiring on our fide to concur towards the glorious end, which is propofed for re-eftablifhing the public tranquility, and for preventing the fears which the rights of our birth, or all others, which might appertain unto us, might occafion, have refolved, to make this relinquifhment, this abdication, and this renunciation of all our rights, for ourfelves, and in the name of all our fucceffors and defcendants ; and for the accomplifhing of this refolution, which we have taken of our meer, free, and frank will, we declare and hold ourfelves from this prefent, us, our children and defcendants, for excluded and difabled, abfolutely, and for ever, and without limitation or diftinction of perfons, of degrees, and of fexes, from every act, and from all right of fucceeding to the crown of Spain. We will and confent, for us and our defcendants, that from this time, and for ever, we be held, we and ours, for excluded, difabled, and incapacitated, in whatever degree we may happen to be, and in what manner foever the fucceffion may fall to our line, and to all others, whether of the houfe of France, or of that of Auftria, and of all the defcendants both of the one and the other houfe, which, as it is faid and fuppofed, ought likewife to hold themfelves for cut off and excluded ; and that for this reafon the fucceffion to the faid crown of Spain be deemed to be devolved, and tranferred to him to whom the fucceffion of Spain ought to be transferred, in fuch cafe, and at any time whatfoever ; fo that we do take and hold him for true and lawful fucceffor, becaufe neither we, nor our defcendants, ought any more to be
con-

confidered as having any foundation of reprefentation,
active or paffive, or making a continuation of a line effective, or contentive of fubftance, blood, or quality, nor
ought we to derive any right from our defcent, or reckon
the degrees from Queen Anne of Auftria, our moft honored Lady and grandmother, nor from the glorious kings
her anceftors. On the contrary, we ratify the renunciation which the faid lady Queen Anne made, and all the
claufes which the Kings Philip III. and Philip IV. inferted
in their wills. We renounce in like manner all the right
which may appertain to us, and to our children and defcendants, by virtue of the declaration made at Madrid,
the 29th of October, 1703, by Philip V. King of Spain,
our nephew ; and any right which might appertain to us,
for us, and our defcendants, we relinquifh the fame, and
renounce it for us and for them ; we promife and engage
for us, our faid children and defcendants, prefent and to
come, to employ ourfelves with all our might, in caufing
thefe prefents to be obferved and fulfilled, without allowing, or fuffering that, directly or indirectly, the fame be
violated, whether in the whole, or in part. And we relinquifh all means, ordinary or extraordinary, which by
common right, or any fpecial privilege might appertain to
us, our children and defcendants, which means we renounce abfolutely, and in particular that of evident, enormous, and moft enormous prejudice, which may be found
in the renunciation of the fucceffion to the faid crown of
Spain ; and we will that any of the faid means neither may,
nor can ferve, or avail us. And if under this pretext, or
any other colour whatever, we would poffefs ourfelves of
the faid kingdom of Spain by force of arms, that the war
which we fhould make, or ftir up, be held for unjuft, unlawful, and unduly undertaken ; and that on the contrary,
that which he fhould make upon us, who by virtue of this
renunciation fhould have right to fucceed to the crown
of Spain, be held for juft and allowable ; and that all the
fubjects and people of Spain do acknowledge him, obey
him, defend him, do homage to him, and take the oath
of fealty to him, as to their King, and lawful Lord.
And for the greater affurance, and fecurity of all that
we fay and promife, for us, and in the name of our fucceffors

fors and defcendants, we fwear folemnly on the Holy Gofpels, contained in this miffal, whereon we lay our right
hand, that we will keep, maintain, and fulfil the fame
wholly and entirely; and that we will at no time afk to have
ourfelves relieved therefrom; and if any perfon afks it, or
if it is granted us *motu proprio*, we will not make ufe, or
avail ourfelves thereof; but rather, in cafe it fhould be
granted us, we make another oath, that this fhall fubfift
and remain for ever, what difpenfation foever may be
granted us. We further fwear and promife, that we have
not made, neither will we make, either in public, or in
fecret, any proteftation or reclamation to the contrary,
which may hinder that which is contained in thefe prefents, or leffen the force thereof, and if we fhould make
any, what oath foever they may be attended with, they
fhall not have either force or virtue, or produce any
effect.

And for greater fecurity, we have paffed, and do pafs
the prefent act of renunciation, abdication and relinquifhment, before mafters Anthony le Moyne, and Alexander le Fevre, counfellors to the King, notaries, minute-
keepers, and feal-keepers at the Chatelet of Paris, hereunder written, in our palace royal at Paris, 1712, the 19th
of November, before noon; and for caufing thefe prefents to be infinuated and regiftered in every place, where
it fhall appertain, we have conftituted the bearer to be our
attorney, and we have figned thefe prefents, and the minute thereof remaining in the poffeffion of the faid Le
Fevre, notary.

PHILIP, *of Orleans.*
*Le Moyne, Le Fevre.*

*The* KING's LETTERS PATENTS *of the Month of Decem-*
ber, 1700.

LEWIS, by the grace of God, King of France and
Navarre, to all prefent and to come, greeting. The
profperity which it has pleafed God to heap upon us during the courfe of our reign, are fo many motives to us, to
apply ourfelves, not only for the time prefent, but alfo
for the future, to the happinefs and tranquillity of the people

ple whereof Divine Providence has entrusted to us the government. His impenetrable judgments, let us only see, that we ought not to place our confidence, neither in our forces, nor in the extent of our dominions, nor in a numerous posterity, and that these advantages, which we receive from his goodness alone, have no other solidity than what it pleases him to give them. But as it is, however, his will that the kings, whom he chuses to lead his people, should foresee afar off the events able to produce disorders, and the most bloody wars; that they should make use of the lights, which his divine wisdom pours upon them; we fulfil his designs, when, in the midst of the universal rejoicings of our kingdom, we look upon, as a possible thing, a sad futurity, which we pray God to avert for ever. At the same time that we accept the will of the late King of Spain; that our most dear and most beloved son the Dauphin renounces his lawful right to that crown, in favour of his second son the Duke of Anjou, our most dear and most beloved grandson, instituted by the late King of Spain, his universal heir; that this Prince, known at present by the name of Philip V. king of Spain, is ready to enter his kingdom, and to answer the earnest wishes of his new subjects; this great event does not hinder us from carrying our views beyond the time present, and when our succession appears the best established, we judge it to be equally the duty of a King, and of a father, to declare, for the future, our will conformably to the sentiments which these two qualities inspire in us. Wherefore, being persuaded that the King of Spain, our grandson, will always preserve for us, for our house, for the kingdom wherein he is born, the same tenderness, and the same sentiments, whereof he has given us so many proofs, that his example, uniting his new subjects to ours, is going to form a perpetual amity, and the most perfect correspondence between them; we should think likewise, that we do him an injustice, whereof we are incapable, and occasion an irreparable prejudice to our kingdom, if we should hereafter look upon as a stranger, a Prince, whom we grant to the unanimous requests of the Spanish nation.

For

For thefe caufes, and other great confiderations us hereunto moving, of our fpecial grace, full power, and royal authority, we have refolved, declared, and ordained, and by thefe prefents figned with our hand, we do refolve, declare, and ordain, we will, and it is our pleafure, that our moft dear and moft beloved grandfon the King of Spain, do preferve for ever the rights of his birth, in the fame manner as if he made his actual refidence in our kingdom; wherefore our moft dear and moft beloved only fon the Dauphin, being the true and lawful fucceffor and heir of our crown, and of our dominions, and after him our moft dear and moft beloved grandfon the Duke of Burgundy, if it fhould happen (which God forbid) that our faid grandfon the Duke of Burgundy, fhould come to die without male children, or that thofe which he fhould have in good and lawful marriage, fhould die before him, or if the faid male children fhould not leave any male children after them born in lawful marriage, in fuch cafe our faid grandfon the King of Spain, making ufe of the rights of his birth, is to be the true and lawful fucceffor to our crown, and to our dominions, notwithftanding he fhould be at that time abfent, and refiding out of our faid kingdom; and immediately after his deceafe, his heirs male begot in lawful marriage, fhall come into the faid fucceffion, notwithftanding that they may be born, or that they may dwell out of our kingdom; we will that, for the abovefaid caufes, neither our faid grandfon, the King of Spain, nor his children being males, be deemed and reputed lefs able and capable to enter upon the faid fucceffion, or upon others which may fall to them within our faid kingdom. On the contrary we intend, that all rights, and generally other things whatever, which may at prefent, or for the future, belong and appertain to them, be and remain preferved whole and intire, as if they did refide and dwell conftantly within our kingdom to the time of their deceafe, and as if their heirs had been natives, and inhabitants of the kingdom; having for this purpofe, as far as there is or fhall be need enabled and difpenfed with them, as we do enable and difpenfe with them by thefe prefents. And fo we give it in command to our beloved and trufty Counfellors, the members of our Court of Parliament, and Chamber of our Accounts

counts at Paris, Prefidents and Treafurers General of France in the office of our Exchequer eftablifhed in the fame place, and to all others our officers and juftices to whom it fhall appertain, that they caufe thefe prefents to be regiftered, and our faid grandfon the King of Spain, his children and defcendants, being male, born in lawful marriage, to enjoy and ufe the contents thereof, fully and peaceably, any thing to the contrary notwithftanding; to which, by our grace and authority, as abovefaid, we have derogated, and do derogate; for this is our pleafure. And that this may be a matter firm and lafting for ever, we have caufed our feal to be put to thefe prefents. Given at Verfailles, in the month of December, in the year of our Lord, 1700, and of our reign the 58th. Signed LEWIS, and on the fold, by the king, *Phelipeaux*. And fealed with the great feal on green wax, with ftrings of red and green filk.

Regiftered, the King's Attorney General being heard and requiring the fame, in order to their being executed according to their form and tenor, purfuant to the act of this day. At Paris in Parliament, the 1ft of February, 1701.

*Signed,*                              *DONGOIS.*

NOW whereas it is provided and fettled by the preceding renunciation (which is always to have the force of a pragmatick, fundamental, and inviolable law) that at no time whatever either the Catholic King himfelf, or any one of his lineage, fhall feek to obtain the crown of France, or afcend the throne thereof; and by reciprocal renunciations on the part of France, and by fettlements of the heriditary fucceffion there, tending to the fame purpofe, the crowns of France and Spain are fo divided and feparated from each other, that the aforefaid renunciations, and the other tranfactions relating thereto, remaining in force, and being truly and faithfully obferved, they can never be joined in one. Wherefore the moft ferene Queen of Great Britain, and the moft ferene and the moft Chriftian King, engage to each other folemnly, and on their royal words, that nothing ever fhall be done by them, or their heirs and fucceffors, or allowed to be done by others, whereby the aforefaid renunciations, and the other tranfactions

tranfactions aforementioned, may not have their full effect : but rather on the contrary, their Royal Majefties,
with joint councils and forces, will always fincerely take
that care, and ufe thofe endeavours, that the faid foundations of the public fafety may remain unfhaken, and be
preferved untouched for ever.

Moreover, the moft Chriftian King confents and engages, that he will not, for the intereft of his fubjects,
hereafter endeavour to obtain, or accept of any other
ufage of navigation and trade to Spain, and the Spanifh
Indies, than what was practifed there in the reign of the
late King Charles II. of Spain, or than what fhall likewife
be fully given and granted, at the fame time, to other
nations and people concerned in trade.

VII. That there be a free ufe of navigation and
commerce between the fubjects of both their Royal Majefties, as it was formerly in the time of peace, and before
the declaration of this laft war, and alfo as it is agreed and
concluded by the treaty of commerce this day made between the two nations.

VIII. That the ordinary diftribution of juftice be re-
vived, and open again, through the kingdoms and dominions of each of their Royal Majefties, fo that it may be
free for all the fubjects on both fides, to fue for, and obtain their rights, pretenfions, and actions, according to
the laws, conftitutions, and ftatutes of each kingdom.

IX. The moft Chriftian King fhall take care that all
the fortifications of the city of Dunkirk be razed, that the
harbour be filled up, and that the fluices or moles which
ferve to cleanfe the harbour be levelled, and that at the
faid King's own expence, within the fpace of five months
after the conditions of peace are concluded and figned ;
that is to fay, the fortifications towards the fea, within the
fpace of two months, and thofe towards the land, together
with the faid banks, within three months ; on this exprefs
condition alfo, that the faid fortifications, harbour, moles,
or fluices, be never repaired again. All which fhall not,
however, be begun to be ruined, till after that every
thing is put into his Chriftian Majefty's hands, which is to
be given him, inftead thereof, or as an equivalent.

X. The

**X.** The faid moft Chriftian King fhall reftore to the kingdom and Queen of Great Britain, to be poffeffed in full right for ever, the bay and ftreights of Hudfon, together with all lands, feas, fea-coafts, rivers, and places fituate in the faid bay, and ftreights, and which belong thereunto, no tracts of land or of fea being excepted, which are at prefent poffeffed by the fubjects of France. All which, as well as any buildings there made, in the condition they now are, and likewife all fortreffes there erected, either before or fince the French feized the fame, fhall within fix months from the ratification of the prefent treaty, or fooner, if poffible, be well and truly delivered to the Britifh fubjects, having commiffion from the Queen of Great Britain, to demand and receive the fame, entire and undemolifhed, together with all the cannon and cannon-ball which are therein, as alfo with a quantity of powder, if it be there found, in proportion to the cannon ball, and with the other provifion of war ufually belonging to cannon. It is however provided, that it may be entirely free for the company of Quebec, and all other the fubjects of the moft Chriftian King whatfoever, to go by land, or by fea, whitherfoever they pleafe out of the lands of the faid bay, together with all their goods, merchandizes, arms, and effects, of what nature or condition foever, except fuch things as are above referved in this article. But it is agreed on both fides, to determine within a year, by commiffaries to be forthwith named by each party, the limits which are to be fixed between the faid Bay of Hudfon, and the places appertaining to the French; which limits both the Britifh and French fubjects fhall be wholly forbid to pafs over, or thereby to go to each other by fea or by land. The fame commiffaries fhall alfo have orders to defcribe and fettle, in like manner, the boundaries between the other Britifh and French colonies in thofe parts.

**XI.** The abovementioned moft Chriftian King fhall take care that fatisfaction be given, according to the rule of juftice and equity, to the Englifh company trading to the Bay of Hudfon, for all damages and fpoil done to their colonies, fhips, perfons, and goods, by the hoftile incurfions and depredations of the French, in time of peace, an eftimate being made thereof by commiffaries to

be

be named at the requifition of each party. The fame commiffaries fhall moreover inquire as well into the complaints of the Britifh fubjects concerning fhips taken by the French in time of peace, as alfo concerning the damages fuftained laft year in the ifland called Montferat, and others, as into thofe things of which the French fubjects complain, relating to the capitulation in the ifland of Nevis, and caftle of Gambia, alfo to French fhips, if perchance any fuch have been taken by Britifh fubjects in time of peace. And in like manner into all difputes of this kind, which fhall be found to have arifen between both nations, and which are not yet ended ; and due juftice fhall be done on both fides without delay.

XII. The moft Chriftian King fhall take care to have delivered to the Queen of Great Britain, on the fame day that the ratifications of this treaty fhall be exchanged, folemn and authentic letters, or inftruments, by virtue whereof it fhall appear, that the ifland of St. Chriftophers is to be poffeffed alone hereafter by Britifh fubjects, likewife all Nova Scotia or Acadia, with its ancient boundaries, as alfo the city of Port Royal, now called Annapolis Royal, and all other things in thofe parts, which depend on the faid lands and iflands, together with the dominion, propriety, and poffeffion of the faid iflands, lands, and places, and all right whatfoever, by treaties, or by any other way obtained, which the moft Chriftian King, the crown of France, or any the fubjects thereof, have hitherto had to the faid iflands, lands, and places, and the inhabitants of the fame, are yielded and made over to the Queen of Great Britain, and to her crown for ever, as the moft Chriftian King does at prefent yield and make over all the particulars abovefaid ; and that in fuch ample manner and form, that the fubjects of the moft Chriftian King fhall hereafter be excluded from all kind of fifhing in the faid feas, bays, and other places, on the coafts of Nova Scotia, that is to fay, on thofe which lie towards the Eaft, within 30 leagues, beginning from the ifland commonly called Sable, inclufively, and thence ftretching along towards the South weft.

XIII. The ifland called Newfoundland, with the adjacent iflands, fhall from this time forward, belong of right wholly

wholly to Britain ; and to that end the town and fortrefs of Placentia, and whatever other places in the faid ifland, are in the poffeffion of the French, fhall be yielded and given up, within feven months from the exchange of the ratifications of this treaty, or fooner if poffible, by the moft Chriftian King, to thofe who have a commiffion from the Queen of Great Britain, for that purpofe. Nor fhall the moft Chriftian King, his heirs and fucceffors, or any of their fubjects, at any time hereafter, lay claim to any right to the faid ifland and iflands, or to any part of it, or them. Moreover, it fhall not be lawful for the fubjects of France, to fortify any place in the faid ifland of Newfoundland, or to erect any buildings there, befides ftages made of boards, and huts neceffary and ufual for drying of fifh ; or to refort to the faid ifland, beyond the time neceffary for fifhing, and drying of fifh. But it fhall be allowed to the fubjects of France, to catch fifh, and to dry them on land, in that part only, and in no other befides that, of the faid ifland of Newfoundland, which ftretches from the place called cape Bonavifta, to the northern point of the faid ifland, and from thence running down by the weftern fide, reaches as far as the place called Point Riche. But the ifland called Cape Breton, as alfo all others, both in the mouth of the river of St. Lawrence, and in the gulph of the fame name, fhall hereafter belong of right to the French, and the moft Chriftian King fhall have all manner of liberty to fortify any place, or places there.

XIV. It is exprefsly provided, that in all the faid places and colonies to be yielded and reftored by the moft Chriftian King, in purfuance of this treaty, the fubjects of the faid King may have liberty to remove themfelves within a year to any other place, as they fhall think fit, together with all their moveable effects. But thofe who are willing to remain there, and to be fubject to the kingdom of Great Britain, are to enjoy the free exercife of their religion, according to the ufage of the church of Rome, as far as the laws of Great Britain do allow the fame.

XV. The fubjects of France inhabiting Canada, and others, fhall hereafter give no hindrance or moleftation to the five nations or cantons of Indians, fubject to the dominion of Great Britain, nor to the other natives of America,

rica, who are friends to the same. In like manner, the subjects of Great Britain shall behave themselves peaceably towards the Americans who are subjects or friends to France; and on both sides they shall enjoy full liberty of going and coming on account of trade. As also the natives of those countries shall, with the same liberty, resort, as they please, to the British and French colonies, for promoting trade on one side, and the other, without any molestation or hindrance, either on the part of the British subjects, or of the French. But it is to be exactly and distinctly settled by commissaries, who are, and who ought to be accounted the subjects and friends of Britain or of France.

XVI. That all letters, as well of reprisal, as of mark and counter-mark, which have hitherto on any account been granted on either side, be and remain null, void, and of no effect; and that no letters of this kind be hereafter granted by either of their said Royal Majesties, against the subjects of the other, unless there shall have been plain proof beforehand of a denial, or wrongful delay of justice; and unless the petition of him, who desires the grant of letters of reprisal, be exhibited and shewn to the minister, who resides there in the name of that Prince, against whose subjects those letters are demanded, that he within the space of four months, or sooner, may make enquiry to the contrary, or procure that satisfaction be forthwith given to the plaintiff by the party accused. But in case no minister be residing there from that Prince, against whose subjects reprisals are demanded, that letters of reprisal be not granted till after the space of four months, to be computed from the day whereon the petition was exhibited and presented to the Prince, against whose subjects reprisals are desired, or to his Privy-council.

XVII. Whereas it is expressly stipulated among the conditions of the suspension of arms, made between the abovementioned contracting parties the $\frac{11}{22}$ day of August last past, and afterwards prolonged for four months more, in what cases ships, merchandizes, and other moveable effects, taken on either side, should either become prize to the captor, or be restored to the former proprietor; it is therefore agreed, that in those cases the conditions of
the

the aforesaid suspension of arms shall remain in full force, and that all things relating to such captures, made either in the British and Northern seas, or in any other place, shall be well and truly executed according to the tenor of the same.

XVIII. But in case it happens through inadvertency, or imprudence, or any other cause whatsoever, that any subject of their aforesaid Royal Majesties do, or commit any thing by land, by sea, or on fresh waters, in any part of the world, whereby this present treaty be not observed, or whereby any particular article of the same hath not its effect, this peace and good correspondence between the Queen of Great Brieain, and the most Christian King, shall not be therefore interrupted or broken, but shall remain in its former strength, force, and vigour. But that subject alone shall be answerable for his own fact, and shall suffer the punishment which is inflicted by the rules and directions of the law of nations.

XIX. However, in case (which God Almighty forbid) the diffentions which have been laid asleep, should at any time be renewed, between their said Royal Majesties, or their successors, and break out into open war, the ships, merchandizes, and all the effects both moveable and immoveable, on both sides, which shall be fouund to be and remain in the ports, and in the dominions of the adverse party, shall not be confiscated, or any wise endamaged; but the entire space of six months, to be reckoned from the day of the rupture, shall be allowed to the said subjects of each of their Royal Majesties, in which they may sell the aforesaid things, or any part else of their effects, or carry and remove them from thence whither they please, without any molestation, and retire from thence themselves.

XX. Just and reasonable satisfaction shall be given to all and singular the allies of the Queen of Great Britain, in those matters which they have a right to demand from France.

XXI. The most Christian King will, in consideration of the friendship of the Queen of Great Britain, grant, that in making the treaty with the Empire, all things concerning the state of religion in the aforesaid Empire, shall
be

be fettled conformable to the tenor of the treaties of Weft-phalia, fo that it fhall plainly appear, that the moft Chri-ftian King neither will have, nor would have had any al-teration made in the faid treaties.

XXII. Moreover, the moft Chriftian King engages, that he will forthwith, after the peace is made, caufe juf-tice to be done to the family of Hamilton, concerning the dukedom of Chatelraut; to the Duke of Richmond, concerning fuch requefts as he has to make in France, as alfo to Charles Douglas, concerning certain lands to be reclaimed by him, and to others.

XXIII. By the mutual confent of the Queen of Great Britain, and of the moft Chriftian King, the fubjects of each party, who were taken prifoners during the war, fhall be fet at liberty, without any diftinction or ranfom, paying fuch debts as they fhall have contracted during the time of their being prifoners.

XXIV. It is mutually agreed, that all and fingular the conditions of the peace, made this day between his facred royal moft Chriftian Majefty, and his facred Royal Ma-jefty of Portugal, be confirmed by this treaty; and her fa-cred Royal Majefty of Great Britain takes upon herfelf the guaranty of the fame, to the end that it may be more firmly and inviolably obferved.

XXV. The treaty of peace made this day between his facred royal moft Chriftian Majefty, and his Royal High-nefs the Duke of Savoy, is particularly included in this treaty, as an effential part of it, and is confirmed by it, in the fame manner as if it were word for word inferted therein; her Royal Majefty of Great Britain declaring ex-prefsly, that fhe will be bound by the ftipulations of fecu-rity and guaranty promifed therein, as well as by thofe which fhe has formerly taken upon herfelf.

XXVI. The moft ferene King of Sweden, with his kingdoms, dominions, provinces, and rights, as alfo the Great Duke of Tufcany, the republic of Genoa, and the Duke of Parma, are in the beft manner included in this treaty.

XXVII. Their Majefties have alfo been pleafed to comprehend, in this treaty, the Hans-Towns, namely, Lu-beck, Bremen, and Hamburg, and the city of Dantzick,

w th

with this effect, that as soon as the general peace shall be concluded, the Hans-Towns and the city of Dantzick may, for the future, as common friends, enjoy the ancient advantages which they have heretofore had in the business of trade, either by treaties, or by old custom.

XXVIII. Those shall be comprehended in this present treaty of peace, who shall be named by common consent, on the one part and on the other, before the exchange of the ratifications, or within six months after.

XXIX. Lastly, Solemn ratifications of this present treaty, and made in due form, shall be exhibited on both sides at Utrecht, and mutually and duly exchanged within the space of four weeks, to be computed from the day of the signing, or sooner, if possible.

XXX. In witness whereof, we the underwritten Ambassadors Extraordinary and Plenipotentiaries of the Queen of Great Britain, and of the most Christian King, have put our seals to these present instruments, subscribed with our own hands, at Utrecht the $\frac{3\ 1}{1\ 1}$th day of $\frac{\text{March}}{\text{April}}$ in the year 1713.

(L. S.) *Joh. Bristol, C. P. S.*   (L. S.) *Huxelles.*
(L. S.) *Strafford.*   (L. S.) *Mesnager.*

---

*Treaty of Navigation and Commerce between the Most Serene and Most Potent Princess* Anne, *by the Grace of* God, *Queen of* Great Britain, France, *and* Ireland, *and the Most Serene and Most Potent Prince* Lewis XIV. *the Most Christian King*; *concluded at* Utrecht *the* $\frac{3\ 1}{1\ 1}$ *Day of* $\frac{\text{March}}{\text{April}}$

1713. Reprinted from the copy published by the Queen's special command.

I. IT is agreed and concluded between the Most Serene and Most Potent Queen of Great Britain, and the Most Serene and Most Potent the Most Christian King, that there shall be a reciprocal and entirely perfect liberty of navigation and commerce, between the subjects on each part, through all and every the kingdoms, states, dominions, and provinces of their Royal Majesties in Europe, concerning

concerning all and fingular kinds of goods, in thofe places, and on thofe conditions, and in fuch manner and form, as is fettled and adjufted in the following articles.

II. But that the commerce and friendfhip between the fubjects of the abovefaid parties may be hereafter fecure, and free from all trouble and moleftation, it is agreed and concluded, that if at any time any ill underftanding and breach of friendfhip, or rupture fhould happen between the crowns of their Royal Majefties (which God forbid) in fuch cafe the term of fix months fhall be allowed, after the faid rupture, to the fubjects and inhabitants on each part, refiding in the dominions of the other, in which they themfelves may retire, together with their families, goods, merchandizes, and effects, and carry them whitherfoever they fhall pleafe; as likewife at the fame time the felling and difpofing of their goods, both moveable and immoveable, fhall be allowed them freely, and without any difturbance; and in the mean time their goods, effects, wares, and merchandizes, and particularly their perfons, fhall not be detained or troubled by arreft or feizure: but rather, in the mean while, the fubjects on each fide fhall have and enjoy good and fpeedy juftice, fo that during the faid fpace of fix months, they may be able to recover their goods and effects entrufted, as well to the public, as to private perfons.

III. It is likewife agreed and concluded, that the fubjects and inhabitants of the kingdoms, provinces, and dominions of each of their Royal Majefties, fhall exercife no acts of hoftility and violence againft each other, neither by fea, nor by land, nor in rivers, ftreams, ports, or havens, under any colour or pretence whatfoever, fo that the fubjects of either party fhall receive no patent, commiffion, or inftruction, for arming and acting at fea as privateers, nor letters of reprifal, as they are called, from any princes or ftates, which are enemies to one fide or the other; nor by virtue, or under colour of fuch patents, commiffions, or reprifals, fhall they difturb, infeft, or any way prejudice or damage the aforefaid fubjects and inhabitants of the Queen of Great Britain, or of the moft Chriftian King; neither fhall they arm fhips in fuch manner as is abovefaid, or go out to fea therewith. To which end, as often as it is required by either fide, ftrict and exprefs prohibitions fhall be renewed and publifhed in all the regions, dominions, and territories of each party wherefoever, that no one fhall in any wife ufe fuch commiffions or letters of reprifal, under the fevereft punifhment that can be inflicted on the tranfgreffors, befides reftitution and full fatisfaction to be given to thofe, to whom they have done any damage; neither fhall any letters of reprifal be hereafter granted on either fide by the faid confederates, to the detriment or difadvantage of the fubjects of the other, except in fuch cafe only as juftice is denied or delayed; to which denial or delay, credit fhall not be given, unlefs the petition of the perfon who defires the faid letters of reprifal be communicated to the Minifter refiding there on the part of the Prince, againft whofe fubjects they are to be granted, that within the fpace of four months, or fooner, if it be poffible, he may evince the contrary, or procure the performance of what is due to juftice.

IV. The fubjects and inhabitants of each of the aforefaid confederates, fhall have liberty, freely and fecurely, without licence or paffport, general or fpecial, by land or by fea, or any other way, to go into the kingdoms, countries, provinces, lands, iflands, cities, villages, towns, walled or unwalled, fortified or unfortified, ports, dominions, or territories whatfoever, of the other confederate in Europe, there to enter, and to return from thence, to abide there, or to pafs through the fame, and in the mean time to buy and purchafe as they pleafe, all things neceffary for their fubfiftence and ufe, and they fhall be treated with all mutual kindnefs and favour. Provided, however, that in all thefe matters they behave and comport themfelves conformably to the laws and ftatutes, and live and converfe with each other friendly and peaceably, and keep up reciprocal concord by all manner of good underftanding.

V. The fubjects of each of their Royal Majefties may have leave and licence to come with their fhips, as alfo with the merchandizes and goods on board the fame (the trade and importation whereof are not prohibited by the laws of either kingdoms) to the lands, countries, cities, ports, places, and rivers of either fide in Europe, to enter

into

into the fame, to refort thereto, to remain and refide there, without any limitation of time; alfo to hire houfes, or to lodge with other people, and to buy all lawful kinds of merchandizes, where they think fit, from the firft workman or feller, or in any other manner, whether in the public market for the fale of things, in mart-towns, fairs, or wherefoever thofe goods are manufactured or fold; they may likewife lay up and keep in their magazines and warehoufes, and from thence expofe to fale merchandizes brought from other parts; neither fhall they be in any wife obliged, unlefs willingly and of their own accord, to bring their faid merchandizes to the marts and fairs, on this condition, however, that they fhall not fell the fame by retail in fhops, or any where elfe. But they are not to be loaded with any impofitions, or taxes, on account of the faid freedom of trade, or for any other caufe whatfoever, except what are to be paid for their fhips and goods, according to the laws and cuftoms received in each kingdom. And moreover, they fhall have free leave, without any moleftation, to remove themfelves; alfo if they fhall happen to be married, their wives, children, and fervants, together with their merchandizes, wares, goods, and effects, either bought or imported, whenfoever and whitherfoever they fhall think fit, out of the bounds of each kingdom, by land and by fea, on the rivers and frefh waters, difcharging the ufual duties, notwithftanding any law, privilege, grant, immunity, or cuftom, in any wife importing the contrary. But in the bufinefs of religion, there fhall be an entire liberty allowed to the fubjects of each of the confederates, as alfo, if they are married, to their wives and children, neither fhall they be compelled to go to the churches, or to be prefent at the religious worfhip in any other place. On the contrary, they may, without any kind of moleftation, perform their religious exercifes after their own way, although it be forbid by the laws of the kingdom, privately and within their own walls, and without the admittance of any other perfons whatfoever. Moreover, liberty fhall not be refufed to bury the fubjects of either party, who die in the territories of the other, in convenient and decent places, to be appointed for that purpofe, as occafion fhall require; neither fhall the dead

bodies

bodies of those that are buried be any ways molested. The laws and statutes of each kingdom shall remain in full force, and shall be duly put in execution, whether they relate to commerce and navigation, or to any other right, those cases only being excepted, concerning which it is otherwise determined in the articles of this present treaty.

VI. The subjects of each party shall pay the tolls, customs, and duties of import and export through all the dominions and provinces of either party, as are due and accustomed. And, that it may be certainly known to every one what are all the said tolls, customs, and duties of import and export, it is likewise agreed, that tables shewing the customs, port-duties, and imposts, shall be kept in public places, both at London, and in other towns within the dominions of the Queen of Great Britain, and at Roan, and other towns of France, where trading is used, whereunto recourse may be had, as often as any question or dispute arises concerning such port-duties, customs, and imposts, which are to be demanded in such manner, and no otherwise, as shall be agreeable to the plain words, and genuine sense of the abovesaid tables. And if any officer, or other person in his name, shall, under any pretence, publicly or privately, directly or indirectly, ask or take of a merchant, or of any other person, any sum of money, or any thing else on account of right, dues, stipend, exhibition, or compensation, although it be under the name of a free gift, or in any other manner, or under any other pretence, more, or otherwise, than what is prescribed above, in such case the said officer, or his deputy, if he be found guilty, and convicted of the same before a competent judge, in the country where the crime was committed, shall give full satisfaction to the party that is wronged, and shall likewise be punished according to the direction of the laws.

VII. Merchants, masters of ships, owners, mariners, men of all kinds, ships, and all merchandizes in general, and effects of one of the confederates, and of his subjects and inhabitants, shall on no public or private account, by virtue of any general or special edict, be seized in any the lands, ports, havens, shores, or dominions whatsoever of
the

the other confederate for puplic ufe, for warlike expeditions, or for any other caufe, much lefs for the private
ufe of any one, fhall they be detained by arrefts, compelled by violence, or under any colour thereof, or in any
wife molefted or injured. Moreover, it fhall be unlawful
for the fubjects of both parties, to take any thing, or to
extort it by force, except the perfon to whom it belongs
confent, and it be paid for with ready money. Which,
however is not to be underftood of that detention and
feizure which fhall be made by the command and authority of juftice, and by the ordinary methods, on account
of debt, or crimes, in refpect whereof the proceeding muft
be by way of law, according to the form of juftice.

VIII. Furthermore, it is agreed and concluded as a
general rule, that all and fingular the fubjects of the moft
ferene Queen of Great Britain, and of the moft ferene
the moft Chriftian King, in all countries and places fubject to their power on each fide, as to all duties, impofitions, or cuftoms whatfoever, concerning perfons, goods
and merchandizes, fhips, freights, feamen, navigation and
commerce, fhall ufe and enjoy the fame privileges, liberties, and immunities at leaft, and have the like favour
in all things, as well in the courts of juftice, as in all fuch
things as relate either to commerce, or to any other right
whatever, with any foreign nation, the moft favoured,
has, ufes, and enjoys, or may hereafter have, ufe, and
enjoy.

IX. It is further agreed, that within the fpace of two
months after a law fhall be made in Great Britain, whereby it fhall be fufficiently provided, that no more cuftoms
or duties be paid for goods and merchandifes brought
from France to Great Britain, than what are payable for
goods and merchandizes of the like nature, imported into
Great Britain, from any other country in Eurpe; and
that all laws made in Great Britain fince the year 1664,
for prohibiting the importation of any goods and merchandizes coming from France, which are not prohibited before that time, be repealed, the general tariff made
in France the 18th day of September, in the year 1664,
fhall take place there again, and the duties payable in
France by the fubjects of Great Britain, for goods imported

ported and exported, fhall be paid according to the tenor of the tariff abovementioned, and fhall not exceed the rule therein fettled, in the provinces whereof mention is there made, and in the other provinces the duty fhall not be payable, otherwife than according to the rule at that time preſcribed ; and all prohibitions, tariffs, edicts, declarations or decrees, made in France fince the ſaid tariff of the year 1664, and contrary thereto in refpect to the goods and merchandizes of Great Britain, fhall be repealed. But whereas it is urged on the part of France, that certain merchandizes, that is to fay, manufactures of wool, fugar, falted fifh, and the product of whales, be excepted out of the rule of the abovementioned tariff, and likewife other heads of matters belonging to this treaty remain, which having been propoſed on the part of Great Britain, have not yet been mutually adjufted, a fpecification of all which is contained in a feperate inftrument fubfcribed by the Ambaffadors Extraordinary and Plenipotentiaries on both fides ; it is hereby provided and agreed, that within two months from the exchange of the ratifications of this treaty, commiffaries on both fides fhall meet at London, to confider of and remove the difficulties concerning the merchandizes to be excepted out of the tariff of the year 1664, and concerning the other heads, which, as is abovefaid, are not yet wholly adjufted. And at the fame time the ſaid Commiffaries fhall likewife endeavour, (which feems to be very much for the intereft of both nations) to have the methods of commerce on one part, and of the other, more thoroughly examined, and to find out and eftablifh juft and beneficial means on both fides for removing the difficulties in this matter, and for regulating the duties mutually. But it is always underftood and provided, that all and fingular the articles of this treaty, do in the mean while remain in their full force, and efpecially that nothing be deemed, under any pretence whatfoever, to hinder the benefit of the general tariff of the year 1664, from being granted to the fubjects of her royal Majefty of Great Britain, and the ſaid Britifh fubjects, from having and enjoying the fame, without any delay or tergiverfation, within the fpace of two months after a law is made in Great Britain, as abovefaid, in as ample manner and form as the

fubjects

subjects of any nation, the moſt favoured might have and enjoy the benefit of the aforeſaid tariff, any thing to be done or diſcuſſed by the ſaid commiſſioners, to the contrary in any wiſe notwithſtanding.

X. The duties on tobacco, imported into France, either in the leaf, or prepared, ſhall be reduced hereafter to the ſame moderate rate as the ſame tobacco, of the growth of any country in Europe or America being brought into France, does or ſhall pay. The ſubjects on both ſides ſhall alſo pay the ſame duties in France for the ſaid tobacco; there ſhall be likewiſe an equal liberty of ſelling it; and the Britiſh ſubjects ſhall have the ſame laws as the merchants of France themſelves have and enjoy.

XI. It is likewiſe concluded, that the impoſition or tax of 50 *Sols Tournois*, laid on Britiſh ſhips in France for every tun, ſhall wholly ceaſe, and be from henceforward annulled. In like manner the tax of five ſhillings ſterling, laid on French ſhips in Great Britain for every tun, ſhall ceaſe; neither ſhall the ſame, or any the like impoſitions, be laid hereafter on the ſhips of the ſubjects on either ſide.

XII. It is further agreed and concluded, that it ſhall be wholly free for all merchants, commanders of ſhips, and other the ſubjects of the Queen of Great Britain, in all places of France, to manage their own Buſineſs themſelves, or to commit them to the management of whomſoever they pleaſe, nor ſhall they be obliged to make uſe of any interpreter, or broker, nor to pay them any ſalary, unleſs they chuſe to make uſe of them. Moreover maſters of ſhips ſhall not be obliged, in loading or unloading their ſhips, to make uſe of thoſe workmen, either at Bourdeaux, or in any other places, as may be appointed by public authority for that purpoſe; but it ſhall be entirely free for them to load or unload their ſhips by themſelves, or to make uſe of ſuch perſons in loading or unloading the ſame, as they ſhall think fit, without the payment of any ſalary to any other whomſoever; neither ſhall they be forced to unload any ſort of merchandizes, either into other ſhips, or to receive them into their own, or to wait for their being loaded longer than they pleaſe. And all and every the ſubjects of the moſt Chriſtian King, ſhall

ſhall reciprocally have and enjoy the ſame privileges and liberty, in all places in Europe ſubject to the dominion of Great Britain.

XIII. It ſhall be wholly lawful and free for merchants and others, being ſubjects either to the Queen of Great Britain, or to the moſt Chriſtian King, by will, and any other diſpoſition made, either during the time of ſickneſs, or at any other time before, or at the point of death, to deviſe or give away their merchandizes, effects, money, debts, belonging to them, and all moveable goods, which they have, or ought to have at the time of their death, within the dominions, and any other places belonging to the Queen of Great Britain, and to the moſt Chriſtian King. Moreover, whether they die, having made their will, or inteſtate, their lawful heirs and executors, or adminiſtrators, reſiding in either of the kingdoms, or coming from any other part, although they be not naturalized, ſhall freely and quietly receive and take poſſeſſion of all the ſaid goods and effects whatſoever, according to the laws of Great Britain and France reſpectively; in ſuch manner however, that the wills and rights of entering upon the inheritances of perſons inteſtate, muſt be proved according to law, as well by the ſubjects of the Queen of Great Britain, as by the ſubjects of the moſt Chriſtian King, in thoſe places where each perſon died, whether that may happen in Great Britain, or in France, any law, ſtatute, edict, cuſtom, or *Droit d' Aubene* whatever to the contrary notwithſtanding.

XIV. A diſpute ariſing between any commander of the ſhips on both ſides, and his ſeamen in any port of the other party, concerning wages due to the ſaid ſeamen, or other civil cauſes, the magiſtrate of the place ſhall require no more from the perſon accuſed, than that he give to the accuſer a declaration in writing, witneſſed by the magiſtrate, whereby he ſhall be bound to anſwer that matter before a competent judge in his own country, which being done, it ſhall not be lawful either for the ſeamen to deſert their ſhip, or to hinder the commander from proſecuting his voyage. It ſhall moreover be lawful for the merchants on both ſides, in the places of their abode, or elſewhere, to keep books of their accounts, and affairs,

affairs, as they ſhall think fit, and to have an intercourſe of letters, in ſuch language or idiom, as they ſhall pleaſe, without any moleſtation or ſearch whatſoever. But if it ſhould happen to be neceſſary for them to produce their books of accounts for deciding any diſpute or controverſy, in ſuch caſe they ſhall be obliged to bring into court the entire books or writings, but ſo as that the judge may not have liberty to inſpect any other articles in the ſaid books, than ſuch as ſhall relate to the teſtimony or authority in queſtion, or ſuch as ſhall be neceſſary to give credit to the ſaid books; neither ſhall it be lawful, under any pretence, to take the, ſaid books or writings forcibly out of the hands of the owners, or to retain them; the caſe of bankruptcy only excepted: neither ſhall the ſaid ſubjects of the Queen of Great Britain be obliged to write their accounts, copies of letters, acts or inſtruments relating to trade, on ſtamped paper, in French, *Papier Timbre*, except their day-book, which, that it may be produced as evidence in any law-ſuit, ought, according to the laws, which all perſons trading in France are to obſerve, to be ſubſcribed gratis by the judge, and ſigned with his own hand.

XV. It ſhall not be lawful for any foreign privateers, not being ſubjects of one or the other of the confederates, who have commiſſions from any other prince or ſtate, in enmity with either nation, to fit their ſhips in the ports of one or the other of the aforeſaid parties, to ſell what they have taken, or in any other manner whatever to exchange either ſhips, merchandizes, or any other ladings; neither ſhall they be allowed even to purchaſe victuals, except ſuch as ſhall be neceſſary for their going to the next port of that prince from whom they have commiſſions.

XVI. The ſhips of both parties being laden, ſailing along the coaſts or ſhores of the other, and being forced by ſtorm into the havens or ports, or coming to land in any other manner, ſhall not be obliged there to unlade their goods, or any part thereof, or to pay any duty, unleſs they do, of their own accord, unlade their goods there, or diſpoſe of any part of their lading: but it may be lawful to take out of the ſhip, and to ſell, leave being firſt

firſt obtained from thoſe who have the inſpection of ſea affairs, a ſmall part of their lading, for this end only, that neceſſaries, either for the refreſhment or victualing of the ſhip may be purchaſed; and in that caſe the whole lading of the ſhip ſhall not be ſubject to pay the duties, but that ſmall part only which has been taken out and ſold.

XVII. It ſhall be lawful for all and ſingular the ſub-jects of the Queen of Great Britain, and of the moſt Chriſ-tian King, to ſail with their ſhips with all manner of li-berty and ſecurity, no diſtinction being made, who are the proprietors of the merchandizes laden thereon, from any port to the places of thoſe who are now, or ſhall be hereafter at enmity with the Queen of Great Britain, or the moſt Chriſtian King; it ſhall likewiſe be lawful for the ſubjects and inhabitants aforeſaid, to ſail with the ſhips and merchandizes aforementioned, and to trade with the ſame liberty and ſecurity from the places, ports, and ha-vens of thoſe who are enemies of both, or of either par-ty, without any oppoſition or diſturbance whatſoever, not only directly from the places of the enemy aforemention-ed to neutral places, but alſo from one place belonging to an enemy, to anothar place belonging to an enemy, whe-ther they be under the juriſdiction of the ſame prince, or under ſeveral. And it is now ſtipulated concerning ſhips and goods, that free ſhips ſhall alſo give a freedom to goods, and that every thing ſhall be deemed to be free and ex-empt, which ſhall be found on board the ſhips belonging to the ſubjects of either of the confederates, although the whole lading, or any part thereof, ſhould appertain to the enemies of either of their Majeſties, contraband goods be-ing always excepted, on the diſcovery whereof matters ſhall be managed according to the ſenſe of the ſubſequent articles. It is alſo agreed in like manner, that the ſame liberty be extended to perſons who are on board a free ſhip, with this effect, that although they be enemies to both, or either party, they are not to be taken out of that free ſhip, unleſs they are ſoldiers, and in actual ſer-vice of the enemies.

XVIII. The liberty of navigation and commerce ſhall extend to all kinds of merchandizes, excepting thoſe only which

which follow in the next article, and which are fignified by the name of contraband.

XIX. Under this name of contraband, or prohibited goods, fhall be comprehended arms, great guns, bombs, with their fufees and other things belonging to them; fire-balls, gunpowder, match, cannon-ball, pikes, fwords, lances, fpears, halberds, morters, petards, granadoes, falt-petre, mufkets, mufket-ball, helmets, head-pieces, breaft-plates, coats of mail, and the like kinds of arms, proper for arming foldiers, mufket-refts, belts, horfes with their furniture, and all other warlike inftruments whatever.

XX. Thefe merchandizes which follow fhall not be reckoned among prohibited goods, that is to fay, all forts of clothes, and all other manufactures woven of any wool, flax, filk, cotton, or any other materials whatever; all kinds of clothes and wearing apparel, together with the fpecies whereof they are ufed to be made; gold and filver, as well coined as uncoined, tin, iron, lead, copper, brafs, coals; as alfo wheat and barley, and any other kind of corn, and pulfe; tobacco, and likewife all manner of fpices, falted and fmoaked flefh, falted fifh, cheefe and butter, beer, oils, wines, fugars, and all forts of falt, and, in ge-neral, all provifions which ferve for the nourifhment of mankind, and the fuftenance of life. Furthermore, all kinds of cotton, hemp, flax, tar, pitch, ropes, cables, fails, failcloths, anchors, and any parts of anchors; alfo fhip-mafts, planks, boards and beams of what trees foever; and all other things proper either for building or repairing fhips; and all other goods whatever, which have not been worked into the form of any inftrument, or thing pre-pared for war, by land or by fea, fhall not be reputed contraband, much lefs fuch as have been already wrought and made up for any other ufe; all which fhall wholly be reckoned among free goods, as likewife all other merchan-dizes and things which are not comprehended, and par-ticularly mentioned in the preceding article, fo that they may be tranfported, and carried in the freeft manner by the fubjects of both confederates, even to places belong-ing to an enemy, fuch towns or places being only except-ed, as are at that time befieged, blocked up round about, or invefted.

XXI. To

XXI. To the end that all manner of diffentions and quarrels may be avoided and prevented on one fide, and the other, it is agreed, that in cafe either of their royal Majefties who are allied, fhould be engaged in war, the fhips and veffels belonging to the fubjects of the other ally, muft be furnifhed with fea-letters or paffports, expreffing the name, property, and bulk of the fhip, as alfo the name of the place of habitation of the mafter or commander of the faid fhip, that it may appear thereby, that the fhip really and truly belongs to the fubjects of one of the princes; which paffports fhall be made out and granted, according to the form annexed to this treaty; they fhall likewife be recalled every year, that is, if the fhip happens to return home within the fpace of a year. It is likewife agreed, that fuch fhips being laden, are to be provided, not only, with paffports, as abovementioned, but alfo with certificates containing the feveral particulars of the cargo, the place whence the fhip failed, and whither fhe is bound, that fo it may be known, whether any forbidden or contraband goods, as are enumerated in the 19th article of this treaty, be on board the fame, which certificates fhall be made out by the officers of the place whence the fhip fet fail, in the accuftomed form. And if any one fhall think it fit, or advifable, to exprefs in the faid certificates, the perfon to whom they belong, he may freely do fo.

XXII. The fhips of the fubjects and inhabitants of both their moft ferene royal Majefties, coming to any of the fea-coafts within the dominions of either of the confederates, but not willing to enter into port, or being entered, yet not being willing to fhew or to fell the cargoes of their fhips, fhall not be obliged to give an account of their lading, unlefs they are fufpected upon fure evidence, of carrying to the enemies of the other confederate prohibited goods, called contraband.

XXIII. And in cafe of the faid manifeft fufpicion, the faid fubjects and inhabitants of the dominions of both their moft ferene royal Majefties, fhall be obliged to exhibit in the ports their paffports and certificates, in the manner before fpecified.

XXIV. But in cafe the fhips of the fubjects and inhabitants of both their moft ferene royal Majefties, either on

the

the fea-coaft, or on the high feas, fhall meet with the men of war of the other, or with privateers, the faid men of war and privateers, for preventing any inconveniencies, are to remain out of cannon-fhot, and to fend a boat to the merchant-fhip, which has been met with, and fhall enter her with two or three men only, to whom the mafter or commander of fuch fhip or veffel fhall fhew his paffport, concerning the property thereof, made out according to the form annexed to this prefent treaty ; and the fhip which fhall exhibit one, fhall have free paffage, and it fhall be wholly unlawful any way to moleft her, fearch, or compel her to quit her intended courfe.

XXV. But that merchant fhips of the other party, which intends to go to a port at enmity with the other confederate, or concerning whofe voyage, and the fort of goods on board, there may be juft fufpicion, fhall be obliged to exhibit, either on the high feas, or in the ports and havens, not only her paffports, but her certificates, expreffing that they are not of the kind of goods prohibited, which are fpecified in the 19th article.

XXVI. But if one party, on the exhibiting the abovefaid certificates, mentioning the particulars of the things on board, fhould difcover any goods of that kind which are declared contraband or prohibited by the 19th article of this treaty, defigned for a port fubject to the enemy of the other, it fhall be unlawful to break up the hatches of that fhip, wherein the fame fhall happen to be found, whether fhe belong to the fubjects of Great Britain, or of France, to open the chefts, packs, or cafks therein, or to remove even the fmalleft parcel of the goods, unlefs the lading be brought on fhore, in the prefence of the officers of the court of Admiralty, and an inventory thereof made ; but there fhall be no allowance to fell, exchange, or alienate the fame in any manner, unlefs after that due and lawful procefs fhall have been had againft fuch prohibited goods, and the judges of the Admiralty refpectively fhall, by a fentence pronounced, have confifcated the fame, faving always as well the fhip itfelf, as the other goods found therein, which by this treaty are to be efteemed free ; neither may they be detained on pretence of their being, as it were, infected by the prohibited goods, much lefs fhall

they

they be confifcated as lawful prize: but if not the whole cargo, but only part thereof, fhall confift of prohibited or contraband goods, and the commander of the fhip fhall be ready and willing to deliver them to the captor, who has difcovered them, in fuch cafe the captor having received thofe goods, fhall forthwith difcharge the fhip, and not hinder her, by any means, freely to profecute the voyage on which fhe was bound.

XXVII. On the contrary it is agreed, that whatever fhall be found to be laden by the fubjects and inhabitants of either party, on any fhip belonging to the enemy of the other, and his fubjects the whole, although it be not of the fort of prohibited goods, may be confifcated, in the fame mrnner as if it belonged to the enemy himfelf; except thofe goods and merchandizes as were put on board fuch fhip before the declaration of war, or even after fuch declaration, if fo be it were done within the time and limits following: that is to fay, if they were put on board fuch fhip, in any port and place within the fpace of fix weeks after fuch declaration, within the bounds called the Naze in Norway, and the Soundings; of two months from the Soundings to the city of Gibraltar; of ten weeks in the Mediterranean Sea; and of eight months in any other country or place in the world; fo that the goods of the fubjects of either prince, whether they be of the nature of fuch as are prohibited, or otherwife, which, as is aforefaid, were put on board any fhip belonging to an enemy before the war, or after the declaration of the fame, within the time and limits abovefaid, fhall no ways be liable to confifcation, but fhall well and truly be reftored, without delay, to the proprietors demanding the fame; but fo as that if the faid merchandizes be contraband, it fhall not be any ways lawful to carry them afterwards to the ports belonging to the enemy.

XXVIII. And that more abundant care may be taken for the fecurity of the fubjects of both their moft ferene royal Majefties, that they fuffer no injury by the men of war or privateers of the other party, all the commanders of the fhips of the Queen of Great Britain, and of the moft Chriftian King, and all their fubjects, fhall be forbid doing any injury or damage to the other fide; and if they

act

act to the contrary, they fhall be punifhed, and fhall moreover be bound to make fatisfaction for all caufe of damage, and the intereft thereof, by reparation, under the bond and obligation of their perfon and goods.

XXIX. For this caufe all commanders of privateers, before they receive their patents, or fpecial commiffions, fhall hereafter be obliged to give, before a competent judge, fufficient fecurity by good bail, who are men able to pay, and have no intereft in the faid fhip, and are each bound in the whole, for the fum of 1500l. fterling, or 16500 *Livres Tournois*; or if fuch fhip be provided with above one hundred and fifty feamen or foldiers, for the fum of 3000l. fterling, or 33000 *Livres Tournois*, that they will make entire fatisfaction for any damages and injuries whatfoever, which they, or their officers, or others in their fervice, commit during their courfe at fea, contrary to this prefent treaty, or the edicts of either of their moft ferene royal Majefties, publifhed by virtue thereof ; under penalty likewife of having their fpecial commiffions and patents revoked and annulled.

XXX. Both the abovenamed royal Majefties being willing to fhew a mutual and equal favour in all their dominions refpectively, to the fubjects of each other, in the fame manner as if they were their own fubjects, will give fuch orders as fhall be neceffary and effectual, that juftice be adminiftered concerning prizes in the court of Admiralty, according to the rule of equity and right, and the articles of this treaty, by judges who are above all fufpicion, and who have no manner of intereft in the caufe in difpute.

XXXI. Whenfoever the Ambaffadors of each of their royal Majefties abovenamed, and other their minifters, having a public character, and refiding in the court of the other Prince, fhall complain of the unjuftnefs of the fentences which have been given, their Majefties on each fide fhall take care, that the fame be revifed and re-examined in their refpective councils, that it may appear whether the directions and provifions prefcribed in this treaty have been obferved, and have had their due effect . they fhall likewife take care, that this matter be effectually provided for, and that right be done to every com-
plainant

plainant within the fpace of three months. However, before or after judgment given, the revifion thereof ftill depending, for the avoiding of all damage, it fhall not be lawful to fell the goods in difpute, or to unlade them, unlefs with the confent of the perfons concerned.

XXXII. A fuit being commenced between the captors of prizes on one part, and the reclaimers of the fame on the other, and a fentence or decree being given in favour of the reclaimer; that fame fentence or decree, fecurity being given, fhall be put in execution, the appeal of the captor to a fuperior judge in any wife notwithftanding; which, however, is not to be obferved when judgment has been given againft the reclaimer.

XXXIII. In cafe that either fhips of war, or merchant-men, forced by ftorm, or other misfortune, be driven on rocks or fhelves on the coafts of one or the other party, and are there broken to pieces and fhip-wrecked, whatever part of the fhips, or tackling thereof, as alfo of the goods and merchandizes fhall be faved, or the produce thereof, fhall be faithfully reftored to the proprietors, reclaimers, or their factors, paying only the expences of preferving the fame, in fuch manner as it may be fettled on both fides concerning the rate of falvage : faving, at the fame time, the rights and cuftoms of each nation : and both their moft ferene royal Majefties will interpofe their authority, that fuch of their fubjects may be feverely punifhed, who in the like accident fhall be found guilty of inhumanity.

XXXIV. It fhall be free for the fubjects of each party, to employ fuch advocates, attornies, notaries, folicitors, and factors, as they fhall think fit; to which end the faid advocates, and others abovementioned, may be appointed by the ordinary judges, if it be needful, and the judges be required thereunto.

XXXV. And that commerce and navigation may be more fecurely and freely followed, it is further agreed, that neither the Queen of Great Britain, nor the moft Chriftian King, fhall receive any pirates and robbers, into any of their ports, havens, cities or towns, neither fhall they permit them to be received into their ports to be protected or affifted, by any manner of harbouring, or

fupport,

fupport, by any the fubjects or inhabitants of either of
them ; but they fhall rather caufe all fuch pirates and fea-
robbers, or whoever fhall receive, conceal, or affift them,
to be apprehended and punifhed as they deferve, for a
terror and example to others. And all the fhips, goods,
or merchandizes, being piratically taken by them, and
brought into the ports of the kingdom of either, as
much as can be found, although they have by fale been
conveyed to others, fhall be reftored to the lawful owners,
or their deputies, having inftruments of delegation, and
an authority of procuration for reclaiming the fame; and
indemnifation fhall be made, proper evidence being firft
given in the court of Admiralty, for proving the property.
And all fhips and merchandizes, of what nature foever,
which can be refcued out of their hands on the high feas,
fhall be brought into fome port of either kingdom, and
fhall be delivered to the cuftody of the officers of that
port, with this intention, that they be delivered entire to
the true proprietor, as foon as due and fufficient proof
fhall have been made concerning the property thereof.

XXXVI. It fhall be lawful, as well for rhe fhips of war
of both their moft ferene royal Majefties, as for privateers, to carry whitherfoever they pleafe, the fhips and
goods taken from their enemies, neither fhall they be
obliged to pay any thing to the officers of the Admiralty,
or to any other judges, nor fhall the aforementioned
prizes, when they come to and enter the ports of either of
their moft ferene royal Majefties, be detained by arreft,
neither fhall fearchers, or other officers of thofe places,
make examination concerning them, or the validity thereof; but rather they fhall have liberty to hoift fail at any
time, to depart, and to carry their prizes to that place,
which is mentioned in their commiffion of patent, which
the commanders of fuch fhips of war fhall be obliged to
fhew : on the contrary, no fhelter or refuge fhall be given
in their ports to fuch as have made a prize upon the fubjects of either of their Royal Majefties. And if perchance
fuch fhips fhall come in, being forced by ftrefs of weather,
or the danger of the fea, particular care fhall be taken,
as far as it is not repugnant to former treaties made with
other

other Kings and States) that they go from thence, and retire elfewhere, as foon as poffible.

XXXVII. Neither of their moft ferene royal Majefties fhall permit that the fhips or goods of the other be taken upon the coafts, or in the ports, or rivers of their dominions, by fhips of war, or others having commiffion from any prince, commonwealth, or town whatfoever. And in cafe fuch a thing fhould happen, both parties fhall ufe their authority and united force, that the damage done be made good.

XXXVIII. If hereafter it fhall happen through inadvertency, or otherwife, that any contraventions, or inconveniencies on either fide arife concerning the obfervation of this treaty, the friendfhip and good intelligence fhall not immediately thereupon be broke off; but this treaty fhall fubfift in all its force, and a proper remedy for removing the inconveniencies fhall be procured, as likewife reparation of the contraventions; and if the fubjects of the one or the other be found in fault, they only fhall be feverely punifhed and chaftized.

XXXIX. But if it fhall appear that a captor made ufe of any kind of torture upon the mafter of the fhip, the fhip's crew, or others who fhall be on board any fhip belonging to the fubjects of the other party; in fuch cafe, not only the fhip itfelf, together with the perfons, merchandizes, and goods whatfoever, fhall be forthwith releafed without any further delay, and fet entirely free, but alfo fuch as fhall be found guilty of fo great a crime, as alfo the acceffaries thereunto, fhall fuffer the moft fevere punifhment, fuitable to their crime; this the Queen of Great Britain, and the moft Chriftian King, do mutually engage fhall be done, without any refpect of perfons.

*Form of the Paffports to be defired of, and given by the Lord High Admiral of Great Britain, &c. or by the Lords Commiffioners for executing the Office of High Admiral of Great Britain, &c. according to the Direction of the 21ft Article of this Taeaty.*

TO all to whom thefe prefents fhall come, greeting. We          High Admiral of Great Britain, &c.

(or)

(or) We            commiffioners for executing the cf-
fice of High Admiral of Great Britain, &c. do make
known and teftify by thefe prefents, that A. B.        of
C.            the ufual place of his dwelling, mafter or
commander of the fhip called D.        appeared before
us, and declared by folemn oath, (or) produced a certificate under the feal of the magiftrate, or of the officers of
the cuftoms of the town and port of E.        Dated the
            day of the month of        in the year of our
Lord 17        of and concerning the oath made before
them, that the faid fhip and veffel D. burthen        tons,
whereof he himfelf is at this time mafter or commander,
doth really and truly belong to the fubjects of her moft ferene Majefty our moft gracious Sovereign. And whereas
it would be moft acceptable to us, that the faid mafter or
commander fhould be affifted in the affairs wherein he is
juftly and honeftly employed, we defire you, and all and
every of you, that wherefoever the faid mafter or commander fhall bring his fhip, and the goods on board
thereof, you would caufe him to be kindly received, to be
civily treated, and in paying the lawful and accuftomed
duties, and other things, to be admitted to enter, to remain in, to depart out of your ports, rivers, and dominions, and to enjoy all manner of right, and all kind of
navigation, traffic, and commerce, in all places where he
fhall think it proper and convenient. For which we fhall
always be moft willing and ready to make returns to you
in a grateful manner. In witnefs and confirmation whereof,
we have figned thefe prefents, and caufed our feal to be
put thereunto. Given at        the        day of the
month of        in the year 17

*Form of the Certificates to be required of; and to be given by*
*the Magiftrate, or Officers of the Cuftoms of the Town and*
*Port, in their refpective Towns and Ports, to the Ships and*
*Veffels which fail from thence, according to the direction of*
*the 21ft Article of this prefent Treaty.*

WE A. B.        magiftrate (or) officers of the
    cuftoms of the town and port of C.        do
certify and atteft, that on the        day of the month
                                                    of

**of**　　　in the year of our Lord 17　　D. E. of F.
　　　　perfonally appeared before us, and declared by
a folemn oath, that the fhip or veffel called G.　　of
about　　　tons, whereof H. I. of K. his ufual place of
habitation, is mafter or commander, does rightfully and
properly belong to him and others, fubjects of her moft
ferene Majefty, our moft gracious Sovereign, and to them
alone : that fhe is now bound from the port of L.
to the port of M.　　　laden with the goods and merchandizes hereunder particularly defcribed and enumerated, that is to fay, as follows :

In witnefs whereof we have figned this certificate, and
fealed it with the feal of our office.　Given the
day of the month of　　in the year of our Lord 17

*Form of the Paſſports and Letters, which are to be given in
the Admiralty of France, to the Ships and Barks, which
ſhall go from thence, according to the 21ſt Article of this
preſent Treaty.*

LEWIS, Count of Thouloufe, Admiral of France, to
all who fhall fee thefe prefents, greeting.　We make
known, that we have given leave and permiffion to
mafter and commander of the fhip called　　　of
the town of　　　burthen　　　tons, or thereabouts,
lying at prefent in the port and haven of　　　and
bound for　　　and laden with　　　after that his
fhip has been vifited, and before failing, he fhall make
oath before the officers, who have the jurifdiction of maritime affairs, that the faid fhip belongs to one or more of
the fubjects of his Majefty, the act whereof fhall be put at
the end of thefe prefents, as likewife that he will keep,
and caufe to be kept by his crew on board, the marine ordinances and regulations, and enter in the proper office a
lift figned and witneffed, containing the names and fur-
names, the places of birth and abode of the crew of his
fhip, and of all who fhall embark on board her, whom he
fhall not take on board, without the knowledge and permiffion of the officers of the marine; and in every port or
haven where he fhall enter with his fhip, he fhall fhew this
prefent leave to the officers and judges of the marine,
and

and shall give a faithful account to them of what passed and was done during his voyage. And he shall carry the colours, arms, and ensigns of the king, and of us during his voyage. In witness whereof we have signed these presents, and put the seal of our arms thereunto, and caused the same to be countersigned by our secretary of the marine at the        day of        17        signed LEWIS, count of Thoulouse, and underneath by

### Form of the Act containing the Oath.

WE        of the Admiralty of        do certify, that        master of the ship named in the above passport, has taken the oath mentioned therein. Done at        the        day of        17

XL. The present treaty shall be ratified by the Queen of Great Britain, and by the most Christian King, and the ratifications thereof shall be duly exchanged at Utrecht within four weeks, or sooner, if possible.

XLI. In witness whereof we, the underwritten ambassadors extraordinary and plenipotentiaries of the Queen of Great Britain, and of the most Christian King, have set our hands and seals to this present treaty, at Utrecht the $\frac{31}{11}$ day of $\frac{March}{April}$ in the year of our Lord 1713.

(L. S.) *Joh. Bristol*, C. P. S.        (L. S.) *Huxelles*.
(L. S.) *Strafford*.        (L. S.) *Mesnager*.

BE it known unto all men, that whereas in the 9th article of the treaty of commerce, concluded this day between the most serene Queen of Great Britain, and the most serene the most Christian King, by their Majesties ambassadors extraordinary, and plenipotentiaries, mention is made of some heads of matters, which being proposed on the part of Great Britain, have not as yet been mutually adjusted ; and therefore it was thought fit to refer them to be discussed and determined by commissioners : we therefore the underwritten ambassadors, that it may certainly appear what are those heads of matters which are to be referred to commissioners, have resolved

to

to give a particular defcription of them in this writing; declaring that they are the fame, and no other than what follow :

I. NO manufactures of either kingdom, and the dominions belonging thereunto, fhall hereafter be fubject to be infpected and confifcated, under any pretence of fraud or defect in making or working them, or becaufe of any other imperfection therein; but abfolute freedom fhall be allowed to the buyer and feller to bargain and agree for the fame as they fhall fee good; any law, ftatute, edict, arreft, privilege, grant, or cuftom, to the contrary notwithftanding.

II. And forafmuch as a certain ufage, not confirmed by any law, has obtained in feveral towns of Great Britain and France; that is to fay, that every one for coming in, and going out, fhall pay a kind of tax, called in Englifh *Head-Money*, and in French, *Du Chef*, it is concluded, that neither the fame, nor any other duty on that account, fhall any more be exacted.

III. And the Britifh merchants fhall not hereafter be forbidden to fell the faid tobacco to any buyer whom they pleafe, for which purpofe, the letting out the duties on the faid tobacco to farmers, which has been hitherto practifed, fhall ceafe, neither fhall fuch farming be ufed again hereafter.

IV. The following cafe only being excepted, that is to fay where Britifh fhips fhall take up merchandizes in one port, and carry them to another port of France, in which cafe, and in no other, the Britifh fubjects fhall be obliged to pay the duties abrogated and abolifhed by this article, only in proportion to the goods which they take in, and not according to the bulk of the fhip.

V. Whereas feveral kinds of goods, contained in caiks, chefts, or other cafes, for which the duties are paid by weight, will be exported from, and imported into France by Britifh fubjects, it is therefore agreed, that in fuch cafe the aforefaid duties fhall be payable only according to the weight of the goods themfelves; but the weight of the cafks, chefts, and other cafes whatever, fhall be deducted

in

in fuch manner, and in fuch proportion, as has been hitherto in ufe in England, and is ftill practifed.

VI. It is further agreed, that if any miftake or error fhall on either fide be committed by any mafter of a fhip, his interpreter, or factor, or by others employed by him, in making the entry or declaration of the goods on board his fhip, for fuch defect, if fo be fome fraud does not evidently appear, neither the fhip nor the lading thereof fhall be fubject to be confifcated, but it fhall be free for the proprietors to take back again fuch goods as were omitted in the entry or declaration of the mafter of the fhip, paying only the accuftomed duties according to the rates fettled in the books; neither fhall the merchants, or the mafter of the fhip, lofe the faid goods, or fuffer any other punifhment, if fo be that the faid goods, fo omitted, were not brought on fhore, before the declaration made, and the cuftoms paid for the fame.

VII. And whereas the quality of the fhip, mafter, and goods, will fufficiently appear from fuch paffports and certificates, it fhall not be lawful for the commanders of men of war to exact any other verification under any title whatfoever. But if any merchant fhip fhall want fuch paffports or certificates, then it may be examined by a proper judge, but in fuch manner, as if it fhall be found from other proofs and documents, that it does truly belong to the fubjects of either of the confederates, and does not contain any prohibited goods, defigned to be carried to the enemy of the other, it fhall not be liable to confifcation, but fhall be releafed, together with its cargo, in order to proceed on its voyage, fince it may often happen that fuch papers could not come to the fhip when fhe was fetting fail from any port, or that they have been loft by fome chance or other, or that they have been taken away from the fhip. And if, befides the paffports and certificates made according to the form of their treaty, other paffports and certificates happen to be found in the fhip, in another form, and perhaps according to the prefcription of treaties made with others, no pretence fhall be taken from thence, of detaining, or in any wife molefting, either the fhip, or men, or goods. If the mafter of the fhip named in the paffports be removed by death, or any other caufe,

caufe, and another be put in his place, the paffports fhall neverthelefs retain their force, and the fhips, and goods laden thereon, fhall be fecure.

VIII. It is further provided on both fides, and fhall be taken for a general rule, that a fhip and goods, although they have remained in the enemies power for four and twenty hours, fhall not therefore be efteemed as capture, and be immediately made prize; but, if on other accounts they ought to be reftored, they may be reclaimed, and fhall be given again to the proprietors.

IX. It fhall be free for both their royal Majefties, for the advantage of their fubjects, trading to the kingdoms and dominions of the other, to conftitute national confuls of their own fubjects, who fhall enjoy that right and liberty which belongs to them by reafon of the exercife of their function; but as to the places where fuch confuls are to be appointed, both fides fhall afterwards agree between themfelves.

In witnefs whereof, we the Ambaffadors Extraordinary and Plenipotentiaries of her Sacred Royal Majefty of Great Britain, and of his Sacred Royal Moft Chriftian Majefty, have fubfcribed this prefent inftrument with our hands, and fet our feals thereunto. At Utrecht, the $\frac{31}{11}$ day of the month of $\frac{March}{April}$ in the year 1713.

(L. S.) *Joh. Briftol, C. P. S.*　　(L. S.) *Huxelles.*
(L. S.) *Strafford.*　　　　　　　(L. S.) *Mefnager.*

BE it known unto all men, that whereas in the 9th article of the treaty of navigation and commerce, concluded the $\frac{31}{11}$ day of $\frac{March}{April}$ 1713, between the Moft Serene Queen of Great Britain, and the Moft Serene the Moft Chriftian King, by the Ambaffadors Extraordinary and Plenipotentiaries of their Majefties, certain merchandizes, namely, woollen manufactures, fugar, falt fifh, and what is produced from whales, are excepted in general words from the rule of the Tariff made the 18th day of the month of September, in the year 1664, in order to be afterwards referred to the difcuffion of commiffaries; to prevent therefore all miftakes and ambiguity, which might perhaps arife

from

from such general terms, and to make it more evidently appear what particular sorts of goods are to come under the consideration of the aforesaid commissaries. We the underwritten Ambassadors Extraordinary and Plenipotentiaries, have declared by these presents, and do declare, that the exception of the abovementioned merchandizes, is to be understood in the manner following :

I. WHalebone cut and prepared, fins and oils of whales, shall pay at all places of importation in the kingdom, the duties appointed by the Tariff of the 7th of December 1699.

II. Cloths, ratines, and serges, shall be likewise subject to the same duties of the Tariff of the 7th of December 1699, and in order to facilitate the trade thereof, it shall be allowed to import them by St. Valery upon the Somme, by Rouen, and by Bourdeaux, where these goods shall be subject to visitation in the same manner as those which are made in the kingdom.

III. Salt fish in barrels only is to be imported into the kingdom, and at all places of entrance in the kingdom, countries, and territories under the dominion of the King, even at all free ports, the duties of landing and of consumption shall be paid, which were appointed before the Tariff of 1664, and besides 40 livres per last, consisting of 12 barrels, weighing each 300 lb. for the duty of entry, which entry shall not be permitted but by St. Valery upon the Somme, Rouen, Nantz, Libourne, and Bourdeaux, and shall remain prohibited at all other harbours or ports, as well in the Ocean as in the Mediterranean.

IV. Refined sugar, in loaf or in powder, white and brown sugar candy, shall pay the duties appointed by the Tariff of 1699.

In confirmation of which, we the underwritten Ambassadors Extraordinary, and Plenipotentiaries of her Majesty the Queen of Great Britain, and the Most Christian King, have signed and sealed these presents at Utrecht, the $\frac{2}{9}$ day of $\frac{\text{April}}{\text{May}}$ in the year 1713.

(L. S.) *Joh. Bristol, C. P. S.*　　　(L. S) *Huxelles.*
(L. S.) *Strafford.*　　　　　　　　(L. S.) *Mesnager.*

*Treaty*

*Treaty of Peace and Friendſhip between the Moſt Serene and Moſt Potent Princeſs* Anne, *by the Grace of God Queen of* Great Britain, France, *and* Ireland, *Defender of the Faith, &c. and the Moſt Serene and Moſt Potent Prince* Philip V. *the Catholic King of* Spain, *concluded at* Utrecht, *the* ¹³⁄₁ *Day of July* 1713. Reprinted from the Copy publiſhed by the Queen's ſpecial Command.

I. THAT there be a Chriſtian univerſal peace, and a perpetual and true friendſhip, between the Moſt Serene and Moſt Mighty Princeſs Anne, Queen of Great Britain, and the Moſt Serene and Moſt Mighty Prince Philip V. the Catholic King of Spain, and their heirs and ſucceſſors, and alſo the kingdoms, ſtates, dominions, and provinces of both parties, whereſoever ſituated, and their ſubjects; and that the ſame be ſo ſincerely preſerved and cultivated, that neither party do, under any colour whatever, endeavour to attempt any thing to the deſtruction or detriment of the other, or yield any aid, by what name ſoever it be called, to thoſe who attempt the ſame, or who endeavour to do any damage, neither may or ought they to help them by any means. On the contrary, their Royal Majeſties ſhall be obliged, the one to promote the advantage, honour, and intereſt of the other, and to direct their councils to that end with all care, that, by mutual proof of friendſhip, the peace which is now made, may daily receive new additions of ſtrength.

II. But whereas the war, which is ſo happily ended by this peace, was at the beginning undertaken, and was carried on for ſo many years with the utmoſt force, at immenſe charge, and with almoſt infinite ſlaughter, becauſe of the great danger which threatened the liberty and ſafety of all Europe, from the too cloſe conjunction of the kingdoms of Spain and France. And whereas, to take away all uneaſineſs and ſuſpicion, concerning ſuch conjunction, out of the minds of people, and to ſettle and eſtabliſh the peace and tranquillity of Chriſtendom, by an equal balance of power (which is the beſt and moſt ſolid foundation

foundation of a mutual friendfhip, and of a concord which will be lafting on all fides) as well the Catholic King, as the Moft Chriftian King, have confented, that care fhould be taken by fufficient precautions, that the kingdoms of Spain and France fhould never come and be united under the fame dominion, and that one and the fame perfon fhould never become king of both kingdoms. And to this end his Catholic Majefty has, for himfelf, his heirs, and fucceffors, moft folemnly renounced all manner of right, title, and pretenfion to the crown of France, in the form and words following:

[*The inftrumemts of renunciation, are exactly the fame with thofe already inferted in the Treaty with France of this date.*]

His faid Catholic Majefty hereby renews and confirms the moft folemn renunciation abovementioned, made on his part; and as it has obtained the force of a general and fundamental law, he engages again in the moft facred manner poffible, that he w ll obferve and take care that the fame be obferved inviolably, and he will likewife ufe his utmoft d ligence, and provide with the greateft earneft-nefs, that the aforefaid renunciations may be irrevocably obferved, and put in execution, as well on the part of Spain, as on the part of France, forafmuch as while they fubfift in their full force, and are faithfully kept on both fides, as alfo the other tranfactions relating thereto, the crowns of Spain and France will be fo feparated and divided from each other, that they can never hereafter be united in one.

III. That there be a perpetual amnefty on both fides, and oblivion of all things which have been in an hoftile manner committed in any place, or by any way, on one fide and the other, during the late war. So that neither on account thereof, nor by reafon or under pretence of any other matter, fhall the one any way do, or fuffer to be done, any enmity to the other, or give any moleftation, directly or indirectly, under colour of right, or by way of fact.

IV. All and fingular the prifoners on each fide, of what ftate or condition foever they be, fhall immediately after the ratification of this prefent treaty, be reftored to their former liberty, without any ranfom, paying only
   
   such

such debts as they may have contracted, during their being prisoners.

V. Moreover, for giving a greater and more lasting
strength to the peace which is restored, and to this friendship, which is never to be violated, and for cutting off all
occasions of distrust, which may at any time arise from the
established right and order of the hereditary succession
to the crown of Great Britain, and the limitation thereof
by the laws of Great Britain, (made and enacted in the
reign of the late King William III. of glorious memory,
and in the reign of the present Queen) to the issue of the
abovenamed Queen, and in failure thereof to the Most Serene Princess Sophia, Electress Dowager of Brunswick, and
her heirs, in the Protestant line of Hanover. That therefore the said succession may be well and securely preserved,
according to the laws of Great Britain, the Catholic King
sincerely and solemnly acknowleges the abovementioned
limitation of the succession to the kingdom of Great Britain; and declares and engages, on the faith and word of
a King, and on the pledge of his and his successors honour, that the same is, and shall for ever be, approved and
accepted by him, and his heirs and successors; and, under
the same tie of the word of a King and his honour, the
Catholic King does promise, that no person besides the
said Queen, and her successors, according to the order of
limitation established by the laws and statutes of Great
Britain, shall ever be acknowledged, or reputed by him,
or by his heirs and successors, to be King or Queen of
Great Britain.

VI. The Catholic King doth further promise, as well
in his own name, as in that of his heirs and successors,
that they will not at any time disturb or molest the said
Queen of Great Britain, her heirs and successors, of the
Protestant line, as aforesaid, being in possession of the
crown of Great Britain, and the dominions subject thereunto; neither will the aforesaid Catholic King, or any
of his successors, give at any time any aid, succour, favour, or counsel, directly or indirectly, by land or by sea,
in money, arms, ammunition, warlike instruments, ships,
soldiers, seamen, or in any other manner whatever, to any
person or persons, whosoever they be, who on any cause

or

or pretence fhould hereafter endeavour to oppofe the faid fucceffion, either by open war, or by encouraging fedition, and forming confpiracies againft fuch prince and princes, who are in poffeffion of the throne of Great Britain, by virtue of the acts of parliament there made, or againft that prince or princefs to whom the fucceffion to the crown of Great Britain fhall belong, according to the acts of parliament, as abovefaid.

VII. That the ordinary diftribution of juftice be reftored, and open again through the kingdoms and dominions of each of their royal majefties, fo that it may be free for all the fubjects on both fides, to profecute and obtain their rights, pretenfions and actions, according to the laws, conftitutions and ftatutes of each kingdom. And efpecially if there be any complaints concerning injuries or grievances, which have been done contrary to the tenor of the treaties, either in time of peace, or at the beginning of the war lately ended, care fhall be taken that the damages be forthwith made good, according to the rule of juftice.

VIII. That there be a free ufe of navigation and commerce between the fubjects of each kingdom, as it was heretofore, in time of peace, and before the declaration of this late war, in the reign of Charles II. of glorious memory, Catholic King of Spain, according to the treaties of friendfhip, confederation, and commerce, which were formerly made between both nations, according to ancient cuftoms, letters patents, cedulas, and other particular acts; and alfo according to the treaty or treaties of commerce which are now, or will forthwith be made at Madrid. And whereas, among other conditions of the general peace, it is by common confent eftablifhed as a chief and fundamental rule, that the exercife of navigation and commerce to the Spanifh Weft-Indies, fhould remain in the fame ftate as it was in the time of the aforefaid King Charles II. That therefore this rule may hereafter be obferved with inviolable faith, and in a manner never to be broken, and thereby all caufes of diftruft and fufpicion, concerning that matter may be prevented and removed, it is efpecially agreed and concluded, that no licence, nor any permiffion at all, fhall at any time be given, either to the French, or to any nation whatever, in any
name,

name, or under any pretence, directly or indirectly, to
fail, to traffick in, or introduce negroes, goods, merchandizes, or any things whatfoever into the dominions fubject to the crown of Spain in America, except what may
be agreed by the treaty or treaties of commerce abovefaid, and the rights and privileges granted in a certain
convention, commonly called *el Affiento de Negros*, whereof mention is made in the twelfth article; except alfo
whatfoever the faid Catholic King, or his heirs or fucceffors, fhall promife by any contract or contracts for the
introduction of negros into the Spanifh Weft-Indies to
be made after that the convention, or the *Affiento de Negros* abovementioned fhall be determined. And that more
ftrong and full precautions may be taken on all fides, as
abovefaid, concerning the navigation and commerce to the
Weft-Indies, it is hereby further agreed and concluded,
that neither the Catholic King, nor any of his heirs and
fucceffors whatfoever, fhall fell, yield, pawn, transfer, or
by any means, or under any name, alienate from them
and the crown of Spain, to the French, or to any other
nations whatever, any lands, dominions, or territories, or
any part thereof belonging to Spain in America. On the
contrary, that the Spanifh dominions in the Weft-Idies
may be preferved whole and entire, the Queen of Great
Britain engages, that fhe will endeavour, and give affiftance to the Spaniards, that the ancient limits of their dominions in the Weft Indies be reftored, and fettled as they
ftood in the time of the abovefaid Catholic King Charles
II. if it fhall appear that they have in any manner, or under any pretence, been broken into, and leffened in any
part, fince the death of the aforefaid Catholic King
Charles II.

IX. It is further agreed and concluded as a general
rule, that all and fingular the fubjects of each kingdom
fhall, in all countries and places on both fides, have and
enjoy at leaft the fame privileges, liberties and immunities,
as to all duties, impofitions, or cuftoms whatfoever, relating to perfons, goods, and merchandizes, fhips, freight,
feamen, navigation, and commerce; and fhall have the
like favour in all things, as the fubjects of France, or any
other foreign nation, the moft favoured, have, poffefs,
and

and enjoy, or at any time hereafter may have, poffefs, or enjoy.

X. The Catholic King does hereby, for himfelf, his heirs and fucceffors, yield to the crown of Great Britain the full and entire propriety of the town and caftle of Gibraltar, together with the port, fortifications, and forts thereunto belonging; and he gives up the faid propriety to be held and enjoyed abfolutely with all manner of right for ever, without any exception or impediment whatfoever. But that abufes and frauds may be avoided by importing any kinds of goods, the Catholic King wills, and takes it to be underftood, that the abovenamed propriety be yielded to Great Britain, without any territorial jurifdiction, and without any open communication by land with the country round about. Yet whereas the communication by fea with the coaft of Spain, may not at all times be fafe or open, and thereby it may happen that the garrifon, and other inhabitants of Gibraltar, may be brought to great ftraits; and as it is the intention of the Catholic King, only that fraudulent importations of goods fhould, as is abovefaid, be hindered by an inland communication, it is therefore provided, that in fuch cafes it may be lawful to purchafe, for ready money, in the neighbouring territories of Spain, provifions, and other things neceffary for the ufe of the garrifon, the inhabitants, and the fhips which lie in the harbour. But if any goods be found imported by Gibraltar, either by way of barter for purchafing provifions, or under any other pretence, the fame fhall be confifcated, and complaint being made thereof, thofe perfons who have acted contrary to the faith of this treaty, fhall be feverely punifhed. And her Britannic Majefty, at the requeft of the Catholic King, does confent and agree, that no leave fhall be given, under any pretence whatfoever, either to Jews or Moors, to refide, or have their dwellings, in the faid town of Gibraltar; and that no refuge or fhelter fhall be allowed to any Moorifh fhips of war in the harbour of the faid town, whereby the communication between Spain and Ceuta may be obftructed, or the coafts of Spain be infefted by the excurfions of the Moors. But whereas treaties of friendfhip, and a liberty and intercourfe of commerce, are between the Britifh and certain territories,

fituate

fituate on the coaft of Africa, it is always to be underftood, that the Britifh fubjects cannot refufe the Moors, and their fhips, entry into the port of Gibraltar, purely upon the account of merchandizing. Her Majefty the Queen of Great Britain does further promife, that the free exercife of their religion fhall be indulged to the Roman Catholic inhabitants of the aforefaid town. And in cafe it fhall hereafter feem meet to the crown of Great Britain, to grant, fell, or by any means to alienate therefrom the propriety of the faid town of Gibraltar, it is hereby agreed, and concluded, that the preference of having the fame, fhall always be given to the crown of Spain before any others.

XI. Moreover, the Catholic King doth in like manner for himfelf, his heirs and fucceffors, yield to the crown of Great Britain, the whole ifland of Minorca, and doth transfer thereunto for ever, all right, and the moft abfolute dominion over the faid ifland, and in particular over the town, caftle, harbour, and fortifications of the bay of Minorca, commonly called Port Mahon, together with the other ports, places, and towns, fituated in the aforefaid ifland. But it is provided, as in the above written article, that no refuge or fhelter fhall be open to any fhips of war of the Moors in Port Mahon, or in any other port of the faid ifland of Minorca, whereby the Spanifh coafts may be infefted by their excurfions: and the Moors and their fhips fhall only be allowed to enter the ifland aforefaid, on account of traffick, according to the agreement of treaties. The Queen of Great Britain promifes alfo on her part, that if at any time it fhall happen, that the ifland of Minorca, and the ports, towns, and places therein fituated, be by any means hereafter alienated from the crown of her kingdoms, the preference fhall be given to the crown of Spain, before any other nation whatever, of redeeming the poffeffion and propriety of the aforefaid ifland. Her royal Majefty of Great Britain moreover engages, that fhe will take care, that all the inhabitants of the faid ifland, both ecclefiaftical and fecular, fhall fafely and peaceably enjoy all their eftates and honours, and the free ufe of the Roman Catholic religion fhall be permitted: and meafures fhall be taken for preferving the aforefaid religion in that ifland, provided the fame be confiftent with the civil government

and

and laws of Great Britain. Those likewise who are now in the service of his Catholic Majesty, shall enjoy their honours and estates, though they continue in the said service; and it shall be lawful for any person who is desirous to leave the said island, to sell his estate, and pass freely with the value thereof into Spain.

XII. The Catholic King doth furthermore hereby give and grant to her Britannic Majesty, and to the company of her subjects appointed for that purpose, as well the subjects of Spain, as all others, being excluded, the contract for introducing negroes into several parts of the dominions of his Catholic Majesty in America, commonly called *el Pacto de el Assiento de Negros*, for the space of thirty years successively, beginning from the first day of the month of May, in the year 1713, with the same conditions on which the French enjoyed it, or at any time might or ought to enjoy the same, together with a tract or tracts of land to be allotted by the said Catholic King, and to be granted to the company aforesaid, commonly called *la Compania de el Assiento*, in some convenient place on the river of Plata, (no duties or revenues being payable by the said company on that account, during the time of the abovementioned contract, and no longer) and this settlement of the said society, or those tracts of land, shall be proper and sufficient for planting, and sowing, and for feeding cattle for the subsistence of those who are in the service of the said company, and of their negroes; and that the said negroes may be there kept in safety till they are sold; and moreover, that the ships belonging to the said company may come close to land, and be secure from any danger. But it shall always be lawful for the Catholic King, to appoint an officer in the said place or settlement, who may take care that nothing be done or practised contrary to his royal interests. And all who manage the affairs of the said company there, or belong to it, shall be subject to the inspection of the aforesaid officer, as to all matters relating to the tracts of land abovementioned. But if any doubts, difficulties, or controversies, should arise between the said officer and the managers for the said company, they shall be referred to the determination of the governor of Buenos Ayres. The Catholic King has been likewise pleased to

grant

grant to the said company, several other extraordinary advantages, which are more fully and amply explained in the contract of the Assiento, which was made and concluded at Madrid, the 26th day of the month of March, of this present year 1713. Which contract, or *Assiento de Negros*, and all the clauses, conditions, privileges and immunities contained therein, and which are not contrary to this article, are and shall be deemed, and taken to be, part of this treaty, in the same manner as if they had been here inserted word for word.

XIII. Whereas the Queen of Great Britain has continually pressed, and insisted with the greatest earnestness, that all the inhabitants of the principality of Catalonia, of whatever state or condition they may be, should not only obtain a full and perpetual oblivion of all that was done in the late war, and enjoy the entire possession of all their estates and honours, but should also have their ancient privileges preserved safe and untouched; the Catholic King, in compliance with the said Queen of Great Britain, hereby grants and confirms to all the inhabitants of Catalonia whatsoever, not only the amnesty desired, together with the full possession of all their estates and honours, but also gives and grants to them all the privileges which the inhabitants of both Castiles, who, of all the Spaniards, are the most dear to the Catholic King, have and enjoy, or may hereafter have and enjoy.

XIV. And whereas the Catholic King, at the request of her royal Britannic Majesty, has been pleased to yield the kingdom of Sicily to his royal highness Victor Amadeus, Duke of Savoy, and by the treaty this day entered into between his royal Catholic Majesty, and his royal highness of Savoy, does make a cession of the said kingdom, her royal Majesty of Great Britain aforesaid, promises and engages, that she will take great care, that in default of the heirs male of the house of Savoy, the possession of the aforesaid kingdom of Sicily, shall revert again to the crown of Spain; and her abovesaid royal Britannic Majesty, doth further consent, that the kingdom of Sicily may not, under any pretence, or in any manner whatever, be alienated or given to any prince or state, unless to the Catholic King of Spain, and to his heirs and successors.

fors. And whereas the Catholic King hath made known to her royal Britannic Majefty, that it would be both reafonable in itſelf, and acceptable to him, that not only the ſubjects of the kingdom of Sicily, although they may reſide in the dominions of Spain, and be in the ſervice of his ſaid Catholic Majeſty, but alſo the Spaniards and other ſubjects of Spain, who may perhaps have eſtates and honours in the aforeſaid kingdom of Sicily, ſhould without any diminution, entirely enjoy their ſaid eſtates and honours, and ſhould in no wiſe, under pretence of perſonal abſence out of the ſaid kingdom, be troubled or diſquieted. And whereas the aboveſaid Catholic King freely promiſes likewiſe on his part, that he will conſent, that the ſubjects of the ſaid kingdom of Sicily, and other ſubjects of his ſaid Royal Highneſs, if they ſhould chance to have eſtates and honours in Spain, or other the dominions belonging to Spain, ſhall in like manner, without any diminution, intirely enjoy the ſame, and that they ſhall in no wiſe be troubled or diſturbed under pretence of perſonal abſence : therefore her royal Britannic Majeſty promiſes, that ſhe will endeavour, and will give inſtructions to her Ambaſſadors extraordinary, and Plenipotentiaries at Utrecht, that they interpoſe the moſt effectual good offices, that the Catholic King and his Royal Highneſs may mutually agree concerning this matter, and may take care and provide for the ſame, in ſuch manner as ſhall be moſt commodious on both ſides.

XV. Their royal Majeſties on both parts renew and confirm all treaties of peace, friendſhip, confederation, and commerce, made heretofore, and concluded between the crowns of Great Britain and Spain, and the ſaid treaties are hereby renewed and confirmed in as full and ample manner, as if they were now particularly here inſerted ; that is to ſay, as far as they are not found to be contrary to the treaties of peace and commerce which were the laſt made and ſigned. And eſpecially by this treaty thoſe agreements, treaties, and conventions are confirmed and ſtrengthened, which relate as well to the exerciſe of commerce and navigation in Europe, and elſewhere, as to the introduction of negroes into the Spaniſh Weſt Indies, and which either are already made, or will forthwith be made

between

between both nations at Madrid. And whereas it is infiſted on the part of Spain, that certain rights of fiſhing at the iſland of Newfoundland belong to the Guipuſcoans, or other ſubjects of the Catholic King, her Britannic Majeſty conſents and agrees, that all ſuch privileges as the Guipuſcoans and other people of Spain are able to make claim to by right, ſhall be allowed and preſerved to them.

XVI. Whereas, in the convention for making a ſuſpenſion of arms, from the $\frac{11}{22}$ day of the month of Auguſt laſt paſt, for four months, between the Queen of Great Britain, and the moſt Chriſtian King; which the Catholic King alſo approved by his conſent, and does hereby further approve; and which by another convention was prolonged to the $\frac{11}{22}$ of the month of April of this preſent year, among other conditions it is expreſsly ſtipulated, in what caſes the ſhips, merchandizes, and other moveables taken on one ſide and the other, ſhould either become prize to the captor, or be reſtored to the former owner; it is therefore agreed, that in thoſe caſes the conditions of the aforeſaid ſuſpenſion of arms ſhall remain in full force, and all things relating to ſuch captures, made either in the Britiſh and Northern ſeas, or elſewhere, ſhall be well and truly executed according to the tenor thereof.

XVII. But if it happen through inadvertency, or imprudence, or any other cauſe, that any ſubject of either of their aforeſaid royal Majeſties, do or commit any thing by land, ſea, or on freſh waters, in any part of the world, whereby this preſent treaty be not obſerved, or whereby any particular article of the ſame hath not its effect, this peace and good correſpondence between the Queen of Great Britain and the Catholic King, ſhall not therefore be interrupted or broken, but ſhall remain in its former ſtrength, force, and vigour. And that ſubject only ſhall be anſwerable for his own fact, and ſhall ſuffer ſuch puniſhment as is inflicted by law, and according to the preſcription of the law of nations.

XVIII. But if (which God forbid) the diſputes which are compoſed, ſhould at any time be renewed between their ſaid royal Majeſties, and break out into open war, the ſhips, merchandizes, and goods, both moveable and immoveable,

moveable, of the subjects on both sides, which shall be found to be and remain in the ports and dominions of the adverse party, shall not be confiscated, or suffer any damage ; but the space of six months, on the one part, and on the other, shall be granted to the said subjects of each of their said royal Majesties, in order to their selling the aforesaid things, or any other their effects, or carrying away and transporting the same from thence, whithersoever they please, without any molestation.

XIX. The Kings, Princes, and States, mentioned in the following articles, and all others who shall be nominated on either side, by common consent, before the ratifications are exchanged, or within six months after, shall, for a mark of mutual friendship, be included and comprehended in this treaty, their royal Majesties aforenamed being persuaded, that they will approve all the settlements made and established by it,

XX. Whatsoever shall be contained in the treaty of peace next entered into between his sacred royal Majesty of Spain, and his sacred royal Majesty of Portugal, with the previous approbation of her royal Majesty of Great Britain, shall be deemed an essential part of this treaty, in the same manner as if it was transcribed here word for word. Moreover, her sacred royal Majesty of Great Britain, offers herself to be a surety, or guarantee of the aforesaid agreement of peace, which she promises to fulfil according to the substance and words thereof, to the end that it may be observed the more sacred and inviolable.

XXI. The treaty of peace this day entered into between his royal Catholic Majesty, and his royal highness the Duke of Savoy, is specially included in, and confirmed by this treaty, as an essential part thereof, as fully as if it was inserted therein word for word, her royal Majesty of Great Britain expressly declaring, that she will be obliged by the terms of the promise and guarantee therein made.

XXII. The most serene King of Sweden, together with his realms, dominions, provinces, and rights, and the most serene princes the Great Duke of Tuscany, and the Duke of Parma, together with their people and subjects, and the liberties and advantages of their subjects in matters of trade,

shall

fhall be included in this treaty in the moft effectual manner.

XXIII. The moft ferene republic of Venice, for the fake of the neutrality, which during the war they exactly obferved between the parties in hoftility, and for the fake of many acts of humanity performed by it, (the dignity, power, and fecurity of the eftates and dominions thereof, remaining ever inviolable) fhall be particularly comprehended and included in this treaty, in the beft manner poffible as a common friend, and one to whom their royal Majefties, at all times, defire to repay the offices of a faithful friendfhip, according to the exigencies of the faid republic.

XXIV. It has been thought good to comprehend in the prefent treaty, the moft ferene Republic of Genoa, which by a conftant neutrality, during the war, hath cultivated the ancient friendfhip with the crowns of Great Britain and Spain, that the benefit of this peace may be extended to every thing that concerns that republic, and the fubjects thereof, may in all things, and every where, fully enjoy the fame liberty of commerce hereafter, as they enjoyed formerly, and during the life of Charles II. the Catholic King of Spain.

XXV. The city of Geneva is likewife included in this agreement, to the end that it may, for the future, enjoy all the advantages in trade, which it has heretofore enjoyed in either kingdom, either by treaties or ancient cuftom.

XXVI. Solemn ratifications of this treaty, and drawn up in the proper form, fhall be duly and reciprocally exchanged on both fides, within fix weeks, to be computed from the time of figning, or fooner, if poffible.

In witnefs whereof the Ambaffadors Extraordinary and Plenipotentiaries abovenamed, having on each fide exhibited and duly exchanged their letters of full powers, figned and fealed this prefent treaty at Utrecht, the $\frac{2}{1}$ day of the month of July, in the year of our Lord 1713.

(L. S.) *Joh. Briftol,* C. P. S.     (L. S.) *Duc de Offuna.*
(L. S.) *Strafford.*     (L. S.) *El Marque le Monteleone.*

W E

WE having feen and confidered the treaty of peace and friendfhip above-written, have approved, ratified, and confirmed the fame, in all and every one of its articles, as we do by thefe prefents approve, ratify, and confirm it, for ourielves, our heirs, and fucceffors, promifing and engaging our royal word, that we will faithfully and inviolably perform and obferve the aforefaid treaty, and all and every one of the things contained therein, and that we will never fuffer the fame to be violated or tranfgreffed by any one, as far as it lies in our power. For the greater teftimony and validity whereof, we have caufed our great feal of Great Britain to be affixed to thefe prefents, which we have figned with our royal hand. Given at our court at Kenfington the 31ft day of July, 1713, in the twelfth year of our reign.

#### The firft SEPARATE ARTICLE.

I. BESIDES thofe things which have been ftipulated between the Lord Baron of Lexington, on the part of her royal Majefty of Great Britain, and the Lord Marquis of Bedmar, on the part of his royal Catholic Majefty, by the treaty of the 27th of March laft at Madrid, it is further agreed by this feparate article, which fhall be of the fame force, as if it was inferted word for word in the treaty this day concluded between their royal Majefties, that fince his royal Catholic Majefty is ftedfaftly refolved, and does folemnly promife by thefe prefents, that he will not confent to any further alienation of countries, provinces or lands of any fort, or wherever fituate, belonging to the crown of Spain; her royal Majefty of Great Britain does likewife reciprocally promife, that fhe will perfift in thofe meafures and councils, by which fhe has provided and taken care, that none of the parties in war fhall require or obtain of his Catholic Majefty, that any farther part of the Spanifh monarchy be torn from it; but that any new demand of that kind being made, and the fame refufed by his Catholic Majefty, her royal Majefty of Great Britain will ufe her endeavours that fuch demands fhall be receded from.

And when it fhall feem to her royal Majefty of Great
Britain

Britain, to be for the common benefit, that a new treaty be entered into, between her Britannic Majesty, the Catholic King, and King of Portugal, that the security of the crown of Portugal may be provided for, his Catholic Majesty does, by these presents, give his consent to so wholesome a work, and does hereby testify it.

This article shall be ratified, and the ratifications thereof shall be exchanged at Utrecht, within six weeks, or sooner, if it can be.

In testimony whereof, we the Ambassadors Extraordinary, and Plenipotentiaries of their royal Britannic and Catholic Majesties, by virtue of the full powers exchanged this day, have signed and sealed the present article, at Utrecht, the 17/5 of July, in the year of our Lord 1713.

(L. S.) *Joh. Bristol*, C. P. S.     (L. S.) *Duc d' Ossuna.*
(L. S.) *Strafford.*                 (L. S.) *Marquis de Monteleone.*

### The *second* SEPARATE ARTICLE.

II. THAT it may appear what consideration her sacred Majesty the Queen of Great Britain has for the Princess of Ursini, her said Majesty the Queen of Great Britain, in the 21st article of the conventions of peace, made between the Baron of Lexington, on the part of her said Britannic Majesty, and the Marquis de Bedmar, on the part of his Catholic Majesty, at Madrid, the 27th day of March last, did oblige herself, as by the present article she does oblige herself, and promises and agrees for herself and her successors, that she will really procure and effect that forthwith, and without any delay, the said Lady Princess of Ursini be put into real and actual possession of the duchy of Limburg, or of other countries in the Netherlands, which shall be substituted in lieu thereof, to the full satisfaction of the Lady Princess of Ursini, with all manner of absolute and independent superiority, clear from any fee, or other tie whatsoever, which shall produce an annual revenue of 30,000 *Scudos*, according to the form and tenor of the diploma granted by his said Catholic Majesty to the said Princess, the 28th day of September, 1711, to the effect following :

PHILIP

PHILIP, by the grace of God, King of Caftile, Leon, Arragon, both Sicilies, Jerufalem, Navarre, Granada, Toledo, Valencia, Galicia, Majorca, Seville, Sardinia, Cordova, Corfica, Murcia, Jaen, Algarves, Algezira, Gibraltar, Canary Iflands, Eaft and Weft Indies, Iflands, and Terra Firma of the Ocean Sea, Archduke of Auftria, duke of Burgundy, Brabant and Milan, Count of Apfburg, Flanders and Tirol, and of Barcelona, Lord of Bifcay and Molina, &c. To all who fhall fee thefe prefents, or hear them read, greeting. Our deareft and moft well-beloved coufin, the Princefs of Urfini, has, fince the beginning of our reign, rendered us, and continues to render us fo many fignal and acceptable fervices, that we thought we could not defer any longer giving her lively teftimonies of our acknowledgments, and of the efteem we have for her perfon. This Princefs having quitted the rank, and the prerogatives fhe had at the court of Rome, to accept the employment of firft Lady of the bed-chamber to the Queen our deareft confort, fhe went to meet her at Nice in Provence, and conducted her to our dominions of Spain, and difcharged her duty with fo much care, exactnefs, and wifdom, that fhe has gained all poffible confidence and confideration.

When we trufted the regency of our kingdoms of Spain to the Queen, our deareft confort, that we might go and command our armies in the kingdoms and ftates of Italy, the Princefs of Urfini redoubled her zeal and affiduity about her perfon; fhe has always affifted her with her care and her counfel, with equal prudence and affection, and in all times, and on all occafions, we have experienced the happy effects of fo judicious, fo faithful, and fo valuable conduct.

Since it has pleafed God to blefs our royal houfe, and to fecure the fucceffion of it by a happy iffue, fhe has likewife taken upon her to beftow her moft tender and effectual care on the education of our deareft and moft beloved fon the Prince of the Afturias, in whom we already obferve the benefit and progrefs of it. All thefe fervices, fo diftinguifhing, and fo important to the welfare of our dominions, and to the felicity of our reign, the application

with

with which this Princefs gives us ftill frefh proofs of an entire affection to the perfon of us, the Queen our deareft confort, and the Princes our children, and the good fuccefs that has attended the wholefome counfels fhe has given us, have engaged us to find out means to grant her a reward fuitable to fo many fervices, and that might ferve for the future as a certain proof of the greatnefs of our gratitude, as well as of the merit and virtues of this Princefs. This has given us occafion to think of fecuring to her not only a confiderable revenue, but alfo a country fhe might enjoy with the title of Sovereign; which we have embraced with the greater readinefs, that this Princefs, being born of the houfe of *la Trimouille*, one of the moft ancient and moft illuftrious of France, is not only allied to the Princes of the blood of the houfe of France, but likewife to feveral other fovereign houfes of Europe, and that knowing the endowments of her mind, and the wifdom of her conduct in all things, we are perfuaded fhe will govern with juftice the country and people that fhall be under her fubjection; and that this great favour will ever be looked upon as the juft effect of the juftice and magnificence of the Sovereigns towards thofe who have been fo happy as to render them important fervices. Know ye therefore, that, out of our full power, meer motion, and royal and abfolute authority, we have given, yielded and transferred, as we do give, yield and transfer by thefe prefents, to our deareft and moft well-beloved coufin, Mary Anne de la Trimouille, Princefs of Urfini, for herfelf, her heirs, fucceffors, and affigns, the duchy, town, and caftle of Limbourg, being part of the Spanifh Netherlands, with the towns, boroughs, villages, caftles, houfes, lands, and other appurtenances of the faid duchy, to enjoy the fame to herfelf the faid Princefs of Urfini, her heirs, fucceffors, or affigns, in full property and perfect fovereignty, without referving or detaining any part thereof, to ourfelves, and to our fucceffors, the Kings of Spain, under any title whatfoever, either of refort or feodality, as alfo without return or reverfion in any cafe, or at any time, whereof we have exempted the faid duchy of Limbourg, and its dependencies comprehended in the prefent donation; to which end, fo far as is, or fhould be neceffary, we have extinguifhed
and

and suppressed, as we do extinguish and suppress the said rights; willing that the said Princess of Ursini do exercise, in her name, all the rights of soverignty within the said duchy of Limbourg, the territories and jurisdictions thereto annexed, with the same authority as we exercised, and had right to exercise the same before these presents, and that she enjoy there all the revenues, fruits, profits, and emoluments whatsoever, as well ordinary, as extraordinary and casual, of what nature soever, either for the collation and patronage of the livings, the provision and destitution of offices, the customs, entries, subsidies, impositions, and other rights, expressed, and not expressed, the defence of the country, and the tranquillity of the people, the raising the revenues of the said duchy, and its dependencies; all which rights and revenues the said Princess of Ursini shall commence to enjoy from the day of these presents, from the reckoning of which, the agents, receivers, clerks, or others appointed to receive the said revenues, shall be accountable, and remit the produce into the hands of the bearers of the powers of the said Princess, and in so doing they shall be duly acquitted and discharged thereof towards us, as by these presents we discharge them thereof; and consequently the said Princess of Ursini, shall remain unalterable proprietor of the duchy of Limbourg, and its dependencies, as well for the sovereignty, as for all the revenues, as the whole belonging to her, in full, free, and entire property, with power to dispose thereof, by donation between persons alive, or legacy to such person, and with such clauses and conditions, as she shall think fit, and even to treat thereof by exchange or otherwise, and the same rights and powers shall belong successively, after her, to her nearest heir, in case she has not otherwise disposed thereof. To which end we have discharged, absolved, and freed, as by these presents we discharge, absolve, and free the inhabitants of the said duchy of Limbourg, and its dependencies, of what state, quality, or dignity they are, as well ecclesiastical as secular, political, military, and of what other ranks and conditions they are, or may be, and each of them in general and in particular, of the oaths of fidelity, faith, and obedience, promises, obligations, and duties they owed us, as their Lord and Sovereign Prince:

order-

ordering and enjoining them moſt expreſsly, that by virtue of theſe preſents, they do own and acknowledge the ſaid Princeſs of Urſini, and after her, her heirs, ſucceſſors, or ſuch as have a right thereto, ſucceſſively for their Princes and ſovereign Lords; that they take and ſwear to her the oaths of fidelity and obedience in the uſual manner, and moreover, that they pay all homage, reverence, affection, obedience, fidelity, and ſervices, as good and loyal ſubjects are obliged to do to their ſovereign Lord, and as they have done hitherto to the Kings our predeceſſors, and to us. And farther, our intention being, that the ſaid duchy of Limbourg, and its dependencies, ſhould produce at leaſt the effectual and real revenue yearly to the profit of the ſaid Princeſs of Urſini, her heirs, ſucceſſors, and aſſigns, thirty thouſand crowns, each crown of eight ſilver reals, old double money of Caſtile, deduction being made of local employments, maintenance of places, and officers that uſed to be paid and maintained out of the revenues of the ſaid duchy. Our will and pleaſure is, that during the firſt year of enjoyment by the ſaid Princeſs of Urſini, after her having taken poſſeſſion of the ſaid duchy of Limbourg, and after the publication of the peace, a ſtate be made of the revenues and employments of the duchy of Limbourg, and its dependencies, in the preſence of perſons appointed for that purpoſe, as well on our part, as on that of the ſaid Princeſs of Urſini, and in caſe, after deduction is made for the ſaid employments, the revenues for the neat remainder to the profit of the ſaid Princeſs of Urſini, do not amount to the ſaid thirty thouſand crowns per annum, whether by reaſon of the alienations that might have been made of ſome part of that duchy, or whether becauſe any of the ſaid rights, revenues, and appurtenances, ſhould have been ſold, engaged, or charged with ſome rents, even ſome debts for ſums taken by loan, or anticipation, in this caſe, we ordain, and our will and pleaſure is, that the whole be redeemed and diſengaged, and the purchaſers, mortgagers, tenants, and other creditors, reimburſed, paid, and ſatisfied out of the produce of the moſt liquid revenues of the other provinces of the Spaniſh Netherlands, ſo as that the ſaid Princeſs enjoy, fully, really, and without any charge, the ſaid thirty thouſand crowns yearly; to

which

which end, and until the full reimburſement for the redeeming the ſaid alienations or engagements, conſtitutions
of rents, anticipations, or other loans whatever they may
be, the purchaſers of the funds alienated, or mortgagers,
tenants, and all other creditors, ſhall be, and remain aſſigned, as from this time we aſſign them to receive their
arrears, or intereſts of their capitals, out of the ſaid revenues of the other provinces of the Spaniſh Netherlands;
and conſequently, we have from this time yielded and
transferred, as we do yield and transfer all and ſuch of our
revenues as ſhall be requiſite to the mortgagers and creditors, and until the concurrence of what is due to them
for principal intereſts, to take, have, and receive out of
the moſt liquid and effective part of the ſaid revenues of
the ſaid Spaniſh Netherlands, except thoſe of the ſaid duchy
of Limbourg, to enjoy the ſame themſelves, until they
ſhall be fully reimburſed. And if it ſhould happen, that
notwithſtanding the ſaid redemption and reimburſement
being made or aſſigned, the revenue of the ſaid duchy of
Limbourg ſhould not amount to the ſaid ſum of thirty
thouſand crowns yearly, all charges deducted, we will, that
there be diſmembered, as from this time we diſmember,
from the other countries belonging to us, adjacent, or lying convenient to the ſaid duchy of Limbourg, ſuch
other towns, boroughs, villages and territories, as ſhall be
requiſite to make up by their yearly produce and revenue, what ſhall be wanting of the ſaid thirty thouſand
crowns yearly in the duchy of Limbourg, which towns,
boroughs, villages and territories, together with the revenue and appurtenances, ſhall remain diſmembered from
our other lordſhips, and ſhall be united and joined for the
future, and for ever, to the ſaid duchy of Limbourg, to
be poſſeſſed by the ſaid Princeſs of Urſini, with the ſame
title of ſovereignty, juriſdiction, and prerogative before
mentioned, and as making part of the ſaid duchy of Limbourg. And whereas, by the ſeveral propoſals that are
from time to time made to us, to attain the peace ſo much
deſired by us, and other princes and ſtates of Europe engaged in the preſent war, ſome of them tend to certain
diſmemberings of the ſaid Spaniſh Netherlands, from the
other dominions that make up our monarchy, we declare,

that

that our intention is, that thefe prefents fhall not be prejudiced by the treaties of peace that fhall be made, and
that all the princes and potentates interefted in the faid
propofals, do ratify the difmembering we make by thefe
prefents of the faid duchy of Limbourg, and the erecting
of that in fovereignty, in favour of the Princefs Urfini,
fo as that fhe be put, and remain in full poffeffion, and
peaceable enjoyment thereof, within the full extent of
thefe prefents, according to their form and tenor, and
without any referve or reftriction whatfoever; it being
our will, that the prefent donation be one of the conditions of the treaties that may be made, in what fhall concern the faid Spanifh Netherlands, to the end the faid
Princefs of Urfini, her heirs, fucceffors and affigns, may
enjoy the faid duchy of Limbourg and its appurtenances,
fully, peaceably, perpetually, and for ever, with the title
of fovereignty, without any trouble and hindrance; on
the contrary, to effect the fame, and to conftrain thereto
all thofe whom it fhall concern, or that are therefore to
be conftrained, we have, out of our full power and royal
authority, fupplied, as we do hereby fupply all defects or
omiffions of right or fact, that might be found or happen
in this donation, ceffion, and conveyance, either by the
fault of expreffion, of the value of the revenues, and of
the employments of the faid duchy of Limbourg, that are
not therein fpecified or declared, and that might be requifite by former ordinances, to which, and the derogatories
of the derogatories therein contained, we have exprefsly
derogated, as we derogate by thefe prefents; for fuch is
our will and good pleafure: willing that thefe prefent letters patents be delivered to the faid Princefs of Urfini,
that fhe may caufe the fame to be regiftered and publifhed
where it fhall be neceffary, and even to caufe them to be
inferted, with the donation and ceffion therein contained,
in the treaty of peace to be negotiated, therein to be included and acknowledged in the quality of fovereign princefs of the duchy of Limbourg, and in that quality to
exercife the rights thereof, and there to make treaties and
alliances with the princes and fovereigns that fhall intervene, enjoining the minifters and ambaffadors who fhall
be there on our part, to acknowledge her as fuch, and all
our

our officers of the said duchy of Limbourg, to obey these presents from the moment they shall be notified to them; and to the end this present donation be firm and lasting for ever, we have signed these present letters with our own hand, and caused our great seal to be affixed to them, willing and ordaining that they be registered in all and every one of our councils, and chambers of account where it shall belong. Given at our city of Corella, in our kingdom of Navarre, the 28th day of September, in the year of our Lord, 1711, and of our reign the eleventh.

And her said Majesty of Great Britain promises, that she will maintain the said Lady Princess of Ursini, or her assigns, in the real, actual, and peaceable possession of the said sovereignty and territory, against all and every one, at any time, and for ever, and that she will not permit, that the said Lady Princess be disturbed or molested in the said possession by any body, by right or fact. And whereas, the real possession of the sovereignty of the said duchy of Limbourg, or of the territories as aforesaid to be subrogated, ought, by virtue of the before-mentioned convention, concluded the 27th of March last past, to have been already given to the said Lady Princess, although it is not yet given: therefore her said royal Majesty of Great Britain, as a farther surety, promises, and engages her royal word, that she will not yield or remit, nor suffer to be yielded or remitted to any body, the said Spanish Netherlands, but will keep, or cause the same to be kept, not only until the said Lady Princess of Ursini be put in actual and peaceable possession of the said sovereignty, but also, that the said Lady Princess of Ursini be, as aforesaid, acknowledged sovereign Lady of the said sovereignty, and put in possession thereof by the Prince to whom the said Spanish Netherlands are to be yielded and remitted.

This present article shall be ratified, and the exchange of the ratifications shall be made at Utrecht within six weeks, or sooner, if possible.

In witness whereof we, the Ambassadors Extraordinary and Plenipotentiaries of her sacred royal Majesty of Great Britain have subscribed this present article, and
sealed

fealed the fame with our feals, at Utrecht, the $\frac{2}{13}$ of July in the year of our Lord, 1713.

(L. S.) *Joh. Briftol*, C. P. S.    (L. S.) *Duque de Ofuna.*
(L. S.) *Strafford.*        (L. S.) *El Marque le Monteleone.*

---

*Treaty of Navigation and Commerce between the Moft Serene and Moft Potent Princefs* Anne, *by the Grace of God Queen of* Great Britain, France, *and* Ireland, *Defender of the Faith, &c. and the Moft Serene and Moft Potent Prince* Philip V. *the Catholic King of* Spain, *concluded at* Utrecht, *the* $\frac{28}{?}$ *Day of* $\frac{\text{November}}{\text{December}}$ 1713. Reprinted from the Copy printed by Her Majefty's fpecial Command.

ANNE, by the grace of God, Queen of Great Britain, France, and Ireland, defender of the faith, &c. to all and fingular to whom thefe prefents fhall come, greeting. Whereas the right reverend father in God, our right trufty and well-beloved counfellor, John, bifhop of Briftol, our ambaffador extraordinary and plenipotentiary, dean of Windfor, and regifter of our moft noble order of the garter, did on our part, together with the plenipotentiaries of his Catholic Majefty, conclude and fign at Utrecht, on the $\frac{8}{9}$ day of $\frac{\text{November}}{\text{December}}$ 1713, a treaty of commerce between the fubjects of Great Britain and Spain, as follows:

A Good and firm peace, and a true and fincere friend-fhip having, by the merciful affiftance of God, been happily eftablifhed between the moft ferene and potent Prince and Lady, Anne, by the grace of God, Queen of Great Britain, France, and Ireland, &c. and the moft ferene and potent Prince and Lord, Philip V. by the grace of God Catholic King of Spain, &c. and their heirs and fucceffors, kingdoms and fubjects, by a treaty of pacification, concluded at Utrecht the $\frac{2}{13}$ day of the month of July laft paft, their Majefties before all things made it their care, that the mutual advantage of their fubjects in

matters

matters of trade, might be provided for after the beft manner; and therefore they moft gracioufly gave inftruftions
to their ambaffadors extraordinary and plenipotentiaries,
(by whofe means the peace had been happily concluded)
to draw up into a folemn treaty of commerce, whatfoever,
after all things had been thoroughly confidered at the conferences held for that purpofe at Madrid, fhould feem to
conduce moft to this good end; the faid ambaffadors
therefore, by virtue of their full powers, (copies whereof
are inferted word for word at the end of this inftrument)
agreed upon articles of commerce for the explanation of
former treaties, and greater eafe and convenience of trade,
in the manner and form following:

I. THE treaty of peace, commerce, and alliance, concluded at Madrid, between the crowns of Great
Britain and Spain, the $\frac{13}{23}$ day of May, 1667, is ratified
and confirmed by this treaty, and for the greater ftrengthening and confirmation of the fame, it has been thought
proper to infert it word for word in this place, together
with the royal fchedules or ordinations annexed to it, as
follows:

The treaty of peace and friendfhip between the crowns
of Great Britain and Spain, concluded at Madrid the $\frac{13}{23}$
day of May, in the year of our Lord, 1667, entered into
and concluded by the moft excellent Lord Edward, Earl of
Sandwich, privy-counfellor to the moft ferene and potent
King of Great Britain, and his ambaffador extraordinary
to Spain, in the name of the moft ferene King his mafter;
and the moft excellent Lords Don John Eberardo Nidardo, confeffor to the moft ferene Catholic Queen, inquifitor general and counfellor of ftate, Don Ramiro Pheli-
pez Nunez de Guzman, duke of San Lucar Mayor, and
of Medina de las Torres, counfellor of ftate, and prefident
of Italy, and Don Gafpar of Bracamonte and Guzman,
count of Penaranda, counfellor of ftate, and prefident of
the Indies, in the name of the moft ferene and potent
King and Queen of Spain, at Madrid the $\frac{13}{23}$ day of May,
1667.

*In the name of the moſt Holy Trinity, Father, Son, and Holy Ghoſt, three diſtinct Perſons, and One only true God.*

## ARTICLE I.

FIRST, it is agreed and concluded, that from this day forward there ſhall be, between the two crowns of Great Britain and Spain, a general, good, ſincere, true, firm, and perfect amity, confederation and peace, which ſhall endure for ever, and be obſerved inviolably, as well by land, as by ſea, and freſh-waters ; and alſo between the lands, countries, kingdoms, dominions, and territories, belonging unto, or under the obedience of either of them. And that their ſubjects, people, and inhabitants reſpectively, of what condition, degree, or quality ſoever, from henceforth reciprocally, ſhall help, aſſiſt, and ſhew to one another all manner of love, good offices, and friendſhip.

II. That neither of the ſaid Kings, nor their reſpective people, ſubjects, or inhabitants, within their dominions, upon any pretence, may in public or ſecret, do, or procure to be done, any thing againſt the other, in any place, by ſea or land, nor in the ports or rivers of the one or the other, but ſhall treat one another with all love and friendſhip; and may, by water and by land, freely and ſecurely paſs into the confines, countries, lands, kingdoms, iſlands, dominions, cities, towns, villages, walled or without wall, fortified or unfortified, their havens and ports (where hitherto trade and commerce hath been accuſtomed) and there trade, buy and ſell, as well of and to the inhabitants of the reſpective places, as thoſe of their own nation, or any other nation that ſhall be or come there.

III. That the ſaid Kings of Great Britain and Spain, ſhall take care that their reſpective people and ſubjects, from henceforward, do abſtain from all force, violence, or wrong; and if any injury ſhall be done by either of the ſaid Kings, or by the people or ſubjects of either of them, to the people or ſubjects of the other, againſt the articles of this alliance, or againſt common right, there ſhall not therefore be given letters of repriſal, marque, or counter-marque, by any of the confederates, until ſuch

time

time as juſtice is ſought and followed in the ordinary courſe of law. But if juſtice be denied or delayed, then the King whoſe people or inhabitants have received harm, ſhall aſk it of the other, by whom (as is ſaid) the juſtice ſhall have been denied or delayed, or of the commiſſioners that ſhall be, by the one King or the other, appointed to receive and hear ſuch demands, to the end that all ſuch differences may be compounded in friendſhip, or according to law. But if there ſhould be yet a delay, or juſtice ſhould not be done, nor ſatisfaction given within ſix months after having the ſame ſo demanded, then may be given letters of repriſal, marque or counter-marque.

IV. That between the King of Great Britain, and the King of Spain, and their reſpective people, ſubjects and inhabitants, as well upon ſea as upon land, and freſh-waters, in all and every their kingdoms, lands, countries, dominions, confines, territories, provinces, iſlands, plantations, cities, villages, towns, ports, rivers, creeks, bays, ſtreights, and currents, where hitherto trade and commerce hath been accuſtomed, there ſhall be trade and commerce, in ſuch way and manner, that without ſafe conduct, and without general or particular licence, the people and ſubjects of each other may freely, as well by land as by ſea, and freſh-waters, navigate and go into their ſaid countries, kingdoms, dominions, and all the cities, ports, currents, bays, diſtricts, and other places thereof; and may enter into any port with their ſhips laden or empty, carriage or carriages, wherein to bring their merchandize, and there buy and ſell what, and how much they pleaſe, and alſo at juſt and reaſonable rates provide themſelves with proviſions, and other neceſſary things, for their ſubſiſtence and voyage; and alſo may repair their ſhips and carriages, and from thence again freely depart with their ſhips, carriages, goods, merchandize and eſtate, and return to their own countries, or to ſuch other places as they ſhall think fit, without any moleſtation or impediment, ſo that they pay the duties and cuſtoms which ſhall be due, and ſaving to either ſide the laws and ordinances of their country.

V. *Item*, It is likewiſe agreed, that for the merchandizes which the ſubjects of the King of Great Britain ſhall buy in Spain, or other the kingdoms or dominions of the
King

**King of** Spain, and fhall carry in their own fhips, or in fhips hired or lent unto them, no new cuftoms, toll, tenths, fub-fidies, or other rights or duties whatfoever, fhall be taken or increafed, other than thofe which in the like cafe the natives themfelves, and all other ftrangers are obliged to pay ; and the fubjects aforefaid buying, felling and con-tracting for their merchandizes, as well in refpect of the prices, as of all duties to be paid, fhall enjoy the fame pri-vileges which are allowed to the natural fubjects of Spain; and may buy, and lade their fhips with fuch goods and merchandizes; which faid fhips being laden, and cuftoms paid for the goods, fhall not be detained in port upon any pretence whatfoever; nor fhall the laders, merchants, or factors, who bought and loaded the goods aforefaid, be queftioned after the departure of the faid fhips, for any matter or thing whatfoever concerning the fame.

VI. And to the end that the officers and minifters of all cities, towns, and villages belonging to either, may nei-ther demand nor take from the refpective merchants and people, greater taxes, duties, ftipends, recompences, gifts, or any other charges, than what ought to be taken by vir-tue of this treaty; and that the faid merchants and people may know and underftand with certainty what is ordained in all things touching this, it is agreed and concluded, that tables and lifts fhall be put up at the doors of the cuf-tom-houfes and regiftries of all the cities, villages, and towns of, or pertaining to one or the other King, where fuch rights and excifes, or cuftoms, are ufually paid; in which, how much, and of what quality, fuch rights, cuf-toms, fubfidies, and payments, either to the Kings, or any the aforefaid officers are allowed, fhall be put down in wri-ting, declaring as well the fpecies of what is imported, as what is carried out. And if any officer, or any other in his name, upon any pretence whatfoever, in public or fecret, directly or indirectly, fhall afk or receive of any merchant, or other perfon refpectively, any fum of mo-ney or other thing, by the name of right, due, ftipend, allowance, or recompence, (though it be by the way of voluntary donative) more or otherwife than aforefaid, the faid officer or his deputy being in fuch manner guilty, and convicted before a competent judge in the country where
the

the crime is committed, fhall be put in prifon for three months, and fhall pay thrice the value of the thing fo received; of which, the half fhall be for the King of the country where the crime is committed, and the other half for the denunciator, for the which he may fue his right before any competent judge of the country where it fhall happen.

VII. That fhall be lawful for the fubjects of the King of Great Britain, to bring out and carry into Spain, and all or any lands and dominions of the King of Spain, (where heretofore they have ufed trade and commerce) and trade there with all kind of merchandize, clothes, manufactures, and things of the kingdom of Great Britain, and the manufactures, goods, fruits, and kinds of the iflands, towns, and plantations to him appertaining, and what fhall have been bought by Englifh factors on this fide, or farther on the other fide of the cape of Buena Efperanca, without being enforced to declare to whom, or for what price they fell their faid merchandize and provifions, or being molefted for the errors of the mafters of the fhips, or others, in the entry of the goods; and at their pleafure to return again out of the dominions of the King of Spain, with all, or any goods, eftates, and merchandize, to any of the territories, iflands, dominions, and countries of the King of England, or to any other place, paying the rights and tributes mentioned in the antecedent chapters; and the reft of all their lading which is not brought to land, they may detain, keep and carry away in their faid fhip or fhips, veffel or veffels, again, without paying any right or impofition whatfoever for it, as if therewith they had never been within any bay or port of the Catholic King. And all the goods, eftates, merchandize, fhips, or other veffels, with any things introduced into the dominions or places of the crown of Great Britain as prizes, and judged for fuch in the faid dominions and places, fhall be taken for goods and merchandize of Great Britain, comprehended fo by the intention of this article.

VIII. That the fubjects and vaffals of the moft ferene King of Great Britain, may bring and carry to all and fingular the dominions of the King of Spain, any fruits and commodities of the Eaft Indies, it appearing by teftimony

of

of the deputies of the East-India Company in London, that they are of, or have come from the English conquests, plantations or factories, with like privilege, and according to what is allowed to the subjects of the United Provinces, by the royal cedulas of Contravando, bearing date the 27th of June, and the 3d of July, 1663, and published on the 30th of June, and 4th of July, the same year. And for what may concern both the Indies, and any other parts whatsoever, the crown of Spain doth grant to the King of Great Britain and his subjects, all that is granted to the United States of the Low Countries, and their subjects, in their treaty of Munster, 1648, point for point, in as full and ample manner as if the same were herein particularly inserted, the same rules being to be observed, whereunto the subjects of the said United States are obliged, and mutual offices of friendship to be performed from one side to the other.

IX. That the subjects of the King of Great Britain, trading, buying, and selling in any of the kingdoms, governments, islands, ports, or territories, of the said King of Spain, shall have, use, and enjoy all the privileges and immunities, which the said King hath granted and confirmed to the English merchants that reside in Andaluzia, by his royal cedulas or orders, dated the 19th day of March, the 26th day of June, and the 9th day of November, 1645, his Catholic Majesty, by these presents, reconfirming the same as a part of this treaty between the two crowns. And to the end that it may be manifest to all, it is consented, that the said schedules (as to the whole substance thereof) be passed and transferred to the body of the present articles, in the name and favour of all and singular the subjects of the King of Great Britain, residing and trading in any places whatsoever, within his Catholic Majesty's dominions.

X. That the ships, or any other vessels that shall belong to the King of Great Britain, or his subjects, navigating into the King of Spain's dominions, or any of his ports, shall not be visited by the judges of counterband, or by any other officer or person, by his own, or by any other authority; nor shall any soldiers, armed men, or other officers or persons, be put on board any of the said ships or

veffels ;

veffels; nor fhall the officers of the cuftom-houfe of the one or the other party, fearch in any veffels or fhips belonging to the people of the one or the other, which fhall enter into their regions, dominions, or refpective ports, until their faid fhips or veffels are unladen, or until they have carried on fhore all the lading and merchandize which they declare they refolve to difembark in the faid port; nor fhall the captain, mafter, or any other of the company of the faid fhips, be imprifoned, or they or their boats detained on fhore; but in the interim, officers of the cuftom-houfe may be put on board the faid veffels or fhips, fo they exceed not the number of three for each fhip, to fee that no goods or merchandize be landed out of the faid fhips and veffels, without paying fuch duties as by thefe articles either party is obliged to pay; which faid officers are to be without any charge to the fhip or fhips, veffel or veffels, their commanders, mariners, company, merchants, factors, or proprietors. And when it happens that the mafter or owner of any fhip fhall declare the whole lading of his faid fhip is to be difcharged in any port, the entry of the faid lading fhall be made in the cuftom-houfe, after the ufual manner; and if, after the entry made, any other goods be found in the faid fhip or fhips, more than what are contained in the faid entry, eight working days fhall be allowed them, on which they may work, (which fhall be reckoned from the day they began to unlade) to the end that the concealed goods may be entered, and the confifcation of them prevented : and in cafe that in the time limited, the entry or manifeftation of them, fhall not have been made, then fuch particular goods only, which fhall be found, as aforefaid, though the unlading be not finifhed, fhall be confifcated, and not any other, nor fhall other trouble be given, or punifhment inflicted on the merchant or owner of the fhip; and when the fhips or veffels are reladen, they may have freedom to go out again.

XI. That the fhip or fhips appertaining to the one or the other King, or to their refpective people and fubjects that fhall enter into any ports, lands, or dominions of the one or the other, and fhall difcharge any part of their goods and merchandizes in any port or haven, being configned

with

with the reft to other places, within or without the faid dominions, fhall not be obliged to regifter or pay the rights
of any other goods or merchandizes, than of that which
they fhall unlade in the faid port or haven, nor be conftrained to give bond for the goods they fhall carry to
other places, nor any other fecurity, if it be not in cafe
of felony, debt, treafon, or other capital crime.

XII. Whereas, the one moiety of the cuftom of all foreign goods and merchandizes imported into England, is
allowed and returned back to the importer, if the faid
goods be exported out of the faid kingdom within twelve
months after the firft landing, upon oath made that they
are the fame goods which paid cuftom inwards, and that if
they be not refhip'd within the faid twelve months, yet
they may at all times be exported without paying any cuftom or duty outwards : it is therefore agreed, that if any
the fubjects of the King of Great Britain, fhall hereafter
land any goods or merchandizes, of what growth or nature
foever they be, in any of the ports of his Catholic Majefty,
and having entered them, and paid the cuftom which by
this treaty ought to be paid, and fhall afterwards defire to
tranfport them, or any part of them, to any other place
whatfoever, for a better market, it fhall and may be lawful, for him or them, fo to do freely, without paying, or
being demanded any other cuftom or duty at all for the
fame, he or they making oath, if required thereunto, that
they are the fame goods for which cuftom was paid at the
landing : and in cafe that the fubjects, people, and inhabitants of the dominions of either part fhall unlade, or
have in any city, town, or village refpectively, any
goods, merchandizes, fruits, or eftates, and have paid the
cuftoms due, according to what hath been declared, and
after that, not being able to put them off, fhall refolve to
remit them to fome other city, town, or village of the faid
dominions, they may not only do it without difficulty or
impediment, and without paying other rights than what
were due at their entry, but likewife the cuftom or rights
fhall not be paid again in any other part of the faid dominions, bringing certificates from the officers of the cuftom-houfe, that they were paid before in the due form.
And the chief farmers and commiffioners of the King of
Spain's

Spain's rents in all places, or some other officer or officers to be appointed for that purpose, shall at all times permit and suffer the transportation of all such goods and merchandizes from place to place, and give sufficient certificate to the owners thereof, or their assigns, of their having paid their custom at their first landing whereby they may be carried to, and landed at any other port or place of the said jurisdiction, free from all dutes or impediments whatsoever, as aforesaid, saving always the right of any third person.

XIII. That it shall be lawful for the ships belonging to the subjects of the one or the other King, to anchor in the roads or bays of either, without being constrained to enter into port; and in case they be necessitated to enter thereinto, either by distress of weather, fear of enemies, pirates, or any other accident, in case the said ships be not bound to an enemy's port, and carrying thither contraband goods, (whereof without some clear proof they shall not be questioned) it shall be lawful for the said subjects to return to sea freely when they please, with their ships and goods, so as they do not break bulk, or expose any thing to sale; and that when they cast anchor, or enter the ports aforesaid, they be not molested or visited; and it shall suffice, that in this case they shew their passports, or sea-papers, which being seen by the respective officers of either King, the said ships shall return freely to sea without any molestation.

XIV. And if any ship or ships belonging to the subjects and merchants of the one or the other, entering into bays, or in the open sea, shall be encountered by the ships of the said Kings, or of privateers their subjects, the said ships, to prevent all disorders, shall not come within cannon shot, but shall send their long-boat, or pinnace, to the merchant-ship, and only two or three men on board, to whom the master or owner shall shew his passports and sea-letters, according to the form which shall be inserted at the end of this treaty, whereby not only the ship's lading, but the place to which she belongs, and as well the master and owner's name, as the name of the ship, may appear; by which means the quality of the ship, and her master or owner, will be sufficiently known, as also the commodities

she

fhe carries, whether they be contraband, or not ; to the which paffports and fea-letters, entire faith and credit fhall be given, fo much the rather, for that as well on the part of the King of England, as of the King of Spain, fome counter-figns fhall be given, if it fhall be found neceffary, whereby their authenticalnefs may the better appear, and that they may not be in any ways falfified.

XV. If any prohibited merchandize or goods fhall be exported from the kingdoms, dominions, and territories of either of the faid Kings, by the refpective people or fub-jects of the one or the other, in fuch cafe the prohibited goods fhall be only confifcated, and not the other goods ; neither fhall the delinquent incur any other punifhment, encept the faid delinquent fhall carry out from the refpec-tive kingdoms or dominions of the King of Great Britain, the proper coin, wool, or fullers-earth of the faid king-doms ; or fhall carry out of the refpective kingdoms or dominions of the faid King of Spain, any gold or filver, wrought or unwrought; in either of which cafes, the laws of the refpective countries are to take place.

XVI. That it fhall be lawful for the people and fub-jects of both Kings, to have accefs to the refpective ports of the one and the other, and there remain, and depart again with the fame freedom, not only with their fhips, and other veffels for trade and commerce, but alfo with their other fhips fitted for war, armed, and difpofed to refift and engage the enemy, and arriving by ftrefs of weather to re-pair their fhips, or furnifh themfelves with provifions ; fo that entering willingly, they be not fo numerous, that they give juft occafion of fufpicion, to which end they are not to exeeed the number of eight, nor continue in their ha-vens, nor about their ports, longer time than they fhall have juft caufe for the repair of their fhips, to take in provifions, or other neceffary things, much lefs be the oc-cafion of interrupting the free commerce, and coming in of other fhips, of nations in amity with either King; and when an unufual number of men of war by accident fhall come unto any port, it fhall not be lawful for them to come into the faid ports or havens, not having firft ob-tained permiffion of the King unto whom the faid ports do belong, or the governor of the faid ports, if they be not
forced

forced thereinto by ſtreſs of weather, or other neceſſity, to avoid the danger of the ſea; and in ſuch caſe they ſhall preſently acquaint the governor, or chief magiſtrate of the place, with the cauſe of their coming; nor ſhall they remain there any longer time than the ſaid governor or magiſtrate ſhall think convenient, or do any act of hoſtility in ſuch ports, that may prove of prejudice to the one or the other of the ſaid Kings.

XVII. That neither the ſaid King of Great Britain, nor the King of Spain, by any mandate general, nor particular, nor for any cauſe whatſoever, ſhall embark or detain, hinder or take, for his reſpective ſervice, any merchant, maſter of a ſhip, pilot, or mariner, their ſhips, merchandize, cloaths, or other goods belonging unto the one or the other, in their ports or waters, if it be not that either of the ſaid Kings, or the perſons to whom the ſhips belong, be firſt advertiſed thereof and do agree thereunto: provided that this ſhall not be conſtrued to hinder or interrupt the ordinary courſe of juſtice and law in either country.

XVIII. That the merchants and ſubjects of the one and the other King, their factors and ſervants, as alſo their ſhips, maſters, or mariners, may as well going as coming, upon ſea and other waters, as in the havens and ports of the one and the other reſpectively, carry and uſe all kind of arms, defenſive and offenſive, without being obliged to regiſter them, as alſo upon land to carry and uſe them for their defence, according to the cuſtom of the place.

XIX. That the captains, officers, and mariners, of the ſhips belonging to the people and ſubjects of either party, may not commence an action, nor hinder or bring trouble upon their own ſhips, their captains, officers, or mariners, in the reſpective kingdoms, dominions, lands, countries, or places of the other, for their wages or ſalaries, or under any other pretence. Nor may they put themſelves, or be received, by what pretext or colour ſoever into the ſervice or protection of the King of England, or King of Spain, or their arms; but if any controverſy happen between merchants and maſters of ſhips, or between maſters and mariners, the compoſing thereof ſhall be left to the

conſul

conful of the nation, but after fuch manner, as he who
fhall not fubmit to the arbitrement, may appeal to the ordinary juftice of the place where he is fubject.

XX. And to the end that all impediments be taken
away, and that the merchants and adventurers of the kingdoms of Great Britain, be permitted to return to Brabant,
Flanders, and other the provinces of the Low Countries,
under the jurifdiction of the King of Spain ; forafmuch as
it hath been thought convenient, that all, and any the
laws, edicts, and acts, by which the importation of cloth,
or any cloth, or any other woollen manufacture, of what
kind foever, dyed or undyed, milled or unmilled, into
Flanders, or the other provinces, hath been prohibited,
be revoked and difannulled; and that if any right, tribute, impofition, charge, or money, hath been, with permiffion, or otherwife, put upon cloths, or any of the aforefaid woollen manufactures fo imported, (except the ancient
tribute upon every piece of cloth, and proportionably upon
every other woollen manufacture, agreeable to the ancient treaties and agreements between the then Kings of
England, and the Dukes of Burgundy, and Governors of
the Low Countries) the fame fhould be altogether void,
and no fuch tribute or impofition from henceforth impofed,
or put upon the faid cloths or manufactures, for any caufe
or pretext whatfoever; and that all the Englifh merchants,
trading in any of the faid provinces, their factors, fervants,
or commiffioners, fhould enjoy from henceforward, all the
privileges, exemptions, immunities, and benefits, which
formerly have been agreed and given by the aforefaid ancient treaties and agreements, between the then Kings of
England, and the Dukes of Burgundy, and Governors of
the Low-Countries : it is therefore agreed, that deputies
fhall be named by the King of Great Britain, who meeting with the Marquis of Caftel-Rodrigo, or the governor
of thofe provinces for the time being, or any other minifters of the King of Spain, fufficiently authorifed in this behalf, fhall friendly treat and conclude hereupon ; and
alfo fuch further privileges, immunities, and neceffary exemptions, fuitable to the prefent ftate of affairs, fhall be
granted for the encouragement of the faid merchants and
adventurers, and for the fecurity of their trade and commerce,

merce, as fhall be agreed upon in a fpecial treaty, that fhall be made between both the kings, touching this particular.

XXI. The fubjects and inhabitants of the kingdoms and dominions of the moft ferene King of Great Britain and Spain refpectively, fhall with all fecurity and liberty fail to, and traffic in all the kingdoms, eftates, or countries, which are or fhall be in peace, amity, or neutrality, with the one or the other.

XXII. And they fhall not be difturbed or difquieted in that liberty, by the fhips or fubjects of the faid kings refpectively, by reafon of the hoftilities which are, or may be hereafter, between either of the faid kings, and the aforefaid kingdoms, countries, and ftates, or any of them, which fhall be in friendfhip or neutrality with the other.

XXIII. And in cafe that within the faid fhips refpectively, be found by the abovefaid means, any merchandize hereunder mentioned, being of contraband and prohibited, they fhall be taken out and confifcated, before the Admiralty, or other competent judges; but for this reafon the fhip, and the other free and allowed commodities which fhall be found therein, fhall in no wife be either feized or confifcated.

XXIV. Moreover, for better prevention of the differences which might arife touching the meaning of forbidden merchandize and of contraband; it is declared and agreed, that under this name fhall be comprehended all fire-arms, as ordnance, mufkets, mortar-pieces, petards, bombs, granadoes, fire-crancels, fire-balls, mufketrefts, bandeliers, gunpowder, match, falt-petre, and bullets; likewife under the name of forbidden merchandize, are underftood all other arms, as pikes, fwords, pots, helmets, backs and breafts, halberds, javelins, and fuch like armour; under this name is likewife forbidden the tranfportation of foldiers, horfes, their harnefles, cafes of piftols, holfters, belts, and other furniture, formed and compofed for the ufe of war.

XXV. Likewife, to prevent all manner of difpute and contention, it is agreed, that under the name of forbidden merchandize, and of contraband, fhall not be comprehended wheat, rye, barley, or other grain, or pulfe, salt, falt, wine, oil, and generally whatfoever belongs to the fuftaining and nourifhing of life, but they fhall remain free, as likewife all other merchandizes not comprehended in the preceding articles; and the tranfportation of them fhall be free and permitted, although it be to the towns and places of enemies, unlefs fuch towns and places be befieged, and blocked up, or furrounded.

XXVI. It is alfo agreed, that whatfoever fhall be found laden by the fubjects or inhabitants of the kingdoms and dominions of either of the faid Kings of England and Spain, aboard the fhips of the enemies of the other, though it be not forbidden merchandize, fhall be confifcated, with all things elfe which fhall be found within the faid fhips, without exception or referve.

XXVII. That the conful which hereafter fhall refide in any of the dominions of the King of Spain, for the help and protection of the fubjects of the King of Great Britain, fhall be named by the King of Great Britain, and he fo named, fhall have and exercife the fame power and authority in the execution of his charge, as any other conful hath formerly had in the dominions of the faid King of Spain : and in like manner the Spanifh conful refiding in England, fhall enjoy as much authority as the confuls of any other nation have hitherto enjoyed in that kingdom.

XXVIII. And that the laws of commerce that are obtained by peace, may not remain unfruitful, as would fall out if the fubjects of the King of Great Britain, when they go to, come from, or remain in the dominions or lordfhips of the King of Spain, by reafon of their commerce or other bufinefs, fhould be molefted for cafe of confcience; therefore, that the commerce be fecure, and without danger, as well upon land as fea, the faid King of Spain fhall provide, that the fubjects of the faid King of Great Britain, fhall not be aggrieved contrary to the laws of commerce, and that none of them fhall be molefted or difturbed for their confcience, fo long as they give no public fcandal or offence; and the faid King of Great Britain fhall likewife provide, for the fame reafons, that the fubjects of the King of Spain fhall not be molefted or difturbed for their confcience, againft the laws of commerce, fo long as they give no public fcandal or offence.

XXIX. That the people and fubjects refpectively of one
kingdom

kingdom, in the dominions, territories, regions, or colonies of the other, fhall not be compelled to fell their merchandize for brafs-metal coin, or exchange them for other coin or things, againft their will; or having fold them, to receive the payment in other fpecies than what they bargained for, notwithftanding any law, or other cuftom, contrary to this article.

XXX. That the merchants of both nations, and their factors, fervants, and families, commiffioners, or others by them employed; as alfo mafters of fhips, pilots, and mariners, may remain freely and fecurely in the faid dominions, kingdoms, and territories, of either of the faid kings, and alfo in their ports and rivers; and the people and fubjects of the one king, may have, and with all freedom and fecurity enjoy, in all the lands and dominions whatfoever of the other, their proper houfes to live in, their warehoufes and magazines for their goods and merchandize, which they fhall poffefs during the time for which they fhall have taken, hired, and agreed for them, without any impediment.

XXXI. The inhabitants and fubjects of the faid confederate kings, in all the lands and places under the obedience of the one or the other, fhall ufe and employ thofe advocates, proctors, fcriveners, agents, and folicitors, whom they think fit, the which fhall be left to their choice, and confented to by the ordinary judges, as often as there fhall be occafion; and they fhall not be conftrained to fhew their books and papers of account to any perfon, if it be not to give evidence for the avoiding law-fuits and controverfies; neither fhall they be embarked, detained, or taken out of their hands, upon any pretence whatfoever. And it fhall be permitted to the people and fubjects of either king, in the refpective places where they fhall refide, to keep their books of account, traffick and correfpondence, in what language they pleafe, in Englifh, Spanifh, Dutch, or any other, the which fhall not be molefted, or fubject to any inquifition. And whatfoever elfe hath been granted by either party, concerning this particular, to any other nation, fhall be underftood likewife to be granted here.

XXXII. That in cafe the eftate of any perfon or perfons fhall be fequeftered, or feized on by any court of
juftice

juſtice or tribunal whatſoever, within the kingdoms and dominions of either party, and any eſtate or debt happen to lie in the hands of the delinquents belonging *bona fide* to the people and ſubjects of the other, the ſaid eſtate or debts ſhall not be confiſcated by any of the ſaid tribunals, but ſhall be reſtored to the true owners *in ſpecie*, if they yet remain, and if not, the value of them, (according to the contract and agreement which was made between the parties ſhall be reſtored within three months after the ſaid ſequeſtration.

XXXIII. That the goods and eſtates of the people and ſubjects of the one king, that ſhall die in the countries, lands, and dominions of the other, ſhall be preſerved for the lawful heirs and ſucceſſors of the deceaſed; the right of any third perſon always reſerved.

XXXIV. That the goods and eſtates of the ſubjects of the King of Great Britain, that ſhall die without making a will in the dominions of the King of Spain, ſhall be put into inventory, with their papers, writings, and books of account, by the conſul, or other public miniſter of the King of Great Britain, and depoſited in the hands of two or three merchants, that ſhall be named by the ſaid conſul or public miniſter, to be kept for the proprietors and creditors; and neither the Cruzada, nor any other judicatory whatſoever, ſhall intermeddle therein; which alſo, in the like caſe, ſhall be obſerved in England, towards the ſubjects of the King of Spain.

XXXV. That a decent and convenient burial-place ſhall be granted and appointed to bury the bodies of the ſubjects of the King of Great Britain, who ſhall die within the dominions of the King of Spain.

XXXVI. If it ſhall happen hereafter that any difference fall out, (which God forbid) between the King of Great Britain and the King of Spain, whereby the mutual commerce and good correſpondence may be endangered, the reſpective ſubjects and people of each party ſhall have notice thereof given them in time, that is to ſay, the ſpace of ſix months, to tranſport their merchandize and effects, without giving them in that time any moleſtation or trouble, or retaining or embarking their goods or perſons.

XXXVII. All goods and rights concealed or embarked,

ed, moveables, immoveables, rents, deeds, debts, credits, and the like, which have not, with a formal notice of the cause, and by a legal condemnation, according to the ordinary juftice, been brought into the royal exchequer at the time of concluding this treaty, fhall remain at the full and free difpofal of the proprietors, their heirs, or of thofe who fhall have their right, with all the fruits, rents, and emoluments thereof, and neither thofe who have concealed the faid goods, nor their heirs, fhall be molefted for this caufe, by the exchequers refpectively ; but the proprietors, their heirs, or thofe who fhall have their right, fhall have, for the faid goods and rights, their action at law, as for their own proper goods and eftate.

XXXVIII. It is agreed and concluded, that the people and fubjects of the King of Great Britain, and of the King of Spain, fhall have and enjoy in the refpective lands, feas, ports, havens, roads, and territories of the one or the other, and in all places whatfoever, the fame privileges, fecurities, liberties, and immunities, whether they concern their perfons or trade, with all the beneficial claufes and circumftances which have been granted, or fhall be hereafter granted by either of the faid kings, to the moft Chriftian King, the States General of the United Provinces, the Hans-Towns, or any other kingdom or ftate whatfoever, in as full, ample, and beneficial manner, as if the fame were particularly mentioned and inferted in this treaty.

XXXIX. In cafe any difference or difpute fhall happen on either fide concerning thefe articles of trade and commerce, by either the officers of the Admiralty, or other perfon whatfoever, in the one or the other kingdom ; the complaint being prefented by the party concerned, to their Majefties, or to any of their council, their faid Majefties fhall caufe the damages forthwith to be repaired, and all things, as they are above agreed, to be duly executed ; and in cafe, that in progrefs of time any frauds or inconveniencies be difcovered in the navigation and commerce between both kingdoms, againft which fufficient prevention hath not been made in thefe articles, other provifions may be hereafter mutually agreed on, as fhall be judged convenient, the prefent treaty remaining ftill in full force and vigour.                    XL. It

XL. It is likewise accorded and concluded, that the moſt ſerene and renowned Kings of Great Britain and Spain, ſhall ſincerely and faithfully obſerve and keep, and procure to be obſerved and kept, by their ſubjects and inhabitants reſpectively, all and ſingular the capitulations in this preſent treaty agreed and concluded, neither ſhall they, directly or indirectly, infringe the ſame, or conſent that the ſame ſhall be infringed by any of their ſubjects or inhabitants. And they ſhall ratify and confirm all and ſingular the conventions before accorded by letters patents reciprocally, in ſufficient, full, and effectual form, and the ſame ſo formed and made, ſhall interchangeably deliver, or cauſe to be delivered, faithfully and really, within four months after the date of theſe preſents; and they ſhall then, as ſoon as conveniently may be, cauſe this preſent treaty of peace and amity to be publiſhed in all places, and in the manner accuſtomed.

In witneſs whereof, we the abovementioned Ambaſſador Extraordinary of the moſt ſerene King of Great Britain, and the Commiſſaries of the moſt ſerene King and Queen of Spain, have put our ſeals to this preſent treaty, ſubſcribed with our own hands, at Madrid the $\frac{13}{23}$ day of May, in the year 1667.

(L. S.) *Sandwich.*          (L. S.) *J. Eberardo Nidardo.*
(L. S.) *Duc. de St. Lucar, &c.*  (L. S.) *Conde de Penaranda.*

*The Form of Letters which ought to be given by the Towns and Sea-Ports, to the Ships and Veſſels ſetting ſail from thence.*

TO all unto whom theſe preſents ſhall come. We the governors, conſuls, or chief magiſtrate, or commiſſioners of the cuſtoms, of the city, town, or province of N. do teſtify and make known, that N. N. maſter of the ſhip N. hath before us, under ſolemn oath, declared, that the ſhip N. of          tons, (more or leſs) of which he is at preſent maſter, doth belong to the inhabitants of N. in the dominions of the moſt ſerene King of Great Britain.
And

And we, defiring that the faid mafter may be affifted in his voyage and bufinefs, do entreat all perfons in general and particular, who fhall meet him, and thofe of all places where the faid mafter fhall come with the faid fhip and her merchandize, that they would admit him favourably, treat him kindly, and receive the faid fhip into their ports, bays, havens, rivers, and dominions, permitting her quietly to fail, pafs, frequent, and negotiate there, or in any other places, as fhall feem good to the faid mafter, paying ftill the toll and cuftoms which of right fhall be due. Which we will acknowledge gratefully upon the like occafions. In witnefs whereof, we have figned thefe prefents, and fealed them with the feal of our town.

*Will. Godolphin.*
*Don Pedro Fernandez del Campo y Angulo.*

## PETITION.

I Don Brian Johnfon, conful of the Englifh nation, in the beft form I can, do declare, that his Majefty hath been pleafed to difpatch divers cedulas, or grants, in favour of the faid nation, whereby they may have a particular judge confervator, that may take cognizance of their caufes, as well being plaintiffs as defendants of the faid nation; and in the articles of peace, in the ninth article, and the thirty-eighth, it is exprefsly ordered and agreed, that they fhould be kept with all the exemptions granted to the faid Englifh nation, together with the rights and privileges granted to any other nation whatfoever, or to the Hans-Cities: as alfo doth appear by another cedula fet forth by the Queen our Lady; and thefe Hans-Towns, have the privilege of a judge confervator, being either plaintiffs or defendants, as the faid Englifh nation hath, as appears by a copy of the faid cedula, and the cedula which I now prefent and fwear to: Given in Madrid the 20th day of March, in the year 1670. I entreat your Lordfhip therefore, to command the faid cedulas, and articles of peace be perufed, and to order, that they be obferved, and executed in all refpects; let thofe of the Englifh nation, be either
                                              plaintiffs

plaintiffs or defendants, providing as much as may be, in favour of the said nation : I ask justice, &c.

*Don Brian Johnson, Lic.*
*D. Juan de Oliver.*

*The* QUEEN *Governess.*

## CEDULA.

FOrasmuch as the merchants of the English nation, which trade in the city of Sevilla, have represented, that they receive many vexations from the ministers which reside therein, contravening the articles between this crown and that, humbly entreating me, that for the future they may not be prejudiced in any thing that hath been agreed to, or ordered in the articles of the peace, and that I would order the necessary dispatches to be given for the observance thereof : as also that the cedulas which the King my Lord (now in glory) granted them, in the year 1645, may have their full force and vigour, as being part of the last treaty adjusted between me, and the most serene King of Great Britain, as is referred to in the ninth article, I have consented thereunto : wherefore I order and command the president of the court of degrees of the city of Sevilla, and all other ministers thereof, to whom belongs the performance of the one and the other, that in all respects whatsoever, they inviolably execute all what is contained in the said articles of peace, and granted by the cedula referred to, whensoever they are required by them, or authentic copies, without going against the tenor thereof in any wise, for such is my will. Given in Madrid, the 20th of March, 1670.

*I THE QUEEN.*
*D. Diego de la Torre.*

## PETITION.

I Don Brian Johnson, consul of the English nation, appear before your lordships, and say, that it is convenient for the said nation, that Andrez Perez de Mansilla, notary of the government of this city (before whom were
pub-

publifhed the articles of peace, which were adjufted in the year 1677, between this crown and that of England) do give a copy of the ninth and thirty eighth articles, wherefore I defire your Lordfhips, and humbly entreat, that you caufe to be iffued out your compulfory mandate, to the end that the faid Andrez Perez de Manfilla, may give an abftract of the faid articles: I afk juftice.

*Don Brian Johnfon.*

## THE ACT.

THAT the faid Andrez Perez de Manfilla do give, on the behalf of the faid conful, an authentic copy, attefted in due form, of the two articles of the peace, which this petition refers to, and that this act ferve for a mandate. His Lordfhip Don Rodrigo Serrano y Trillo, of his Majefty's council, prefident of the royal court of this city, judge confervator of the Englifh nation, has ordered it in Sevilla, the 13th day of the month of September, in the year 1670.

*Don Rodrigo Serrano y Trillo.*

Before me,
*Juan Goncales de Avellaneda.*

## CERTIFICATE.

ANDREZ Perez de Manfilla, notary public for our Lord the King, and for the government of this city, do certify, that by the regifters of public acts made upon what hath been adjufted, and concluded between this crown and that of England, for renewing the articles of peace, and commerce, which were publifhed in this city, the 29th day of the month of December, in the year 1677, by virtue of the cedula from our Lady the Queen, directed to the Count de Humanes, who was then governor, and colonel of the forces in this city and its diftricts, and which copy, authorized and compared, is in the faid acts, and with them a copy for the continuation and renewing of the peace and amity between the two crowns of Spain and Great Britain, printed in quarto, which is that which was remitted to Madrid with the faid cedula, and is the fame which was publifhed in this faid city, and in the public

places

places thereof, and amongst the articles of the said treaty of peace, there are two, the one number nine, and the other number thirty-eight, which are of the tenor following, viz.

*Article* **T**HAT the subjects of the King of Great Britain, trading, buying and selling, in any of the kingdoms, governments, islands, ports, or territories of the said King of Spain, shall hold, use, and enjoy, all the privileges and immunities which the said King hath granted and cofirmed to the English merchants which reside in Andalucia, by his royal cedulas or orders, made the 19th of March, the 26th of June, and 9th of November, 1645; his Catholic Majesty, by these presents, ratifying the same, as part of this treaty between the two crowns; and to the end that it may be manifest to all people, he hath confented that the faid cedulas, as to their entire subftance, be brought, transferred, and incorporated in these present articles, in the name, and in behalf, of all and every of the subjects of the King of Great Britain, residing and trading in any part whatfoever, within the dominions of his Catholic Majesty.

*Article* **I**T is agreed and concluded, that the people XXXVIII. and subjects of the one and the other of their said Majesties, shall have and enjoy in their respective lands, seas, ports, roads, coasts, territories, and places belonging to each other, the fame privileges, securities, liberties and immunities, as well touching their persons, as their trade, which have been given, or shall be given by one or the o her part, to the most Chriftian King, or the States General of the United Provinces of the Low Countries, or to the Hans-cities, or any other kingdom or state whatfoever, and that it be with all the claufes and circumftances in their favour, in as full, ample, and beneficial a manner, as if the fame was here particularly referred unto and inferted.

As is manifeft and appears from the said treaty of peace and amity between this crown and that of Great Britain, which now remains in my cuftody, to which I refer myfelf; and that it may be manifeft, in virtue of the act paffed

by

by Don Rodrigo Serrano y Trillo, of his Majesty's council, and his president in the royal court of this city; and at the request of Don Brian Johnson, I have given these presents in Sevilla, the 15th day of the month of September, 1670. In testimony of the truth,

*Andrez Perez de Mansilla.*

*Cedula of Privileges granted by his Majesty to the English which reside in* Sevilla, St. Lucar, Cadiz, *and* Malaga.

DON Philip, by the grace of God, King of Castile, of Leon, of Arragon, of the two Sicilies, of Jerusalem, of Portugal, of Navarre, of Granada, of Toledo, of Valencia, of Majorca, of Sevilla, of Sardinia, of Cordova, of Corcega, of Murcia, of Jaen, of the Algarves, of Algezira, of Gibraltar, of the islands of the Canaries, of the East and West Indies, Islands, and Terra Firma of the ocean, Archduke of Austria, Duke of Burgona, of Brabant, and of Milan, Count of Apsburg, of Flanders, Lord of Biscay and of Molina, &c.

Forasmuch as on the part of you Richard Anthony, consul of the English nation, by you, and in the name of the vassals of the King of Great Britain, information hath been given to me, that by means of the peace, which between this and that kingdom is settled, those which do reside and commerce in Andaluzia, principally in the city of Sevilla, San Lucar, Cadiz, and Malaga, humbly entreat me, that I would be pleased to confirm to you the privileges, exemptions, and liberties which appertain to you, as well by the articles of the said peace, as by the confirmations of them, and other favours and indultos, which the King my Lord and father (now in glory) granted you, and all others whatsoever, that have been granted by my crowns of these my kingdoms of Castile and of Portugal, commanding that they be observed and accomplished in all, and through all, without any limitation, and that they may be of more force, to grant them anew, with the qualities, amplifications, conditions, and declarations, which may be most convenient for you, imposing punishments upon

whom

whom fhall contradict them, and not obferve them ; and
that it may be known what they are, that there be given
copies of them, of what favour I have granted them, having a due regard to the aforefaid, and becaufe that for the
occafions which I have of wars, you have offered to affift
me with two thoufand five hundred ducats of filver, paying one thoufand down, and the other thoufand five hundred remaining, in the month of April, of this prefent
year, for which Don Francifco Moreno, with the intervention of Don Antonio de Campo-Redondo y Rio, Knight
of the order of St. James, of my privy council, and of my
exchequer, in your name, and by virtue of your power,
paffed a writing or obligation in form, before John Cortez
de la Cruz, my notary, I have thought fit, and by thefe
prefents, of my own proper motive, certain knowledge,
and royal and abfolute power, which in this part I will
ufe, and do ufe, as King and natural Lord, not acknowledging any fuperior in temporals, I confirm and approve
the faid privileges of exemptions, and liberties which appertain to you, as well by the articles of the faid peace,
as by the confirmations of them, and the reft of the favours, indultos, which the King my Lord and father
granted you, and any others whatfoever, which have been
granted by my crowns of Caftile and Portugal, to the faid
vaffals in all, and through all, as therein, and in every
thing, and in part thereof is fpecified, contained, and
declared, that they may be firm, ftable, and valid to you,
and be obferved to you, kept and fulfilled, becaufe that
my intention and deliberate will is, that all thofe of the faid
nation may enjoy, and do enjoy them without any limitation, with condition, that during the time they fhall refide
in Andaluzia, the faid Englifh may not be put upon any
office, or in any public poft, nor made guardians, truf-
tees, nor collectors, although they may be of the duties of
Alcavalus, and Millones, or other duties which relate to
my royal treafury ; nor fhall they demand from you loans,
or donatives, nor oblige you to farm any rents, nor take
your horfes or flaves.

   And to do you further favour, in conformity of what
is capitulated in the faid peace, I will and permit that you
may, and do trade and commerce freely, and fell your
                                                    mer-

merchandizes and goods, and buy thofe of my kingdoms, and carry them thence, obferving what is ordained by the laws and decrees that treat thereof, paying into my royal treafury the duties that ought to be paid, prohibiting as I do prohibt and command, that they do not take from you by force, any merchandizes, as wheat or barley, although it be for difpatch of my armadas, fleets, or galloons, neither for the Affentiftas, nor Eftranqueros, and the faid privileges fhall be as to wheat and barley, according to the tax ; and as to other things and merchandizes, as you fhall covenant and agree for, without taking them from you till they have paid you for them, and that they fhall not, upon the account aforefaid, give you any manner of trouble or vexation.

And becaufe that many of you trade in bringing to the ports of Andaluzia, city of Sevilla, and other parts, a great quantity of bacallao, and other kinds of fifh dry and falted, which being the moft neceffary provifions that can be, and creates you a great deal of coft and trouble, I will and command that you enjoy the cuftom of the city of Sevilla, in which it is ordered, that thofe which arrive with any fifh dry and falted there, may not be impofed any rate, but that they fell at the price they will, without that it be neceffary that they manifeft it to more than to the minifters which recovers my royal revenues, and that if the fhips in which they bring the faid bacallao be great, that they cannot come up the river, and fhall unload them in barks, the Judge of the Admiralty, or any other, may not put in the faid barks any guards at the coft of the owners of them. In like fort I command, that in cafe it appears that the faid fifh is rotten, and cannot be fpent, it be burnt or caft into the fea, without that by reafon thereof there may be made any procefs againft the owners, or perfons that fold it, or be imprifoned or informed againft.

And becaufe that the adminiftrator of the Almonarifargos, and divers other duties, which are recovered on goods and merchandizes, have been ufed, upon information given, to feize the perfon they fufpect, which, to men of trade, occafions much difcredit, cofts, and vexations ; my will is, and I command, that upon the faid in-

for-

formations, they only proceed againft the merchandizes, and not againft the perfons, permitting them, as I do permit them, that they may make, and do make their defences againft the faid vexations.

And whereas, according to one article of the faid peace, which treats in matter of religion, notwithftanding that in fome law-fuit, it haih been endeavoured that they declare whether they be Roman-catholics, or not, excufing giving credit to the oath which they make, as being parties, or as witneffes, I command, therefore, that in thofe matters they fhall not meddle with the natives of the faid kingdom ; but that the faid condition be fully obferved, without making them any fuch queftions ; and to the oath you fhall tender them in court, the fame faith and credit fhall be given, as if they were natural Spaniards, without that upon this account they are molefted, or troubled, or receive any grievance.

And by reafon that for juftification of fome caufes, the judges and juftices pretend that the merchants fhould exhibit their books of trade, and thereupon they receive vexation and trouble, I command and will, that the books of the merchants of the faid nation be not taken from them, but that they produce them in their own houfes, to take out the article which fhall be appointed, without demanding others ; nor may be taken from them any other papers, upon punifhment of him that fhall contravene herein, to be chaftifed according to law.

And becaufe likewife the merchants enter their goods in the cuftom-houfe of the city of Sevilla, of all the duties, which, becaufe they are many, is made upon one fheet of paper, and firmed and figned by all the officers, and remains in poffeffion of the warehoufe-keeper of the cuftom-houfe, that by virtue thereof, he may deliver fuch goods as go in bales, packs, trunks, and chefts ; and after they have taken them out, and put them in their houfes and warehoufes, the head waiter of the cuftom-houfe, and the officers of the half per cent, fhall not fearch your houfes, nor goods, caufing you trouble and vexation, afking of you the difpatches, it being manifeft that you cannot have them, having left them in the power of the faid head waiter. I prohibit therefore and command, that the houfes of the
faid

said merchants shall not be visited, nor be asked of them the dispatches of their goods, which doth not remain in their custody, so that this is to be understood, and is understood of the houses which are within the walls of the said city. And that it may be known, those who are of the said nation, let copies be given of the said privileges, and exemptions which concerns you, and were granted you, as well by the articles of the said peace, as in any other manner whatsoever ; and for the execution and accomplishing of all the aforesaid, I command those of my privy council, and the rest of my counsellors, juntas, and tribunals of my court, and the presidents, and justices of my courts, as also the judges, and justices of the peace belonging to my house, court, and chancery, and the regent, and judges of my court *de Grados*, in the city of Sevilla, and the chief magistrate of the court thereof, and all mayors, governors, magistrates, and other inferior officers, as well of the said cities of Sevilla, Cadiz, and Malaga, and San Lucar de Barrameda, as of all other cities, towns, and places of these my kingdoms, and dominions, and judges, and justices thereof, of whatever quality and condition they may be, to whom principally or accidentally it shall concern in any manner whatsoever, the accomplishing of all that is contained in this my letter, that as soon as they shall have been required herewith, or with a copy thereof signed by a public notary, (to which shall be given as much credit as to the original) each one for that part which shall concern him, observe and accomplish, cause to be observed and accomplished, in all, and through all, as is contained therein, without that in the whole, or in part, there be put any, impediment, or other doubt, or difficulty that shall oppose or contravene its tenor, and form, nor consent, or allow that it be interpreted, limited, or suspended in whole, or in part, contrary to the cedulas, provisions, or other orders for observance thereof, in that part which shall relate to each of you, and that they provide, and give the necessary orders for the greater security of the favour, which by this my letter I grant you, and that at all times, this favour may be certain and secure to you, that you may have a judge conservator for Andaluzia, principally for the said cities of Sevilla, Malaga, Cadiz, and San Lucar de
Barrameda,

Barrameda, to whom I fhall give fufficient commiffion for the prefervation and accomplifhing of the faid privileges, lib rties and exemptions, (which may oblige and compel all and every perfon whatfoever, of whatfoever condition, or quality foever they be) as fhall concern the faid nation, as well in thofe in which they fhall be defendants, as in thofe in which they fhall be plaintiffs, although the perfon which fhall fue them, and of whom they fhall be fued, may have any other fpecial judges whatfoever, as well by covenant or contract which they may have made, as by the preeminencies or immunities which they may have, becaufe that of the faid caufes only the faid judge confervator may take cognizance, and no other judge or tribunal whatfoever, although it be for any excefs or notorious crimes, or in any other manner and form whatfoever; and the faid judge confervator for the prefent, fhall be doctor Don Francifco de Vergara, judge of my court of degrees of the city of Sevilla, during the time that he fhall act therein, and, in his abfence, doctor Don Francifco de Medrano, judge of the fame court, who, for matters and law-fuits which fhall offer in the faid cities of Cadiz, Malaga, and San Lucar, may fubftitute his confervatorfhip in the perfon that fhall be propofed by the faid nation, that they may be laid before, and remitted to him, for the determination thereof; and of that which fhall be fo determined by him, they may appeal to my council, and not to any other tribunal, and becaufe that my will is, that each one in his time may have jurifdiction and fpecial commiffion, to protect and defend you in all that is contained in this my letter, and that all of it may be obferved, and accomplifhed, in the form that it is offered to you; I have thought fit to give charge, as by thefe prefents I give them charge of the protection and defence thereof, and command them, that they fee this my letter, and the qualities, and conditions, and preeminencies, and amplifications, contained therein, and caufe all of it to be obferved and accomplifhed, in the form accordingly, and in the manner that is contained therein, and declared, without confenting or allowing that in whole or in part, they may put, or do put any doubt or difficulty therein; and before the faid Don Francifco de Vergara, and in his abfence

before

before the said Don Francisco de Medrano, and not before any other special judge, the first motion shall pass,
and be followed in all causes and law-suits for what relates
thereunto, and cause the same to be executed, and a chaf-
tisement of the disobedient, for such is my will ; and that
the cognizance and determination of all that is contained
in this special letter, shall concern them, and doth concern them, that they proceed against those that shall be
guilty, executing on them such penalties as the law requires,
reserving, as I do reserve to my council, the appeals,
which by their acts and scentences they shall interpose, and
not for any other tribunal, without that any of the rest of
my councils, tribunals, courts or chanceries, or any other
judges or justices of these my kingdoms and dominions, of
whatsoever quality they be, may intermeddle, or do intermeddle therein, neither in the practice nor exercise of the
special jurisdiction, by which this my cedula I grant them,
be it by way of excess, appeal, or any other recourse
whatsoever; to whom and to each of them I inhibit, and
hold for inhibited their cognizance, and declare them for
judges incompetent thereof, for the whole, and in each
thing and part thereof, granting them as full and compleat power, and most ample commission as in law is required, and is necessary, with their incidencies, dependencies, annexities, and connexities ; and that, after them, the
said English nation of the said city of Sevilla, may name
in the said commission, one of the judges of the said court,
whom the said nation shall think fit ; and I command the
president, and those of my privy council, that presenting
before them his name, in case the said commission be vacant by promotion, or vacation of the said Don Francisco de Vergara, or Don Francisco de Medrano, or in any
other manner, they shall be dispatched by him that shall be
named, in the form accordingly, and as by this my letter
is ordained : and for the better performance hereof, for
time to come, I grant them power, licence, and authority,
that they may substitute, and do substitute this commission
for matters and law-suits, which shall offer in the said cities of Cadiz and Malaga, and San Lucar de Barrameda,
in the person which by you shall be proposed to them,
that they may examine matters, and bring them to a conclusion,

fion, and remit them the caufes and law-fuits you fhall have, to determine them in the form they fhall think fit, and fee convenient for the fecurity of what is contained in this my letter; and I encharge the moft ferene Prince, Don Balthafar Carlos, my very dear and beloved fon, and commanded the infantes, prelates, dukes, marqueffes, counts, barons, knights, efquires, governors of caftles, fortreffes and plains, and thofe of my council, prefident and judges of my courts, officers of my houfe and court, and chancery, and all mayors, governors, deputy-governors, juftices of the peace, and other whatfoever juftices and judges of my kingdoms and dominions, that they obferve to you and accomplifh, and caufe to be obferved and accomplifhed, this my letter and favour, which I do grant you, and againft the tenor and form thereof, not to go, nor act now, nor at any time, nor by any manner perpetually, for ever, nor confent, nor allow that they be limited to you, or fufpended in the whole, or in part, all its contents, whatfoever laws, or orders of thefe my kingdoms, and dominions, ordinances, ftile, ufe and cuftom of the faid cities of Sevilla, Cadiz, Malaga, and San Lucar, and all others which they have or may have to the contrary notwithftanding, forafmuch as doth concern thefe prefents, accounting it to be here inferted and incorporated, as if it had been word for word, and of this my letter Geronimo de Canencia, my chief treafurer and accountant, and my fecretary de la Media Anata, is to take cognizance, to whofe charge is committed the account of the faid duty; and I declare, that of this favour you have payed the duty of Media Anata, which imports thirty and five thoufand, one hundred, fifty and five maravedis in filver, which you are to pay every fifteen years perpetually, and that being complied with, you fhall not have the power to ufe this favour, without that it firft appears that you have fatisfied this duty, and alfo that you pay the judge confervator you fhall name, the falary which he fhall enjoy by the faid occupation, which is to be manifefted by certificate from the office of this duty. Given in Zaragoza, the 19th day of March, 1645.

*I THE KING.*

*Second*

*Second cedula, amplifying and confirming the privileges granted to the English nation.*

TO doctor Don Francisco de Medrano, judge of my court of degrees of the city of Sevilla; know ye, that by one of my letters and degrees of the 19th of March, of this present year, I did grant (to Richard Anthony, consul of the English nation, and to the subjects of the kingdom of England, which reside and trade in Andaluzia, principally in this city, and in that of Cadiz, and in that of San Lucar de Barrameda) the privileges, exemptions and licences, which appertain to them, as well as by the articles of the peace, as by the confirmation, and other favours and indultos, which the King my Lord and Father (now in glory) granted them, and with the other qualities, conditions, preeminences, and amplifications in the said decree declared, for having offered to serve me with two thousand five hundred ducats of silver, according as more largely thereby doth appear, to which I refer myself, and one of the conditions which I did grant them, was, that I would name and allow them a judge conservator for Andaluzia, principally for the said two cities, and San Lucar de Barrameda, to whom should be given sufficient commission, for the observance and accomplishment of the said privileges, liberties and exemptions, who should take cognizance of all causes, both civil and criminal, which should be brought against them, in which they were made defendants, that before him should come all law-suits, and causes whatsoever, which should concern the said English, or any other persons whatsoever, of whatsoever quality they may be, as well those in which they shall be defendants, as in those in which they shall be plaintiffs, although the persons that shall sue them may have special judges, as well by agreement or contract, which they may have made, by the preeminence or immunity which they may have, because of the said causes, only shall take special cognizance the said judge conservator, and no other judge, or tribunal, although it may be by way of excess, or in any other manner or form whatsoever, and that for the causes and suits that shall offer in the said cities of Cadiz and Malaga, and

San

San Lucar, may be fubftituted their commiffion in the
perfon, which by the faid nation fhall be propofed, that he
may bring things to a conclufion, and that they be remitted
to him to determine, and of that which the faid judge
fhall fo determine, they may appeal to my council, and
not to any other tribunal, and that the time you fhall act
in the faid court, you fhall be efteemed as fuch, and in
your abfence, and after you, he whom the faid nation, in
the faid city of Sevilla fhall appoint, and becaufe that my
will is, that all this be obferved and accomplifhed in the
form as is expreffed, I have thought fit to give charge to
you, and by this prefent do give charge of the protection and defence hereof, and command you that you fee
the faid decree, and the conditions, preeminences, and amplifications therein contained, and all of it to be obferved,
and accomplifhed in form accordingly, and after the manner that in the faid decree, and in this my cedula is declared, without confenting, or allowing that in the whole
or in part, may put or be put, any doubt or difficulty,
and before you, and not before any other judge, at the
firft inftance fhall be brought and followed, all caufes and
law-fuits, which thereupon, or any other thing or part
thereof, fhall be made, and caufe cognizance to be taken
of all caufes, civil and criminal, in which they fhall be
profecuted, or againft them fhall be attempted, and before you fhall be brought whatfoever law-fuits and caufes
which fhall concern the faid Englifh, between whatfoever
perfons, or whatfoever quality they may be, and the execution, and chaftifement of thofe that fhall difobey; becaufe that my will is, that the cognizance and determination of all that is contained in the faid provifion, and in
this my cedula of amplification, fpecially fhall and do concern you, proceeding fully againft thofe that fhall be guilty,
executing upon them the punifhment you fhall find by juftice due to them, without that any of the tribunals, courts
of chancery, or any other judges, or juftices of my kingdoms and dominions of Caftile, of whatfoever quality they
may be, may intermeddle, or do intermeddle herein, neither in the ufe nor exercife of the fpecial jurifdiction in the
faid firft inftance, which by this my cedula I grant you,
be it by way of excefs, appeal, or any other recourfe or
manner,

manner, to whom, and to each of you, I inhibit, and hold
for inhibited their cognizance, declaring you for judges incompetent thereof, as for the whole, and every thing, and
part thereof, and I grant you the moſt full and compleat
power, and moſt ample commiſſion, as by law required
and neceſſary, with their incidencies, dependencies, annexities and connexities, and that after you, the ſaid Eng-
liſh nation of the ſaid city of Sevilla, may have power to
name in the ſaid commiſſion, one of the judges of this
court, whom the ſaid nation ſhall think fit, and I command
thoſe of my privy council, that preſenting before them his
name, the ſaid commiſſion being vacant by promotion or
otherwiſe, him who ſhall be named, ſhall have his diſpatches
in due form, according as in this my cedula is ordained,
and that it may be better accompliſhed all that is contained in the ſaid decree, and in this my cedula, I grant
you licence, power, and authority, that you may ſubſtitute,
and do ſubſtitute this commiſſion for matters, and law-ſuits
that ſhall offer in the ſaid cities of Cadiz, Malaga, and
San Lucar, in the perſon that by the ſaid nation ſhall be
poropoſed to you, that you may conclude matters, you re-
miting to him the termination thereof, in the form you
ſhall think fit, ſuch as may be for the ſecurity of the ſaid
decree, and that all may be obſerved in the form, which
by it is ordained and commanded, any laws and pragmaticas of my ſaid kidgdoms, and dominions, ordonances,
ſtile, uſe and cuſtom, or any thing whatſoever, to the contrary notwithſtanding: All which, and foraſmuch as relates to theſe preſents, I diſpenſe with, abrogate, and derogate, make void and annul, count for nothing, and of no
value and force, and that theſe preſents remain in full
force and vigour for the future. Done in Zaragoza, the
26th of June, in the year 1645.

*I THE KING.*

By command of our Lord the King.

*Antonio Cannero.*

DON Philip, by the grace of God, King of Caſtile, of
Leon, of Arragon, of the two Sicilies, of Jeruſa-
lem, of Navarra, of Granada, of Toledo, of Valencia, of
Galicia,

Galicia, of Majorca, of Sevilla, of Sardinia, of Corcega, of Murcia, of Jaen, of Algarves, of Algecira, of Gibraltar, of the iflands of Canary, of the Indies Eaft and Weft, iflands and Terra Firma of the ocean fea, Archduke of Auftria, Duke of Borgona, of Brabant, and Millan, Count of Abfpurg, of Flanders, of Tiroll, of Barcelona, Lord of Bifcay and Molina, &c.

Forafmuch as by my letter and decree of the 19th of March, of this prefent year, I did grant to you, the fubjects of the King of Great Britain, who refide in Andaluzia, a confirmation and approbation of the privileges, cedulas, and franchifes which were granted you by the crown of Caftile and Portugal, and commanded that they fhould be kept and obferved to you the faid articles of peace, made between my crowns and that of England, and that by my other cedula, of the 26th of June of the fame year, you may name a judge confervator, that fhall take cognizance of all your caufs civil and criminal, as well in thofe in which you fhall be plantiffs as in thofe in which you fhall be defendants, with other conditions, amplifications, and preeminences in the faid decree and cedula contained, referring myfelf to the tenor thereof.

And now on your part relation having been made to me, that having prefented the laft cedula in the affembly of the court of degrees of the city of Sevilla, a copy thereof was ordered to be given to Don Juan de Villalva, my Fifcal of the faid court, who kept it in his poffeffion from the 15th of July, without having anfwered it till now, which had hindered and deprived you of the benefit and performance of the faid decree and cedula, to your great prejudice and detriment, although by what is ordained thereby, the judge confervator ought to take cognizance of all caufes, civil and criminal, as well being plaintiffs as defendants, with any perfon whatfoever you fhould trade with, your intent being only to enjoy the faid peivileges and judge confervator, when there fhould be any law-fuits between thofe of your nation, whether you be plaintiffs or defendants, and whether the caufes be civil, or whether they be criminal, and when the fuits fhall be with Spaniards, or with other perfons of different nations, the confervator is to take cognizance fo far only of the caufes in

which

which you fhall be civilly or criminally profecuted as defendants, and not in which you fhall be plaintiffs, humbly
intreating me, that whereas in this particular you have
waved and defifted from the faid privilege before Alonfo
de Alarcon, that I would be pleafed to declare it, with the
conditions, amplifications, and preeminences, as may be
moft convenient for you, and fhall be moft neceffary for
the greater force of what is infifted, of what my pleafure
fhall be; and becaufe that for the fervice of the wars, you have
offered to affift me with one thoufand five hundred ducats in
filver, payable at certain fixed days, I have thought
fit, and by thefe prefents I will and declare, that when the
fuits fhall be between thofe of your nation, whether you be
plaintiffs or defendants, or the caufes fhall be civil or
criminal, you fhall enjoy the fame privilege and its conditions : and when the faid fuits fhall be with Spaniards, or
with other perfons of divers nations, then the judge confervator fhall take cognizance, and do take cognizance
only of the caufes in which you fhall be civilly or criminally defendants, and not when you fhall be plaintiffs.

And becaufe that the duties of excife of millones, which
are impofed on bacallao dry and frefh, pilchards, herrings,
and falmon and other kinds of fifh, frefh and falted, it
was ordered that it fhould be recovered of thofe which
confume it; and by reafon the farmers of thefe duties,
and judges which take cognizance of thefe caufes, do occafion you great grievances, and oblige you to pay two
hundred marvedis for each quintail of bacallao, and accordingly on other forts as are permitted, and upon the
arrival of the fhips at the ports of Malaga, Cadiz and San
Lucar, they oblige you to declare the quantity of fifh you
bring, charging you by the great for the whole, obliging you to the payment thereof, as Money due to me,
and oblige you to the payment thereof in four months of
what it amounts to, which is unjuft, becaufe that thofe
who buy thefe kinds, are clergymen, fryars, monks, and
other perfons which have privileges and habits, mayors,
aldermen, and common-councilmen, for which caufe the
farmers of thefe duties will not recover them of fuch, but
recover them of you for the whole, without confidering
the quantity they fteal from you, that which is rotten, and
what

what you spend in your own families, and if you infist on the recovery thereof of such persons, they treat you ill, and do not pay you; therefore I will and command, that this duty be recovered of the buyers and consumers, and that the farmers put a person for their account, that may recover the same, as is done in the revenues of alcavala and almoxarifazgo, with this condition, that you be obliged, as I oblige you, that you shall register all the said kinds of fish aforesaid, as you are obliged to do, according to the general dispatches, without that this may be in any manner avoided.

And because from the visits which the farmers of duties make you, there results a great deal of trouble, I will and command, that in the cities of Malaga, San Lucar and Cadiz, be observed to you, and kept the privilege, that they may not examine the merchandizes which are in your houses, according to what is ordered and commanded by the said decree, of the nineteenth of March of this present year, being the same which is granted to those who reside in the city of Sevilla: and likewise I command that the said search may not be made by any farmer, if in the Custom-house you have paid all the duties, and that this be observed to you, and accomplished inviolably.

And because that all ships that come to these my said kingdoms, from those of England, Ireland and Scotland, the minister of the contrabands, and of the almoxarifazgo upon searching them as they enter the ports, cause great vexations and trouble to the masters of them, and shut up the holes and hatches of the said ships, deferring the visiting them eight or fifteen days, putting waiters aboard at the cost of the masters, who they will have to maintain them, and make them presents, I command the said ministers, as well of the contraband, as those of the almoxarifazgo, and every of them, that within three days they shall and do make the said visit, without putting waiters aboard them, or taking any duties by reason thereof, and if they shail put them, it shall be at the cost of the chief almoxarifazgo, and the Admiralty, since you owe nothing: and when there shall come into the said ports of Malaga, Cadiz, and San Lucar, any ship with provisions or merchandizes,

chandizes, neither at the time of the vifit, and of the unloading, nor at any other, as aforefaid, I order that the
judges, and officers of the contraband, nor Admiralty,
nor any others, may not put, or do put in them waiters
at the coft of the mafters or owners, nor do give you any
trouble, either the one or the other, upon that account,
according to what is ordered in the fourth article of the
inftitution of the faid Admiralty, by which it is expreft,
relating thereunto, for the fatisfaction of the waiters and
other officers, in the eighth article of the peace, in which
it is ordered, That the vaffals of the one King in the
territory of the other, fhall be treated as the natives themfelves, in whofe fhips never are put waiters at the coft of
the mafters or owners thereof.

And becaufe alfo that the officers of the contraband
in the faid ports, as foon as the fhips caft anchor, demand
of the mafters their manifeft, and if they do not find in
it the merchandizes that come configned to you, they
give you trouble, although you have the bills of lading
that the mafters have figned for them, to deliver them
according to their confignment, in which you receive a
great deal of damage, becaufe that the beft inftrument
you can have is the bills of lading, becaufe that by them,
you may oblige them by juftice to deliver you your goods,
and if the mafters, by neglect or malice, do not write them
in the faid manifeft, it is not juft that they execute the
punifhment upon the owners of the goods, but upon the
mafters and fhips, and in fo doing, the manifeft fhall be
always juftifiable. Wherefore it is my will, and I declare,
that the mafters do comply with exhibiting their manifeft,
within three days after their arrival in the faid ports, and
I command, that by reafon hereof, the owner of the goods
fhewing the bill of lading, you may not give him any
trouble, or moleftation whatfoever.

And becaufe likewife the judges for exportation, and
other officers, caufe you much trouble and vexation if
they find in the fhip any money, and it being neceffary
that the mafters have a fum according to the tonnage, to
buy fails, cables, anchors, and other neceffary ftores, I
give licence and permiffion, that having firft made a regifter, as is ufual, every fhip may have three pieces of eight
for

for every ton, for the faid purpofe, and not for any other, without therefore that upon that account they be put to any trouble.

And becaufe, that alfo they of the excife office of the faid city of Sevilla, occafion you trouble, vexation, and law-fuits, faying, that there is an order that you fhall manifeft the butter, leather, and other merchandizes and provifions, and that you declare the price you fell them at, and to what perfons, by which means it is two years fince, that you have not brought any butter to the faid city, and the order doth not relate to the ftrangers that bring thefe goods and provifions by fea, but only with the retailers that go to buy them in the ports, and bring them to the faid city to gain by them, I declare, that you have no obligation to make the faid manifeft and declaration, nor can they be obliged thereby to make them, nor to make a procefs againft you; and if they do, I command they be remitted to the judge confervator to determine them.

And becaufe that many times you have taken leafes of the houfes in which you live, and keep your merchandizes, and while you are in them, perfons of great authority take them from you, before your leafe is expired, becaufe they be large, and ftand where trade is, and oblige you to remove the goods, whereby they are damaged, and ftolen from you; I will, and command, that during the time of your leafe, the faid houfes may not be taken from you by any perfon, although he may be a judge, and have a particular privilege.

And that all this may be certain and fecure, I command the regent, and judges of my court of degrees of the city of Sevilla, and the judges of the courts thereof, and my governor of the faid city, and his deputy, and the other judges and juftices thereof, and of others whatfoever cities, villages, and places of my kingdoms, and dominions of my crowns of Caftile, to whom principally or accidentally fhall concern what is here contained, that all caufes which fhall be depending, in which you fhall be defendants, being of the qualities in this my letter contained, that they may provide and give order, that they may be remitted prefently to the judge confervator, as I have

have named you, in the posture they shall be, though
they may have been begun before, or after my said decree of the nineteenth of March, of this present year, together with the said decrees, and cedulas (notwithstanding
it having been ordered by my said court of degrees, to give
a copy thereof to my said judge) without making therein
any excuse, reply, doubt, or any difficulty whatsoever;
and I command, that they do not intermeddle, nor may
intermeddle in any thing concerning what is contained in
the said decree and cedulas, and in this my letter, but
that they observe, and fulfil, and cause to be observed,
and fulfilled, and executed in all, and through all, as
therein is contained, and that each of you, in that part
which shall concern him, do cause them to be put in true
and due execution effectually, so as in all respects it may
be complied with, without that it be necessary to have
further recourse to me hereupon, whatsoever laws, and
pragmaticas of these my kingdoms and dominions, ordinances, stiles, use and custom, which they have, or might
have, to the contrary notwithstanding; with which, for as
much as relates to these presents, I dispense, abrogate, and
derogate, make void and null, and give for no value and
effect, these presents remaining in full force and vigour for
the future, and of this my letter the clerks of my royal
treasury are to take notice, and I declare, that for this
grant, you have paid the duty of the *media anata*. Given
in Valencia, the nineteenth day of November, in the year
one thousand six hundred forty-five.

*I THE KING.*

### The Treaty of UTRECHT.

THEIR royal Majesties do mutually promise, that
they will faithfully perform and fulfil all and every
one of the articles of the foregoing treaty, and all privileges,
concessions, agreements, or other advantages whatsoever,
arising to the subjects on either side, which are contained
in them, or in the annexed schedules; and that they will
at all times cause the same to be performed and fulfilled
by their ministers, officers, or other subjects, so that the
subjects on each side may enjoy the full effect of all and
every one of them, (those only excepted, concerning
which

which something elſe ſhall be eſtabliſhed in the following articles, to the mutual ſatisfaction of each party) and
of all thoſe likewiſe which are contained in the following
articles. Moreover, the treaty of 1670, made between the
crowns of Great Britain and Spain, for preventing all differences, reſtraining depredations, and eſtabliſhing peace
between the ſaid crowns in America, is again ratified and
confirmed, without any prejudice, however, to any contract
or other privilege or leave granted by his Catholic Majeſty
to the Queen of Great Britain, or her ſubjects, in the late
treaty of peace, or in the contract of Aſſiento, as likewiſe
without prejudice to any liberty or power, which the ſubjects of Great Britain enjoyed before, either through right,
ſufferance, or indulgence.

II. The ſubjects of their Majeſties, trading reſpectively
in the dominions of their ſaid Majeſties, ſhall not be bound
to pay greater duties, or other imports whatſoever, for
their imports or exports, than ſhall be exacted of, and paid
by the ſubjects of the moſt favoured nation; and if it ſhall
happen in time to come, that any diminutions of duties, or
other advantages, ſhall be granted by either ſide, to any
foreign nation, the ſubjects of each crown ſhall reciprocally and fully enjoy the ſame. And as it has been agreed,
as is abovementioned, concerning the rates of duties, ſo it
is ordained as a general rule between their Majeſties, that
all and every one of their ſubjects ſhall, in all lands and
places ſubject to the command of their reſpective Majeſties,
uſe and enjoy at leaſt the ſame privileges, liberties, and
immunities, concerning all imposts or duties whatſoever,
which relate to perſons, wares, merchandize, ſhips, freight-
ing, mariners, navigation, and commerce, and enjoy the
ſame favour in all things (as well in the courts of juſtice, as
in all thoſe things which relate to trade, or any other right
whatſoever) as the moſt favoured nation uſes and enjoys,
or may uſe and enjoy for the future, as is explained more
at large in the 38th article of the treaty of 1667, which is
ſpecially inſerted in the foregoing article.

III. Whereas by the treaty of peace lately concluded
between their royal Majeſties, it was laid as the baſis and
foundation of the ſaid treaty, that the ſubjects of Great Britain ſhould uſe and enjoy the ſame privileges and liberty
of

of trade throughout all the dominions of Spain, which they enjoyed in the time of Charles II. and therefore the same rule is likewise, and ought to be, the basis and foundation of the present treaty of commerce, (which is understood to extend reciprocally to the subjects of Spain trading in Great Britain, in regard to whatsoever, by agreement, belongs to them:) and whereas a certain, clear, and expeditious method of paying the duties, is of the greatest use in settling trade upon a good foot, and to the mutual advantage of each nation; it is therefore agreed and concluded, that within the space of three months from the ratification of this treaty, commissaries appointed for that purpose by their respective Majesties, shall meet on the part of each of their royal Majesties, either at Madrid or Cadiz; by whom a new book of rates shall, without any delay of time, be made, which book of rates shall be published in every port, and shall contain and severally express the duties which are hereafter to be paid for wares brought into, or carried out of Castile, Arragon, Valencia, and Catalonia, and shall settle them in such a manner, that all the different imposts which in the time of the late King Charles II. were paid under several names, and in different custom-houses, for wares entering into, or going out of the ports of Spain, (the kingdoms of Arragon and Valencia, and the principality of Catalonia being comprehended therein, Guipuscoa and Biscaya, of which mention shall be made hereafter, only excepted) shall be put together, and be contained in one duty, and payable only in one sum.

But whereas the British Ambassador made pressing instances, that it might be given as a rule to the said commissaries, that no greater duties, or other imposts whatsoever, should be made payable in any port, wet or dry, in his said Catholic Majesty's dominions, by the said new book of rates, than what were paid in the custom-houses of the port of St. Mary's, or Cadiz, in the reign of the late King of Spain, Charles II. the Ambassadors of Spain have consented, and it is agreed and stipulated, that that rule shall be observed in those very ports of Cadiz and St. Mary's; and that all augmentations of duties which were introduced in the said ports after the time of Charles II.

on occafion of the war, or under the title of *habilitation*, or any other whatfoever, ceafing and being taken away, the Britifh fubjects fhall not, before or after the faid book of rates is fettled, be bound to pay any greater duties, of what fort foever, or under what name foever, for their imports or exports in the ports of St. Mary's and Cadiz, than what were paid there in the time of King Charles II.

Moreover, in regard to the ports of St. Mary's and Cadiz, the faid commiffaries fhall be ftrictly enjoined not to make the new book of rates according to the old indexes of duties, which, by reafon of the exorbitant rights that were appointed to be paid by them, ceafed to be in ufe in the time of Charles II. but fhall follow the tenor of thofe indexes only (which, whether they were commonly called *arancel* or regifters) fhall be found to have fubfifted in the time of King Charles II. and to have been the rule by which the duties were then paid.

And it is further agreed, that the fubjects of Great Britain, having paid thefe duties for their wares in the faid ports, to wit, thofe, until the new indexes are made, which were paid in the time of Charles II. or elfe fuch as fhall be made payable by the faid new book of rates, fhall have liberty to tranfport the faid wares, either by fea or land, into any other port or place of the aforefaid dominions of Spain, nor fhall the duties which were paid before, be re-exacted on that occafion.

Moreover, for preventing all difputes, which (notwithftanding the exact adminiftration of juftice in Spain in all other refpects) have formerly arifen concerning other duties, which, to the great prejudice of trade and traders, have been exacted formerly; it is agreed, that wares which have paid the duties in the manner aforefaid at Cadiz, or the port of St. Mary's, and are tranfported in order to be fold by wholefale, fhall be free and clear from any other duty whatfoever, throughout all Spain, provided however, that the proprietor of the faid wares or factors bring certificates, that the duties were duly paid in the manner aforefaid, otherwife fuch wares fhall be looked upon as fraudulently tranfported. But as to the payment of the rights commonly called *de Alcavalos*, *Cientos*, and *Millones*, it is agreed,

agreed, that it shall be regulated according to the fifth and eighth article of this treaty.

But because the Spanish Ambassadors are persuaded that the duties in every port of Spain cannot be reduced to the same rule with those which are or may become customary in Cadiz, or the port of St. Mary's, without violating the laws of Spain, and several privileges there, which have the force of laws, nor without the too great prejudice of their King and master; it is therefore thought proper to leave this matter to the determination of the commissaries who shall be appointed to settle the new book of rates.

But his Catholic Majesty promises, that he will immediately take off all augmentations of duties in the said ports, which have been introduced there since the time of Charles II. on occasion of the war, or under the title of *habilitations*, or any other whatsoever, and that either the same rule shall be observed in those ports, which is agreed to in the ports of St. Mary's and Cadiz, or else at least that the same rule shall be observed, as well before as after the said new book of rates shall be made, which had obtained in each respective port in the time of King Charles II. so that hereafter no greater duties shall be exacted there, or in any other place of passage, than what were paid in the said places in the time of Charles II. In the same places shall be likewise observed, what has been above appointed in this article concerning the rights de *Alcavalos, Cientos*, and *Millones*.

As to the ports of Guipuscoa and Biscaya, and others, not subject to the laws of Castile, in which less duties were paid in the time of Charles II. than at Cadiz, or in the port of St. Mary's, his Catholic Majesty promises, that those duties shall not be augmented in the said places by the new book of rates, but shall, in the mean time, remain as they were in the time of Charles II. All wares, however, brought into the ports of Biscaya and Guipuscoa, which shall afterwards be carried by land into the kingdoms of Castile or Arragon, shall be bound to pay such duties in the port where they first enter the said kingdoms, as were paid there in the time of Charles II. or else such as shall be established by the new book of rates,

IV. The

IV. The Catholic King confents and promifes, that for the future, it fhall always be lawful for the fubjects of Great Britain, living in the provinces of Bifcaya and Guipufcoa, to hire houfes or warehoufes fit for the prefervation of their merchandive; and his Majefty will, by renewing his orders to that purpofe, take effectual care that it fhall be in their power to do this in the like manner, and with the fame privileges, with which the faid Britifh fubjects, by virtue of the aforefaid treaty of 1667, or of any diploma or ordinance granted by their Catholic Majefties, did enjoy, or ought to have enjoyed, that liberty in *Andalufia*, or in any other ports and places of Spain whatfoever. The fubjects of Spain fhall enjoy the fame liberty in any ports and places of Great Britain, with all the privileges belonging to them by the aforefaid treaty.

V. To prevent abufes in collecting the rights called *de Alcavalos* and *Cientos*, his Catholic Majefty confents that the fubjects of Great Britain, who fhall bring their wares into any port of Spain; wet or dry, in order to fell them by wholefale, fhall have their choice whether they will pay the faid rights *de Alcavalos* and *Cientos*, in the firft place or port that they arrive at, or elfe according to the laws of Caftile, at the place where, and at the time when they are fold; which faid rights fhall be the fame as were paid in the time of King Charles II. And it is further agreed, that the fubjects of Great Britain may fend or carry the wares, for which the faid rights *de Alcavalos* have once been paid, into any port or place whatfoever, belonging to his Catholic Majefty's dominions in Europe, (in order to fell them there by wholefale) without any moleftation or repetition of the faid duties, or exaction of any others for the firft fale; provided, however, that they who carry the faid wares, fhall bring receipts or certificates from the farmers, or commiffioners of the cuftom-houfes, from whence it may appear, that the faid rights have been paid for thofe wares, and likewife other certificates, proving that the faid wares have not yet been fold; but if any merchant fells his wares by retail, he fhall be bound under fuch penalties as are inflicted by law, to pay all the local and municipal duties which are due and cuftomary at the

fale

fale of them, together with the rights *de Alcavalos & Cientos,* and all others whatfoever.

His Catholic Majefty farther confents, that if after the certificates abovementioned have been fhewn, any officer, or gatherer of duties, fhall exact the faid rights again, or fhall give any trouble, or ftop the paffage of the wares on that account, the officer guilty of the faid fault, fhall incur the penalty of 2000 ducats, payable to the ufe of his Majefty's chamber, or of the general hofpital at Madrid ; the notaries of the cuftom-houfes, or the contraband, fhall not receive above 15 *Ryals Villon,* for difpatching the faid certificates, unlefs it fhall be otherwife agreed in fettling the new book of rates.

VI. And as the fubjects of their Majefties are to enjoy on both fides an entire, fecure, and unmolefted ufe and liberty of navigation and commerce, as long as the peace and friendfhip, entered into by their Majefties, and their crowns, fhall continue, fo likewife their Majefties have provided, that the faid fubjects fhall not be deprived of that fecurity for any little difference which may poffibly arife, but that they fhall, on the contrary, enjoy all the benefits of peace, until war be declared between the two crowns.

And it is further agreed, that if it fhould happen, (which God prevent) that war fhould arife, and be declared between their Majefties and their kingdoms, then according to the contents of the 36th article of the aforementioned treaty of 1667, after the declaration of fuch a rupture, the fpace of fix months fhall be allowed to the fubjects of each party, refiding in the dominions of the other, in which they fhall be permitted to withdraw with their families, goods, merchandizes, effects, and fhips, and to tranfport them, after having paid the due and accuftomed impofts, either by fea or land, to whatfoever place, they pleafe, as they fhall alfo be fuffered to fell and alienate their moveable and immoveable goods, and freely, and without any difturbance, to carry away the price of them, nor fhall their goods, wealth, merchandizes, or effects, much lefs their perfons, be in the mean time detained or molefted, by any feizure or arreft. Moreover, the fubjects of each fide fhall, in the mean time, enjoy and obtain quick and
impartial

impartial juſtice, by means of which they may, before the expiration of the ſix months, recover the goods and effects which they have lent, either to the public, or to private perſons.

VII. And it is further agreed, that all the loſſes which the ſubjects of either crown ſhall duly prove, that they have ſuſtained in the beginning of the late war, (contrary to the tenor of the 36th article of the abovementioned treaty) whether they conſiſted of moveable or immoveable goods, ſhall be reciprocally made good, without any delay to them, their lawful procurators, heirs, or thoſe to whom their cauſe is intruſted, and reſtitution ſhall be made of thoſe goods, whether lands, buildings, or inheritance, or of what ſort ſoever they are, which remain and were confiſcated, and the juſt and lawful price of thoſe goods which cannot be recovered, whether moveable or immoveable, ſhall be paid; and their Majeſties have articled and agreed, that the ſaid payments, the pretenſions to them being, as is aforeſaid, fully proved, ſhall faithfully be performed, and made by their treaſurers on each part.

VIII. It is agreed, and his Catholic Majeſty will give effectual orders to that purpoſe, that the duties upon fiſh, and other proviſion, called *Millon*, ſhall not be demanded in the place where the ſaid wares firſt arrive, but the ſaid duties ſhall be paid according to the ancient cuſtom eſtabliſhed by law, only in the place of conſumption, and when the wares are ſold, and not before.

IX. His Catholic Majeſty promiſes that thoſe merchandizes, which are not particularly mentioned in the catalogue of rates, which is to be made according to the third article of this treaty, ſhall be charged with the ſame duties in proportion to their value, and no greater than thoſe which are laid upon merchandizes named in the ſaid catalogue of rates. And if any difference ariſes between the farmers of the cuſtom-houſes or commiſſaries, and any merchant, concerning the value of any wares, it ſhall be in the choice of the merchant to ſell his wares to the farmer or commiſſary, at the price the farmer of the cuſtom-houſe valued them (which price ſhall be immediately paid in ready money, the duties only deducted) or elſe to give part of his merchandizes at the rate ſet upon them, as hath been mentioned, to the farmer or commiſſary, inſtead of the duty, and retain the reſt.

X. It is agreed, that in caſe the Britiſh ſubjects ſhall bring any wares from any part of the coaſts of Africa, into Spain, and the ſame ſhall be admitted to pay the duties, thoſe being duly paid, the ſaid wares ſhall not afterwards be charged, either by the captains-general of the coaſts, or commanders of the harbours, or any body elſe, with any other duties, under what name or title ſoever: excepting ſuch as are payable in general, for all wares of the ſame ſort, at the time of their ſale.

XI. The maſters of merchant-ſhips, who ſhall enter into any port of Spain with their ſhips, ſhall be obliged, within twenty-four hours after their arrival, to deliver two declarations or inventories of their wares, or of that part of them which they are to unlade there, viz. one declaration to the farmer of the cuſtom-houſes or commiſſary, and another to the judge of the contraband, nor ſhall they open the hatches of their ſhips, till they either have ſearchers with them, or have leave given them by the farmer of the cuſtom-houſes to do it. No wares ſhall be unladen with any other view than that of being immediately carried to the cuſtom-houſes, according to a permiſſion which ſhall be given in writing for that end. It ſhall not be lawful however for any of the judges of contraband, or other officers of the cuſtom-houſes, under any pretence whatſoever, to open any bags, cheſts, hogſheads, or other covers of any wares whatſoever, belonging to the ſubjects of Great Britain, while they are carrying to the cuſtom-houſe, and before they are brought thither, and the proprietor of them, or his factor, is alſo come, who may diſcharge the duties, and take the goods into his own cuſtody. But the ſaid judges of contraband, or their deputies, may be preſent when the wares are taken out of the ſhips, and alſo when they are declared and laid open in the cuſtom-houſe, and if there be ſuſpicion of deceit, as that it is deſigned to lay open one merchandize inſtead of another, it ſhall be lawful for him to open all the bags, cheſts, and hogſheads, ſo this be done in the cuſtom-houſe, and no other place, and in the preſence of the merchant, or his factor, and not otherwiſe. But when the goods have been expoſed, and

and carried away from the cuftom-houfe, and the chefts, hogfheads, or other covers containing them, have been marked with the fign or feal of the proper officer, no judge of the contraband, or other officer, fhall prefume to open them again, or to hinder them from being carried to the merchant's houfe. Neither fhall it be lawful for them, under any pretence whatfoever, to hinder the faid goods from being carried from one houfe or warehoufe to another, within the walls or compafs of the faid city or place; provided that be done between the hours of eight in the morning, and five in the evening, and previous notice be given to the farmers of the rights *de Alcavalos & Cientos*, of the intent with which thofe goods are removed, to wit, whether it be that they fhould be fold, that in that cafe thofe duties, if not paid before, may be paid there, or at the place of fale; or, if they are not to be fold, then a certificate may be given, after the ufual manner, to the merchant. Furthermore, it fhall be lawful to carry wares from any port or place within the King of Spain's dominions, to any other port or place, either by fea or land, under fuch conditions as are expreffed in the fifth article of this treaty,

XII. The duties upon merchandize brougbt into the Canary iflands, exported from thence by Britifh fubjects, fhall not be greater than thofe that were paid in the reign of the late King Charles II. or fuch as fhall become payable by the new book of rates.

XIII. The fubjects of each of their Majefties, who are in debt to the fubjects of the other, whether the debts were contracted before the beginning of the faid war, or within the fpace of fix months after it was begun, or during the war, under the protection of letters of fafe conduct, or laftly, after a truce was made between the two crowns, fhall be bound and obliged faithfully to pay the fame, in the fame manner as if war had never arofe between the two crowns, nor fhall they be permitted to raife any exceptions againft the juft demands of their creditors, on pretence of the war.

XIV. His Catholic Majefty gives leave to the fubjects of Great Britain to fettle themfelves, and dwell in the town called

called St. Ander, upon the terms that are expreſſed in the 39th article of the treaty of 1667.

XV. As to the judge conſervator, and others to be ſubſtituted by him, if this privilege be granted to any other foreign nation whatſoever, the ſubjects of Great Britain ſhall likewiſe enjoy it. In the mean time, however, and until ſomething certain ſhall be determined in this matter, his Catholic Majeſty will give expreſs orders to all and every one of the judges of his kingdom, and to all others whomſoever, who are any ways concerned in the adminiſtration or execution of juſtice, and ſhall enjoin the ſame under the ſtricteſt penalties, to do juſtice, and cauſe it to be executed, without any delay, partiality, favour, or affection, in all cauſes relating to the ſubjects of Great Britain.

The Catholic King conſents, that appeals from ſentences in cauſes concerning the Britiſh ſubjects, may be brought before the tribunal of the council of war at Madrid, and no where elſe.

XVI. If any miniſter, or other ſubject of her Majeſty of Great Britain, or of his Catholic Majeſty, ſhall violate this treaty, or any article of it, he ſhall be reſponſible for all the damage occaſioned by it; and if he be placed in any public office, he ſhall, beſides making ſatisfaction to the injured party, (as is aforeſaid) be deprived of his office alſo.

XVII. The ſubjects of Great Britain having brought by ſea from any other port in Spain, wine, brandy, oil, ſoap, dried grapes, or other merchandizes, and producing certificates that the duties were paid at the place whence they ſet ſail, ſhall be ſuffered to put the ſame into their ſhips lying at Cadiz, or there to remove them from one ſhip to another (with the conſent of the inſpectors of the maritime affairs, and in the preſence of them, or their deputies, if they have a mind to be there, and at a ſeaſonable time to be appointed by the ſaid inſpectors, within four and twenty hours, in order to prevent all frauds whatſoever) and to carry away from thence; with this liberty, that they ſhall not pay the duty called *Hondeaxe,* or any other of entrance, or going out.

The

The prefent treaty fhall be ratified by the moſt ferene Queen of Great Britain, and the moſt ferene Catholic King, and the ratifications fhall be exchanged at Utrecht, within two months, or fooner, if poſſible.

In witneſs whereof, we the underwritten Ambaſſadors Extraordinary and Plenipotentiaries of the Queen of Great Britain, and the Catholic King, have ſigned and ſealed this preſent inſtrument at Utrecht, the $\frac{28}{9}$ day of November December in the year of our Lord, 1713.

(L. S.) *Joh. Briſtol.*  (L. S.) *Duc de Oſſuna.*
(L. S.) *El Marque de Monteleone.*

WE having feen and confidered the above-written treaty, have approved, ratified, and confirmed the ſame, as we do by theſe preſents, for ourſelves, our heirs and fucceſſors, approve, ratify, and confirm it, excepting only three articles thereof, viz. the third, fifth, and eighth, concluded at Utrecht, which are to be obſerved and un-derſtood in the manner and form following:

III. WHEREAS, by the late treaty of peace it is agreed and eſtabliſhed as a baſis and foundation, that the fubjects of Great Britain, in what regards commerce, fhall enjoy the fame liberties and privileges which they enjoyed in the reign of King Charles II. in all parts of the King of Spain's dominions, which rule is what is alſo to ſerve for a baſis and foundation of the preſent treaty of commerce, and is to be underſtood reciprocally in favour of the King of Spain's fubjects trading in the dominions of Great Britain. And as nothing can contri-bute more to eſtabliſh the commerce to a mutual benefit than a fixed, clear, and eaſy rule in paying the duties, efpecially on a moderate footing, and proportionable to the value of the merchandize, in order to prevent the frauds that otherwiſe would be practiſed, to the prejudice of the revenues of either crown, which has been often ex-perienced in Spain, where the eſtabliſhed duties by the ancient books of rates are exceſſive; in confideration whereof his Catholic Maieſty, being defirous to avoid
the

the like confequences, and to favour, augment, and facilitate, in all that depends upon him, the commerce, in as
ample a manner, as her Britannic Majefty defires, hath
confented, on his part, to fupprefs and make void the different duties payable upon importation and exportation,
contained in the ancient books of rates, as alfo thofe that
have been impofed fince, under any name or pretence
whatfoever, and content himfelf with one only duty to be
paid on importation of all goods and merchandize, after
the rate of 10 per cent. of their value; and the like duty
upon all goods and merchandize, which fhall be exported
out of his dominions, whether the valuation made by
weight, meafure, piece, or *ad valorem*; and the fame duty
fhall be collected in all the ports of entry in Spain, comprehending thofe of Arragon, Valencia, and Catalonia,
excepting out of this general rule, Bifcaya and Guipufcoa,
whofe duties of importation and exportation are to remain as they were in the time of Charles II. And that the
faid 10 per cent. being once paid, the farmers or officers
of the cuftom-houfes where thofe goods fhall be entered,
fhall be obliged to mark the fame with the proper feals
and marks of their office, and alfo give the requifite difpatches; by virtue of which, the proprietors of the goods
may freely tranfport them to all the other parts of Spain
where they pleafe, without being liable to pay any other
duty, impofition, or charges, to the ufe or benefit of his
Catholic Majefty, in any ports or parts of Spain whatfoever, in refpect of tranfporting the faid merchandize, over
and above what they have paid, in purfuance of this new
arancel, provided the receipts and marks are produced;
in default of which, they fhall be efteemed to be fraudulently tranfported. But it is to be underftood, that this
is not to extend to the Alcavalas, Cientos, and Millones,
in relation to which, provifion is made in the fifth and
eighth articles of this treaty.

And forafmuch as the Ambaffador of England hath reprefented, that to avoid all differences and difputes for the
future, it is abfolutely neceffary to eftablifh a certain valuation or rate of the feveral forts of merchandize, by
which the faid duty of 10 per cent. fhall always be paid,
and not altered, either by means of the augmentation or

diminution

diminution of the price of the said merchandize, which may hereafter happen in the commerce, in any time, or in any part of the kingdom; it is agreed by their Catholic and Britannic Majesties, by their Ambassadors, that in the term of three months, from the ratification of this treaty, or sooner, if possible, commissaries named and authorised by both their Majesties in due form, shall meet at Madrid, or in Cadiz, who, without loss of time, shall proceed to the forming a new book of rates, in such a manner, as to fix and limit what shall be paid for the future, on all forts of merchandize, as well upon importation as exportation; and so as that all the different duties which were payable, either before or in the time of Charles II. or since, under whatsoever name or pretence, or collected in different custom-houses or offices, shall be comprehended in this only duty; payable in one sum, whether upon importation or exportation, in all the ports of Spain, and shall extend to the kingdoms of Arragon, Valencia, and principality of Catalonia, and their dependencies, excepting only the provinces of Guipuscoa and Biscaya, of which mention has been already made. And whereas great instances have been made by the Ambassador of Great Britain, that directions be given to the said commissaries, that they take care, and above all do observe, as a fixed rule, that this duty be laid equally and generally in the ports and custom-houses of Spain, upon the importation and exportation of all goods and merchandize, after the rate of 10 per cent. of the value which such goods and merchandize bear in the course of trade, between the merchants of Cadiz and port St. Mary's, to which the Ambassadors of Spain have consented; always provided, that the goods and commodities which shall be imported into the kingdom of Spain, by the ports of Biscaya and Guipuscoa, and afterwards transported into the other provinces depending on the kingdoms of Castile and Arragon, shall be obliged to pay at the first custom-house of entry into the said kingdoms, the duties which shall be established in this new book of rates.

V. To prevent the abuses that may be committed in collecting the duties called *Alcavalas & Cientos*, his Catholic Majesty consents, that the subjects of her Britannic Majesty shall not be obliged to pay these duties, during

such

fuch time as they think fit to let their merchandize remain in the magazines of the cuftom-houfes appointed for that purpofe; but when they fhall think fit to take out the faid goods, either to be tranfported farther into the country, fell them in the fame place, or carry them to their own houfes, it fhall be permitted them fo to do, upon giving his bond, with fufficient fecurity, to pay the faid duties of *Alcavalas & Cientos*, for the firft fale, in two months after the date of his bond, upon which he fhall have receipts given him for the faid goods, and the goods fhall be marked w th the proper mark and feal of the farmers of the faid *Alcavalas* and *Cientos*, where fuch bond and fecurity fhall be given for the firft fale, after which the faid merchandize may be tranfported, and fold by wholefale, in any port or place belonging to the King of Spain in Europe; and that no obftruction or hindrance fhall be made upon account of the faid duties, nor the proprietor liable to pay a fecond time in refpect of the firft fale, provided thofe who carry the faid merchandizes produce the receipts and marks of the farmer, or proper officer, concerned in the collection of thefe duties, or making fufficient proof of their not being fold before. But if, on the contrary, any merchant do fell his goods by retail, he fhall be obliged to pay the faid duties of *Alcavalas* and *Cientos* a fecond time, under the pains eftabl fhed by the laws. And his Catholic Majefty declares, that if any officer of the *Alcavalas* and *Cientos* fhall exact a fecond time the faid duties on the fame merchandize, when the faid receipts and marks have been produced, or fhould obftruct their paffage, or tranfportation, or occafion the leaft impediment, fuch officer fhall be fined 2000 crowns, to the benefit of his Majefty's revenues. And the officers of the cuftom-houfes fhall not demand, or take, for making fuch receipts or certificates, more than 15 reals vellon, unlefs it be otherwife fettled in the new book of rates.

VIII. His Catholic Majefty confents, that the duties commonly called *Millones*, which are payable upon fifh, and other forts of domeftic provifions, fhall not be demanded in the firft ports or cuftom-houfes of entry in Spain, during fuch time as the proprietors will let them remain in the warehoufes appointed for that purpofe. But in

cafe

case the owner shall desire to take them out, either to send into the country, sell them on the place, or carry them to their own houses, they are then to give bond, with good security, to pay the said duty of *Millones* in two months after date of the said bond, upon which the necessary dispatches are to be given them. And the said merchandize shall be marked with the seals or marks of the farmers of the *Millones* where the said duties were secured, after which the said goods may be transported to, and sold in the places where they are to be consumed, without paying any new duties of *Millones*. His Majesty also declares, that if after the receipts are produced, any officer belonging to the farmers of the *Millones*, should exact a second time the same duties on the same goods, or should oppose their passage, transport or sale, or occasion the least impediment, the said officer shall be fined 2000 crowns, for the benefit of his Majesty's revenue.

THEREFORE, by virtue of these presents, we do approve and ratify the treaty above written, as likewise the three articles, viz. the third, fifth, and eighth, as they are set forth in this instrument of ratification, and are to be taken as part of the said treaty, and to have the same force and effect, as if they had been inserted therein: promising and engaging our royal word, that we will faithfully and religiously perform and observe, all and singular the things agreed upon in this treaty, and that we will not suffer the same to be violated by any one, as far as lies in our power. For the greater testimony and validity whereof, we have caused our great seal to be affixed to these presents, which we signed with our royal hand. Given at our castle of Windsor, the 7th day of February, 17¼, in the twelfth year of our reign.

ANNE, by the grace of God, Queen of Great Britain, France, and Ireland, defender of the faith, &c. to all and singular to whom these presents shall come, greeting. Whereas the right reverend father in God, our right trusty and well-beloved counsellor, John, bishop of Bristol, our ambassador extraordinary and plenipotentiary,

dean

dean of Windsor, and register of our most noble order of the garter, did on our part, together with the plenipotentiaries of the most serene Catholic King, conclude and sign at Utrecht, on the $\frac{28}{9}$ day of $\frac{November}{December}$ 1713, a treaty of commerce between the crowns of Great Britain and Spain; and, at the same time, a separate article was concluded, made between the said plenipotentiaries, who were severally furnished with sufficient authorities, and is as follows:

### SEPARATE ARTICLE.

BY the present separate article, which shall be altogether of the same validity and force, as if it was inserted word for word in the treaty of commerce this day concluded, between their royal Majesties of Great Britain and Spain, and shall for that end be ratified, as well as the said treaty; his Catholic Majesty consents, that it shall at all times hereafter be lawful for the British subjects, who shall live in the Canary Islands, for the sake of their trade, to nominate some one person, being a subject of Spain, who shall execute the office of judge conservator there, and shall at the first instance take cognizance of all causes relating to the commerce of the British subjects; and his royal Majesty promises, that he will grant commissions to such judge conservator so named, together with the same authority, and all the privileges which the judges conservators have formerly enjoyed in Andalusia. And if the British subjects shall desire to have more judges of that sort there, or to change those that are appointed every three years, it shall be allowed and granted them. His Catholic Majesty consents likewise, that appeals from the sentences of the said judge conservator, shall be brought before the tribunal at the council of war at Madrid, and no where else.

In witness whereof, we the underwritten Ambassadors Extraordinary, and Plenipotentiaries of her sacred Majesty of Great Britain, and of his sacred Catholic Majesty, have

have figned and fealed thefe prefents at Utrecht, the ⁹/₅ day of November/December in the year of our Lord 1713.

(L. S.) *Joh. Briftol.*

(L. S.) *Duc de Offuna.*
(L. S.) *El Marque de Monteleone.*

WE having feen and confidered this feparate article, have approved, ratified, and confirmed, as we do by thefe prefents approve, ratify, and confirm the fame, promifing and engaging our royal word, that we will faithfully and inviolably keep all and fingular the things therein contained, and that we will not fuffer any thing to be done contrary thereunto. For the greater teftimony and validity whereof, we have figned this inftrument with our royal hand, and caufed our great feal of Great Britain to be affixed thereunto. Given at our caftle of Windfor the feventh day of February, 17¹³⁄₁₄, in the twelfth year of our reign.

*ANNE R.*

*Convention made at* London, July 26, O. S. 1715, *relating to the Duties laid on* Britifh *Woollen Cloths exported to the* Auftrian Netherlands.

HIS Britannic Majefty's minifters having complained that the commerce of his faid Britannic Majefty, with the Auftrian Netherlands, is very much prejudiced, by the high duties of importation laid upon the coarfe woollen cloths fent from Great Britain to the faid Auftrian Netherlands: the underwritten minifter and plenipotentiary of his Imperial and Catholic Majefty, for the treaty of Barrier at Antwerp, declares by thefe prefents, that his Imperial and Catholic Majefty will confent to the immediate reducing of the duties on the faid coarfe woollen cloths, according to the following fpecification; and that, in all other refpects, the commerce of the fubjects of his Britannic Majefty with the Auftrian Netherlands, fhall remain, continue, and fubfift wholly on the fame foot as it does at prefent, without any alteration, innovation, diminution, or augmentation to be made, under

any

any pretext whatfoever, till all the parties interefted fhall agree upon a treaty of commerce.

| Dyed woollen cloths. | Fl. | Sols. |
|---|---|---|
| A piece of the value of above 60 florins, up to 90 | 3 | 10 |
| A piece of the value of above 40 florins, up to 60 | 2 | 0 |
| A piece of the value of 40 florins, and under | 1 | 0 |
| Mixed woollen cloths. | | |
| A piece of the value of above 60 florins, up to 90 | 2 | 10 |
| A piece of the value of above 40 florins, up to 60 | 1 | 10 |
| A piece of the value of 40 florins, and under | 1 | 0 |
| White woollen cloths. | | |
| A piece of the value of above 60 florins, up to 90 | 2 | 10 |
| A piece of the value of above 40 florins, up to 60 | 2 | 0 |
| A piece of the value of 40 florins, and under | 1 | 0 |
| Draps de pie (cloth to lie upon floors) of all forts, the piece | 0 | 8 |

Done at London this 26th of July, O. S. 1715.

(L. S.) *J. L. de KINIGSEGG.*

*Requifition made to the Council of State at* Bruffels, *the* 6th *of* November 1715.

IT being abfolutely neceffary for the fervice of his Imperial and Catholic Majefty, to leffen immediately the duties of importation on coarfe woollen cloths coming from Great Britain, and from the United Provinces, on the following foot.

| Woollen cloths dyed. | Fl. | Sols. |
|---|---|---|
| A piece of the value above 60 florins, up to 90 florins | 3 | 10 |
| From 40 to 60 | 2 | 0 |
| Of 40 and under | 1 | 0 |
| Mixed. | | |
| A piece of the value of 60 florins, and fo up to 90 | 2 | 10 |
| From 40 to 60 | 1 | 10 |
| Of 40 and under | 1 | 10 |
| White. | | |
| A piece of the value of 60 florins, and fo up to 90 | 2 | 10 |
| From 40 to 60 | 2 | 0 |
| Of 40 and under | 1 | 0 |
| Draps de pie (cloth to lie upon floors) of all forts, the piece | 0 | 8 |

And

And to reduce the duties of importation on brandies diftilled from corn coming from Great Britain, and from the United Proyinces, to three florins the awm, inftead of eight which is now paid; you are required, gentlemen, to give forthwith the neceffary directions in the finances, that the proper orders may be immediately iffued for this purpofe, and that the collectors of the duties of importation and exportation, may conform themfelves accordingly thereto. Done at the conference at Bruffels, this 6th of November, 1715.

Signed,

*William Cadogan.*
*John Vander Bergh.*
*P. W. Francquen.*

Attefted to be a copy.

*A Copy of the Refolution of the Council of State, minuted in the Margin of the Confultation of the Council of the Finances, the 7th of* November, 1715.

HAVING made our reprefentation to the minifters of the conference, conformably to this confultation, and added alfo other reafons to enforce it, they have newly made this day another more preffing requifition to us, by which they infift abfolutely that the former be put in execution; whereupon the council of the finances fhall iffue the orders therein fpecified; but it is underftood that they fhall not have force nor effect, unlefs they be approved and ratified by his Imperial and Catholic Majefty, in the treaty of barrier. This laft claufe, however, which begins with the words *it is underftood*, and ends with the words, *in the treaty of barrier*, fhall not be inferted in the orders to be fent to the collectors. Signed *Voorfp.*

Attefted to be a copy.

*P. W. Francquen.*

*Order of the Council of Finances to the Collectors of the Duties.*

THE counfellors and commiffioners of the demefnes and finances of his Imperial and Catholic Majefty. Moft dear and fpecial friends, we herewith fend you by exprefs order of the council of ftate appointed for the general

neral government of these countries, a copy of the requisition made to them by the ministers of the conference, relating to the lessening of the duties of importation on the coarse woollen cloths coming from Great Britain, and from the United Provinces; as also for reducing the said duties on brandies distilled from corn: commanding you by express order of the said council of State, to take care to regulate yourselves pursuant thereto, in collecting the said duties, and to give notice of it to your subalterns. Most dear and special friends, God have you in his holy keeping. Brussels, at the council of the said finances, the 12th of November, 1715.

To the collectors of the duties of importation and exportation at

| | |
|---|---|
| Newport, | Fort St. Philip, |
| Ostend, | Borgerhoute, |
| Bruges, | Mechlen, |
| Ghent, | Turnhout, |
| Dendermonde, | Tirlemont. |

This is a copy agreeing with the minutes kept in the registry of the finances.

*P. W. Francquen.*

*Extract from the* TARIFF, *settled the 14th of* November, 1715.

*N. B.* A difficulty having arisen about the intention of the requisition of the 6th of November, 1715, of which mention is made in the 26th article of the treaty of barrier, it is agreed provisionally to cause the duties of importation on all the different sorts comprehended in the above Tariff, under the denomination of woollen cloths, to be collected according to the tenor of the said requisition of the 6th of November, till his Imperial and Catholic Majesty, and his Majesty the King of Great Britain, shall agree upon it otherwise; and, in the mean while, the King's collectors and officers shall permit the said manufactures to be imported, giving notice, and taking security for the payment of the operplus duties of importation, on the foot the same shall be settled.

*A Let-*

*A Letter from the Imperial Envoy, Count* Volkra, *to the Lord Viscount* Townshend, *principal Secretary of State.*

My LORD,

YOU have acquainted me, that complaints are made of contraventions to the 26th article of the treaty of barrier; and I have had the honour to communicate to you what Count Kinigsegg has answered thereupon.

I can declare to you besides, that, for the future, there will be an exact performance of the said 26th article of the treaty of barrier of the 15th of November, 1715, and of the convention at London, of the 26th of July, 1715; as also of the declaration in the Tariff of the 14th of November, 1715, that is to say, that the duties on the Petite Draperie, (or woollen stuffs) of England, will be collected on the foot of the coarse woollen cloths, according to the diminution expressed in the foresaid convention at London, without any alteration, till it be agreed otherwise between the Emperor and the King, our masters; but in the mean time the merchants are to give security to pay the surplus, if the matter shall be so determined between the two respective courts. I am, &c.

London, $\frac{20}{31}$ August, 1716.          *The Count Volkra.*

---

*Treaty between* Charles VI. *Emperor of the* Romans, *and Catholic King of* Spain, *on the one Part, and* George, *King of* Great Britain, *and the Lords the States General of the United Provinces of the* Netherlands, *on the other Part, for the entire Restitution of the* Spanish Netherlands, *to his Imperial and Catholic Majesty; with the Reserve of a strong and solid Barrier to the said* Netherlands, *in Favour of their High Mightinesses; as also of the yearly Payment of several great Sums, as well for the Maintenance of the said Barrier, as for the Reimbursement of those which were due to them before. Made at* Antwerp *the 15th of November, 1715; together with a separate Article relating to Mortgages of the same Date, and Forms of the Oaths to be taken by the Governors of Places, full Powers and Ratifications.*

FOrasmuch as it pleased the Almighty to restore peace some time ago to Europe, and as nothing is more desirable

firable and neceffary, than as far as poffible to re-eftablifh
and fecure the common and public fafety and tranquility;
and whereas the Lords the States General of the United
Provinces have engaged to remit the Netherlands to his
Imperial and Catholic Majefty Charles VI. as it was ftipulated and agreed by the treaty made at the Hague the
7th of September, 1701, between his Imperial Majefty
Leopold, of glorious memory, his Britannic Majefty William III. alfo of glorious memory, and the faid States
General, that the faid potentates fhould agree upon what
related to their reciprocal interefts; particularly with refpect
to the manner of eftablifhing the fecurity of the Netherlands, to ferve as a Barrier to Great Britain and the United Provinces, and with refpect to the commerce of the
inhabitants of Great Britain and the United Provinces.
And whereas at prefent, his Imperial and Catholic Majefty, Charles VI. to whom the faid Netherlands fhall be
remitted by this treaty, his Britannic Majefty King George,
both at this time reigning, and the lawful heirs and fucceffors of the faid Emperor, and King, and the States General
of the Uunited Provinces, acting therein by the fame prin-
ciples of friendfhip, and with the fame intention to procure and eftablifh the fame mutual fecurity, and the more
to confirm a ftrict union, have for that end named, commiffioned, and appointed for the Minifters Plenipotentiaries, viz. his Imperial and Catholic · Majefty, the Seur
Jofeph Lotharius Count de Konigfegg, his Chamberlain,
Counfellor of war, and Lieutenant General of his armies:
his Britannic Majefty, William Cadagon, Efq; his Envoy
Extraordinary' to their High Mightineffes the States General of the United Provinces, Member of the Parliament of
Great Britain, Mafter of the Wardrobe, Lieutenant General
of his Armies, and Colonel of the fecond Regiment of his
Guards: and the States General, Meffieurs Bruno Vander
Duffen, late Burgomafter, Senator and Counfellor, Pen-
fionary of the city of Gouda, Affeffor in the Councils of
Hemfrades de Schieland, Dykegrave of Crimpenerwaerde;
Adolphus Henry, Count de Rechteren, Lord of Almelo
and Vriefeveen, &c. Prefident of the Lords the States of
the province of Overyffel, and Droffart of the quarter of
Zealand; Scato de Gockinga, Senator of the city of Gro-
ningen

ningen, and Adrian de Broffelle, Lord of Geldermanfen, &c. Senator of the city of Flufhing; the three firft Deputies of the Affembly of the Lords the States General, on the part of the provinces of Holland and Weft Friefeland, Overyffel, Groningen and Omlands, and the fourth, Deputy of the Council of State of the United Provinces. Who being affembled in the city of Antwerp, which by common confent had been named for the place of congrefs, and having exchanged their full powers, copies whereof are inferted at the end of this treaty, after many conferences, have agreed for, and in the name of his Imperial and Catholic Majefty, his Britannic Majefty, and the Lords the States General, in the manner as follows:

I. The States General of the United Provinces, immediately after the exchange of the ratifications of the prefent treaty, fhall, by virtue of the grand alliance in 1701, and of the engagements they have entered into fince, remit to his Imperial and Catholic Majefty all the provinces and towns of the Netherlands, with their dependencies, as well thofe which were poffeffed by the late King of Spain, Charles II. of glorious memory, as thofe which were lately given up by his late Majefty the moft Chriftian King, alfo of glorious memory; which provinces and towns thogether, as well thofe that are remitted by this prefent treaty, as thofe which were remitted before, fhall hereafter be and compofe in the whole or in part but one undividable, unalienable, and unchangeable domain, which fhall be infeparable from the eftates of the houfe of Auftria in Germany, to be enjoyed by his Imperial and Cotholic Majefty, his heirs and fucceffors, in the full and irrevokable fovereignty and propriety; that is to fay, with refpect to the former, as they were enjoyed, or ought to have been enjoyed by the late King Charles II. of glorious memory, purfuant to the treaty of Ryfwick; and with refpect to the latter, in the fame manner, and upon the fame conditions as they were furrendered up, and remitted to the Lords the States General, by the late moft Chriftian King, of glorious memory, in favour of the moft auguft houfe of Auftria, and without any other charges, mortgages or engagements, which may have been conftituted on the part of the States General, and to their profit.

II. His

II. His Imperial and Catholic Majesty promises and engages, that no province, city, place, fortress or territory of the said Netherlands, shall be surrendered, transferred, granted, or descended to the crown of France, nor to any prince or princes of the house and line of France, nor to any other who shall not be the successor, heir and possessor of the dominions of the house of Austria in Germany, either by donation, sale, exchange, marriage-contract, inheritance, testamentary succession, or *ab intestato*, or upon any other title or pretext whatsoever. So that not any province, city, place, fortress or territory of the said Netherlands, shall ever be subject to any other prince, than the successors of the said house of Austria; only excepting what was formerly yielded to the King of Prussia, and what shall be given up by the present treaty to the said Lords the States General.

III. Whereas the safety of the Austrian Netherlands will chiefly depend upon the number of troops that may be kept in the said Netherlands, and places that are to form the barrier which has been promised to the Lords the States General by the grand alliance, his Imperial and Catholic Majesty, and their high Mightinesses, have agreed constantly to maintain therein, at their own expence, a body of from 30 to 35000, whereof his Imperial and Catholic Majesty shall provide three fifths, and the States General two fifths. Provided always, that if his Imperial and Catholic Majesty shall diminish his quota, it shall be in the power of the said States General, to lessen theirs in proportion: and when there is any appearance of war or attack, the said body shall be augmented to 40,000 men, according to the same proportion; and, in case of actual war, a farther force shall be agreed upon, according as shall be found necessary. The repartition of the said troops in time of peace, for as much as concerns the places committed to the guard of the troops of their High Mightinesses, shall be made by them only, and the repartition of the rest by the governor of the Netherlands, by imparting reciprocally to each other the dispositions they shall have made.

IV. His Imperial and Catholic Majesty grants to the States General, a privative or separate garrison of their own

troops,

troops, in the towns and caftles of Namur and Tournay, and in the towns of Menin, Furnes, Warneton, Ypres, and Fort Knoque; and the States General engage themfelves, not to employ any troops in the faid places, which although in their own pay, belong to any prince or nation that may be at war with, or fufpected to be in engagements contrary to the interefts of his Imperial and Catholic Majefty.

V. It is agreed, that in the town of Dendermonde there fhall be a common garrifon, which fhall be compofed, for the prefent, of one batallion of Imperial troops, and one batallion of the troops of the States General; and that if hereafter it fhould be neceffary to augment the faid garrifon, fuch augmentation fhall be made equally by the troops of both parties, and by mutual concert. The governor fhall be put in by his Imperial and Catholic Majefty, and, together with the fubaltern officers, fhall take an oath to the States General, never to do, or fuffer any thing to be done in the faid town, which may be prejudicial to their fervice, with refpect to the prefervation of the town and garrifon: and he fhall be obliged, by the faid oath, to grant free paffage to their troops always, and as often as they fhall defire; provided it be demanded beforehand, and that it be for a moderate number at a time.

VI. His Imperial and Catholic Majefty confents alfo, that in the places hereby granted to the States General, to hold their feparate garrifons in, they may place fuch governors, commanders, and other officers that compofe the ftate major as they fhall think fit, on condition that they fhall be no charge to his Imperial and Catholic Majefty, nor to the provinces and towns, unlefs it be for convenient lodging, and the emoluments accruing from the fortifications, and that they be not perfons who may be difagreeable or fufpected to his Majefty, for particular reafons that may be given.

VII. Which governors, commanders and officers, fhall be entirely and feparately dependent on, and fubject to the fole orders and jurifdiction of the States General, for all that concerns the defence, guard, fecurity, and all other military affairs of their places. But the faid governors, as well as their fubalterns, fhall be obliged to take on oath to

his

his Imperial and Catholic Majesty, to keep the said places true to the sovereignty of the house of Austria, and not to intermeddle in any other affairs, according to the form that is agreed upon and inserted at the end of this treaty.

VIII. The generals shall give to one another reciprocally, as well in the towns where his Imperial and Catholic Majesty has a garrison, as in those intrusted to the guard of the troops of their High Mightinesses the States General, the honours usually paid according to their character, and the nature of their service; and in case the governor-general of the Netherlands come into places committed to the guard of their High Mightinesses, the same honours shall be paid to him which he usually receives in the places garrisoned by the troops of his Imperial and Catholic Majesty; and he shall even give the word there: but all this without prejudice to the 6th article. And the governors, or in their absence the commanders, shall give notice to the said governor-general of the dispositions by them made for the security and guard of the places comitted to their care; and they shall have a due regard for the changes which the said governor-general shall judge proper to make.

IX. His Imperial Catholic Majesty grants to the troops of the States General, wherever they are in garrison, the free exercise of their religion, so as to be in particular places convenient and proportionable to the number of the garrison, which the magistrates shall assign and maintain in every town and place where there has been none assigned already, and to which places no external mark of a church shall be given: and it shall be strictly enjoined by both parties, to the civil and military officers, as also to ecclesiastics, and all others concerned, to hinder all occasion of scandal and controversies that may arise upon the subject of religion; and when any dispute or difficulty shall happen, both parties shall amicably accommodate it. And as for religion, with regard to the inhabitants of the Austrian Netherlands, all things shall continue and remain on the same foot they were during the reign of Charles II. of glorious memory.

X. All

X. All the ammunition, artillery, and arms of the States General, as also materials for the fortifications, corn in time of scarcity, provisions to put into the magazines, when there is an appearance of war; and moreover, the cloth and furniture for cloathing the soldiers, which shall be certified to be designed for that use, shall pass freely, and without paying any customs or tolls, by virtue of passports which shall be demanded and granted, upon the specification signed; on condition nevertheless, that at the first custom-house of his Imperial and Catholic Majesty, where the said provisions, materials, arms and mountings shall enter, and at the place where they are to be unladen, the boats and other carriages may be duly visited, to hinder the mixture of other merchandize therewith, and to prevent fraud and abuse, against which it shall be always lawful to take such precautions, as length of time and experience shall shew to be necessary; and the governors and their subalterns shall not be permitted in any manner whatsoever, to hinder the effect of this article.

XI. The States General may change their garrisons, and the disposition of the troops in the towns and places committed to their particular guard, according as they shall judge proper, and no body shall on any pretence whatsoever, hinder or stop the passage of the troops, which they shall from time to time send thither, or draw from thence. And the said troops may even, in case it be required, pass thro' all the towns of Brabant and Flanders, and thro' all the open country, and make bridges as well over the canal betwixt Bruges and Ghent, as over all other canals and rivers which they shall find in their road; on condition nevertheless, that they shall be the troops of a prince or nation not in war with his Imperial and Catholic Majesty, nor suspected to be in any engagement or league contrary to his interests, as is said above in the fourth article, and that notice shall be given of it beforehand, and request made to the governor-general of the Netherlands, with whom the routs and other affairs shall be regulated, by some person who shall have their High Mightinesses commission. The regulation made by the States General for the passage of the troops, shall be observed here, as it is observed in their own country: and the States

General

General fhall obferve to make the faid change of garrifons, as well as the difpofitions neceffary to it, with as
little charge and inconveniency as poffible to the inhabitants.

XII. For as much as the common fafety demands in
time of war, or in imminent danger of war, that the States
General fhould fend their troops to places that are moft expofed to the danger of being attacked or furprized, it is
agreed between his Imperial and Catholic Majefty, and
the States General, that their troops fhall be received into
the faid places, as far as fhall be neceffary for their defence, when it fhall be evidently the cafe; always provided,
that this be done by agreement and concert with the governor-general of the Netherlands.

XIII. The States General may, at their own coft and
expence, caufe the faid towns and places to be fortified,
either by new works, or by caufing the old to be repaired,
and maintain them, and generally provide all that they
fhall find neceffary for the fecurity and defence of the faid
towns and places, excepting that they fhall not caufe new
fortifications to be built, without giving notice of it beforehand, to the governor-general of the Netherlands, and
having his opinion and advice thereupon, nor bring the
charges thereof to the account of his Imperial and Catholic Majefty, or the country, without his faid Majefty's
confent.

XIV. For the fecurity of the communication between
the United Provinces, and the places of the barrier, his Imperial and Catholic Majefty fhall take care fo to order it,
that the letters and meffengers, as well ordinary as extraordinary, may pafs freely to and from the towns and places of the barrier, and thofe of other countries; on condition that the faid Meffengers carry no letters or packets for
merchants, or other private perfons, which as well for the
places of the barrier, as for all other countries, fhall be
put in at the poft-offices of his Imperial and Catholic
Majefty.

XV. As for the artillery, magazines and military provifions which their High Mightineffes have in the towns
and places which they remit to his Imperial and Catholic Majefty, they fhall be allowed to carry them out without

out any hindrance, and without paying any cuſtoms or tolls, as well thoſe which they brought thither themſelves, as the artillery marked with their arms, and loſt in the late war, or otherwiſe belonging to them, and found in the ſaid places when taken; unleſs his Imperial and Catholic Majeſty deſire to take the ſaid artillery and ammunition upon his own account, and agree with their High Mightineſſes for the price, before the places are ſurrendered. And as for the artillery and ammunition at that time in the places committed to the guard of the troops of the States General, they ſhall be left to their keeping and direction, according to the inventories that ſhall be drawn up and ſigned on both ſides, before the exchange of the ratifications of the preſent treaty; but they ſhall not be tranſported elſewhere without common conſent, and the property ſhall remain to his Imperial and Catholic Majeſty, for as much as they are found in the ſaid places at the time of their ceſſion or ſurrender.

XVI. In caſe the provinces of the Auſtrian Netherlands be attacked, and it happen (which God forbid) that the enemy's forces ſhould enter Brabant, to act there, and lay ſiege to any place in the ſaid province, or any of thoſe that form the barrier, their High Mightineſſes ſhall be permitted to cauſe their troops to enter and take poſt in the towns and places on the Demer, from the Schelde to the Maeſe, as alſo to make retrenchments, lines and inundations there, as much as the circumſtances of the war ſhall require, to hinder the farther progreſs of the enemy; provided the whole be done in concert with the governor-general of the Netherlands.

XVII. As it appears by the experience of the laſt war, that for ſecuring the frontiers of the States General in Flanders, it was neceſſary to leave ſo many conſiderable bodies of troops there, that the army was thereby very much weakened: to prevent this inconvenience, and the better to ſecure the ſaid frontiers for the future, his Imperial and Catholic Majeſty yields to the States General ſuch forts, and as much of the territory of the Auſtrian Flanders bordering upon the ſaid frontiers, as they ſhall want to make the neceſſary inundations, and for covering them from the Bebelde to the ſea, in places where they are not already

ſuf-

sufficiently secured, and where they cannot be secured by making inundations upon those lands only that already belong to the States General.

For this purpose his Imperial and Catholic Majesty agrees and approves, that the limits of the States General in Flanders, shall hereafter begin at the sea between Blankenberg and Heyst, at the place where there are no downs; provided they do not cause or permit any villages or houses to be built near that post, nor suffer fishermen to settle there, nor make any sluices to the sea there.

And their High Mightinesses promise moreover, that if they think fit to cause any fortifications to be built at the head of their new limits, they will take care not to weaken the dyke; and they will not only defray the extraordinary expences that may be incurred on account of the said fortifications, but will also indemnify the inhabitants of the Austrian Netherlands from all losses they may sustain, in case the sea comes to make inundations through the said fortifications.

There shall be drawn from the post abovenamed, a direct line to Grootewege, from whence the line shall be continued towards Heyst, and from Heyst it shall go to the Drie-hoeck and Swarte-sluice, from thence to Fort St. Donas, which his Imperial and Catholic Majesty yields in full propriety and sovereignty to their High Mightinesses, (provided the gates of the sluices of the said fort be left open in time of peace;) and in like manner he gives up the land situate on the north side of the above-mentioned line.

Grom fort St. Donas, the new limits of the States General shall extend to fort St. Job, from whence they shall fall in with the old ones near the town of Middleburg; which limits shall be continued along the Zydelings Dyke, as far as the place where the Eckelose Watercourse and the Water-loop meet at a sluice.

After this the limits shall run from the Graaf-Jaans Dyke to the village of Bouchout, (the proprietors of whose sluices are permitted to place them where they were before) and from Bouchout the line shall be continued strait forward to the antient limits of the States General.

His

His Imperial and Catholic Majefty gives up alfo, in full and entire fovereignty to the States General, the territory fituate on the north fide of the line.

And in regard it is neceffary for their entire fecurity, that the inundation be continued from Bouchout, as far as the canal of Sas van Ghent, along the Graaf-Jaans Dyke, their High Mightineffes fhall be permitted, in time of war, to take poffeffion of, and fortify all the fluices that they fhall find in the Graaf-Jaans Dyke, and the Zydelings Dyke.

As for the town of Sas van Ghent, the limits fhall be extended to the diftance of two thoufand geometrical paces; provided that no villages be included in that fpace.

And for the prefervation of the lower Schelde, and the communication between Brabant and Dutch Flanders, his Imperial and Catholic Majefty gives up to the States General, the full and entire property and fovereignty of the village and Polder of Doel, together with the Polders of St. Anne and Keteniffe.

And whereas, in time of war it will be neceffary, for the better fecurity, to make inundations through the fluices, between the forts of the Meer and the Perle, his Imperial and Catholic Majefty fhall, as foon as the barrier is attacked, or a war begun, remit the guard of the Perle fort, and the fluices, to their High Mightineffes; provided that as foon as the war is over their High Mightineffes fhall reftore the faid fluices and fort to his Imperial and Catholic Majefty, together with thofe which they fhall, in that time have taken poffeffion of on the Graaf-Jaans dyke, and Zydelings dyke. The States General fhall not make any inundation in time of peace, and when they find themfelves obliged to make any in time of war, they fhall give previous notice of it to the governor-general of the Netherlands, and concert the affair with the generals that command the armies in the Netherlands; promifing moreover, that if upon occafion of the giving up to them fome fluices (whereof the inhabitants of the Auftrian Flanders fhall retain the free ufe in time of peace) they fhould happen to fuffer any damage or prejudice, either from the com-

commanders, or other military officers of the States General shall not only remedy it immediately, but shall also give satisfaction to those concerned.

And because by this new situation of the limits, it will be necessary to alter the toll-houses, for preventing frauds, which is a case wherein his Imperial and Catholic Majesty, and their High Mightinesses, are equally concerned, the places shall be agreed on for establishing the great offices, and for such farther precautions as it shall be thought convenient to take.

It is moreover stipulated by this article, that a just valuation shall be made before the ratification of the present treaty of the revenues arising to the sovereign, from the lands which shall be yielded to their High Mightinesses by this article, as also of what profit accrued to the sovereign, by the renewing of grants on the foot that they were agreed to for thirty years last past, to be deducted and set off from the annual subsidy of 500,000 crowns.

And the Roman-catholic religion shall be preserved and maintained in the places given up as above, on the same footing as it is now, and was exercised in the reign of King Charles II. of glorious memory; and all the privileges of the inhabitants shall be preserved and maintained in like manner.

The fort of Rodenhuysen shall be razed, and the differences touching the canal of Bruges shall be referred to the decision of neutral arbitrators chose by both parties; provided, that by the giving up of the fort of St. Donas, the people of the town of Sluys shall not have more right upon that canal, than they had before that place was yielded up.

XVIII. His Imperial and Catholic Majesty yields to their High Mightnesses the States General for ever, in full sovereignty and propriety, the town of Venlo in the upper part of Guelderland, with its precinct and jurisdiction, and the fort of St. Michael, and moreover the fort of Stevenswaert, with its territory or jurisdiction; as also as much land as shall be necessary to augment their fortifications on this side the Maese: And his said Majesty promises, that he will never cause to be built, or permit any other to build any fortification, of what name soever, withIn

within the diftance of half a league from the faid fortrefs. Moreover, his Imperial and Catholic Majefty gives up to the States General, the ammanie of Montfort, confifting (with exception to the villages of Swalmt and Elmt, which he referves to himfelf) of the little towns of Nieuftadt and Echt, with the following villages, viz. Ohe and Lack, Rooftern, Braght, Beefel, Belfen, Vlodorp, Poftert, Berg, Lin and Montfort, to be poffeffed by the faid States General, in the manner as they were enjoyed by his Majefty King Charles II. of glorious memory, with the perfectures, burghs, fiefs, lands, funds, quit-rents, revenues, tolls, of what nature foever, fubfidies, contributions and collections, fealties, demefnes, and others whatfoever, belonging to the faid places given up as aforefaid. The whole however, without prejudice to, and faving all the rights which may belong to the King of Pruffia, &c. and notwithftanding all exceptions, pretentions, or cavils already made, or that may hereafter be formed to difturb the States General in the peaceable poffeffion of the places yielded up by the prefent article; all compacts, conventions, or difpofitions, contrary to the prefent article, being deemed null and void.

Provided, and be it underftood, that this furrender is made with this exprefs claufe, that the ftatutes, antient cuftoms, and in general, all privileges civil and ecclefiaftical, as well with regard to the magiftrates and private perfons, as to the churches, convents, monafteries, fchools, feminaries, hofpitals, and other public places, with all their appurtenancies and dependencies, as alfo the diocefan right of bifhop of the Ruremonde, and in general every thing that concerns the rights, liberties, immunities, functions, ufages, ceremonies, and the exercife of the Catholic religion, fhall be preferved and fubfift without any charge or innovation, either directly or indirectly, in all the places yielded as above, in the fame manner as in the time of King Charles II. of glorious memory, and as it fhall be explained on both fides more fully, in cafe any difpute happens on that account; and the officers of the magiftracy and the police, fhall be given to none but perfons of the Catholic religion.

The

The right of collation to benefices, which has been hitherto in the fovereign, fhall hereafter belong to the bifhop of Ruremonde; on condition that the faid benefices fhall not be given to perfons difagreeable to the States General, for particular reafons that may be alledged.

It is alfo ftipulated, that the States General fhall not pretend to have acquired by the ceffion of the town of Echt, any right of judicature or appeal, with refpect to the chapter of Thorn, or other lands of the Empire; and it fhall be free for his Imperial and Catholic Majefty, to nominate fuch place as he fhall think fit for the faid judicature or appeal.

And becaufe the inhabitants of that part of the upper quarter which is hereby furrendered, can no longer carry their procefs, in cafe of appeal, to the court of Ruremonde, it fhall be free for their High Mightineffes to eftablifh a court of appeal for their fubjects, in what part of the province they think fit.

It is moreover agreed, that all the duties on import and export, which are levied along the Maefe, fhall not be encreafed or leffened, in the whole or in part but by common confent; of which duties his Imperial and Catholic Majefty fhall receive to his own profit, thofe which are collected at Ruremonde and Navaigne, and the Lords the States General thofe which are paid at Venlo; and for as much as the faid duties upon the Maefe in general, as alfo thofe upon the Schelde by way of fubfidy, are appropriated to the payment of two diftiftinct annuities, viz. one of 80,000 florins a year, and another of 70,000, by virtue of a tranfaction paffed and concluded the 26th of December, 1687, with his late Majefty of Great Britain King William III. it is agreed that their High Mightineffes, by reafon of the ceffion abovementioned, fhall give a yearly fupply to his Imperial and Catholic Majefty in the payment of the faid annuities and other debts, which may be there mortgaged, in proportion to the produce of the duties of import and export which they fhall receive, the whole according to the very conftitution of the faid annuities.

And as for the debts contracted and conftituted upon the generality of the upper quarter of Guelderland, the States General fhall concur in the payment thereof for fo

much

much as is their quota, according to the proportion fet forth in the matricula of all the faid upper quarter. All the documents and papers which concern the upper quarter of Guelderland, fhall remain as heretofore in the archives of Ruremonde. But it is agreed, that an inventory, or Regifter of them fhall be formed at the meeting of commiffaries from his Imperial and Catholic Majefty, his Majefty of Pruffia, and the Lords the States General; and an authentic copy of the faid inventory fhall be given to each of thofe three powers, that they may always have free accefs to all the papers and documents, whereof they may have occafion, for the part which they feverally poffefs in the faid upper quarter of Guelderland; and an authentic copy of fuch papers fhall be delivered to them on the firft demand.

XIX. In confideration of the great charge and extraordinary expence which the States General are unavoidably obliged to be at, as well for maintaining the great number of troops which they are engaged by the prefent treaty to keep in the towns above named, as for fupplying the great fums abfolutely neceffary for the maintenance and repair of the fortifications of the faid places, and for furnifhing them with ammunition and provifions, his Imperial and Catholic Majefty engages and promifes to caufe to be annually paid to the States General, the Sum of 500,000 crowns, or 1,250,000 florins Dutch money over and above the revenue of the part of the upper quarter of Guelderland, given up by his Imperial and Catholic Majefty in propriety to the States General, by the 18th article of the prefent treaty, as alfo over and above the coft of lodging the ttoops, according to the regulation made in the year 1698, in the manner as fhall be particularly agreed upon: which fum of 500,000 crowns, or 1,250,000 florins Dutch money, fhall be fecured and mortgaged, as it is by this article fecured and mortgaged upon all the revenues of the Auftrian Netherlands in general, including therein the countries yielded up by France; and in particular, upon the clear neat revenues of the provinces of Brabant and Flanders, and of the countries, towns, chatellanies and dependencies yielded up by France, according as it is more particularly fpecified by a feparate article, as well for the

faid

faid mortgage, as for the means and terms of receiving the faid fums.

And the faid payment of the fubfidy of 500,000 crowns, or 1,250,000 florins Dutch money, fhall commence from the day of the figning the prefent treaty, from which fhall be deducted the revenues of the towns, chatellanies, and dependencies yielded by France, in proportion to the term elapfed from the fame day, till the day on which the faid countries fhall be remitted to his Imperial and Catholic Majefty, in proportion to what the States General fhall receive.

XX. His Imperial and Catholic Majefty, by this article, confirms and ratifies the capitulations granted to the provinces and towns of the Netherlands, heretofore called Spanifh, at the time of their reduction to the obedience of his faid Majefty, together with the general adminiftration of the faid country therein, exercifed by Great Britain, and the States General of the United Provinces, the lawful fovereign having been reprefented by their minifters who refided at Bruffels, and by the council of ftate commiffioned to the general government of the faid Netherlands, in purfuance of the power and inftructions that were given them, and of the requefts that were made on the part of the two powers, as well in matters of regale, juftice and police, as of the finances ; as alfo the particular adminiftration of the ftates, provinces, colleges, towns and communities in the open country, as alfo in the fovereign courts of juftice, and the other fubaltern courts and judges.

Which acts of police, regale, juftice, and the finances, fhall fubfift and have their full and entire effect, according to the tenor of the faid acts and fentences paffed : the whole in the fame manner, as if they had been done by the lawful fovereign of the country, and under his government.

XXI. Every thing that is comprifed in the foregoing article fhall alfo be obferved, ratified and maintained, on the part of his Imperial and Catholic Majefty, with refpect to the upper quarter of Guelderland, and the countries conquered from France, (of which King Charles II. of glorious memory, was not in poffeffion at his deceafe) for all the

dif-

difpofitions made in the name, and on the part of the States General of the United Provinces.

And as for what concerns ecclefiaftical benefices and dignities, thofe who have been preferred to them, and are now in poffeffion, fhall not be difplaced; and thofe who are not yet in poffeffion, fhall be admitted to them without any oppofition, but by the ways, and in the order of juftice, according to the laws and cuftoms of the country.

XXII. His Imperial and Catholic Majefty acknowledges, and promifes to fatisfy the obligations entered into by his Catholic Majefty Charles II. of glorious memory, for the levies of money which their High Mightineffes caufed to be negociated for his faid Majefty, a lift whereof is fubjoined to this article: and as they have not yet been remitted to the States General the obligations of the Spanifh Netherlands, for the fum of 200,000 florins a year, for payment of the intereft, and reimburfing the principal of 1,400,000 florins, taken up at intereft in the year 1698, to be employed on the neceffary occafions of the frontiers of the faid Spanifh Netherlands, and four years intereft, amounting to the fum of 224,000 florins wherewith the faid capital of 1,400,000 florins, is encreafed; which obligations the faid King Charles II. of glorious memory, promifed to caufe to be given, though they were not; his Imperial and Catholic Majefty promifes hereby, to caufe the obligations to be given by the States of the provinces of the faid Netherlands, and immediately after to be delivered to the faid States General, according to the tenor of the faid obligation of his Catholic Majefty, of the 30th of May, 1698, at the firft meeting of the States, or at fartheft within the term of two month after the exchange of the ratifications of this treaty.

*A Lift of the feveral Sums negociated by the States General, at the Requeft of his Catholic Majefty Charles II.*

1. THE firft advance was of one million five hundred feventy-five thoufand florins, at five per cent on the duties of import and ex-

port

*Florins.*

port by fea, made by an act of December 13, 1690. — — — 1575000

2. Upon the fame fund, at five per cent. raifed by an act of March 21, 1691. — — 525000

3. At five per cent. alfo upon the revenues of the upper quarter of Guelderland, by an act of Jan. 15, 1692. — — 567000

4 and 5. At fix per cent. upon the import and export, purfuant to two acts of the 4th and 22d of May, 1693. — — — 700000

6. At five per cent. upon the fame fund, raifed the 11th of April, 1695. — — 665000

7. At five per cent. upon the fame fund, raifed by an act of Nov. 24, 1695. — — 1440000

8, 9, 10. At five per cent. upon the revenues of the province of Namur, and by way of fubfidy, on the fea revenues, and the domains of the province of Luxemburg, by the feveral acts of Dec. 10, 1695, Sept. 12, 1696, and March 6, 1697, amounting in all to — — 800000

11. At fix per cent. upon the revenues of the provofty of Mons, raifed by an act of April 30, 1696. — — — 500000

12. The fum of one million and 400,000 florins, at four per cent. was raifed upon the fubfidies of the provinces of the Netherlands, upon the remittances from Spain, and fubfidiarily upon the fea-revenues. Item, 224,000 florins for four years intereft of the faid capital, conformably to the tenor of the obligation of the 30th of May, 1698, which both together make the fum of — — 1624000

Total 8396000

XXIII. In like manner his Imperial and Catholic Majefty acknowledges, approves, and confirms all levies of money (a lift whereof is fubjoined to this article) which there have been occafion to make for things indifpenfibly neceffary for the prefervation of the Spanifh Netherlands,
and

and for the maintenance of the troops of his Imperial and Catholic Majesty, during the provisional government of Great Britain, and the States General of the United Provinces, and made by their High Mightinesses, in concert with her Britannic Majesty; his Imperial and Catholic Majesty promising to satisfy and cause the said negociations duly to be registered in the chambers of the finances and accounts, and to cause an act thereof to be delivered to their High Mightinesses in form, also to cause the capital and interests thereof, without funds and mortgages, as well principal as subsidiary, appropriated for that end, to be paid: and his Imperial and Catholic Majesty shall not, without leave of the States General, make any alteration in the direction or administration of the mortgages, upon which negociations have been made, but shall leave the same to their High Mightinesses, conformably to the tenor of the obligation; and if those funds are not sufficient, what is wanting shall be supplied by the states of the provinces of the said Austrian Netherlands.

*A List of the Money negociated during the provisional Government of her Britannic Majesty, and their High Mightinesses, in the Netherlands.*

Florins.

IN 1707, 300,000 florins were advanced at five per cent. interest upon the revenue of the post-office, to be sent to Barcelona for the King.

And 400,000 florins more, at five per cent. upon the customs of import and export in Flanders, for the service of the necessities of the Netherlands; the interest of which 400,000 florins, was settled on the post-office.  —  —  700000

In February, 1709, 250,000 florins were raised at five per cent. upon the sea-duties, to maintain the Imperial and Palatine troops. —  —  250000

In May, 1709, a sum of 500,000 florins was advanced at five per cent. upon the same conditions, on the same funds, and for the same use.  500000

In

*Florins.*

In Auguſt the fame year, was alſo raiſed a fum of ten hundred thouſand florins, on the fame conditions and funds, and for the fame uſe.     1000000

In the year 1710, a fum of three hundred thouſand florins was negociated at fix per cent. upon the revenue of the poſt-office, to provide for the charge of the Imperial and Palatine troops, in the ſervice of his Imperial and Catholic Majeſty. ——— ———     300000

Item upon the duties of import and export in Flanders, at fix per cent. viz. five per cent. on the cuſtoms in Flanders, and one per cent. on the revenues of the ſea, to defray the charges of the Imperial troops. ———     400000

Item upon the fame funds, and at fix per cent. viz. five per cent. on the duties of import and export in Flanders, and one per cent. on the revenues of the ſea, for the fame uſe.     300000

Item more upon the fame funds, at the fame intereſt, and for the fame uſe. ———     340625

Item upon the ſea revenues at five per cent. for the fame uſe. ——— ———     300000

In March, 1711, upon the revenues of the poſt-office, at fix per cent. for the fame uſe.     300000

In December, 1712, upon the ſea-revenues at five per cent. for the neceſſities and fortifications of Mons, St. Ghiſlain, and Aeth. —     228330

Making together the fum of 4,618,955, the employment whereof, as alſo of the fum of 550,000 florins, which the receivers of the duties of export and import in Flanders, furniſhed by bills of exchange to the States-General in 1710, of 100,000 florins, which they received of the receiver of the Medianaters, and of 105,000 florins (ſaving any miſtake in the calculation) which they have received of the third chamber of the council of Flanders, has been verified to the Plenipotentiary Miniſter of his Imperial and Catholic Majeſty, in the manner as it is more particularly explained by the declaration ſubjoined to the account of the negociations and monies furniſhed, and of the employment thereof, ſigned upon the fame day.

XXIV. A

XXIV. A liquidation of the payment made of the interest and principal of the loans mentioned in the two foregoing articles, shall be proceeded on as soon as possible; by which liquidation nothing shall be brought to the account of their High Mightinesses, but what has been actually and really paid by virtue of the said obligations; and on the part of his Imperial and Catholic Majesty, no difficulty or pretence of abatement or diminution shall be made against the payment of the said interest, by reason of the non-possession of the securities, confiscation in time of war, depravation of the mortgages, because of the diminution of the duties of export and import, or for any other cause or pretext whatever. Neither shall his Imperial and Catholic Majesty discontinue payment for the re-recovery of the interest or the terms of re-imburfement, by reason of this liquidation, but the payment shall be continued according to the conditions of the obligations, till it shall appear that all the loans, and the interests upon them, be entirely acquitted and reimbursed; after which the mortages shall be duly discharged and restored.

XXV. Moreover, by the present article are ratified and confirmed all contracts for bread waggons, and the forage of the Imperial and Palatine troops, made by the ministers of the two powers at Brussels, or by the council of state commissioned for the government of the Netherlands, at the request of the said ministers; and in like manner are confirmed and ratified all the payments already made for that purpose by the council of the finances, and the orders given by the said council for assigning the remainder of what is due for the said bread, forage, and waggons, upon the growing duties of the four species, pursuant to the request of the council of state; and the said growing duties shall not be diverted to any other uses, under any pretence whatsoever, before the undertakers who have delivered the said bread, forage, and waggons, be entirely satisfied, according to the tenor of their contracts, pursuant to the requests of the ministers of the two potentates, and to the orders of the council of state, and the council of the finances.

XXVI. As to commerce, it is agreed, that the ships, merchandize and commodities coming from Great-Britain and

and the United Provinces, and entering into the Auftrian Netherlands, and alfo the fhips, merchandize, and commodities going from the faid Netherlands to Great Britain and the United Provinces, fhall pay no other duties of importation or exportation, than what are paid upon the prefent foot, and particularly fuch as were regulated before the figning of the prefent treaty, according to the requeft made to the council of ftate at Bruffels, by the minifters of the two powers, dated the 6th of November : and fo every thing fhall remain, continue, and fubfift generally upon the fame foot, without any alteration, innovation, diminution, or augmentation, under any pretence whatfoever, till his Imperial and Catholic Majefty, his Britannic Majefty, and the Lords the States General fhall otherwife appoint by a treaty of commerce to be made as foon as poffible. In the mean time, the commerce, and all that depends on it between the fubjects of his Imperial and Catholic Majefty in the Auftrian Netherlands, and thofe of the United Provinces, in the whole and in part, fhall remain upon the foot eftablifhed, and in the manner appointed by the articles of the treaty concerning commerce, made at Munfter, the 30th of January, 1648, between his Majefty King Philip IV. of glorious memory, and the faid Lords the States General of the United Provinces ; which articles are now confirmed by the prefent treaty.

XXVII. That the fortifications and all the works of the citadel of Liege, as alfo thofe of the caftle of Huy, and all the forts and works fhall be razed and demolifhed, fo as never to be rebuilt or reftored. Provided and be it underftood, that the faid demolition fhall be made at the expence of the ftates of the country of Liege, to whom the materials fhall remain, to be fold and tranfported elfewhere. The whole by the order and under the direction of the States General, who fhall for that end fend perfons capable of having the direction of the faid demolitions, which fhall be begun immediately after the figning of the prefent treaty ; and fhall be finifhed in three months, or fooner if poffible ; and that in the mean time, the garrifons of the States General of the United Provinces fhall not go out of the faid places before the demolition is finifhed.

XXVIII. And

XXVIII. And for the further fecurity and performance of the prefent treaty, his Britannic Majefty promifes and engages to confirm and guarantee it, in all its points and articles, as he does by thefe prefents accordingly confirm and enter into a guaranty of it.

XXIX. The prefent treaty fhall be ratified and approved by his Imperial and Catholic Majefty, by his Britannic Majefty, and by the Lords the States General of the United Provinces ; and the ratifications fhall be delivered within fix weeks, or fooner, if poffible, to be computed from the day of figning. In witnefs whereof, we the Minifters Plenipotentiary of his Imperial and Catholic Majefty, his Britannic Majefty, and the Lords the States General, by virtue of our refpective full powers, have in their names figned thefe prefents, and thereto affixed the feal of our arms. Done at Antwerp, Nov. 15, 1715.

(L. S.) *J. L. C. a Konigfegg.*
(L. S.) *W. Cadogan.*
(L. S.) *B. v. Duffen.*
(L. S.) *The Count de Rechteren.*
(L. S.) *S. L. Gockinga.*
(L. S.) *Adr. v. Borffele Sig. v. Geldermalfen.*

*Form of the Oath for the Governor of* Dendermonde.

I N. N. who, by the appointment of his Imperial and Catholic Majefty, am governor of Dendermonde, do promife and fwear that I will never do any thing, nor fuffer any thing to be done in the faid town, which may be prejudicial to the fervice of their High Mightineffes the States General of the United Provinces, with refpect to the prefervation of the town and garrifon: and that I will always, and as often as they defire, give free paffage to their troops, provided it be required beforehand, and that the faid troops do not pafs in too great a number at one time. The whole conformably to the fifth article of the Barrier Treaty, a copy of which has been communicated to me. So help me God.

*A*

*A Form of the Oath for the Governors of the places.*

I N. N. swear and promise faithfully to keep
which has been committed to my government, in full
sovereignty and property for his Imperial and Catholic
Majesty, and never to give it up to any other power; and
that I will not meddle, directly nor indirectly, nor suffer
any one whatsoever, under my command, to meddle with
any affair concerning the political government, religion, and
things ecclesiastic, justice and the finances, nor even in any
matter whatsoever, contrary to the rights, privileges, and
immunities of the inhabitants, whether clergy or laymen,
or in any other affair which does not directly relate to the
preservation of the place, and to the maintenance of the
garrison committed to my care ; but that I will leave all
those matters to his Imperial and Catholic Majesty, as the
lawful sovereign, and to the states and magistrates, whether
spiritual or temporal, as far as it appertains to each of them;
promising on the contrary to assist them with force of arms
always, and as often as I shall be required, for the maintenance of the orders of the state, and the preservation of
the tranquillity against all those that shall offer to oppose
them. Provided, and be it understood, that it shall be
lawful for me to execute the orders which the States General shall give me, conformably to and in pursuance of
the treaty between his Imperial and Catholic Majesty and
their High Mightinesses. So help me God.

### SEPARATE ARTICLE.

WHEREAS in the 19th article of the treaty of barrier for the States General of the United Provinces
in the Austrian Netherlands, concluded this day, being the
15th of November, 1715, between his Imperial and Catholic Majesty, his Britannic Majesty, and the said
Lords the States General, it was agreed that there should
be a more specific explanation by a separate article, with
regard to the mortgages, and to ways and means for collecting the subsidy therein mentioned ; his Imperial and
Catholic Majesty, for the better securing and facilitating
the payment of the said subsidy of 500,000 crowns, or

1,250,000

1,250,000 florins Dutch money, granted annually, and stipulated by the said article, has particularly charged the sum of 610,000 florins Duch money annually, upon the countries, towns, chatellanies, and dependencies, yielded by France, according to the following repartition, viz. Upon the city of Tournay 55,000 florins ; upon the chatellany of Tournay called the Tournefis, 25,000 florins ; upon the city and verge of Menin 90,000 florins ; and upon that part of Weft Flanders which was yielded by France, fhare and fhare alike among the towns, chatellanies, and dependencies, 44,000 florins ; and the refidue thus, viz. One-third upon the fubfidies of the province of Brabant, amounting to the fum of 213,333½ florins ; and upon thofe of the province of Flanders, two-thirds, amounting to the fum of 426,666⅓ florins, making all together the faid total fum of 500,000 crowns, or 1,250,000 florins Dutch money.

The portion of the province of Brabant is charged upon the contingent of the feven quarters of Antwerp, and the other diftrict of Brabant, in the fubfidies of that province.

And the quota of the province of Flanders, upon the contingent of the country of Waes, including therein Beveren, the county of Oudenburg, the frank of Bruges, country of Aloft, and the town and country of Dendermonde, in the fubfidies of that province. And for the better fecuring the regular payment of the faid refpective fums, his Imperial and Catholic Majefty promifes and engages that it fhall be made quarterly, viz. at the end of every three months from the day of the figning of the prefent treaty : and on failure of payment at the end of the faid three months, his Imperial and Catholic Majefty from this time, and by this treaty, orders the ftates of the provinces and jurifdictions, and the receivers of the fubfidies, both ordinary and extraordinary, together with thofe of his rights and demefnes, by whom the payment ought to be made, conformably to the foregoing repartition, that by virtue of this article, and according to a copy thereof, they immediately pay the fums abovementioned at the expiration of each term, to the receiver general of the States General, or his orders, without expecting any other notice or affignment, this prefent article being to ferve them inftead of an order and affignment, from the prefent time, and for that time too.                                    And

And the said payment shall be allowed them in the accompt, by his Imperial and Catholic Majesty, as much as if it had been paid to himself.

On failure whereof, or rather in case the said States should not grant the subsidy with the necessary speed, the States General may proceed to methods of compulsion and execution, and even to violence against the receivers, states and demesnes of the said provinces and jurisdictions, which his Imperial and Catholic Majesty renders thereto liable, by virtue of this article. The whole without prejudice to the right of their High Mightinesses to the other revenues of the sovereign, over and above the subsidy of the provinces, such as the duties of import and export, taxes, taillers, tolls, and other domains.

Moreover, it is agreed that the payment of the said subsiy shall not be retarded, much less refused on pretence of compensation, liquidation, or any other claims, of what name or nature soever they be.

And this separate article shall have the same force as the said treaty of barrier, altogether as much as if it was therein insertd verbatim, and it shall be ratified at the same time as this treaty.

In witness whereof, we the Ministers Plenipotentiary of his Imperial and Catholic Majesty, his Britannic Majesty, and the Lords the States General, have signed this present article, and caused it to be sealed with the seals of our arms. Done at Antwerp the 15th of November, 1715.

(L. S.) *J. L. C. Konigsegg*.
(L. S.) *W. Cadogan*.
(L. S.) *B. v. Duffen*.
(L. S.) The Count de *Rechteren*.
(L. S.) *S. L. Gockinga*.
(L. S.) *Adr. v. Borssele* Lord of *Geldermalsen*.

*Treaty of Commerce between* Great Britain *and* Spain, *concluded at* Madrid, *the* 14th *of* December 1715.

WHEREAS since the treaties of peace and commerce, lately concluded at Utrecht, the 13th of July and the 9th of December 1713, between his Catholic Majesty jefty and her late Majefty the Queen of Great Britain of glorious memory, there remained ftill fome differences about trade and the courfe thereof ; and his Catholic Majefty and the King of Great Britain, being inclined to maintain and cultivate a firm and inviolable peace and friendfhip, in order to attain to this good end they have by their two minifters underwritten, mutually and duly qualified, caufed the following articles to be concluded and figned.

I. The Britifh fubjects fhall not be obliged to pay higher or other duties, for goods coming in or going out of the feveral ports of his Catholic Majefty, than thofe they paid for the fame goods in King Charles the Second's time, fettled by cedules and ordonances of the faid King or his predeceffors : and although the Gratias commonly called Pie del fardo, be not grounded on any royal ordonance, neverthelefs his Catholic Majefty declares,` wills and ordains, that it be obferved now and hereafter as an inviolable law ; which duties fhall be exacted and raifed now and for the future, with the fame advantages and favours to the faid fubjects.

II. His Majefty confirms the treaty made by the Britifh fubjects with the magiftrates of St. Andero, in the year 1700.

III. His Catholic Majefty permits the faid fubjects to gather falt in the ifle of Tortugas, they having enjoyed this liberty in the reign of King Charles II. without interruption.

IV. The faid fubjects fhall pay no where any higher or other duties than thofe paid by the fubjects of his Catholic Majefty in the fame places.

V. The faid fubjects fhall enjoy all the rights, privileges, franchifes, exemptions, and immunities whatever, which they enjoyed before the laft war, by virtue of the royal cedules or ordonances, and by the articles of the treaty of peace and commerce made at Madrid in 1667, which is hereby fully confirmed ; and the fame fubjects fhall be ufed in Spain in the fame manner as the moft favoured nation, and confequently all nations fhall pay the fame duties on wool and other merchandizes coming in and going out by fea : and all the rights, privileges, franchifes, exemptions, and immunities

munities that fhall be granted and allowed to the faid fubjects, the like fhall be granted, obferved and permitted to
the fubjects of Spain, the kingdoms of his Majefty the
King of Great Britain.

VI. And as innovations may have been made in
trade, his Catholic Majefty promifes on his part to ufe
his utmoft endeavours to abolifh them, and for the future
to caufe them to be avoided : in like manner the King of
Great Britain promifes to ufe all poffible endeavours to
abolifh all innovations on his part, and for the future to
caufe them by all means to be avoided.

VII. The treaty of commerce made at Utrecht, the
9'h of December 1713, fhall continue in force, except the
articles that fhall be found contrary to what is this day concluded and figned, which fhall be abolifhed and rendered
of no force, and efpecially the three articles commonly
called explanatory : and thefe prefents fhall be approved,
ratified and exchanged on each fide, within the fpace of
fix weeks, or fooner, if poffible. In witnefs whereof, and
by virtue of our full powers, we have figned thefe prefents
at Madrid, the 14th of December, in the year 1715.

(L. S.) *M. de Bedmar.*
(L. S.) *George Bubb.*

---

*Treaty of mutual Defence between the moft ferene and moft po-*
*tent Prince* Charles VI. *Emperor of* Germany, *&c. and*
*the moft ferene and moft potent Prince* George, *by the*
*Grace of God, King of* Great Britain, France *and* Ireland, *Defender of the Faith, &c. concluded at* Weftminfter *on the 25th of* May, 1716. Reprinted from the
copy printed by authority.

*In the name of the moft Holy and Undivided Trinity.*

BE it known to all and every one whom it may concern. The auguft Emperor of the Romans, Charles
VI. King of Spain, Hungary and Bohemia, Archduke of
Auftria, Duke of Burgundy, &c. and the moft ferene and
moft potent Prince George, by the Grace of God, King
of Great Britain, France and Ireland, Duke of Brunfwick
and Lunenburgh, Elector of the Holy Roman Empire, &c.
having

having reflected on the eminent advantages which were derived from the fincere and conftant union of their predeceffors, and therefore confidering the more attentively the circumftances of the prefent time, they applied their minds to the renewing of the fame for the common good.

Whereupon, by the bleffing of God, concerting counfels, they have agreed in form upon a treaty and mutual alliance confifting of the following articles.

I. That there be between his abovementioned Imperial and royal Catholic Majefty, and his facred royal Majefty of Great Britain, a fincere friendfhip and union of counfels, and perfect alliance, that each of them look upon the other's interefts as his own, and earneftly endeavour to promote them, and prevent by the beft means he is able, all damages.

II. That the defign and end of this defenfive alliance be no other than mutually to defend each other, and to preferve themfelves in the poffeffion of the kingdoms, provinces and rights, in the condition they now are, which either of them actually has and enjoys ; if therefore it fhall happen, that the one or the other of thefe allies fhall be hoftilely invaded or molefted by any power, it is agreed, that the honour, dignity, as alfo the kingdoms, provinces, and rights abovementioned, which that ally poffeffes in any part of Europe at the time of this alliance, or which during the fame they fhall by mutual confent acquire, fhall with common aid and affiftance by land and by fea, be preferved, defended and maintained inviolable, againft all aggreffors whatfoever ; and likewife that a juft fatisfaction fhall be procured for any injury which fhall happen to be done.

III. For obtaining this wholefome end, in the aforefaid cafe of any hoftile invafion, the party attacked fhall notify the fame to his ally, who fhall ufe all his endeavours with the aggreffor, to induce him to abftain without delay from farther hoftility, to make due fatisfaction for the damage done, and fhall take care for the future fecurity of his ally.

IV. If this fair means do not fucceed within the fpace of two months, affiftance fhall immediately be fent by the ally to the party attacked, nor fhall the fame be recalled till what is expreffed in the foregoing fecond article be obtained.

V. The

V. The fuccours, which when this cafe happens, are to be furnifhed by the allies, fhall be as follows : On the part of his Imperial and Catholic Majefty, twelve thoufand men, that is to fay, eight thoufand foot, and four thoufand horfe. And on the part of his facred royal Majefty of Great Britain, as many thoufand men ; that is to fay, eight thoufand foot, and four thoufand horfe. But if the nature of the war fhould require rather maritime fuccours, in whole or in part, the ally fhall be obliged to furnifh, inftead of the faid land forces, fo many fhips of war as fhall be equal in expence to the faid number of men : So likewife in cafe greater fuccours, either of land or fea forces, fhould be neceffary, the allies fhall without delay come to an agreement about them, and fhow an amicable difpofition on both fides.

VI. It is agreed, that no other prince or power fhall be invited or admitted into this alliance, unlefs by the unanimous and mutual confent of the allies, and in fuch manner as fhall be ftipulated and agreed between them.

VII. But whereas nothing is more defired by either ally, than, this treaty being made, to fecure by mutual affiftance the common fafety, and preferve inviolable the public peace ; and there being no doubt but the mighty States General of the United Provinces of the Netherlands are difpofed moft readily to affift and promote, by their acceffion, fo ufeful and fo neceffary a work, it is therefore now thought fit not only willingly to admit the faid States General into this prefent alliance, but to invite them amicably without delay, to enter into it.

In witnefs whereof the Plenipotentiaries as well of his facred Imperial and Catholic Majefty, as of his facred royal Majefty of Great Britain, have figned thefe prefents with their hands, and fet their feals thereto. Done at Weftminfter on the 25th of May 1716.

(L. S.) *Otto Chriftophorus*    (L. S.) *W. Cant.*
      *Comes Volkra.*      (L. S.) *Cowper C.*
(L. S.) *Joannes Phillippus*    (L. S.) *Sunderland C. P. S.*
      *Hoffman.*        (L. S.) *Devonfhire.*
                 (L. S.) *Marlborough.*
                 (L. S.) *Roxburghe.*
                           (L. S.)

(L. S.) *Orford.*
(L. S.) *Townshend.*
(L. S.) *James Stanhope.*
(L. S.) *R. Walpole.*

SEPARATE ARTICLE.

IT is farther agreed, that if in procefs of time war fhould break out between his facred Imperial and Catholic Majefty, and the Ottoman Empire, the treaty of alliance concluded this day with his facred royal Majefty of Great Britain, fhall not be deemed in any wife to relate or extend thereto ; nor fhall war with the Turks, (reafon of ftate fo requiring) be underftood to be a cafe intended by this treaty. *This feparate article is dated and figned as the treaty.*

*Additional Separate and Secret Article.*

WHEREAS it is the principal fcope and intention of the treaty of alliance concluded the laft year between his facred Imperial and royal Catholic Majefty and his royal Majefty of Great Britain, that the union and friendfhip betwixt their faid Majefties may be bound in the clofeft engagements that are poffible, and that on every occafion that offers they may mutually promote each other's interefts, and may faithfully and fincerely fecure themfelves againft all enemies whatfoever : and whereas, fince the conclufion of the faid alliance, many of his Britannic Majefty's rebel fubjects have come into feveral of the hereditary provinces of his Imperial and Catholic Majefty, whereby they found means and opportunity of carrying on a pernicious correfpondence with other ill-affected and feditious inhabitants of Great Britain, and ufe all their endeavours to ftir up a new rebellion in the faid kingdom ; whence both the government of his Britannic Majefty, and the tranquillity and repofe of his faithful fubjects may be continually difturbed by thefe fecret factions and confpiracies, to their very great detriment. It is therefore declared by thefe prefents on the part of his imperial and royal Catholic Majefty, that he will grant no entertainment, refuge, or paffage, under any pretext whatfoever

foever within his hereditary provinces fituated in Germany and the Auftrian Netherlands, to his Britannic Majefty's rebel fubjects, who are or fhall be declared fuch, nor to the perfon commonly called the Pretender. As likewife his royal Majefty of Great Britain doth promife, that he never will grant any paffage, entertainment, or refuge, to the rebel fubjects of his Imperial and royal Catholic Majefty, who are or fhall be declared fuch within his kingdoms of Great Britain and Provinces of the Roman Empire. Wherefore it is on both fides provided that they will mutually compel the aforefaid rebel fubjects to depart out of the faid kingdoms and provinces within the fpace of eight days, from the time that the minifter of him, whofe fubjects thofe rebels are reputed, fhall have made fuch application to his faid Imperial Majefty, or his royal Majefty, in the name of his mafter. In witnefs whereof we the Commiffioners and Plenipotentiaries of his facred Imperial and royal Catholic Majefty, and of his facred royal Majefty of Great Britain, by virtue of our full powers refpectively (the copies whereof are added at the end of this article) have figned this inftrument with our hands. Done at Vienna Sept. 1, 1717.

(L. S.) *A Stanyan.*

---

*Convention for explaining the articles of the* Affiento, *or contract for* Negroes, *between the moft ferene and moft potent Prince* George, *by the Grace of God, King of* Great Britain, France, *and* Ireland, *Defender of the Faith, &c. and the moft ferene and moft potent Prince* Philip V. *the Catholic King of* Spain. *Concluded at* Madrid, *the* $\frac{16}{15}$ *of* May, 1716.

GEORGE, by the Grace of God, King of Great Britain, France, and Ireland, Defender of the Faith, &c. To all and fingular to whom thefe prefent letters fhall come, greeting : whereas a certain convention, for explaining the articles of the treaty commonly called El Affiento de los Negros, the Contract for Negroes, between us and our good brother Philip V. the Catholic King of Spain and

and the Indies, was concluded and figned by Minifters Plenipotentiaries impowered with fufficient authority on both
fides, at Madrid on the ?? day of the month of May laft,
in the form and words following:

AFTER a long war, which had afflicted almoft all Europe,
and had produced difmal effects, it appearing that the continuance of it would create yet more, it was agreed with
the Queen of Great Britain of glorious memory, to put a
ftop to it, by a good and fincere peace; and in order to
render it firm and folid, and to maintain the union between the two nations, it was determined that the Affiento
for furnifhing our Weft Indies with Negroes, fhould for the
future, and during the time expreffed in the treaty of Affiento, be on the accompt of the royal company of England; which faid company having thereupon made feveral reprefentations to us by the Minifter of Great Britain,
after they had made the fame to the King their mafter,
concerning fome difficulties which related to certain articles of the faid treaty; and we being defirous, not only to
maintain the peace eftablifhed with the Englifh nation, but
to preferve and augment it by a perfect good underftanding, have commanded our minifters to confer on the faid
affair of the Affiento with the Minifter Plenipotentiary of
the King of Great Britain, to the end that, as equity requires, fome agreement might be made on the faid articles,
as has actually been done by the following declarations.

In the treaty of Affiento made between their Britannic
and Catholic Majefties on March 26, 1713, for the carrying of Negroes to the Indies by the company of England,
and for the term of thirty years, which were to commence
from May 1, 1713, his Catholic Majefty was pleafed to
grant to the faid Company the favour of fending to the
Indies every year (during the faid Affiento) a fhip of 500
ton, as is mentioned in the faid treaty: on condition that
the goods with which the faid annual fhip fhould be laden,
fhould not be allowed to be fold but in the time of the
fair; and that if the fhip arrived in the Indies before the
fhips from Spain, the factors employed by the faid company fhould be obliged to land all the goods, and depofit
them in truft in the Catholic King's warehoufes, to be
kept under two keys, and with other circumftances fpecified

fied in the faid treaty, till they could be fold at the time of the fair.

It has been reprefented on the part of his Britannic Majefty and of the faid company, that the faid favour was granted by the Catholic King to make good the loffes which the company might fuffer by the Affiento; fo that if the condition, not to difpofe of the goods but in the time of the fair, were to be obferved, and the fair not being held regularly every year, as experience has fhewn heretofore, and as may happen hereafter, the company inftead of gaining profit, would lofe the prime coft of the cargo; it being very well known that goods will not keep long in that country, and particularly at Porto Bello. For this reafon the company defires an affurance that the fair fhall be held every year, either at Carthagena, Porto-Bello, or *Vera Cruz*; and that notice may be given them at which of thofe three ports it is intended to keep the fair, that they may know where to fend out their fhip; which arriving at the faid ports, if no fair be there held, the company may vend the goods after a certain limited time, to be reckoned from the day of the arrival of the faid fhip at fuch port.

His Majefty being willing to give the King of Great Britain new proofs of his friendfhip, and to corroborate the union and good correfpondence between the two nations, has declared, and declares, that the fair fhall be held regularly every year, either in Peru, or in New Spain, and that notice fhall be given to the court of England of the exact time when the Flota or Galleons will fail for the In-dies, to the end the company may at the fame time dif-patch the fhip granted by his Catholic Majefty; and in cafe the Flota and Galleons fhall not depart from Cadiz before the month of June expires, the faid company fhall be allowed to fend away their fhip, giving notice of the day of her failing to the court of Madrid, or to the mi-minifter of his Catholic Majefty who fhall be at London; and when fhe fhall arrive at one of the three ports of Car-thagena, Porto-Bello, or Vera Cruz, fhe fhall be obliged to wait there for the Flota or Galleons four months, to be reckoned from the day of the arrival of the faid fhip; which term being expired, the company fhall be allowed

to

to fell their goods without any hindrance; but it is to be underftood, that if this fhip of the company's be bound for Peru, fhe fhall go directly to Carthagena and Porto-Bello, without paffing into the South-Sea.

The faid company has alfo reprefented, that the number and price of Negroes to be bought in Africa being uncertain; and as they muft be purchafed with goods, not with money, the quantity of merchandize to be carried to that country cannot be exactly fettled; and it being improper to run any hazard of having too few goods for that trade, it may happen that there will be an overplus: wherefore the faid company defire that the goods which fhall remain undifpofed of in exchange for the Negroes, may be carried to the Indies, otherwife they fhould be obliged to caft them into the fea; for obtaining this the faid company offer, for the greater fecurity, to depofit the faid goods which fhall remain overplus, in the firft port belonging to his Catholic Majefty which their fhip fhall reach, and in the King's warehoufes, to take the fame on board again when the fhip fhall be on her return to Europe.

As to the article, importing that the overplus goods which fhall not be difpofed of in purchafing Negroes, and for want of warehoufes in Africa, are propofed to be carried to the Indies, to be laid up in his Catholic Majefty's ports, under two keys, one to be kept by the King's officers, and the other by the factors of the faid company, his Catholic Majefty will grant it to be done only at the port of Buenos Ayres; becaufe between Africa and the faid port of Buenos Ayres, there is not any ifland or place under the dominion of the King of Great Britain, where the fhips belonging to the Affiento for Negroes can put in; but it is quite the contrary with refpect to the navigation between Africa and the ports of Caracas, Carthagena, Porto-Bello, Vera Cruz, Havanna, Porto-Rico, and St. Domingo: for his Britannic Majefty is among the windward iflands poffeffed of the iflands of Barbadoes, Jamaica, and feveral others; at which the faid Affiento fhips may touch, and leave the faid overplus goods, which fhall not have been exchanged for the Negroes, and take them in again when they return to Europe. By this means all manner of fufpicion is taken away, and the proceedings in the

the affair of the Affiento fhall be with good faith, which ought to be defired on both fides, and is moft convenient. The factors of the faid company fhall be obliged, as foon as the fhip fhall arrive in the port of Buenos Ayres, to give a declaration of all the faid goods to his Catholic Majefty's officers, on condition that all the goods which fhall not be declared, fhall be immediately confifcated and adjudged to his Catholic Majefty.

The faid company has likewife reprefented to his Catholic Majefty fome difficulty that has rifen about the payment of the duties of the year 1713, ftipulated and agreed on by the treaty of Affiento, in which it is faid, that the Affiento was to begin on the 1ft day of May in the faid year: but the company having at the fame time purchafed the whole number of Negroes, to keep them under his Catholic Majefty's protection till the figning of the treaty, the importing thofe Negroes into the Indies was not permitted, by reafon of the claufe which was inferted in the 18th article, namely, that the execution of the treaty fhould not take place till the peace fhould be proclaimed; fo that the company was obliged to caufe them to be fold to the Britifh colonies at confiderable lofs. And though the company have not received any profit, but fuffered lofs, by reafon of the faid article, and of the faid claufe inferted in the faid treaty by his Catholic Majefty's minifters; yet the faid company are willing to give proofs of their moft humble refpect to his Catholic Majefty, and propofe to pay for the year 1714, that is to fay, from the 1ft of May, that year forwards, fubmitting intirely to the pretenfion for two years, on condition his Catholic Majefty will be pleafed to grant to the faid company the permiffion of fending the fhip on the terms above expreffed, in which his Majefty is interefted for the fourth part of the gain, with five per cent. on the other three parts; fo that the faid company oblige themfelves to pay to his Catholic Majefty's order, as foon as they fhall have a favorable anfwer, not only the 200,000 pieces of eight by way of anticipation, but alfo the money due for the two years: which two fums together amount to 466,666 pieces of eight and two-thirds.

His

His Catholic Majefty having confidered the faid repre- fentation, has been pleafed to grant, as he does grant to the faid company, that the faid Affiento fhall commence from May 1, 1714; and confequently that the faid com- pany fhall be obliged to pay the duties of the two years, which began on May 1, 1714, and ended on May 1, 1716, as well as the 200,000 pieces of eight, by way of anticipation; which fum the faid company are obliged to pay at Amfterdam, Paris, London, or Madrid, all in one payment, or divided into feveral, as his Catholic Majefty fhall think fit; and in the like manner fhall the payments be made for the future, as long as the faid Affiento lafts; for which payments the effects of the faid company fhall be anfwerable.

As to the yearly fhip which his Majefty has granted to the company, and which they have not fent to the Indies in the three years 1714, 1715, and 1716; the company having obliged themfelves to pay his Catholic Majefty the duties and revenues of the aforefaid three years, his Majefty is pleafed to make the faid company amends, by allowing them to divide the 1,500 tuns into ten annual parts, to be- gin the enfuing year 1717, and end in the year 1727; fo that the fhip granted by the treaty of Affiento, inftead of being but of 500 tun, fhall be of 650 tun, (each tun being to be computed at two pipes of Malaga in meafure, and at 20 quintals in weight, as is the ordinary computation be- tween Spain and England) during the faid ten years, on condition that the faid fhip fhall be fearched and regiftered by his Catholic Majefty's minifters and officers, who fhall be at the ports of Vera Cruz, Carthagena, and Porto-Bello.

The treaty of Affiento made at Madrid on March 26, 1713, fhall remain in force, thofe articles excepted which fhall appear to be contrary to what is concluded and figned this day, which fhall be abolifhed and of no vali- dity; and thefe prefents fhall be approved, ratified, and exchanged on both fides, within the term of fix weeks, or fooner if it be poffible. In witnefs whereof, and by virtue of our full powers, we have figned thefe prefents, at Ma- drid, the $\frac{26}{15}$ of May, in the year 1716.

(L. S.) *George Bubb.*

(L. S.) *El. Marq. de Bedmar.*

*A Treaty*

*A Treaty of Alliance between* Lewis XV. *King of* France *and* Navarre, George *King of* Great Britain, *and the Lords the States General of the* United Provinces, *for the Maintenance and Guarantee of the Treaties of Peace made at* Utrecht *in* 1713, *and particularly for maintaining the Order of the Succeſſion to the Crowns of* France *and* England, *as eſtabliſhed by the ſaid Treaties, and for the Demolition of the Port of* Mardyke. *Concluded at the* Hague, Jan. 4, 1717.

LEWIS by the Grace of God King of France and Navarre, to all who ſhall ſee theſe preſents, greeting. Whereas our truſty and well-beloved the Abbot du Bois, Counſellor in ordinary in our Council of State ; and our truſty and well-beloved the Sieur de Chateauneuf, Marquis de Caſtagnere, Honorary Counſellor of our Court of Parliament at Paris, our Ambaſſadors Extraordinary and Plenipotentiary, have by virtue of the full powers which we gave them, agreed to conclude and ſign the following treaty of defenſive alliance, on the 4th of this preſent month of January with William Lord Cadogan, Baron of Reading, Knight of the order of St. Andrew, Maſter of the Robes to our moſt dearly beloved brother the King of Great Britain, Lieutenant General of his armies, Colonel of the ſecond regiment of his Guards, Governor of the Iſle of Wight, and his Ambaſſador Extraordinary and Plenipotentiary, who was alſo furniſhed with full powers ; and with the Sieur John Van Eſſen, Burgomaſter of Zutphen, Curator of the Univerſity of Harderwick ; Wigbold Vander Does, Lord of Nortwick, of the order of the Nobility of Holland and Weſtfrieſland ; Samuel Coninck, Senator of the town of Veere ; Frederick Adrian, Baron de Rheede, Lord de Renſwoude, Emminckhuyſen and Moerkerken, &c. Preſident of the nobility of the province of Utrecht; Ulbe Aylva Van Burmania, Bailiff of the Nobility of Leewarden ; Anthony Eckout, Burgomaſter of the town of Campen ; and Wicher Wichers, Burgomaſter of the town of Groningen ; all deputies in their aſſembly, on the part of the States of Guelderland, Holland, and Weſtfrieſland, Zealand, Utrecht, Frieſland, Overyſſel, Groningen, and Ommelands,

melands, in quality of Plenipotentiaries from their High Mightineſſes, our very dear and great friends the States General of the United Provinces of the Netherlands, likewiſe furniſhed with full powers.

Foraſmuch as the moſt ſerene and moſt mighty Prince Lewis XV. by the grace of God, moſt Chriſtian King of France and Navarre, the moſt ſerene and moſt mighty Prince George, by the grace of God King of Great Britain, Duke of Brunſwick and Lunenberg, Elector of the Holy Roman Empire, &c. and the high and mighty Lords the States General of the United Provinces of the Netherlands, being deſirous to corroborate more and more the peace that is eſtabliſhed between their kingdoms and ſtates reſpectively to remove entirely on every ſide, all cauſe of jealouſy, which might in any manner whatſoever diſturb the tranquillity of their dominions, and to bind yet more ſtrongly by new ties, that friendſhip which is between them, in order to attain ſo ſalutary an end, they have thought it neceſſary to come to an agreement between themſelves : and to that purpoſe their Majeſties aforeſaid, and the ſaid Lords the States General have named, viz.

The moſt Chriſtian King, his Ambaſſadors Extraordinary and Plenipotentiaries, the Sieur William du Bois, Abbot of St. Peter d' Airvault, of St. Juſt, and of Nogent, formerly preceptor to his royal highneſs the Duke of Orleans, regent of the kingdom of France, counſellor of ſtate in ordinary ; and the Sieurs Peter Anthony de Chaſteauneuf, Marquiſs de Caſtagnere, honorary counſellor to the parliament of Paris, and ambaſſador from his moſt Chriſtian Majeſty to the Lords the States General of the United Provinces.

The King of Great Britain has named his ambaſſador extraordinary and plenipotentiary, the Lord William Cadogan, baron of Reading, knight of the order of St. Andrew, maſter of the robes to the King of Great Britain, lieutenant general of his armies, colonel of the ſecond regiment of his guards, and governor of the Iſle of Wight.

And the Lords the States General have named their deputies and plenipotentiaries, the Sieurs John van Eſſen, burgomaſter of the town of Zutphen, curator of the univerſity at Harderwick ; Wigbold Vander Does, Lord of Nortwick,

Nortwick, of the order of the nobility of Holland and Weftfriefland, grand baily and dykegrave of Rhynland ; Anthony Heinfius, counfellor, penfionary keeper of the great feal, and fuperintendant of the fiefs of the province of Holland and Weftfriefland ; Samuel Coninck, fenator of the town of Veere; Frederick Adrian, baron de Rheede, lord of Renfwoude, Emminckhuyfen and Moerkerken, &c. prefident of the nobility of the province of Utrecht; Ulbe Aylva van Burmania, baily of the nobility of Leewarden : Anthony Eckhout, burgomafter of the town of Campen ; and Wicher Wichers, burgomafter of the town of Groningen, all deputies in their affembly, on the part of the ftates of Guelderland, Holland, and Weftfriefland, Zealand, Utrecht, Friefland, Overyffel, Groningen, and the Ommelands.

Who after having communicated their full powers to one another, and after having exchanged the fame according to cuftom, agreed upon a treaty of defenfive alliance, between the moft Chriftian King, the King of Great Britain, and the lords the States General of the United Provinces, their kingdoms, dominions, and fubjects on the following conditions.

I. That from this day forth and for ever, there fhall be a true, firm, and inviolable peace, a moft fincere and intimate friendfhip, and a moft ftrict alliance and union between the faid moft ferene Kings, their heirs and fucceffors, and the lords the States General, their lands, countries, and towns refpectively, and their fubjects and inhabitants, as well within as out of Europe : and that the fame be preferved and cultivated in fuch manner, that the contracting parties may faithfully and reciprocally reap their profit and advantage thereby ; and that by the moft convenient meafures all loffes and damages which might befal them, may be averted and prevented.

II. And forafmuch as it is known by experience, that the near abode of the perfon, who in the life-time of King James II. did take upon him the title of Prince of Wales, and fince the death of the faid King has taken the title of King of Great Britain, may excite commotions

and

and troubles in Great Britain, and the dominions depending thereon, it is agreed upon and determined, that his moſt ſerene Majeſty the moſt Chriſtian King do oblige himſelf, by the preſent treaty, to engage the ſaid perſon to depart out of the country of Avignon, and to go and take up his reſidence on the other ſide of the Alps, immediately after the ſigning of the treaty, and before the exchange of the ratifications. And the moſt Chriſtian King, yet farther to teſtify his ſincere deſire, not only to obſerve all the engagements which the crown of France has formerly entered into concerning the ſaid perſon, religiouſly and inviolably, but alſo to prevent all manner of ſuſpicion and diffidence for the future; does again promiſe and engage for himſelf, his heirs and ſucceſſors, not to give, or furniſh at any time whatever, directly or indirectly, either by ſea or by land, any advice, aid, or aſſiſtance, by money, arms, ammunition, military ſtores, ſhips, ſoldiers, ſeamen, or any other manner of help whatſoever, to the ſaid perſon, who takes upon himſelf the title before mentioned, or to any other perſons whatever, who having commiſſion from him may in conſequence thereof diſturb the tranquillity of Great Britain by open war, or by ſecret conſpiracies, or inſurrections and rebellions, and make oppoſition to the government of his Britannic Majeſty.

Moreover, the moſt Chriſtian King promiſes and engages, not to permit the perſon above deſigned to return at any time hereafter to Avignon, or to paſs through the lands depending on the crown of France; on pretence of returning either to Avignon or to Lorrain, or ſo much as to ſet foot on any part of his moſt Chriſtian Majeſty's dominions, much leſs to reſide there under any name or appearance whatſoever.

III. The ſaid moſt ſerene Kings and the ſaid Lords the States General do alſo promiſe and engage themſelves, reciprocally to refuſe all kind of refuge and protection to the ſubjects of either of them, who have been, or ſhall be declared rebels, whenever it ſhall be requeſted by the contracting party, whoſe ſubjects thoſe rebels ſhall be known to be, and likewiſe to compel the ſaid rebels to depart out of the dominions under their obedience, in a week's time after

after the minifter of the faid ally fhall have required it in his mafter's name.

IV. And the moft Chriftian King being fincerely defirous, that every thing heretofore agreed on with the crown of France, concerning the town of Dunkirk, may be fully executed, and that nothing be omitted which the King of Great Britain may think neceffary for the entire deftruction of the port of Dunkirk, and to prevent all manner of fufpicion that there is an intention to make a new port at the canal at Mardyke, and to put it to fome other ufe than draining off the waters which might drown the country, and carrying on the commerce neceffary for the fubfiftence and maintenance of the people on that part of the Netherlands, which is only to be carried on by fmall boats, that are not allowed to be above 16 feet wide ; his moft Chriftian Majefty doth engage, and promife to caufe every thing to be executed, which the Sieur d'Ibberville, his moft Chriftian Majefty's envoy, having full power for that purpofe, did agree to, at Hampton-Court, as is contained in a memorial of the $\frac{19}{30}$ of November, 1716, figned by the Sieur d'Ibberville, and by the Lord Vifcount Townfhend, and Mr. Methuen, fecretaries of ftate for Great Britain, which is as follows:

*An explanation of what fhould be inferted in the IVth article of the treaty, concerning the canal and fluices of* Mardyke.

1. THAT the great paffage of the new fluice of Mardyke, which is 44 feet wide, fhall be demolifhed from top to bottom, that is to fay, by taking away its * bajoyers, planks, * bufks, * longrines, and * traverfines, from one end to the other; and by taking off the gates, the wood and iron-work of which fhall be taken to pieces, and all thefe materials be employed elfewhere, to fuch ufes as his moft Chriftian Majefty fhall think fit; provided neverthelefs, that they be never made ufe of for any

* Thefe are terms for beams, &c. which cannot be rendered into Englifh.

port

port, haven or fluice, at Dunkirk or Mardyke, or in any other place whatfoever, within two leagues from either of thofe two places : it being the intention of the contracting parties, and the end they propofe to themfelves by this treaty, that no port, haven, fortification, fluice, or bafon, be made or built at Dunkirk, the fluice of Mardyke, or any other place whatever along the fhore, at fuch diftance upon that coaft.

2. That the little fluice fhall remain as it is at prefent, with refpect to its depth, provided the breadth thereof be reduced to 16 feet; that is to fay, by advancing the Bajoyer de la Pille ten feet on the weft fide, after having taken away fix feet of the flooring, and the bufks of the * radier all along on the fame fide, the remaining four feet of plank or flooring being neceffary to ferve for the foundation of a new * bajoyer; and forafmuch as the faid bajoyer muft be advanced ten feet towards the eaft-fide, there fhall likewife be demolifhed ten feet of the fame pile on the weft-fide from the foundation, to the end that the prefent radier may never ferve for a fluice of 26 feet broad, as this is at prefent.

3. The jettees and fafcine-work from the Downs, or the place where the tide rifes upon the ftrand, when it is high water, down to the loweft ebb, fhall be demolifhed, on both fides of the new canal, and made level with the fhore; and the ftones and facine-work that are above the faid level, may be carried away and employed to fuch ufe as his moft Chriftian Majefty fhall think fit; provided however, that they be never made ufe of for any port or haven at Dunkirk, or Mardyke, or any other place whatfoever, within two leagues from either of thofe two places : the intention of the parties contracting, and the end they propofe to themfelves by this treaty being, that no more jettees or fafcine-work fhall ever be made again upon the fhore of this coaft, within that diftance on either fide.

4. It is alfo ftipulated, that immediately after the ratification of this prefent treaty, a fufficient number of workmen fhall be employed in the demolition of the faid jettees along the new canal, to the end that they may be razed, and the work finifhed, if poffible, within two months after
the

the ratification. But forafmuch as it has been reprefented, that becaufe the feafon is fo far advanced, they cannot
begin to narrow the radier of the fmall paffage, nor demo-
lifh the great radier till next fpring, it is agreed that this
work fhall be begun $\frac{\text{April 25}}{\text{May 5}}$, and entirely perfected, if
poffible, in the manner abovementioned, by the end of
June, 1717.

5. The demolition of the jettees or piers on both fides
of the old canal or port of Dunkirk, fhall be entirely
finifhed and made level with the ground, all the way from
the loweft ebb, as far as within the town of Dunkirk; and
if there fhall remain any pieces of Fort Blanc, Chateau
Verd, and Bonne Efperance, they fhall be totally laid flat
to the ground.

When this treaty fhall be ratified, the King of Great
Britain, and the Lords the States General of the United
Provinces may fend commiffioners to the fpot, to be eye-
witneffes of the execution of this article.

We have figned this article provifionally, and upon condition that it be approved by his moft Chriftian Majefty,
his Britannic Majefty, and the Lords the States General
of the United Provinces. At Hampton-Court the $\frac{19}{30}$ of
September, in the year 1716. Signed by d'Ibberville,
Townfhend, and P. Methuen.

V. It being the true end and purpofe of this alliance,
between the faid moft ferene Kings, and the Lords the
States General, to preferve and maintain reciprocally the
peace and tranquillity of their kingdoms, dominions, and
provinces, eftablifhed by the late treaties of peace, concluded and figned at Utrecht the 11th of April, 1713, between their moft ferene Majefties the moft Chriftian King,
the Queen of Great Britain, and the faid high and mighty
Lords the States General of the United Provinces: it is
agreed upon and concluded, that all and fingular the articles of the faid treaties of peace, as far as they relate to
the intereft of the faid three powers refpectively, and of
each of them in particular, and likewife the fucceffions to
the crown of Great Britain in the Proteftant line, and to
the

the crown of France, according to the said treaties, shall
remain in their full force and vigour; and that the said
most serene Kings and the said Lords the States General
do promise their reciprocal guarantee for the execution of
all the conventions contained in the said articles, so far as
they regard the successions and interests of the said kingdoms and states as above said, and likewise for the maintaining and defending of all the kingdoms, provinces,
states, rights, immunities, and advantages, which each of
the said allies respectively shall really be possessed of, at the
time of the signing of this alliance. And for this end the
said most serene Kings, and the Lords the States General,
have agreed and concluded between themselves, that if
any one of the said allies be attacked by the arms of any
prince or state whatever, the other allies shall interpose their
good offices with the aggressor, to procure satisfaction to
the party offended, and to engage the aggressor to abstain
entirely from all kinds of hostility.

VI. But if such good offices have not the expected effect,
to reconcile the two parties, and to obtain a satisfaction
and reparation of damages within two months, then those
of the allies who have not been attacked, shall be obliged
without delay to assist their ally, and to furnish him the
succours hereafter mentioned, viz.

The most Christian King, 8,000 foot and 2,000 horse.
The King of Great Britain, 8,000 foot and 2,000 horse.
The States General, 4,000 foot and 1,000 horse.

But if the ally who shall be engaged in a war, as aforesaid, chuse rather to have succours by sea, or even prefers
money to either sea or land forces, the same shall be left
to his discretion, provided a proportion be always observed
between the sums given, and the number of troops above
specified.

And to the end that there may be no dispute about this
point, it is stipulated, that 1000 foot soldiers shall be valued at the sum of 10,000 livres per month, and 1000 horse
at the sum of 30,000 livers per month, Dutch money, reckoning 12 months in the year; and succours by sea shall
be valued at the same proportion.

VII.

VII. It is likewife ftipulated and agreed upon, that if the kingdoms, countries or provinces, of any of the allies are difturbed by inteftine quarrels, or by rebellions on account of the faid fucceffions, or under any other pretext whatever, the ally thus in trouble fhall have full right to demand of his allies the fuccours abovementioned, or fuch part thereof as he fhall judge neceffary, at the coft and expence of the allies that are obliged to furnifh thefe fuccours, which fhall be fent within the fpace of two months after they are demanded; faving, however, as is aforefaid, to the party that requires them, his free choice to demand fuccours either by land or fea: and the allies fhall be reimburfed of what charges they fhall be at for the fuccours given, by virtue of this article, within the fpace of a year after thofe troubles are pacified and appeafed. But in cafe the faid fuccours be not fufficient, the faid allies fhall agree in concert to furnifh a greater number, and alfo if the cafe require it, they fhall declare war againft the aggreffors, and affift one another with all their forces.

VIII. The prefent treaty fhall be ratified by their moft Chriftian and Britannic Majefties, and the Lords the States General, and the letters of ratification fhall be delivered in due form on all fides, within the fpace of four weeks, or fooner if poffible, counting from the day of figning thefe prefents.

In witnefs whereof we the underwritten, being vefted with full powers from their moft Chriftian and Britannic Majefties, and the Lords the States General of the United Provinces, have in their names figned this prefent treaty, and caufed the feals of our arms to be thereto affixed. Done at the Hague, Jan. 4, 1717.

Signed by the plenipotentiaries above named in the preamble to the treaty.

*The feparate Article, figned and ratified between* France *and* Holland.

WHEREAS, in the fifth article of the treaty of alliance, concluded this day between their moft ferene Majefties, the moft Chriftian King and the King of
Great

Great Britain, and the high and mighty Lords the States General of the United Provinces, a reciprocal guarantee was agreed upon, for the execution of all the conditions mentioned in the said article, and likewise for maintaining and defending all the kingdoms, provinces, states, dominions, immunities and advantages, which each of the said allies respectively shall really be possessed of at the time of the signing of the said alliance; the underwritten Ambassadors Extraordinary and Plenipotentiaries of his most Christian Majesty, and the deputies and Plenipotentiaries of the said Lords the States General, have agreed, that without any manner of derogation from the first article of the said alliance, according to which there shall be an inviolable peace, and a strict alliance between their said Majesties, and the said Lords the States General, their dominions and subjects, as well within Europe as out of it, the guarantee stipulated in the 5th article of the same treaty, shall not take place in regard of his most Christian Majesty, and the Lords the States General, but only for the dominions and possessions which they have respectively in Europe; which is also to be understood of the succours stipulated and promised mutually in the 6th article of this treaty: which succours shall also be limited within Europe, with regard to his most Christian Majesty, and the Lords the States General.

The present separate article shall be of the same force as if it was inserted *verbatim* in the treaty, and shall be ratified at the same time as the treaty, and the ratifications shall also be exchanged at the same time with those of the treaty.

In witness whereof; we the underwritten, vested with the full powers of his most Christian Majesty, and the Lords the States General of the United Provinces, have in their names signed the present article, and thereto caused the seals of our arms to be affixed. Done at the Hague the 4th day of January, 1717. Signed by the ministers of France and Hollan mentioned in the preamble.

*Convention*

*Convention between the Moſt Serene and Moſt Potent Prince* George, *by the Grace of God King of* Great Britain, France, *and* Ireland, *Defender of the Faith, &c. and the Moſt Serene and Moſt Potent Prince* Lewis XV. *the Moſt Chriſtian King, for propoſing ultimate Conditions of Peace, between the Emperor and the King of* Spain, *and between the Emperor and the King of* Sicily. *Concluded at* Paris *the* 18*th of* July, *N. S.* 1718. Reprinted from the Copy printed by Authority.

I. THEY will propoſe forthwith and by concert to the Emperor, the ſaid plan of a treaty as an *ultimatum*, in which they oblige themſelves not to make any alteration, as alſo not to admit of the making of any.

II. Their Britannic and moſt Chriſtian Majeſties, promiſe and oblige themſelves reciprocally, to cauſe to be ſigned, and to ratify the ſaid treaty, according to the plan above inſerted; and they will forthwith give to their plenipotentiaries the neceſſary orders and powers for ſigning it at London, without any further delay, as ſoon as the Emperor's miniſter plenipotentiary ſhall be authorized to do it, in the name of his Imperial Majeſty.

III. Until the time the ſaid ſigning ſhall be perfected, their ſaid Majeſties ſhall continue to employ in concert, all their moſt preſſing offices, with the King of Spain, the King of Sicily, and every where elſe, where it may be proper, for cauſing the ſaid treaty to be approved and accepted.

IV. The preſent convention ſhall be ratified by their Britannic and moſt Chriſtian Majeſties, and the letters of ratification in due form ſhall be delivered on both ſides at London, within the ſpace of 15 days, or ſooner if poſſible, to be reckoned from the day of ſigning.

In witneſs whereof we, the underwritten, being furniſhed with the full powers of their Britannic and moſt Chriſtian Majeſties, have in their names ſigned the preſent convention, and have cauſed the ſeal of our arms to be affixed thereto. Done at Paris the 18th day of July, 1718.

(L. S.) *Stair.*    (L. S.) *Huxelles.*
(L. S.) *Stanhope.*   (L. S.) *L. de Clermont Cheverny.*

*Convention between the Most Serene and Most Potent Prince*
George, *by the Grace of God, King of* Great Britain,
France, *and* Ireland, *Defender of the Faith, &c. and the
Most Serene and Most Potent Prince* Lewis XV. *the Most
Christian King, for settling separate and secret Articles be-
longing to the foregoing ultimate Conditions of Peace. Con-
cluded at Paris the 18th of* July, *N. S.* 1718. Reprinted
from the Copy printed by Authority.

### Separate Article, No. 1.

WHEREAS the treaty this day made and signed between his Imperial Majesty, his Britannic Majesty,
and his most Christian Majesty, containing (as well such
conditions as have been thought most equitable and proper for establishing a peace betwixt the Emperor and the
Catholic King, and betwixt the said Emperor and the King
of Sicily, as the conditions of an alliance made for preserving the public peace between the said contracting
powers) hath been communicated to the high and mighty
Lords the States General of the United Netherlands: and
whereas the separate and secret articles likewise signed this
day, and containing the measures which it has been
thought fit to take for putting the abovesaid treaty in execution, are likewise shortly to be proposed to the States
General aforesaid. The inclination which that Republic
has shewn for restoring and establishing the public tranquillity, leaves no room of doubt but they will most readily accede thereto. The States General aforesaid are therefore by name inserted as contracting parties in the said
treaty, in most certain hope that they will enter therein,
as soon as the usual forms of their government will allow.

But if, contrary to the hopes and wishes of the contracting parties (which nevertheless is not in the least to be
suspected) the said Lords the States General shall not take
their resolution to accede to the said treaty; it is expressly
agreed and covenanted between the said contracting parties, that the treaty abovementioned and this day signed,
shall nevertheless have its effect among them, and shall in
all its clauses and articles be put in execution in the same
manner

manner as therein is fet forth, and the ratifications thereof
fhall be exhibited at the times above fpecified.

This feparate article fhall have the fame force as if it
had been word for word inferted in the treaty this day concluded and figned, and fhall be ratified in the fame manner,
and the inftruments of ratification fhall be delivered within the fame time with the treaty itfelf.

In witnefs whereof we the underwritten, by virtue of the
full powers this day mutually exhibited, have figned this
feparate article, and thereto have affixed our feals. Done
at London the 22d of July O. S. in the year 1718.
                      2d of Aug. N. S.

(L. S.) *Chrif. Pemerridter*    (L. S.) *W. Cant.* (L. S.) *Dubois.*
   *ab Adelfhaufen.*      (L. S.) *Parker C.*
                    (L. S.) *Sunderland P.*

(L. S). *Jo. Phil. Hoffman.*   (L. S.) *Kingfton C. P. S.*
                    (L. S.) *Kent.*
                    (L. S.) *Holles Newcaftle.*
                    (L. S.) *Bolton.*
                    (L. S.) *Roxburghe.*
                    (L. S.) *Berkeley.*
                    (L. S.) *J. Craggs.*

## SEPARATE ARTICLE. No. 2.

BUT if the Lords the States General of the United Netherlands fhould happen to think it too hard for them
to contribute their fhare of pay to the Swifs Cantons, for
maintaining the garrifons of Leghorn, Porto-Ferraio,
Parma, and Placentia, according to the tenor of the treaty
of alliance this day concluded; it is exprefsly provided by
this feparate article, and agreed between the four contracting powers, that in fuch cafe the Catholic King may
take upon him the faid fhare of the Lords the States Generals.

This feparate article fhall have the fame force as if it
had been word for word inferted in the treaty this day concluded and figned, and fhall be ratified in the fame manner, and the inftruments of ratification fhall be delivered
within the fame time with the treaty itfelf.

In

In witnefs whereof we the underwritten, by virtue of the full powers this day mutually exhibited, have figned this feparate article, and thereto have affixed our feals. Done at London the $\frac{22d\ of\ July,\ O.\ S.}{2d\ of\ Aug.\ N.\ S.}$ in the year 1718.

*Signed as before.*

### SEPARATE ARTICLE. No. 3.

WHEREAS in the treaty of alliance this day to be figned with his Imperial and Catholick Majefty, as likewife in the conditions of peace inferted therein, their facred royal Britannick, and moft Chriftian Majefties, and the Lords the States General of the United Netherlands, do ftyle the prefent poffeffor of Spain and the Indies Catholic King, and the Duke of Savoy king of Sicily, or alfo king of Sardinia: and whereas his Sacred Imperial and Catholick Majefty cannot acknowledge thefe two princes as kings, before they fhall have acceded to this treaty: his Sacred and Imperial Catholick Majefty, by this feparate article which was figned before the treaty of alliance, doth therefore declare and proteft, that by the titles there either given or omitted, he doth not mean in the leaft to prejudice himfelf, or to grant or allow the titles of king to the faid two princes, only in that cafe when they fhall have acceded to the treaty this day to be figned, and fhall have agreed to the conditions of peace fpecified therein.

This feparate article fhall have the fame force as if it had been word for word inferted in the treaty this day concluded and figned, and fhall be ratified in the fame manner, and the inftruments of ratification fhall be delivered within the fame time, with the treaty itfelf.

In witnefs whereof we the underwritten, by virtue of the full powers this day mutually exhibted, have figned this feparate article, and thereto have affixed our feals. Done at London the $\frac{22d\ of\ July\ O.\ S.}{2d\ of\ Aug.\ N.\ S.}$ in the year 1718.

*Signed as before.*

### SEPARATE ARTICLE. No. 4.

WHEREAS fome of the titles, which his Sacred Imperial Majefty, makes ufe of, either in his full powers, or in the treaty of alliance this day to be figned with

with him, cannot be acknowledged by his facred royal moft Chriftian Majefty ; he doth declare and proteft by this feparate article, which was figned before the treaty of alliance, by the faid titles given in this treaty, he doth not mean to prejudice either himfelf or any other, or that he in the leaft gives any right thereby to his Imperial Majefty.

This feparate article fhall have the fame force as if it had been word for word inferted in the treaty this day concluded and figned, and fhall be ratified in the fame manner, and the inftruments of ratification fhall be delivered within the fame time, with the treaty itfelf.

In witnefs whereof we the underwritten, by virtue of the full powers this day mutually exhibited, have figned this feparate article, and thereto have affixed our feals. Done at London the 2zd of July, O. S. in the year 1718.
2d of Aug. N. S.

*Signed as before.*

*N. B. The king of Sardinia acceded to this convention.*

---

*Treaty of alliance for fettling the publick Peace. Signed at* London July 22, 1718. Reprinted from the copy, printed at *London*, by authority. *Note*, This treaty is commonly called THE QUADRUPLE ALLIANCE.

*In the name of the Moft Holy and Undivided Trinity.*

BE it known to all whom it doth concern, or may any way concern.

Whereas the moft ferene and moft potent prince, George, of Great Britain, France, and Ireland, king, duke of Brunfwick and Lunenburgh, electtor of the holy Roman Empire, &c. and the moft ferene and moft potent prince Lewis XV. the moft Chriftian King, &c. as likewife the High and Mighty States General of the United Provinces of the Netherlands ; being continually intent on preferving the bleffing of peace, have duly confidered, that however by the triple alliance concluded by them on the 4th day of January, 1717, their own kingdoms and

pro•

provinces were provided for, yet that the provifion was neither fo general nor fo folid, as that the publick tranquillity could long flourifh and laft, unlefs at the fame time the jealoufies which were ftill increafing between fome of the princes of Europe as perpetual occafions of varience could be removed; and being convinced by experience from the war kindled the laft year in Italy, for the timely extinguifhing whereof by a treaty made the 18th day of July, N. S. in the year 1718, they agreed among themfelves upon certain articles of pacificat on according to which a peace might be brought about and eftablifhed between his facred Imperial Majefty and the king of Spain; as likewife between his faid Imperial Majefty and the king of Sicily, and farther gave a friendly invitation to his Imperial Majefty, that out of his love for the public peace and quiet, he would receive and approve the faid articles of convention in his own name, and accordingly that he himfelf would accede to the treaty made by them, the tenor of which is as followeth :

*Conditio s of Peace between his Imperial Majefty and his royal Catholick Majefty.*

*Art.* I. For quieting the difturbances lately raifed contrary to the peace of Baden, concluded the 7th day of September, 1714, as likewife to the neutrality eftablifhed for Italy by the treaty of the 14th day of March, 1713, the moft ferene and moft potent King of Spain obliges himfelf to reftore to his Imperial Majefty, and accordingly fhall immediately, or at the fartheft after two months to be reckoned from the exchange of the ratifications of this prefent treaty, actually reftore to his faid Imperial Majefty the ifland and kingdom of Sardinia in the condition wherein he feized it, and fhall renounce in favour of his Imperial Majefty all rights, pretenfions, interefts, and claims upon the faid kingdom; fo that his Imperial Majefty fully and freely, and in the manner which he judges beft, out of his love to the publick good, may difpofe of it as of his own property.

II. Whereas the only method which could be found out for fixing a durable balance in Europe was judged to be

be this, that it fhould be an eftablifhed rule that the kingdoms of France and Spain fhould never go together, or be
united in one and the fame perfon, or in one and the fame
line, and that thofe two monarchies fhould henceforward
for ever remain feparate; and whereas for confirming this
rule fo neceffary for the public tranquillity, thofe Princes,
to whom the prerogative of birth might have given a right
of fucceeding in both kingdoms, have folemnly renounced
one of thofe two kingdoms for themfelves and all their pofterity; fo that this feparation of the two monarchies has
paffed into a fundamental law in the general affembly
commonly called *Las Kortes*, which was received at Madrid
the 9th day of November, 1712, and confolidated by the
treaties of Utrecht, the 11th day of April, 1713, his Imperial Majefty being willing to give the utmoft perfection
to fo neceffary and wholefome a law, to take away all ground
of fufpicion, and to promote the public tranquillity, doth
accept and agree to thofe things which were done, ratified,
and eftablifhed in the treaty of Utrecht, with regard to the
right and order of fucceffion to the kingdoms of France
and Spain, and doth renounce as well for himfelf, as for
his heirs, defcendants, and fucceffors, male and female,
all rights, and all and every pretenfion whatfoever, not
one in the leaft excepted, on any kingdoms whatfoever,
dominions and provinces of the Spanifh monarchy, whereof the Catholic King was acknowledged to be the rightful
poffeffor by the treaty of Utrecht, and will caufe to be
made out in due form accordingly folemn acts of renunciation, which he will caufe to be publifhed and regiftered in the proper courts, and promifes that he will exhibit
the ufual inftruments thereupon to his Catholic Majefty and
to the contracting powers.

III. By virtue of the faid renunciation, which his Imperial Majefty has made out of regard to the fecurity of all
Europe; and in confideration likewife that the Duke of
Orleans has for himfelf and for his defcendants renounced
all his rights and claims upon the kingdom of Spain, on
condition that neither the Emperor, nor any of his defcendants, fhall ever fucceed to the faid kingdom; his Imperial Majefty doth acknowledge Philip V. to be lawful
king of Spain and of the Indies, and doth promife to give
him

him the titles and prerogatives belonging to his dignity and his kingdoms; and moreover, he will allow him, his defcendents, heirs and fucceffors, male and female, peaceably to enjoy all thofe dominions of the Spanifh monarchy in Europe, the Indies, and elfewhere; the poffeffion whereof was allowed him by the treaties of Utrecht, nor will he directly or indirectly difturb him in the faid poffeffion at any time, nor will he claim to himfelf any right to the faid kingdoms and provinces.

IV. In return for the renunciation and acknowledgment made by his Imperial Majefty in the two forgoing articles, the Catholick King as well as in his own, as in the name of his heirs, defcendents, and fucceffors, male and female, doth renounce in favour of his Imperial Majefty, his fucceffors, heirs and defcendents male and female, all rights and claims whatfoever, none in the leaft being exeepted, upon all and every the kingdoms, provinces, and dominions, which his Imperial Majefty doth poffefs in Italy or the Netherlands, or may accrue to him by virtue of this prefent treaty; and he doth wholly abdicate all rights, kingdoms, and provinces in Italy, which heretofore belonged to the Spanifh monarchy, among which the marquifat of Final yielded by his Imperial Majefty to the republic of Genoa in the year 1713, is underftood to be exprefsly comprehended, and he will caufe to be made out accordingly folemn acts of renunciation in due form, which he will caufe to be publifhed and regiftered in the proper courts and promifes that he will exhibit the ufual inftruments thereupon to his Imperial Majefty and the contracting powers. His Catholic Majefty doth in the like manner renounce the right of reverfion of the kingdom of Sicily to the crown of Spain, which he had referved for himfelf, and all other claims and pretenfions under pretext whereof he might difturb his Imperial Majefty, his heirs and fucceffors, directly or indirectly, as well in the forefaid kingdoms and provinces, as in all other dominions, which he actually poffeffes in the Netherlands or elfewhere.

V. Whereas in cafe the grand duke of Tufcany, or the duke of Parma and Placentia, or their fucceffors, fhould die without male iffue, the pretentions of fucceffion to the dominions

minions poffeffed by them might kindle a new war in Italy, on account of the different rights of fucceffion, whereby, after the deceafe of the next heirs before her, the prefent Queen of Spain born Dutchefs of Parma, claims the faid dukedoms to herfelf on the one part, and the emperor and empire on the other part. To the end that the great difputes, and the evils arifing from them, may be timely obviated; it is agreed that the ftates and duchies at prefent poffeffed by the grand Duke of Tufcany, and Duke of Parma and Placentia aforefaid, fhall in time to come be held and acknowledged by all the contracting powers as undoubted male fiefs of the Holy Roman Empire. His Imperial Majefty on his part doth confent by himfelf as head of the empire, that whenever it fhall happen that the faid duchies fhall lie open for want of heirs male, the firft-born fon of the faid queen of Spain, and his defcendents, being males, born in lawful matrimony; and in default of them the fecond born, or other the younger fons of the faid queen, if any fhall be born, together with their male defcendents, born in lawful marriage, fhall in like manner fucceed to all the provinces aforefaid. To which end it being neceffary that the confent of the empire be alfo given, his Imperial Majefty will ufe all his endeavours to obtain it; and having obtained it, he will caufe the letters of expectative, containing the eventual inveftiture for the fon of the faid queen, or her fons, and their legitimate male defcendents, to be expedited in due form; and he will caufe the faid letters to be delivered to the Catholic King immediately, or at leaft after two months from the exchange of the ratifications: without any damage neverthelefs, or prejudice, to the princes who now have poffeffion of the faid duchies, which poffeffion is to remain entirely fafe to them.

It is further agreed, between his facred Imperial Majefty, and the Catholick King, that the town of Leghorn may, and ought, perpetually to remain a free port, in the fame manner as it now is.

By virtue of the renunciation made by the king of Spain, of all the dominions, kingdoms, and provinces in Italy, which heretofore belonged to the Kings of Spain, that king fhall yield to the aforefaid prince his fon, the

town

town of Porto-Longone, together with that part of the island Elba, which he actually possesses therein ; and shall deliver the same up to him, as soon as that prince, on the extinction of the male posterity of the grand Duke of Tuscany, shall be admitted into the actual possession of his territories.

It is moreover agreed to, and provided by solemn contract, that none of the aforesaid duchies or dominions, at any time, or in any case, may or ought to be possest by a prince, who at the same time holds the kingdom of Spain; and that no king of Spain can ever take upon him the guardianship of that prince, or may be allowed to exercise the same.

Lastly it is agreed, and thereto all and singular the parties contracting have equally bound themselves, that it never shall be allowed during the lives of the present possessors of the duchies of Tuscany and Parma, or of their male successors, that any forces of any country whatsoever, whether their own or hired, shall either by the emperor, the king of Spain and France, or even by the prince appointed, as above, to the succession, be introduced into the provinces and lands of the said duchies ; nor shall any of them place any garrison in the cities, ports, towns, or fortresses therein situated.

But the said son of the queen of Spain, appointed by this treaty to the succession of the great duke of Tuscany and the duke of Parma and Placentia, may be more fully secured against all events, and may more certainly depend on the execution of the succession promised him : and likewise that the fief, constituted as above, may remain inviolable to the Emperor and empire ; it is agreed on both sides, that garrisons, not exceeding however the number of 6,000 men, which shall be put into the principal towns thereof, viz. Leghorn, Porto Ferraro, Parma, and Placentia, be taken from among the Swiss Cantons, which Cantons are for this purpose to be payed by the three contracting powers, who have taken upon them the part of mediators. And the said garrisons are therein to be continued till the case of the said succession shall happen, when they shall be obliged to deliver the towns to the said prince appointed to the succession. Nevertheless without any

trouble

trouble or charge to the present possessors, and their successors be males, to whom likewise the said garrisons are to take an oath of fidelity, and are to assume to themselves no other authority than only the guard of the cities committed to their charge.

But whereas this beneficial work may be longer delayed than is convenient, before an agreement can be made with the Swiss Cantons about the number, pay, and manner of establishing such a force; his sacred royal Britannic Majesty out of his singular zeal for the said work, and the public tranquillity, and for the earlier obtaining the end proposed, will not in the mean time refuse to lend his own forces for the use abovementioned, if the rest of the contracting powers think good, till the forces to be raised in the Swiss Cantons can take upon them the guard and custody of the said cities.

VI. His Catholic Majesty, to testify his sincere inclination for the public tranquillity, doth consent to all things hereafter mentioned, with regard to what is settled about the kingdom of Sicily for the advantage of his Imperial Majesty, and doth renounce for himself, his heirs and successors male and female, the right of reversion of that kingdom to the crown of Spain, which he expressly reserved to himself by the instrument of cession dated the 10th of June 1713. Out of love to the public good he moreover departs from the said act of the 10th of June 1713, as far as is necessary, as likewise from the sixth article of the treaty of Utrecht betwixt himself and his royal highness the Duke of Savoy, as likewise in general from every thing that may oppose the retrocession, disposition and permutation of the above-mentioned kingdom of Sicily by this present treaty established. On condition nevertheless that the right of reversion of the island and kingdom of Sardinia to the said crown may be yielded and allowed to him, as hereafter in the second article of the conventions between his sacred Imperial Majesty and the King of Sicily is farther explained.

VII. The Emperor and the Catholic King mutually promise and bind themselves to a reciprocal defence and guaranty of all the kingdoms and provinces which they
actually

actually poſſeſs, or the poſſeſſion whereof ought to belong to them by virtue of the preſent treaty.

VIII. His Imperial Majeſty and his royal Catholic Majeſty ſhall immediately after exchange of the ratifications of theſe preſent conventions, put in execution all and every the conditions therein comprehended, and that within the ſpace of two months at the fartheſt, and the inſtruments of the ratifications of the ſaid conventions ſhall be exchanged at London within the ſpace of two months, to be computed from the day of ſigning, or ſooner if poſſible. Which execution of the conditions being previouſly performed, their Miniſters and Plenipotentiaries, by them to be named, ſhall in the place of Congreſs, which they ſhall agree upon, with all ſpeed ſeverally ſettle and determine the other points of their particular peace, under the mediation of the three contracting powers.

It is farther agreed, that in the treaty of peace particularly to be made between the Emperor and the King of Spain, a general amneſty ſhall be granted to all perſons of any ſtate, dignity, degree, or ſex whatſoever, whether eccleſiaſtical or military, political or civil, who followed the party of the one or the other prince during the late war; in virtue whereof all and ſingular the ſaid perſons ſhall be permitted to receive, and they may receive full poſſeſſion and uſe of their goods, rights, privileges, honours, dignities, and immunities, and ſhall uſe and enjoy the ſame as freely as they did enjoy them at the beginning of the laſt war, or at the time when they begun to join themſelves to the one or the other party, all confiſcations, arreſts, and ſentences made, paſſed, or pronounced, during the war to the contrary notwithſtanding, which ſhall be held as null and of no effect. In virtue moreover of the aforeſaid amneſty, it ſhall be lawful and free for all and ſingular the ſaid perſons, who followed one or the other party, to return to their country, and to enjoy their goods in the ſame manner as if no war had happened : and a full licence is given them to take care of the ſaid effects, either by themſelves if they ſhould be preſent, or by their attornies, if they ſhould chooſe rather to abſent themſelves from their country, and they may eitheir ſell, or any other way, according to their pleaſure, diſpoſe of them entirely

after

after the fame manner they might have done before the beginning of the war.

*Conditions of the Treaty to be compleated between his Imperial Majefty and the King of* Sicily.

*Art.* I. Whereas the ceffion of Sicily, by the treaties of Utrecht to the houfe of Savoy, being folely made for rendering that peace folid, and not on the account of any right the King of Sicily had thereto, has been fo far from bringing about the end propofed, that, as all Europe can witnefs, it has rather proved the great obftacle which hindered the Emperor from acceding to the faid treaties, inafmuch as the feparation of the kindoms of Naples and Sicily, fo long ufed to remain under the fame dominion and to be called by the name of Both the Sicilies, has not only been found oppofite to the common interefts and mutual prefervation of both kingdoms, but likewife to the repofe of all Italy, being conftantly productive of new commotions, while neither the ancient intercourfe and mutual relation between the two nations can be deftroyed, nor the interefts of the different princes can be eafily reconciled: for this reafon it is that the princes, who firft made the Utrecht treaties, have thought it lawful for them even without the confent of the parties concerned, to abrogate that one article of thofe treaties which regards the kingdom of Sicily, and is not any principal part of the faid treaty, founding themfelves chiefly upon thefe reafons; that the prefent treaty will receive its increafe and completion from the Emperor's renunciation; and that by the exchange of Sicily for Sardinia, the wars which threaten Italy may be prevented, inafmuch as the Emperor might rightfully attack Sicily, which he never yet renounced, and which fince the infraction of the neutrality of Italy by the feizure of Sardinia, he may rightfully recover by force of arms: befides that the King of Sicily may become poffeffed of a certain and durable dominion by the benefit of fo folemn a treaty with his Imperial Majefty, and guarantied by the chief princes of Europe. Being moved therefore by fo great reafons they have agreed that the King of Sicily fhall reftore to his Imperial Majefty the ifland and

kingdom

kingdom of Sicily with all its dependencies and appendages in the ftate wherein they now are, immediately, or in two months at the fartheft from the exchange of the ratifications of the prefent treaty. And he fhall in favour of the Emperor, his heirs, and fucceffors of both fexes, renounce all rights and pretenfions whatfoever to the faid kingdom, as well for himfelf as his heirs and fucceffors, male and female ; the reverfion thereof to the crown of Spain being entirely taken away.

II. In return his Imperial Majefty fhall yield to the King of Sicily the ifland and kingdom of Sardinia, in the fame condition wherein he fhall receive it from the Catholic King, and fhall renounce all rights and interefts in the faid kingdom for himfelf, his heirs and fucceffors of both fexes, in favour of the King of Sicily, his heirs and fucceffors, that he may hereafter perpetually poffefs the fame with a title of a kingdom, and all other honours annexed to the royal dignity in the fame manner as he poffeffed the kingdom of Sicily ; on condition neverthelefs that the reverfion of the faid kingdom of Sardinia fhall be referved to the crown of Spain, whenever it may happen that the King of Sicily fhall be without heirs male, and all the houfe of Savoy fhall likewife be deftitute of heirs male. But in the fame manner altogether as the faid reverfion was fettled and ordained for the kingdom of Sicily by the treaties of Utrecht, and by the act of ceffion in purfuance thereof made by the King of Spain.

III. His Imperial Majefty fhall confirm to the King of Sicily all the ceffions made to him by the treaty figned at Turin the 8th day of November 1703, as well of that part of the duchy of Montferrat, as of the provinces, cities, towns, caftles, lands, places, rights, and revenues of the ftate of Milan, which he now doth poffefs, in the manner wherein he actually doth poffefs them; and he will ftipulate for himfelf, his defcendents, and fucceffors, that he never will difturb him, his heirs, or fucceffors, in the poffeffion aforefaid : on condition neverthelefs that all other claims and pretenfions which he may poffibly make in virtue of the faid treaty fhall be and remain void.

IV. His Imperial Majefty fhall acknowledge the right of the King of Sicily, and his houfe to fucceed immediately
to

to the kingdom of Spain and of the Indies, in cafe of the failure of King Philip V. and his pofterity, in manner as is fettled by the renunciations of the Catholic King, the Duke of Berry, and the Duke of Orleans, and by the treaties of Utrecht; and his Imperial Majefty fhall promife as well for himfelf as for his fucceffors and defcendents, that at no time he will directly or indirectly oppofe, or any way act contrary to the fame. It is declared neverthelefs that no prince of the houfe of Savoy who fhall fucceed to the crown of Spain, may poffefs at the fame time any province or dominion on the continent of Italy, and that in fuch cafe thofe provinces fhall devolve to the collateral princes of that houfe who fhall fucceed therein one after another according to the proximity of blood.

V. His Imperial Majefty and the King of Sicily fhall give mutual guaranties for all the kingdoms and provinces which they actually poffefs in Italy, or which fhall accrue to them by virtue of this prefent treaty.

VI. His Imperial Majefty and the King of Sicily immediately after the exchange of the ratifications of thefe conventions fhall put in execution all and every the conditions therein contained, and that within the fpace of two months at the fartheft : and the inftruments of the ratifications of the faid conventions fhall be exchanged at London within two months from the day of figning, or fooner if poffible. And immediately after the previous execution of the faid conditions, their Minifters and Plenipotentiaries, by them to be named, fhall, in the place of congrefs they fhall agree upon, with all fpeed feverally fettle the other points of their particular peace, under the mediation of the three contracting powers.

His abovenamed Imperial and Catholic Majefty being extremely inclined to promote the peace propofed, and to avert the dreadful calamities of war, and out of his fincere defire to fettle an univerfal pacification, hath accepted the afore-mentioned conventions, and all and fingular the articles thereof, and hereby doth accept the fame, and accordingly has entered into a particular treaty with the three powers abovefaid on the following conditions.

*Art.* I. That there be and remain between his facred Imperial Catholic Majefty, his facred Royal Majefty of
Great

Great Britain, his facred royal and moft Chriftian Majefty, and the High and Mighty Lords the States General of the United Netherlands, and their heirs and fucceffors, a moft ftrict alliance, in virtue whereof each of them are bound to preferve the dominions and fubjects of the others, as likewife to maintain peace, to promote mutually the interefts of the others as their own, and to prevent and repel all damages and injuries whatfoever.

II. The treaties made at Utrecht and Baden fhall remain in their full ftrength and force, and fhall be a part of this treaty, thofe articles excepted, from which it has been judged for the public good to depart; as likewife thofe articles of the Utrecht treaties excepted, which were abolifhed by the treaty of Baden. The treaty of alliance made at Weftminfter the 25th day of May 1716, between his facred Imperial and Catholic Majefty, and his facred Royal Majefty of Great Britain, as likewife the treaty made at the Hague the 4th day of January 1717, between the king of Great Britain and the moft Chriftian King, and the States General of the United Provinces, fhall neverthelefs remain in full force in every particular.

III. His facred Britannic Majefty, as likewife his facred moft Chriftian Majefty, and the Lords the States General of the United Netherlands, do covenant for themfelves their heirs and fucceffors, that they never will directly or indirectly difturb his facred Imperial and Catholic Majefty, his heirs and fucceffors, in any of his kingdoms, dominions, and provinces, which he poffeffes by virtue of the treaties of Utrecht and Baden, or which he fhall gain poffeffion of by virtue of this prefent treaty. On the contrary they both will and ought to defend and guarantee the provinces, kingdoms, and jurifdictions, which he now poffeffes, or which fhall accrue to him in virtue of this treaty, as well in Germany as in the Netherlands and in Italy, and they promife that they fhall defend the faid kingdoms and provinces of his Imperial and Catholic Majefty againft all and fingular who may attempt to invade the fame in a hoftile manner: and that they both will and ought, when the cafe happens, to furnifh him with fuch fuccours as he fhall need, according to the conditions and repartition, which they have agreed upon as hereafter mentioned. In like

manner

manner their royal Britannic and moſt Chriſtian Majeſties and the States General expreſsly bind themſelves, that they will not at any time give or grant any protection or refuge in any part of their dominions to the ſubjects of his Imperial and Catholic Majeſty, who actually are, or hereafter ſhall be by him declared rebels, and in caſe any ſuch ſhall be found in their kingdoms, provinces, or dominions, they ſincerely promiſe that they will take effectual care to expel them out of their territories within eight days after application made by his Imperial Majeſty.

IV. On the other hand his ſacred Imperial and Catholic Majeſty, his ſacred royal Britannic Majeſty, and the States General of the United Provinces, promiſe for themſelves, their heirs and ſucceſſors, that they never will, directly or indirectly, diſturb his ſacred moſt Chriſtian Majeſty in any of his dominions to the crown of France now belonging. On the contrary they will and ought to guard and defend the ſame againſt all and ſingular who may attempt to invade them in a hoſtile manner, and in that caſe they will and ought to furniſh ſuch ſuccours as his moſt Chriſtian Majeſty ſhall want, as according as hereafter is agreed upon.

His ſacred Imperial and Catholic Majeſty, his ſacred royal Majeſty of Great Britain, and the Lords the States General, do likewiſe promiſe and oblige themſelves that they will and ought to maintain, guarantee, and defend the right of ſucceſſion in the kingdom of France, according to the tenor of the treaties made at Utrecht the 11th day of April 1713, obliging themſelves to ſtand by the ſaid ſucceſſion plainly according to the form of the renunciation made by the king of Spain the 5th day of November 1712, and by a ſolemn act accepted in the general aſſembly of the ſtates of Spain the 9th day of the month and year aforeſaid, which thereupon paſſed into a law the 18th of March 1713, and laſtly was eſtabliſhed and ſettled by the treaties of Utrecht: and this they ſhall perform againſt all perſons whatſoever who may preſume to diſturb the order of the ſaid ſucceſſion in contradiction to the previous acts and treaties ſubſequent thereon. To which end they ſhall furniſh the ſuccours, according to the repartition agreed on below. Farther, when the mat-

ter

ter may require it, they fhall defend the faid order of fucceffion with all their forces, by likewife declaring war
againft him who may attempt to infringe or impugn the
fame.

Moreover his Imperial royal Catholic Majefty, and
his royal Britannic Majefty, and the States General,
do likewife promife that they will not at any time give
or grant any protection or refuge in their dominions to
the fubjects of his royal moft Chriftian Majefty, who actually are, or hereafter fhall be declared rebels; and in
cafe any fuch fhall be found in their kingdoms, provinces,
and dominions, they fhall command them to depart the
fame within the fpace of eight days after application made
by the faid king.

V. His facred Imperial royal and Catholic Majefty,
as alfo his royal moft Chriftian Majefty, and the States
General of the United Provinces do bind themfelves, their
heirs, and fucceffors, to maintain and guarantee the fucceffion in the kingdom of Great Britain, as eftablifhed by
the laws of that kingdom in the houfe of his Britannic
Majefty now reigning, as likewife to defend all the dominions and provinces poffeffed by his Majefty. And
they fhall not give or grant any protection or refuge in
any part of their dominions to the perfon, or his defcendents, if he fhould have any, who during the life of
James II. took on him the title of Prince of Wales, and
fince the death of that king, affumed the royal title of
King of Great Britain. Promifing alike for themfelves,
their heirs, and fucceffors, that they will not give to the
faid perfon or his defcendents, directly or indirectly, by
fea or by land, any fuccour, council or affiftance whatfoever,
either in money, arms, military ftores, fhips, foldiers,
mariners, or any other manner whatfoever. The fame
they fhall obferve with regard to thofe who may be ordered
or commiffioned by the faid perfon or his defcendents, to
difturb the government of his Britannic Majefty, or the
tranquillity of his kingdom, whether by open war or clandeftine confpiracies, by raifing feditions and rebellions, or
by exercifing piracy on his Britannic Majefty's fubjects.
In which laft cafe his Imperial and royal Catholic Majefty doth promife, that he will in no wife allow that there
be

be any receptacle granted to such pirates in his ports in the Netherlands. The same do his sacred most Christian Majesty and the States General of the United Provinces stipulate, with regard to the ports in their respective dominions; as on the other hand his Britannic Majesty doth promise, that he will refuse any refuge in the ports of his kingdoms to pirates infesting the subjects of his sacred Imperial and royal Catholic Majesty, of his sacred royal most Christian Majesty, or of the Lords the States General. Lastly, his Imperial and royal Catholic Majesty, his sacred royal most Christian Majesty, and the Lords the States General oblige themselves, that they never will give any refuge or protection, in any part of their dominions, to such of his Britannic Majesty's subjects as actually are, or hereafter shall be declared rebels; and in case any such shall be found in any of their kingdoms provinces, or dominions, they shall command them, within eight days after application made by the said King, to depart out of their territories. And if it should happen that his sacred Britannic Majesty should be invaded in any part in a hostile manner, his Imperial and royal Catholic Majesty, as likewise his royal most Christian Majesty, and the States General of the United Provinces, do oblige themselves, in that case, to furnish the succours hereafter specified. The same they are to do in favour of his descendents, if ever it should happen that they should be disturbed in the succession of the kingdom of Great Britain.

VI. His Imperial and royal Catholic Majesty, and their royal Britannic and most Christian Majesties do bind themselves, their heirs, and successors, to protect and guarantee all the dominions, jurisdictions, and provinces, which the Lords the States General of the United Provinces actually possess, against all persons whatsoever who may disturb or invade them, promising to furnish them in such case with the succours hereafter mentioned. His Imperial and royal Catholic Majesty, and their royal Britannic and most Christian Majesties, likewise oblige themselves, that they will give no refuge or protection in any of their kingdoms to the subjects of the States General, who are, or hereafter shall be declared rebels; and if any such shall be found in any of their kingdoms, dominions,

or

or provinces, they will take care to fend them out of their dominions within the fpace of eight days after application made by the Republic.

VII. When it fhall happen that any one of the four contracting powers fhall be invaded by any other prince or ftate, or difturbed in the poffeffion of their kingdoms or dominions, by the violent detention of their fubjects, fhips, goods, or merchandize, by fea or by land, then the three remaining powers fhall, as foon as they are required thereto, ufe their good offices that the party fuffering may have fatisfaction for the damage and injury received, and that the aggreffor may abftain from the profecution of his hoftility. But when thefe friendly offices for reconciliation and procuring fatisfaction and reparation to the injured party fhall have proved infufficient, in that cafe the high allies, within two months after application made, fhall furnifh the party invaded with the following fuccours, jointly or feparately, viz.

His Imperial and royal Catholic Majefty, 8,000 foot, and 4,000 horfe.

His Britannic Majefty, 8,000 foot, and 4,000 horfe.

His moft Chriftian Majefty, 8,000 foot, and 4,000 horfe.

And the Lords the States General, 4,000 foot, and 2,000 horfe.

But if the prince or party injured, inftead of foldiers, chufes rather fhips of war, or tranfports, or fubfidies in money, which is left to his difcretion, in that cafe, the fhips or money defired fhall be granted him in proportion to the charge of the foldiers to be furnifhed. And that all ambiguity with regard to the calculation and charge of fuch fums may be taken away, it is agreed, that 1,000 foot by the month, fhall be reckoned at 10,000 florins of Holland, and 1,000 horfe fhall be reckoned at 30,000 florins of Holland by the month; the fame proportion being obferved with refpect to the fhips.

When the above-named fuccours fhall be found infufficient for the neceffity impending, the contracting powers fhall without delay agree on contributing more ample fupplies. And farter, in cafe of exigency, they fhall affift

their

their injured ally with all their forces, and declare war against the aggreffor.

VIII. The princes and ftates upon whom the contracting powers fhall unanimoufly agree, may accede to this treaty; and the King of Portugal by name.

This treaty fhall be approved and ratified by their Imperial, Britannic, and moft Chriftian Majefties, and by the high and mighty Lords the States General of the United Provinces, and the inftruments of ratification fhall be exchanged at London, and reciprocally delivered within two months, or fooner, if poffible.

In witnefs whereof we the underwritten (being furnifhed with full powers, which have been mutually communicated, and the copies whereof having been in due form by us collated and examined with the originals, are word for word inferted at the end of this inftrument) have fubfcribed this prefent treaty, and thereto put our feals. Done at London the $\frac{\text{22d of July O. S.}}{\text{2d of Aug. N. S.}}$ in the year 1718.

(L. S.) *Chrif. Penterridter* (L. S.) *W. Cant.* (L. S.) *Dubois.*
   *ab Adelfhaufen.*   (L. S.) *Parker C.*
                  (L. S.) *Sunderland P.*
(L. S.) *Jo. Phil. Hoffman.* (L. S.) *Kingfton C. P. S.*
                  (L. S.) *Kent.*
                  (L. S.) *Holles Newcaftle.*
                  (L. S.) *Bolton.*
                  (L. S.) *Roxburghe.*
                  (L. S.) *Berkeley.*
                  (L. S.) *J. Craggs.*

WE, having feen and confidered the above-written treaty, have approved, ratified, and confirmed, as by thefe prefents we do, for us, our heirs, and fucceffors, approve, ratify, and confirm the fame, in all and fingular its articles and claufes, engaging and promifing upon our royal word, fincerely and faithfully to perform all and fingular the contents of the faid treaty, and never to fuffer, as far as in us les, any perfon to violate the fame, or in any manner to act contrary thereunto. In witnefs whereof, we have caufed our great feal of Great Britain to be affixed
ed

ed' to thefe prefents, figned with our royal hand. Given at our palace at Kenfington, the 7th day of Auguft, in the year of our Lord, 1718, and of our reign the fifth.

GEORGE.

## Separate *and* Secret Articles.

*Art.* I. WHEREAS the moft ferene and moft potent King of Great Britain, and the moft ferene and moft potent the moft Chriftian King, as likewife the high and mighty Lords the States General of the United Netherlands, by virtue of the treaty between them this day concluded and figned, have agreed on certain conditions, whereby a peace may be made between the moft ferene and moft potent Emperor of the Romans, and the moft ferene and moft potent King of Spain, as alfo between his facred Imperial Majefty aforefaid, and the King of Sicily, (whom hereafter it is thought fit to call the King of Sardinia) which conditions they have communicated to the three Princes aforefaid, as a bafis of the peace to be eftablifhed between them. His facred Imperial Majefty, being moved by the moft weighty reafons which induced the King of Great Britain, the moft Chriftian King, and the States General aforefaid, to take upon themfelves fo great and fo wholefome a work, and, yielding to their circumfpect and urgent counfels and perfuafions, declares that he doth accept the faid conditions or articles, none of them excepted, as fixed and immutable conditions, according to which he agrees to conclude a perpetual peace with the King of Spain, and the King of Sardinia.

II. But becaufe the King of Spain and the King of Sardinia have not yet confented to the faid conditions, his Imperial Majefty, as likewife their royal Britannic and moft Chriftian Majefties, and the States General aforefaid, have agreed to allow them for confenting thereto, the fpace of three months, to be computed from the day of figning this prefent treaty, as judging this interval of time fufficient for them duly to weigh the faid conditions, and finally determine and declare themfelves whether they are willing to accept them as fixed and immutable conditions of their pacification with his Imperial Majefty, as from their piety

and

and prudence it may be hoped they will do, and, following the example of his Imperial Majefty, that they will be
induced to moderate their paffions, and out of regard to
humanity, that they will prefer the public tranquillity to
their own private opinions; and at the fame time not only
fpare the effufion of their own people's blood, but avert
the calamities of war from the other nations of Europe:
to which end their Britannic and moft Chriftian Majefties,
and the States General of the United Netherlands, will
jointly and feparately contribute their moft effectual offices, for inclining the faid Princes to fuch an acceptation.

III. But if, contrary to all expectation of the parties
above contracting, and the wifhes of all Europe; the King
of Spain and the King of Sardinia, after the term of three
months elapfed, fhould decline to accept the faid conditions
of pacification propofed betwixt them and his Imperial
Majefty, fince it is not reafonable that the tranquillity of
Europe fhould depend upon their refufal, or private defigns, their Britannic and moft Chriftian Majefties, and
the States General, do promife that they will join their
forces with thofe of his Imperial Majefty, in order to compel them to the acceptance and execution of the aforefaid
conditions. To which end they will furnifh his Imperial
Majefty, jointly and feparately, with the felf-fame fuccours
which they have agreed upon for their reciprocal defence
by the feventh article of the treaty figned th·s day, unanimoufly confenting that the moft Chriftian King fhall, inftead of foldiers contribute his quota in money. And if
the fuccours fpecified in the faid feventh article fhall not
be fufficient for compaffing the end propofed, then the
four contracting parties fhall, without delay, agree of more
ample fuccours to be furnifhed to his Imperial Majefty,
and fhall continue the fame till his Imperial Majefty fhall
have reduced the kingdom of Sicil , and till his kingdoms
and provinces in Italy fhall enjoy full fecurity. It is farther agreed, and that in exprefs words, that if, by reafon
of the fuccours which their Britannic and moft Chriftian
Majefties, and the Lords the States General fhall furnifh to
his Imperial Majefty, by virtue, and in execution of the
prefent treaty, the Kings of Spain and Sardinia, or either
of them, fhall declare and wage war againft any one of the
faid

said contractors, either by attacking them in their dominions, or by violently detaining their subjects or ships,
their goods and merchandizes by sea or land, in that case
the two other of the contracting powers shall immediately
declare war against the said Kings of Spain and Sardinia,
or against him of the two Kings who shall have denounc-
ed or waged war against any one of the said contracting
powers; nor shall they lay down their arms before the
Emperor shall be possessed of Sicily, and made secure with
regard to his kingdoms and provinces in Italy, and likewise just satisfaction shall be given to him of the three
contracting powers, who shall have been invaded or suffered damage by reason of the present treaty.

IV. When only one of the two Kings aforesaid who have
not yet consented to the conditions of peace to be made
with his Imperial Majesty shall accept them, he likewise
shall join himself with the four contracting powers, to
compel him that shall refuse the said conditions, and shall
furnish his quota of succours according to the distribution
to be made thereupon.

V. If the Catholic King out of regard to the public
good, and a persuasion that an exchange of the kingdoms
of Sicily and Sardinia is necessary for the maintenance of
the general peace, shall agree thereto, and embrace the
conditions of peace to be made with the Emperor as above;
and on the other hand, if the King of Sardinia shall reject
such an exchange, and persist in retaining Sicily; in that
case the King of Spain shall restore Sardinia to the Emperor, who (saving his supreme dominion over it) shall
put the same into the custody of the most serene King of
Great Britain, and of the Lords the States General, for so
long time, till Sicily being reduced, the King of Sardinia
shall sign the above-mentioned conditions of a treaty with
the Emperor, and shall agree to accept the kingdom of
Sardinia as an equivalent for the kingdom of Sicily; which
being done, he shall be admitted into the possession thereof by the King of Great Britain and the States General.
But if his Imperial Majesty should not be able to conquer
Sicily, and reduce it under his power, in that case the
King of Great Britain and the States General shall restore
to him the kingdom of Sardinia; and in the mean time
his

his Imperial Majesty shall enjoy the revenues of the said kingdom, which shall exceed the charge of keeping it.

VI. But in case the King of Sardinia shall consent to the said exchange, and the King of Spain shall refuse, in this case the Emperor, being aided by the succours of the rest of the contractors, shall attack Sardinia, with which succours they on their part promise to furnish him; as the Emperor promises on his part, that he will not lay down his arms till he shall have possessed himself of the whole kingdom of Sardinia, which immediately after such possession he shall give up to the King of Sardinia.

VII. But if both the Kings of Spain and Sardinia shall oppose the exchange of Sicily and Sardinia, the Emperor, together with the succours of the allies, shall, in the first place attack Sicily, and having reduced it, he shall turn his arms against Sardinia with such a number of forces, besides the succours of the allies, as he shall judge necessary for both expeditions: and, having likewise reduced Sardinia, his Imperial Majesty shall commit the custody thereof to the King of Great Britain, and to the Lords the States General, till the King of Sardinia shall have signed the conditions of peace to be made with the Emperor, and shall consent to accept the kingdom of Sardinia as an equivalent for the kingdom of Sicily, which then is to be delivered up to him by his Britannic Majesty and the States General, and in the mean time his Imperial Majesty shall enjoy the revenues of that kingdom, which shall exceed the charge of keeping it.

VIII. In case the Catholic King and the King of Sardinia, or either of them, shall refuse to accept and execute the abovesaid conditions of peace to them proposed, and for that reason the four contracting powers should be compelled to proceed against them, or either of them, by open force; it is expresly covenanted, that the Emperor (what progress soever his arms may make against the said two Kings, or either of them,) shall be content and ought to acquiesce in the advantages, by mutual consent allotted to him in the said conditions, power nevertheless being reserved to his Imperial Majesty, of recovering the rights which he pretends to have over that part of the duchy of Milan, which the King of Sardinia now possesses, either

by

by war, or by a treaty of peace subsequent opon such war; power being likewise reserved to the other three allies, in case such a war should be undertaken against the Kings of Spain and Sardinia, to agree with his Imperial Majesty in appointing some other Prince, in whose favour his Imperial Majesty may dispose of that part of the duchy of Montferrat, now possessed by the King of Sardinia, in exclusion of the said King; and to what other Prince or Princes he may, with the consent of the Empire, grant the letters of expectative, containing the eventual investiture of the states now possessed by the Grand Duke of Tuscany, and by the Duke of Parma and Placentia, in exclusion of the sons of the present Queen of Spain. This declaration being added, that in no time or case whatsoever, either his Imperial Majesty, or any Prince of the house of Austria, who shall possess the kingdoms, dominions, and provinces of Italy, may assert or gain to himself the said duchies of Tuscany and Parma.

IX. But if his Imperial Majesty, after his efforts by a sufficient number of forces, and the succours and other means of the allies, and by using all convenient diligence, should not be able by arms to subdue, or to establish himself in the possession of Sicily, the contracting powers do agree and declare, that his Imperial Majesty is, and shall be in that case, altogether free and discharged from every obligation entered into by this treaty, of agreeing to make a peace with the Kings of Spain and Sardinia, on the conditions abovementioned. All other the articles of this treaty neverthelefs to remain good, which mutually regard his Imperial Majesty, their Britannic and most Christian Majesties, and the Lords the States General of the United Netherlands.

X. However, as the security and tranquillity of Europe is the end and scope of the renunciations to be made by his Imperial Majesty, and by his Catholic Majesty, for themselves, their descendants and successors, of all pretensions to the kingdom of Spain, and the Indies on the one part; and on the kingdoms, dominions, and provinces of Italy, and the Austrian Netherlands, on the other part: the said renunciations shall be made on the one and the other part, in manner and form as in the second and fourth articles
of

of the conditions of a peace to be made between his Imperial Majefty and his Royal Catholic Majefty has been agreed. And though the Catholic King fhould refufe to accept the aforefaid conditions, the Emperor neverthelefs fhall caufe the inftruments of his renunciation to be difpatched, the publication whereof fhall however be deferred till the day of figning the peace with the Catholic King. And if the Catholic King fhould conftantly perfift in rejecting the faid peace, his Imperial Majefty neverthelefs, at the time when the ratifications of this treaty fhall be exchanged, fhall deliver to the King of Great Britain à folemn act of the faid renunciations, which his Britannic Majefty, purfuant to the common agreement of the contracting powers, doth promife fhall not be exhibited to the moft Chriftian King before his Imperial Majefty fhall come into the poffeffion of Sicily. But that being obtained, then the exhibition, as well as publication of the faid act of his Imperial Majefty's renunciations, fhall be performed upon the firft demand of the moft Chriftian King. And thofe renunciations fhall take place, whether the Catholic King fhall fign the peace with the Emperor or no; by reafon that, in this laft cafe, the guarantee of the contracting parties fhall be to the Emperor in lieu of that fecurity which otherwife the renunciations of the Catholic King would have given to his Imperial Majefty for Sicily, the other ftates of Italy, and the provinces of the Netherlands.

XI. His Imperial Majefty doth promife that he will not attempt or enterprife any thing againft the Catholic King, or the King of Sardinia, or in general, againft the neutrality of Italy, in that fpace of three months allowed them for accepting the conditions of their peace with the Emperor. But, if within the fpace of three months, the Catholic King, inftead of accepting the faid conditions, fhall rather perfift in the profecuting of his hoftilities againft his Imperial Majefty: or if the King of Sardinia fhould with arms attack the provinces which the Emperor poffeffes in Italy; in that cafe their Britannic and moft Chriftian Majefties, and the Lords the States General, oblige themfelves inftantly to furnifh his Imperial Majefty for his defence, with the fuccours, which, in virtue of the treaty

this

this day signed, they have mutually agreed to lend one another for their reciprocal defence: and that jointly or separately, and without waiting the expiration of the two months otherwise prefixed in the said treaty, for the employing of friendly offices. And if the succours specified by the said treaty should not be sufficient for the end proposed, the four contracting parties shall immediately agree amongst themselves to send more powerful assistance to his Imperial Majesty.

XII. The eleven foregoing articles are to be kept secret by his Imperial Majesty, their Britannic and most Christian Majesties, and the States General, for the space of three months, from the day of the signing, unless it shall be unanimously agreed by them to shorten or prolong the said term: and though the said eleven articles be separate from the treaty of alliance, this day signed by the four contracting parties aforesaid, they shall nevertheless have the same power and force, as if they had been word for word inserted therein, since they are deemed to be an essential part thereof.

The ratifications thereof shall moreover be exchanged at the same time, as the other articles of the said treaty.

In witness whereof, we the underwritten, by virtue of the full powers this day mutually exhibited, have subscribed these separate articles, and thereto have affixed our seals. Done at London the $\frac{\text{22d of July, O. S.}}{\text{2d of Aug. N. S.}}$ in the year 1718.

*Signed as before.*

WE having seen and considered the separate and secret articles above-written, have approved, ratified, and confirmed, as by these presents, we do for us, our heirs and successors, approve, ratify, and confirm the same, &c.

GEORGE *R.*

SEPARATE ARTICLE. No. 1.

WHEREAS the treaty this day made and signed between his Imperial Majesty, his Britannic Majesty, and his most Christian Majesty, containing (as well such

such conditions as have been thought most equitable and proper for establishing a peace betwixt the Emperor and the Catholic King, and betwixt the said Emperor and the King of Sicily, as the conditions of an alliance made for preserving the public peace between the said contracting powers) hath been communicated to the high and mighty Lords the States General of the United Netherlands: and whereas the separate and secret articles likewise signed this day, and containing the measures which it has been thought fit to take for putting the abovesaid treaty in execution, are likewise shortly to be proposed to the States General aforesaid. The inclination which that Republic has shewn for restoring and establishing the public tranquillity leaves no room of doubt but they will most readily accede thereto. The States General aforesaid are therefore by name inserted as contracting parties in the said treaty, in most certain hope that they will enter therein, as soon as the usual forms of their government will allow.

But, if contrary to the hopes and wishes of the contracting parties (which nevertheless is not in the least to be suspected) the said Lords the States General shall not take their resolution to accede to the said treaty; it is expressly agreed and covenanted between the said contracting parties, that the treaty abovementioned, and this day signed, shall nevertheless have its effect among them, and shall in all its clauses and articles be put in execution in the same manner as therein is set forth, and the ratifications thereof shall be exhibited at the times above specified.

This separate article shall have the same force as if it had been word for word inserted in the treaty this day concluded and signed, and shall be ratified in the same manner, and the instruments of ratification shall be delivered within the same time, with the treaty itself.

In witness whereof we the underwritten, by virtue of the full powers this day mutually exhibited, have signed this separate article, and thereto have affixed our seals. Done at London the 22d of July, O. S. / 2d of Aug. N. S. in the year 1718.

*Signed as before.*

SEPARATE

## SEPARATE ARTICLE. NO. 2.

BUT if the Lords the States General of the United Netherlands should happen to think it too hard for them to contribute their share of pay to the Swifs Cantons, for maintaining the garrisons of Leghorn, Porto-Ferraro, Parma, and Placentia, according to the tenor of the treaty of alliance this day concluded ; it is expressly provided by this separate article, and agreed between the four contracting powers, that in such case the Catholic King may take upon him the said share of the Lords the States Generals.

This separate article shall have the same force as if it had been word for word inserted in the treaty this day concluded and signed, and shall be ratified in the same manner, and the instruments of ratification shall be delivered with n the same time, with the treaty itself.

In witness whereof we the underwritten, by virtue of the full powers this day mutually exhibited, have signed this separate article, and thereto have affixed our seals. Done at London the 22d of July, O. S. / 2d of Aug. N. S. in the year 1718.

*Signed as before.*

## SEPARATE ARTICLE. NO. 3.

WHEREAS in the treaty of alliance this day to be signed with his Imperial and Catholic Majesty, as likewise in the conditions of peace inserted therein, their sacred royal Britannic, and most Christian Majesties, and the Lords the States General of the United Netherlands, do style the present possessor of Spain and the Indies Catholic King, and the Duke of Savoy, King of Sicily, or also King of Sardinia : and whereas his sacred Imperial and Catholic Majesty cannot acknowledge these two Princes as Kings, before they shall have acceded to this treaty : his sacred Imperial and Catholic Majesty, by this separate article, which was signed before the treaty of alliance, doth therefore declare and protest, that by the titles there either given or omitted, he doth not mean in the least to prejudice

prejudice himſelf, or to grant or allow the titles of King to the ſaid two Princes, only in that caſe when they ſhall have acceded to the treaty this day to be ſigned, and ſhall have agreed to the conditions of peace ſpecified therein.

This ſeparate article ſhall have the ſame force as if it had been word for word inſerted in the treaty this day concluded and ſigned, and ſhall be ratified in the ſame manner, and the inſtruments of ratification ſhall be delivered within the ſame time, with the treaty itſelf.

In witneſs whereof, we the underwritten, by virtue of the full powers this day mutually exhibited, have ſigned this ſeparate article, and thereto have affixed our ſeals. Done at London the $\frac{22d\ of\ July,\ O.\ S.}{2d\ of\ Aug.\ N.\ S.}$ in the year 1718.

*Signed as before.*

## SEPARATE ARTICLE. No. 4.

WHEREAS ſome of the titles, which his ſacred Imperial Majeſty makes uſe of, either in his full powers, or in the treaty of alliance this day to be ſigned with him, cannot be acknowledged by his ſacred royal moſt Chiſtian Majeſty ; he doth declare and proteſt by this ſeparate article, which was ſigned before the treaty of alliance, that by the ſaid titles given in this treaty, he doth not mean to prejudice either himſelf or any other, or that he in the leaſt gives any right thereby to his Imperial Majeſty.

This ſeparate article ſhall have the ſame force as if it had been word for word inſerted in the treaty this day concluded and ſigned, and ſhall be ratified in the ſame manner, and the inſtruments of ratification ſhall be delivered within the ſame time, with the treaty itſelf.

In witneſs whereof, we the underwritten, by virtue of the full powers this day mutually exhibited, have ſigned this ſeparate article, and thereto have affixed our ſeals. Done at London the $\frac{22d\ of\ July,\ O.\ S.}{2d\ of\ Aug.\ N.\ S.}$ in the year 1718.

*Signed as before.*
*Ratified as before.*
*The whole ratified alſo by the Emperor, and the King of* France.

*The*

*The Act of Admission and Accession of the King of Sardinia, &c.*

WHEREAS a certain treaty, and feparate and fecret articles, as likewife four other feparate articles relating thereto, and all of them of the fame force with the principal treaty, have been in due form concluded and fignd, by the Minifters Plenipotentiaries of his Imperial and Catholic Majefty, of his Britannic Majefty, and of his moft Chriftian Majefty, at London the 22d day of July 2d day of Aug. laft paft, between the contracting parties abovementioned, the tenor of all which, word for word, here followeth.

*Here were inferted,*

The treaty.

Separate and fecret articles.

The four feparate articles.

And whereas farther the then King of Sicily, whom it is now agreed to call by the name of King of Sardinia, according to the intention of the treaty and articles above inferted, has been invited to accede fully and amply to all and fingular of them, and to join himfelf in due form to the contracting parties, as if he himfelf from the beginning had been one of the contractors : and whereas the faid King of Sardinia, having maturely weighed the conditions particularly expreffed in the treaty and articles above inferted, has not only declared himfelf willing to accept the fame, and to approve them by 'his acceffion, but has likewife granted fufficient full powers to his minifters appointed to perfect the faid work. That therefore an affair fo beneficial may have the defired fuccefs, we the under-written Minifters Plenipotentiaries of his Imperial and Catholic Majefty, of his Britannic Majefty, and of his moft Chriftian Majefty, in the name and by the authority of their faid Majefties, have admitted, joined and affociate, and by thefe prefents do admit, join, and affociate, the aforefaid King of Sardinia, into a full and total partnerfhip of the treaty above inferted, and of all and fingular the articles thereunto belonging ; promifing by the fame authority that their aforefaid Majefties, jointly and feparately,

ly,

ly, will entirely and exactly perform and fulfil to the said King of Sardinia, all and singular the conditions, cessions, contracts, guarantees, and securities, contained and set forth in the treaty and articles above-mentioned; it being farther provided, that all and singular the things agreed upon by the secret articles against the said King of Sardinia, shall by this his present accession wholly cease, and be abolished. On the other hand also, we the underwritten ministers plenipotentiaries of the King of Sardinia, by virtue of the full power in due form exhibited and allowed, a copy whereof is added at the end of this instrument, do hereby testify and promise in the name of the said King, that our king and master aforesaid doth accede fully and amply to the treaty, and to all and singular the articles therein above inserted. That by this solemn accession he doth join himself, to the contracting parties abovesaid, as if he himself from the beginning had been a party contracting: and that by virtue of this act his said Majesty the King of Sardinia doth mutually oblige and bind himself, both for himself, his heirs and successors, to his Imperial and Catholic Majesty, to his Britannic Majesty, and to his most Christian Majesty, and to their heirs and successors jointly and separately, that he will observe, perform, and fulfil, all and singular the conditions, cessions, contracts, guarantees, and securities, in the abovewritten treaties and articles expressed and set forth, towards all of them jointly, and each of them separately, with the same faith and conscience, as if he had been a contracting party from the beginning, and had made, concluded, and signed, jointly or separately, the same conditions, cessions, contracts, guarantees and securities, with his Imperial and Catholic Majesty, his Britannic Majesty, and his most Christian Majesty.

This instrument of the admission and accession of the said King of Sardinia shall be ratified by all the contracting parties, and the ratifications made out in due form shall be exchanged and mutually delivered at London within the space of two months, or sooner if possible, to be reckoned from the day of the signing

In witness whereof we, the plenipotentiaries of the parties contracting, being on every part furnished with sufficient

cient powers, have figned thefe prefents with our hands, and thereto have put our feals. Namely, the Plenipotentiaries of his Imperial and Catholic Majefty, of his Britannic Majefty, of his Majefty the King of Sardinia, at London the 28th day of Oct. and the Plenipotentiary of his 8th day of Nov. moft Chriftian Majefty at Paris, the      day of November, in the year 1718.

(L. S.) *C. Provana.*
(L. S.) *C. de la Perroufe.*

(L. S.) *Chrif. Penterridter.*  (L. S.) *Parker C.*
    *ab Adelfhaufen.*      (L. S.) *Sunderland P.*
                    (L. S.) *Kent.*
(L. S.) *Jo. Phil. Hoffman.*  (L. S.) *Holles Newcaftle.*
                    (L. S.) *Bolton.*
                    (L. S.) *Roxburghe.*
                    (L. S.) *Stanhope.*
                    (L. S.) *J. Craggs.*

---

*Convention between* Charles VI. *Emperor of the* Romans, *and Catholic King of* Spain, George *King of* Great Britain, *and the* Lords *the* States General *of the* United Provinces, *relating to the execution of certain Articles and Points of the Barrier Treaty, concluded on the* 15th *of* November, 1715. *Signed at the* Hague, *the* 22d *of* December, 1718.

SOME of the articles of the barrier treaty, concluded on the 15th of November, 1715, between his Imperial and Catholic Majefty, his Majefty the King of Great Britain, and the Lords the States General of the United Provinces, being impoffible to be performed, by reafon of certain difficulties that have occurred; and his Majefty the King of Great Britain, and their High Mightineffes, being alike defirous to remove thofe difficulties by the moft agreeable methods, in order to attain to the view propofed by the faid treaty, and the better to eftablifh the foundations of a folid friendfhip and a good underftanding, to which all the parties are inclined, his Imperial and Catholic

lic Majefty, his Majefty the King of Great Britain, and
their High Mightineffes have nominated and appointed to
treat thereof, viz. his Imperial and Catholic Majefty,
the Sieur Hercules Jofeph Lewis Turenetti, Marquis de
Prie & de Pancalier, Count de Mittelevurg & de Caftil-
lon, Lord de St. Servolo & Caftelnovo in Carniola, of Fri-
daw & Rabonftein in Auftria, of Schiurge Belvar & St.
Miclos in Hungary, a Grandee of Spain, Knight of the order of the Annunciadi, Privy Counfellor of his Imperial
and Catholic Majefty, his Minifter Plenipotentiary for the
government of the Netherlands, and his Ambaffador Plenipotentiary, for concluding and figning this prefent treaty,
for the execution of the treaty of the barrier: his Britannic Majefty, William Earl Cadogan, Vifcount Caverfham,
Baron of Reading and Oakley, General of the Foot, Colonel of the 2d regiment of foot guards, Governor of the
Ifle of Wight, Mafter of the Wardrobe, Privy Counfellor,
Knight of the moft noble and moft antient order of St. Andrew, and his Ambaffador Extraordinary and Plenipotentiary to the Lords the States General of the United Provinces: and their High Mightineffes, the Sieurs John van
Wynbergen, Lord of Glinthorft, of the body of the nobles
of the quarter of Veluwe, in the province of Guelderland;
Wigbolt vander Does, Lord of Nortwyck, of the order of
the nobility of Holland and Weft Friefland, High Bailiff
and Dykegrave of Rhynland; Anthony Heinfius, Counfellor
Penfionary, Keeper of the Great Seal, and Superintendant of
the Fiefs of the Province of Holland and Weftfriefland;
Adrian Velters, late Echevin, fenator and penfionary of
the town of Middleburg in Zealand; Gerard Godart Taats
van Amerongen, Canon of the Chapter of St. John at
Utrecht, Affeffor in the Council of Subfidies, conftituting
the Chief Member of the States of the province of Utrecht,
Grand Huntfman of the faid province, and Affeffor in the
Council of the Heemrades of the river of Leck; Dancker
de Kempenaar, Senator of the town of Harlingen, in Friefland; Everard Roufe, Burgomafter of Deventer in Overyffel; and Eger Tamminga, Lord in Zeeryp, Enum,
Leerumus and Zandt, all refpectively Deputies in our Affembly on the part of the States of Guelderland, Holland,
and Weft Friefland, Overyffel and Groningen, and the Ommelands;

melands; who by virtue of their refpective full powers, after having held feveral conferences together, have agreed as follows :

I. Whereas feveral difficulties have arifen with refpect to the 17th article of the faid treaty of Barrier, which relates to the fecurity of the frontiers, and the extending of the limits of their High Mightineffes in Flanders, from whence inconveniencies may arife, which all the parties are defirous to prevent, it is agreed to fubftitute the prefent article in the place of the faid 17th article.

His Imperial and Catholic Majefty agrees and approves, that for the future the boundaries of the States General in Flanders fhall begin at the fea to the N. W. of the fort of St. Paul, now demolifhed, which his Majefty yields to them together with ten rods of land, each rod confifting of 14 feet round the ditch of the counterfcarp, to the weft and fouth fides; and a ftraight line fhall be drawn from the dyke which is to the fouth of the faid fort, marked by the letter A on the map which has been formed and figned by all the parties, through the polder called Hafe-gras, as far as where it joins to the dyke of Crommendyke, marked B, paffing along by a ditch on the weft fide of the faid demolifhed dyke, and from thence to the canal called Neeuwgedhelft marked C, and from thence to the Neeuw-gedhelft Dryhoeck marked C; from whence the new limits fhall run along a watercourfe and ditch, marked E, as far as to the line marked F, which watercourfe and ditch fhall remain to his Majefty. From the letter F they fhall be continued along the faid line beyond the toll-houfe of his Imperial and Catholic Majefty, marked G, in an angle where it fhall enter the dyke again, and run through the little polder level with a ditch as far as the waterfall of the black fluice, and continued on the top of a redoubt or traverfe, which is upon the dyke beyond the two canals of Saute and Soute, marked H, near the fort of St. Do-nat, which his Imperial and Catholic Majefty yields in full fovereignty and propriety to the States General, together with the fovereignty of the land fituate to the north of the line, marked as above ; provided that the gates of the fluices of the faid fort be, and continue taken down in time of peace, and that the proprietors be permitted to fink

the

the threſholds level with that of the black ſluice, and to inſpect them as often as they think neceſſary, to the end that
in time of peace the water may always have a free current
to the ſea.

From the ſaid poſt the new limits ſhall return back
along the foot of the dyke, towards the polder, called the
World's End, and from thence along the ſea dyke, as it is
ſet down in the map, as far as the antient boundaries, to
the cut in the dyke, which cloſes the creek of Lapſchure,
marked I; and the land on the north ſide of the line ſhall
belong to their High Mightineſſes in ſovereignty.

From thence the old limits ſhall be continued as far as
the Barbara polder, at which place the new limits ſhall
enter and begin at the foot of the dyke running along
that polder, and the Lauraine polder, to the long ſtreet
marked K; and from thence in a ſtraight line along the ſaid
ſtreet to the dyke which goes from Bouckhoute, to the
harbour of Bouckhoute, marked L; and from thence
they ſhall enter into the Chapel polder, and continue in
a ſtraight line to an angle of the Grafjanſdyke, marked
M; and from thence along the dyke as far as the Red
polder.

His Imperial and Catholic Majeſty yields to their High
Mightineſſes in full ſovereignty the Barbary polder, Lauraine polder, Chapel polder, and the Red polder, except
what is reſerved by the line above drawn in the Chapel
and the Lauraine polders, which ſhall remain to his Imperial and Catholic Majeſty.

Their High Mightineſſes permit the owners of the
ſluices of Bouckhoute to replace them where they were
before, and that the ſaid ſluices may have their currents
directly to the ſea, as they had before the late war.

Their High Mightineſſes ſhall be permitted in time of
war, when it is neceſſary for the defence and ſecurity of
their frontiers, to occupy and fortify the neceſſary poſts in
the Grafjanſdyke and Zydlingſdyke.

As to the towns of Sas van Ghent, the limits ſhall be extended to the diſtance of two-thirds of two geometrical
miles round the town, beginning at the angles of the baſ-
tions, which ſhall terminate on the ſide towards Zelfate,

at

at the point of the antient limits on the bank of the canal of the Sas.

And for the preservation of the lower Schelde, and for the sake of the communication between Dutch Brabant and Flanders, his Imperial and Catholic Majesty gives up to the States General the full and entire sovereignty of the village and polder of Doel, as also of the polders of St. Anne and Keteniffe; provided nevertheless that the territory of their High Mightineffes shall not extend between the forts of the Pearl and Liefkenshoeck, farther than the midway between the two forts.

His Imperial and Catholic Majesty, as soon as the barrier shall be attacked, or a war begun, shall deliver up the guard of fort Pearl to their High Mightineffes; on condition nevertheless, that as soon as such war is at an end, they shall restore the said fort Pearl to his Imperial and Catholic Majesty, together with the posts they shall have in that time taken posseffion of, on the Grafjanfdyke and Zydlingfdyke.

Their High Mightineffes promise moreover, that if upon occasion of giving up to them some sluices, (whereof the inhabitants of the Austrian Flanders shall retain the free use in time of peace) they should suffer any damage or prejudice, either from the commanders or other military officers, the States General will not only remedy it immediately, but likewise make satisfaction to those concerned.

And because, from this new situation of the limits, there will be a neceffity of changing the toll-houfes to prevent frauds, wherein his Imperial and Catholic Majesty and their High Mightineffes are eqaally interested; other places for establishing the said toll-houfes shall be agreed on, as well as the farther precautions that it shall be thought convenient to take.

It shall moreover be stipulated, that a just valuation shall be made, in three months time, of the revenues which the sovereign receives from the lands that shall be yielded up to their High Mightineffes by this article; as also what have arifen to the sovereign by the renewing of the grants on the foot they have been agreed to for thirty years past, to be deducted and struck off from the annual subfidy of 500,000 crowns; but the payment of the said subfidy shall not be retarded

tarded by reafon of the faid valuation, which lands fhall not be charged with any taxes more than what they now contribute in the public affeffments, according to the rate they are valued at.

The Roman Catholic religion fhall be preferved and maintained in the places abovementioned, in the fame manner and with the fame freedom of public exercife as now; and to the fame extent as this freedom was ftipulated by the 18th article of the barrier treaty.

The proprietors of the lands and other eftates fituate within the limits of the faid ceffion, fhall retain the enjoyment of the fame, in full poffeffion and propriety, with all the prerogatives and rights thereunto annexed, none referved nor excepted; and fhall moreover be continued particular lords of the faid lands and eftates, and maintained in the peaceful propriety and poffeffion of the jurifdictions appertaining to them, in all the degrees of high, mean, and low jurifdiction as they have enjoyed the fame hitherto.

The fort of Rodenhuyfen fhall be demolifhed, and the difputes touching the canal of Bruges fhall be referred to the decifion of neutral arbitrators, to be chofen on both fides; provided neverthelefs, that by giving up of the fort of St. Donat, thofe of the town of Sluys fhall not have more right upon that canal than they had before this ceffion.

In confequence of the ceffions included in this article, their High Mightineffes defift their pretentions to all other lands and places which were yielded to them by the 17th article of the barrier treaty, which fhall remain as they did before under the dominion of his Imperial and Catholic Majefty.

II. Whereas his Imperial and Catholic Majefty promifed by the 19th article of the barrier treaty, to caufe to be paid to the States General the Sum of 500,000 crowns a year, amounting to 1,250,000 florins of Holland, at the terms fpecified by the faid treaty, in confideration of the great charges and extraordinary expences to which the Lords the States General are indifpenfably obliged as well for maintaining the great number of troops which they are obliged by the faid treaty to keep in the towns and places of the faid barrier, as for fupporting the great charge abfolutely neceffary for the maintenance and reparation of
the

the fortification of the said places, and for supplying them with ammunition and provisions.

And his Majesty desires that his promise may be punctually executed according to the tenor of the said 19th article, having for that end shewn their High Mightinesses the difficulties and inconveniences that might arise in the performance of the said article, as also of the separate article of the said treaty, with regard to the assignment made upon the subsidies of the province of Brabant and Flanders, and the quarters, districts and chatellanies therein mentioned, for the sum of 640,000 florins of Holland.

His Imperial and Catholic Majesty and the Lords the States General have agreed upon another reparation, and upon another special mortgage, which shall be substituted in the place of the said mortgages and assignments, upon the subsidies of the provinces of Brabant and Flanders, over and above the general mortgage upon all the revenues of the Austrian Netherlands stipulated by the said treaty.

Namely, that his Imperial and Catholic Majesty, for the better securing and facilitating the payment of the said subsidy of 500,000 crowns, or 1,250,00 florins Dutch money per annum, assigns a sum of 100,000 florins, or 290,000 crowns, in lieu of the sum of 610,000 florins assessed upon the countries, cities, chatellanies, and dependencies, made over again by France, the revenues of which consists in the aids and subsidies payable by the said towns and chatellanies, in the duties of the four members of Flanders, and other duties of domains, in that called the four Patars par Bonnier, and other taxes for the fortifications, the ransom of those called *Contines Militaries*, and in the emoluments and other gratuities, which were paid at the time that the said towns and chatellanies were in the power of France, to the intendants, governors, and other officers on the establishment in the places: and that he does this for all the duties and imposts in general, which their High Mightinesses have enjoyed hitherto in the whole or in part, without any exception whatsoever.

On condition that no diminution or alteration be made in them to the prejudice of the said Mortgage.

The

The awarding of the farm of the faid duties of the four members of Flanders fhall be made in public to the higheſt bidders; provided neverthelefs, that in cafe of infolvency of the farmers and their fecurities, his Imperial and Catholic Majeſty ſhall make good the deficiency out of the other branches and revenues of the towns and chatellanies abovementioned, or out of his demefnes in the other Auſtrian Netherlands, as far as amounts to the fum of 700,000 florins a year.

And when any abatement is folicited, by which the revenues of the faid farm, or of the aids and other duties and impoſts above fpecified, may not be fufficient to produce the entire fum of 700,000 florins, it fhall not be granted till provifion be made for the faid abatement, in fome other fufficient way to their fatisfaction.

His Imperial and Catholic Majeſty affigns and makes over the remaining 550,000 florins of Holland, or 220,000 crowns upon all the revenues of the tolls abovementioned, arifing from the duties of importation and exportation paid in the Auſtrian Netherlands, which are only engaged by way of fubfidy to their High Mightineffes for their levies of Money on feveral occafions, or for annuities in the country, and the like certain charges.

Namely, the toll-houfes of Bruffels, Burgherout, Tirlement, Charleroy, Mons, Aeth, Beaumont, Courtray, Ypres, Tournay, Newport, of the province of Luxemburg, and that of Mechlin, fhall generally and feverally be mortgaged for the faid fum of 550,000 florins.

And for the better fecurity and payment of the faid fum his Majeſty engages, by the way of a fubfidiary and fupplemental fund, the fum of 250,000 Dutch florins per annum, out of the firſt and cleareſt revenue from the duties of import and export of Ghent, Bruges, and Oſtend; promifing that they fhall be entirely paid in five years, out of what remains in arrear of the principal and intereſt of 1,040,600 florins, which were raifed upon thofe three toll-houfes in 1710.

His Majeſty likewife promifes that no alteration fhall be made in the duties of import and export, which may
leffen

leſſen the revenue thereof to the prejudice of the mort-gage.

And if his Majeſty in proceſs of time judges it neceſſary to make any alteration in the levy of the ſaid duties, by which they may happen to be diminiſhed, ſuch alteration ſhall not be eſtabliſhed till a ſufficient fund is appropriated to make good ſuch deficiency.

His Imperial and Catholic Majeſty doth by this convention command the receiver general of his Majeſty's finances, and him that ſhall be eſtabliſhed to preſide in chief in the countries made over again, that by virtue of theſe preſents, and according to a copy hereof, they pay every three months, computing from the firſt of this inſtant December, 1718, to the receiver general of the States General in thoſe countries that are made over again, in ſuch coin, or ſuch money as is received at the toll-houſes and at his Majeſty's general receiving office, an exact quarter part of the ſum of 280,000 crowns, or 700,000 Dutch florins; and to the receiver general of his majeſty's finances in the city of Antwerp, to pay alſo an exact fourth part of the remaining ſum of 550,000 florins, or 220,000 crowns, without ſtaying for any other order or aſſignment; theſe preſents being to ſerve inſtead of an order or aſſignment, both now and hereafter, the ſaid payments ſhall be allowed them in their account with his Imperial and Catholic Majeſty, as much as if they had made them to himſelf.

As for the arrears of the ſaid ſubſidy of 500,000 crowns, or 1,250,000 florins of Holland per annum, to have accrued from the 15th of November 1715, the day on which the barrier treaty was ſigned, on the laſt day of November laſt, it is agreed, for avoiding all manner of diſpute touching the produce in that time, of the revenues of the towns and chatellanies made over again by France, which have not amounted to above 300,000 crowns per annum, all charges deducted, as their High Migtineſſes have ſhewn by eſtimates thereof, which they have cauſed to be drawn up and communicated, and which have been examined by one of the commiſſioners of his Imperial and Catholic Majeſty's finances, and alſo for putting an end to the diſputes that have ariſen on account of the non-performance

of

of certain articles of the said treaty, with regard to the pay of the said arrears of the 15th of November 1715, to the first of January, 1718, which on the part of the States are cast up at above 400,000 crowns; their High Mightinesses will be content to take for all these arrears, from the 15th of November 1715, to the said first of January 1718, 200,000 crowns, or 500,000 florins of Holland, payable by 20,000 crowns a year, till the sum total is discharged; provided that the entire subsidy be paid to them from the beginning of the present year, in manner following.

Namely, that the arrears of the first eight months of the present year, amounting to the sum of 333,333 florins, six sous, eight deniers of Holland money shall be paid in the same manner by 20,000 crowns a year in part of payment, as is aforesaid, immediately after the payment of the said arrears of the preceding years.

For securing the payment of both the one and the other, his Imperial and Catholic Majesty engages, and makes over by way of special mortgage, the duties of import and export of the toll houses of Ghent, Bruges, and Ostend, over and above, and without prejudice to the subsidiary engagement of the said toll-houses for the sum of 250,000 Dutch florins a year, stipulated by the present convention.

For the greater security whereof, the administrators general of the duties of import and export, shall, by the bond which they give for the yearly payment of 550,000 Dutch florins, during the six years of their administration, charge themselves with the payment of the six first portions or terms of the said arrears; and after the expiration of the term of their contract, or receipt, the rest shall be paid by quarter parts by the new administrators, or by those who shall then have the regio and receipt of the said duties at Ghent, Bruges, and Ostend, after the manner and under the engagements stipulated for securing the payment of the 550,000 florins.

The surplus, or the three months remaining of the arrears of the present year, amounting to the sum of 125,000 Dutch florins shall be paid in 1720; his Imperial and Catholic Majesty particularly appropriating for the payment
thereof,

thereof, the revenue of the towns and chatellanies made over again by France, over and above, and without prejudice to the appropriation of the 700,000 florins a year, made by this convention.

Their High Mightineffes fhall enjoy the revenues of the countries made over again to the laft day of laft November, and fhall be at liberty to proceed by way of execution for the recovery of the arrears of the revenues of the faid towns and chatellanies, that are and may become due to the laft day of laft November; and for this purpofe to make ufe of the fame methods of execution againft the States (the ecclefiaftics excepted) magiftrates, towns and chatellanies, farmers and others as they have ftipulated for the recovery of the 700,000 florins a year, affigned upon the faid revenues, and may alfo make ufe of the fame method with regard to the 125,000 florins which are made over to them, conformably to the foregoing article.

And whereas his faid Majefty has put his duties of import and export into adminiftration and direction, and bound the adminiftrators general or directors of the faid duties, to pay a fixed fum yearly for the improvement of his Majefty's finances; the adminiftrators general or directors of the faid duties, fhall enter into an obligation, under a voluntary condemnation, which fhall be decreed by the grand council of Mechlin, and by thofe of Brabant and Flanders, to pay every three months during the time of their adminiftration the faid fourth part of the fum of 550,000 florins of Holland, to the receiver general of the United Provinces or his order, as is faid : and the prefent article fhall fuffice for the difcharge of the faid adminiftrators or directors, with the acquittance of the faid receiver general of the United Provinces.

The faid adminiftrators general, or directors, fhall oblige themfelves by the fame act, to pay off, by equal payments in five years, what remains to be paid to the States General of the faid 1,040,625 florins, raifed in 1710 upon the toll-houfes of Ghent, Bruges, and Oftend, with the interefts that fhall accrue every year ; to the end, that when the five years are expired, the faid toll-houfes may be entirely difcharged from the faid levy.

And

And on the failure of the payment, after the manner above stipulated, as well of the sums of the subsidy of 500,000 crowns, or 1,250,000 Dutch florins, as of the said money raised upon the toll-houses, the Lords the States General may proceed to methods of compulsion and execution even by way of violence against the receiver general of his Majesty's finances, and against the receiver of the countries yielded back again, who shall be both responsible and liable to an execution, for the particular and subaltern receivers of the funds assigned to their respective provinces; if either the receivers general, or the others divert any part of their general or particular receipt to the prejudice of what is contained in the present convention: provided however, that this article shall not take place against the receiver general of the finances, but in case of the management of the duties of import and export.

His Majesty grants the same power to bring an execution, as well against the toll-houses, engaged previously by special mortgage, as against the toll-houses engaged subsidiarily on failure of the former, and against the funds of the said country made over again, as also against the States except the ecclesiastics, and against the magistrates of the towns and chatellanies of the said country, yielded back again, if they make any scruple or too long delays in assessing and furnishing the imposts, which they are obliged to raise for his Imperial and Catholic Majesty.

And this execution against the said States, excepting the clergy, and against the said magistrates, shall be made in the name, and on the part of his Majesty, and in the usual manner; his Majesty for this end authorising the governors of the barrier towns who have taken an oath to him, and subjecting the said States thereto, (except the clergy) and the said magistrates, by virtue of the present convention, as well as the said funds, as those were subjected to it which were specially mortgaged and assigned for the respective sums of the said subsidy by the 19th article, and the separate article of the barrier treaty.

The officers of justice, to whom it shall appertain shall be obliged to give the necessary assistance of their office, when those who bring the writs that shall be ordered and issued in favour of their High Mightinesses, against the

admi-

adminiftrators of his Majefty's duties of import and export, as well as againft their affociates, fhall have recourfe to them, in order to proceed to the execution of the faid writs, according to the received ufage of the tribunals from whence they are difpatched; in the fame manner as they are ufed to execute the fentences which the natives and other inhabitants of the Auftrian Netherlands obtain there. And as to the States of the Netherlands yielded back again, (the ecclefiaftics excepted) magiftrates, toll-houfes and funds, execution may be iffued againft them in the manner as is agreed by the barrier treaty.

And finally, befides the order which fhall be given by his Majefty to the governor general of the Auftrian Netherlands, the prefent convention fhall ferve inftead of a fpecial and irrevocable order and inftruction, for him and his future fucceffors, in purfuance of which they fhall perform and caufe to be performed what is ftipulated by the prefent convention; and are exprefsly forbid not to divert, or fuffer to be diverted by the council of ftate and the finances, by the director general of the finances, or by any other perfon whatfoever, any fum of the revenues abovementioned of the faid towns and chatellanies, nor of the faid adminiftration, management and receipt of the duties of import and export, for any occafion whatfoever, though never fo material and urgent, unlefs of what fhall remain after the payment of the faid quarters; which payment fhall not be retarded, much lefs refufed under colour of compenfations, liquidations, or other pretences of what name or nature foever they be: in confequence of which, their High Mightineffes the States General renounce, and entirely give up, by virtue of the prefent convention, every action and mortgage which had been ftipulated by the 19th article of the barrier treaty, and its feparate article, againft the provinces of Brabant and Flanders, their jurifdictions, chatellanies, the feven quarters of Antwerp, and againft the States and receivers of the provinces.

III. The arrears due of the intereft of the fums raifed upon the revenue of the pofts in the Auftrian Netherlands being very confiderable, his Imperial and Catholic Majefty promifes and engages to remedy it, by caufing

entire

entire payment to be made both of the interest and principal as soon as possible; and till this is performed, his Imperial and Catholic Majesty will give very strict orders that the revenue of the posts may be employed conformably to the bonds, and that no part of it be diverted to the prejudice of their contents.

IV. The Lords the States General having made considerable advances towards paying off the interest of the monies levied, as specified in the barrier treaty, it has been agreed and concluded, that the sum of 705,011 florins, 18 sous and 10 deniers, which his Chtholic Majesty owes to their High Mightinesses, according to the liquidation settled on this day the 22d of December 1718, shall be paid off by equal portions of 20,000 crowns or 50,000 Dutch florins a year, to commence immediately after the six years of the present general administration of the duties of import and export; his Imperial and Catholic Majesty engaging the said duties in Flanders as they are now raised, and as they shall continue to be raised after the end of the said general administration, for paying off the said sum of 705,011 florins, 18 sous and 18 deniers, by way of special mortgage: and till the same is effectually paid off, he shall cause interest to be paid for the said sum, or that part of it which shall remain unpaid, at the rate of two and a half per cent. per annum.

In order to facilitate the payment of the said interest of two and a half per cent. per annum, their High Mightinesses consent that it be compared by the double canon of 800,000 florins per annum, raised upon the revenues of the province of Namur, and subsidiarily upon those of the mayoralty and province of Luxemburgh; on condition that the said double canon be continued proportionably to the time that the reimbursement of the said 800,000 florins shall be retarded by the said diminution.

V. To put an end to the differences touching the artillery and the magazines of war, and particularly concerning the propriety of those of Venlo, St. Michael and Stevenswaert, places yielded to the States General by the treaty of barrier, his Imperial and Catholic Majesty gives up all claim to the said artillery and magazines, on condition that their High Mightinesses recede, as they do

by

by the prefent convention, from the demand of the money
due to them, in purfuance of the act paffed at Antwerp
the 30th of January 1716, by the Count de Konigfegg,
Plenipotentiary of his Imperial and Catholic Majefty took
for the powder, ball, and other ammunition which the
commiffioners of his Imperial and Catholic Majefty
took for his accompt, agreeable to the faid act, and to
lifts figned by the faid commiffioners, which amount in
value to above 100,000 florins: but his Imperial and Catholic Majefty makes no claim on account of the powder
and ammunition belonging to France, which was found
at the reduction of Antwerp, Mechlin, Ghent, and other
places of the Auftrian Netherlands.

VI. The States General immediately after the exchange
of the ratifications of the prefent convention, fhall remit
to his Imperial and Catholic Majefty the poffeffion and
enjoyment of all the towns, chatellanies, diftricts and jurifdictions made over again by France, according to the
tenor of the firft article of the barrier treaty. And his
Imperial and Catholic Majefty fhall likewife remit to
their High Mightineffes, immediately after the exchange
of the faid ratifications, the poffeffion of the land and polders which he has yielded to them in Flanders by the firft
article of this convention.

VII. The barrier treaty, and its feparate article of the
15th of November 1715, fhall be confirmed by thefe prefents, in all and every of its articles.

VIII. Forafmuch as for the greater fecurity and better
performance of the barrier treaty, his Britannic Majefty
has confirmed and guarantied the faid treaty, fo his faid
Majefty doth promife and engage to confirm and guarantee the prefent convention, as he doth confirm and
guarantee it by this article.

IX. The prefent treaty fhall be ratified and approved
by his Imperial and Catholic Majefty, by his Britannic
Majefty, and by the Lords the States General of the
United Provinces, and the ratifications fhall be exchanged
in fix weeks, or fooner if poffible, after the day of its
being figned.

In witnefs whereof, we the Ambaffadors and Plenipotentiaries of his Imperial and Catholic Majefty, and of
his

his Britannic Majefty, and the Deputies and Plenipotentiaries of the Lords the States General, by virtue of our
refpective powers, have in their names figned thefe prefents,
and thereto fet the feals of our arms. Done at the Hague,
the 22d of December, 1718.

(L. S.) The M. *de Prie.*
(L. S.) *Cadogan.*
(L. S.) *J. B. v. Wynbergen.*
(L. S.) *W. Vandor Does.*
(L. S.) *A. Heinfius*
(L. S.) *G. G. Taets van Amerongen.*
(L. S.) *D. D. Kempenaer.*
(L. S.) *Everard Roufe.*
(L. S.) *E. Tamminga.*

---

*Treaty of Peace between* George *King of* Great Britain, *as
Elector and Duke of* Brunfwick, *and* Ulrica Eleonora,
*Queen of* Sweden; *by which, in Purfuance of the Pre-
liminary Treaty, concluded* July $\frac{11}{22}$ 1719, *the Duchies of*
Bremen *and* Verden *are yielded to the faid King as
Elector and Duke of* Brunfwick, *with the fame Prero-
gatives and Titles as the Crown of* Sweden *poffeffed them,
by the Peace of* Weftphalia.

## PARTICULARLY,

*Including therein, the Right of Voice and Seffion in the
Diets of the Empire and Directorfhip of the Circle of*
Lower Saxony, *and the Rights to the Cathedral Chapter of* Hamburg, *and that of* Bremen; *as alfo the Propriety of the Town of* Wilfhaufen, *with its Bailywick
held heretofore by the Duke of* Brunfwick *as a Pledge.
In Exchange whereof, the King, Elector, and Duke pro-
mifeth her* Swedifh *Majefty, to caufe a Million of Crowns
in Money of* Leipfick, *to be paid to her at three Terms,
to maintain the Subjects and Inhabitants in all their
Rights, Liberties, and Privileges, as well with Regard to
Religion, as in other Refpects, and to procure favourable
Juftice to be done according to the Promifes of the late*
King

*King* Charles XII. *to those who shall appear to have been aggrieved in the great and general Reduction, which was made heretofore. The King also promiseth, strictly to maintain all former Treaties made with the Crown of the House of* Holstein, Gottorp, *and likewise to renew them at this Time, in Conformity to the present Union.* Concluded *at* Stockholm, *the $\frac{9}{20}$th of* November 1719.

### In the Name of the Holy Trinity.

BE it known by these presents: whereas the troubles of the North, which began without the holy Roman empire, did likewise in course of time infest some of the provinces depending on the said empire, and afterwards penetrated as far as the circle of Lower Saxony, which was the reason that the most illustrious and most potent Prince and Lord, George King of Great Britain, France, and Ireland, Defender of the Faith, Duke of Brunswick and Lunenburgh, Arch-treasurer and Elector of the holy Roman Empire, as Duke and Elector of Brunswick and Lunenburgh, was involved in the war; the most illustrious and most potent Princess Ulrica Eleonora, Queen of Sweden, the Goths and Vandals, Great Duchess of Finland, Duchess of Schonen, Esthonia, Livonia, Carelia, Bremen, Verden, Stetin, Pomerania, Cassubia, and Vadalina, Princess of Rugen, Lady of Ingria and Wismar, Countess Palatine of the Rhine and Bavaria, Duchess of Juliers, Cleves, and Berg, Landgravine and Hereditary Princess of Hesse, Princess of Hirchsfeld, Countess of Catzenellebogen, Dietz, Ziegenhain, Nidda, and Schaumbourg, &c. and his said Britannic Majesty have with a Christian and laudable intention, considered by what measures they might not only prevent greater misfortunes, and the ruin of countries and nations being occasioned by such a war, but chiefly to restore peace and tranquillity between their said Majesties, and to establish and renew the good harmony and mutual understanding between the two parties. For this end the most illustrious and most potent prince and Lord Lewis XV. the most Christian King of France and Navarre, employed his good offices and mediation by the noble Lord James

de

de Campredon, his minifter refiding at the Swedifh court; and a preliminary treaty of peace was actually agreed on betwen their faid Majeftis, which was concluded at Stockholm the $\frac{11}{22}$ of July laft, in which was ftipulated that peace fhould be formally concluded betwixt them on the foot of the faid treaty, and that a folemn inftrument fhould be drawn up for that purpofe, for the advancing and perfecting a work fo defirable and falutary, the plenipotentiary minifters on both fides being vefted with fufficient full powers, have, in the name of God, entered into a conferrence, viz. on the part of her Swedifh majefty, the Count Guftavus Cronhielm, fenator of her majefty and the kingdom, prefident of the royal chancery, and chancellor of the academy at Upfal; the Count Charles Guftavus Ducker, fenator of her majefty and the kingdom, velt marfhal and counfellor of war; the Count Guftavus Adam Taube, fenator of her majefty and the kingdom, and governor of Stockholm; the Count Magnus de la Gardie, fenator of her majefty and the kingdom, and prefident of the college of commerce; and the Baron Daniel Nicholas de Hopken, fecretary of ftate to her Swedifh Majefty; and on the part of his Baitannick Majefty, as duke and elector of Brunfwick and Lunenburgh, his plenipotentiary, minifter and colonel, Adolphus Frederick de Baffewitz; who have agreed to the following articles:

I. A lafting and fincere peace and friendfhip fhall be eftablifhed and confirmed by thefe prefents between his Swedifh Majefty and the kingdom of Sweden on the one part, and his Britannick Majefty as duke and elector of Brunfwick Lunenburgh, and his ducal and electoral houfe on the other part, both fhall fincerely and conftantly do every thing in their power for ftrengthening the bands of union and confidence between them as much as poffible; and all hoftilities and warlike proceedings of the one part againft the other fhall entirely ceafe from this time.

II. There fhall alfo be on both fides a perpetual oblivion and amnefty of whatever the one has committed hoftilely againft the other, of what nature foever the action was, in fuch manner that nothing done by either party, or by their fubjects, fhall be corrects or revenged, but every

thing

thing fhall by thefe prefents be abolifhed, and for ever buried in oblivion.

III. As to her Swedifh Majefty, by virtue of the preliminary treaty of peace concluded July $\frac{11}{22}$ 1719, with his Britannick Majefty, as duke and elector of Brunfwick and Lunenburg, did then yield, fo fhe does by virtue of thefe prefents again yield for herfelf, the kingdom of Sweden, and her fucceffors and defcendants, to his Britaenick Majefty, as duke and elector of Brunfwick and Lunenburgh, and his fucceffors for ever, the duchies of Bremen and Verden, pleno jure, with all their rights and dependencies, in the fame manner as thofe duchies were among others appropriated, according to the Xth article of the treaty of peace at Ofnaburgh, dated the $\frac{14}{24}$ October 1648, and as the kings and kingdom of Sweden have fince that time poffeffed, do now poffefs, or ought to have poffeffed the faid duchies, with their rights, appendages and appurtenances, without any exception ; and principally the jus pignoris of the bailywick and town of Vilfhaufen, with all its rights and dependencies, which was formerly in the hands of the elector of Brunfwick ; in fuch manner, however, that no demand fhall be formed upon her majefty or the kingdom of Sweden for any engagements with which the fame are, or may be incumbered, either now or hereafter : giving up the whole together, and every particular thereof now and for ever, with the fame prerogatives as her Swedifh Majefty and her predeceffors in the government, as well as the kingdom of Sweden, had poffeffed them, without any diminution or refervation ; as alfo without exception of any rights inteftine or foreign, to keep and poffefs them in propriety, without any difpute, hindrance or interruption on the part of her Swedifh Majefty, or her fucceffors; yielding up, and renouncing by thefe prefents in favour of his faid Britannick Majefty, as duke and elector of Brunfwick and Lunenburg, and his heirs for ever, all the rights fhe hath, or ever had, or ought either one way or another to claim, to the duchies of Bremen and Verden in general and particular, both as to the directorfhip in the circle of Lower Saxony, a feffion and vote in the diets of the empire and the circles, or any thing elfe, by what name foever called, refigning in the fame

fame manner by thefe prefents, to the fubjects and inhabitants of the faid duchies, all their oaths and obligations by which they were bound to her majefty and the kingdom of Sweden, and transferring them by the fame to his majefty of Great Britain, as duke and elector of Brunfwick and Lunenburg, and to his heirs, as their prefent fole and perpetual fovereign lord; and in like manner the chapter of Hamburgh and that of Bremen, together with the perfons appertaining to the latter, fubjects, tenants in fief, farmers and tributaries, as well in the town of Bremen, as thofe who live in what are called the four Gohen of Bremen, and all other places which are there, fhall be by virtue of thefe prefents freed from their faid oaths and engagements taken to the crown and kingdom of Sweden, and made over to his Britannick Majefty, as duke and elector of Brunfwick and Lunenburg, and his heirs.

Her Swedifh Majefty, for herfelf and her Succeffors, does by virtue of thefe prefents, again renounce the jura feudi which fhe and her predeceffors had, on account of the duchies of Bremen and Verden, acquired of the emperors and the holy empire, and hitherto enjoyed; and transfers the faid jura feudi in like manner to his Britannick Majefty and his heirs.

And the archives and documents which relate to the duchies of Bremen and Verden, fhall bona fide, with all the fpeed poffible, be put into the hands of perfons named and authorifed by his Britannick Majefty, to receive them.

IV. His Britannick Majefty, as duke and elector of Brunfwick and Lunenburgh, does as well for himfelf as his heirs, promife and engage on his part to the ftates, fubjects, and all the inhabitants of the country, both in the towns of the faid duchies of Bremen and Verden, and all places that do or may depend thereon, no perfon excepted, and confequently to every one of them, to maintain and defend their juftly acquired liberties, eftates, rights and privileges, in general and particular, in the fame manner as the faid ftates, fubjects and inhabitants enjoyed and poffeffed them, and as they were granted to them by the peace of Weftphalia, as well as the free exercife of the two religions, according to the Augfburg confeffions, as to which
they

they fhall at all times be left to thiir free choice, without moleftation.

And in cafe that either the one or the other is not yet actually confirmed in the expectatives of certain prebends of the chapter of Hamburg, granted by the former kings of Sweden, or bought of others, fuch expectatives, according to their rights and origin, fhall remain entire ; in fuch manner neverthelefs, that for the future when a vacancy happens, no body fhall be preferred to thofe who are the bearers of them.

V. The reduction and liquidation eftablifhed every where by the preceding government of Sweden, having given occafion to many grievances of the fubjects and inhabitants, the late king of Sweden, of glorious memory, in juftice to the caufe was determined to give a fecurity by letters patent, that in cafe any of the fubjects could prove, that any eftate juftly belonging to them had been taken from them, their right fhould be preferved ; in confequence of which feveral were reftored to the poffeffion of their eftates formerly difputed, or fequeftered by virtue of the faid reduction, or any other pretext ; which right has been again confirmed to them fince by their laft affembly of the 30th of May laft.

It is therefore agreed and ftipulated by thefe prefents, between the two contracting fovereigns, that the ceffion made of the duchies of Bremen and Verden by the aforefaid third article of the faid treaty, fhall not prejudice the rights and juft pretenfions of the fubjects and inhabitants of the faid duchies, or their heirs, living intra vel extra territorium ; but the fame fhall be maintained by his Britanick Majefty, as elector of Brunfwick and Lunenburg, to all intents and purpofes in the fame manner as they are now by her Swedifh Majefty, and as they may be certified now or hereafter.

VI. In like manner, purfuant to what is ftipulated by the fecond article concerning the amnefty, the eftates, houfes and properties of any perfon whatfoever, who had been put under arreft by reafon of the war, fhall be reftored and returned to the lawful proprietors, whether they live intra vel extra territorium.

VII.

VII. Neverthelefs, all negociations actually made in the faid duchies, and during the Swedifh regency, publico nomine, till the faid duchies were invaded by his Danifh Majefty, by reafon of the debts and farms which were levied and carried into the royal cheft, and the Sums put into it by the faid regency, fhall remain in full force, in fuch manner that the creditors, and thofe who have legal bonds in confequence of their loans of money, and mortgages truly furrendered, fhall enjoy the contracts which they have in their hands, and the engagements included therein, till by virtue of their contracts they are quite expired, and their monies advanced are all paid; at which time the eftates, and houfes fituate or belonging in and to the faid duchies, fo engaged to the faid creditors fhall become the property of his Britannick Majefty, as duke and elector of Brunfwick and Lunenburg and his fucceffors, and fhall be incorporated in his chamber. But the ftates fhall be obliged to pay every thing negociated upon the bonds and fecurity of the faid ftates.

VIII. His Britannick Majefty promifeth by thefe prefents, not only as king, but alfo as duke and elector of Brunfwick and Lunenburg, to renew from henceforth with her Majefty, and the kingdom of Sweden, the ftrict alliances and treaties of friendfhip heretofore eftablifhed with the predeceffors of her majefty and the kingdom of Sweden, as well as the guarantees, which by virtue of the treaty of peace concluded between the allies of the North, or by that which may be concluded hereafter, fhall be applied to the advantage of the ducal houfe of Holftein Gottorp, and to regulate the fame according to the prefent juncture of affairs.

Moreover his Britannick Majefty, as duke and elector of Brunfwich, engages to pay at Hamburgh to her Swedifh Majefty the fum of a million of rix dollars, in new and valid pieces of fingle and double marks or drittels, according to the allay of Leipfic in the year 1690, of which each fine mark of filver was worth twelve current dollars. And it is fettled, that one-third of the faid fum, viz. $333,333\frac{1}{3}$ rix dollars fhall be paid at Hamburgh to her Swedifh Majefty upon her receipts, before the figning of this inftrument of peace, which fhall accordingly remain

in

in force; and the reſt of the ſaid million of rix dollars ſhall be paid ſpeedily, and without fail at Hamburgh all at once, upon proper aſſignments and acquittances, in five or ſix weeks time after the exchange of the ratification of this treaty of peace.

IX. The treaty of Weſtphalia, except where it is altered by this treaty, or otherwiſe where it may be altered by treaties that may be concluded in the North, ſhall remain in its full force and efficacy; and the two contracting ſovereigns engage themſelves ſeverally to do every thing that ſhall be judged neceſſary for the obſervation of the ſaid treaty of Weſtphalia.

X. The two contracting ſovereigns reſerve to themſelves by this article to demand and accept his Imperial Majeſty's guarantee for this treaty, and that of other powers, according to the circumſtance of affairs.

XI. The ratifications of this peace ſhall be diſpatched in two months time at fartheſt, and exchanged one with the other here at Stockholm.

XII. In witneſs of the above, two copies, both of one and the ſame tenor, have been made, which have been ſigned and ſealed by the·plenipotentiaries of the two contracting ſovereigns, of which one has been given to each party. Done at Stockholm, the 20th of November, 1719.

*Signed,*

(L. S.) *Guſtavus Chronhielm.*
(L. S.) *Charles Guſtavus Ducker.*
(L. S.) *Guſtavus Adam Taube.*
(L. S.) *M. de la Garde.*
(L. S.) *D. N. van Hopken.*
(L. S.) *Adolphus Frederick van Baſſewitz.*

*Treaty between* Ulrica Eleonora, *Queen of* Sweden; *and* George *King of* Great Britain, *for* 18 *years, concluded by the mediation of the moſt Chriſtian King; by which the parties agree to aſſiſt one another mutually, in every caſe of neceſſity, on the baſis of former treaties, which are hereby reaſſumed. And the King promiſes the Queen to aſſiſt her as ſoon as poſſible with ſubſidies and ſoldiers, in the preſent war againſt the Czar of* Muſcovy, *and to continue ſuch aſſiſtance till a peace is reſtored. And the Queen binds her-ſelf and her kingdoms to the perpetual guarantee of the ſucceſſion of the crown of* Great Britain *in the family of* Brunſwick Lunenburg. *Made the* 21ſt *of* January, 1720.

W HEREAS the moſt ſerene and moſt potent Princeſs and Lady, Ulrica Eleonora, Queen of the Swedes, Goths, Vandals, &c. &c. &c. and the moſt ſerene and moſt potent Prince and Lord, George King of Great Britain, France and Ireland, Defender of the Faith, Duke of Brunſwick and Lunenburg, Arch-treaſurer and Elector of the Holy Roman Empire, for the better aſſerting and confirming an intimate friendſhip and cloſe union, and for increaſing and promoting the welfare and ſecurity of the ſaid ſovereigns, and their kingdoms and ſubjects, thought it expedient that the former treaties made between the famous kingdoms of Sweden and Great Britain, and between the former ſovereigns of the ſaid kingdoms, ſhould now be reaſſumed, amended, renewed and accommodated, and applied to the preſent ſtate of affairs by the mediation, and under the guarrantee of his ſacred royal majeſty of France, who for that end was pleaſed to appoint and inſtruct his reſident M. de Campredon, to be his plenipotentiary, and eſpecially that treaty which was made for 18 years at the Hague in 1700, between his royal majeſty of Sweden, Charles XII. of bleſſed and moſt glorious memory then reigning, and his royal majeſty of Great Britaid, William III. alſo of bleſſed and moſt glorious memory then reigning, and which expired in the year 1718. Her ſacred royal majeſty of Sweden has therefore been pleaſed, for perfecting this ſalutary work, lawfully to conſtitute

ſtitute and fully to authoriſe his excellency Count Charles
Guſtavus a Ducker, ſenator of her majeſty and the kingdom, Velt marſhal general, and counſellor at war; and
his excellency Count Guſtavus Adam a Tauble, another of
her majeſty's and the kingdom's ſenotors, Velt marſhal
general, and chief governor of Stockholm; alſo his excellency the Count Magnus de la Gardie, her Majeſty's and
the kingdom's ſenator, and preſident of the college of
commerce; and his excellency John Count Lillienſtedt,
her majeſty's and the kingdom's ſenator and counſellor
of the chancery; and finally, his excellency Daniel Nicholas de Hopken, free baron, and her ſecretary of ſtate: and
his ſacred royal majeſty of Great Britain has commiſſioned
his excellency John Lord Carteret, baron of Hawnes in the
county of Bedford, one of the lords of his bedchamber,
lord lieutenant of the county of Devon, and his ambaſſador extraordinary and plenipotentiary at the court of his
ſacred royal majeſty of Sweden; who having duly exhibited and communicated their full powers in a congreſs at
Stockholm, and held divers conferences on that account,
did, after accurate knowledge and diſquiſition of things, according to the importance of the affair, agree and conclude
to make the treaties of the firſt of March 1665, at Stockholm, and the 6th of June 1700, at Stockholm, the baſis
and foundation; provided nevertheleſs, that the negociation
be entered into immediately without loſs of time, by the
commiſſioners of both parties at Stockholm, concerning
thoſe things which relate to the commerce of both kingdoms, and of their ſubjects, and which conſtitute a part of
the treaties of 1665 and 1700; and as for every thing which
relates to mutual friendſhip, and good correſpondence and
ſecurity, the ſaid treaties of 1665 and 1700 are by this preſent treaty intirely confirmed and corroborated with additions and alterations only to render them better accommodated and more applicable to the preſent ſtate of affairs, as will appear to be more at large ſet forth, provided
and ſtipulated by the following articles:

I. There ſhall be a ſincere, conſtant and perpetual
friendſhip, league and good correſpondence between her
ſacred royal majeſty of Sweden, and the kings her heirs
and ſucceſſors on the one part, and his ſacred royal majeſty

jefty of Great-Britain, and the kings his heirs and fucceffors on the other part, and all fingular their kingdoms,
dominions, provinces, iflands, lands, colonies, cities,
towns, people, fubjects, and inhabitants, and confequently
all their fubjects and vaffals, both now and hereafter, within
Europe and without it, in all places both by land or fea,
and on the frefh-waters ; fo that neither they nor either of
them fhall do any detriment to the other's kingdom, provinces, colonies, wherever fituate, or fubject, nor permit,
much lefs confent that it be done by others ; but fhall embrace each other's interefts with fincere affection, all manner of good will, and mutual affection.

II. In like manner, both of the confederates, and their
heirs and fucceffors, fhall be obliged to take care of and
promote their mutual advantage and honour with all application, to difcover and bring to light all dangers, confpiracies and machinations of the enemy, as foon as they
come to their knowledge, to oppofe the fame as far as lies
in their power, and to employ and unite their counfels and
forces, for averting and hindering them ; for which reafon
it fhall not be lawful for any one of the confederates, either
by himfelf or any others whomfoever, to negotiate or attempt any thing to the detriment of other, or even to
the damage of the other's lands, dominions, or rights wherefoever, fituate either by land or fea ; and they fhall in no
wife fupport the other confedrate's rebels, or enemies, to
his prejudice, nor fhall receive or admit any of his rebels
and traitors into his dominions, much lefs afford them any
advice, aid, and favour, or fuffer or permit fuch advice,
aid, or favour to be given by his fubjects, people or inhabitants.

III. And particularly as to rebels, juft now mentioned,
whofoever fhall be declared a rebel and enemy, by letters
fent from either of the confedrates to the other, he fhall
be inftantly reputed as fuch by that confedrate to whom
fuch letters fhall be fent; and all the ftipulations made by
this alliance againft the enemies and rebels of either, fhall
be put in force.

IV. And to the end that the faid friendfhip and good
correfpondence may be cultivated every day with greater
fuccefs, to the advantage of both the faid princes, and
their

their kingdoms and fubjects, and the protections of the **Pro-**
teftant religion, and that their fecurity may be the better
provided for and guarded, it is agreed on both fides, that
the moft ferene and moft potent kings and kingdoms of
Sweden and Great-Britain, may be united as clofely as poffible, by a particular defenfive alliance, as they are by
thefe prefents joined together by the clofeft alliance,
and reciprocally obliged to the mutual defence of their
kingdoms, dominions, provinces, ftates, fubjects, poffeffions, rights, liberty of navigation and commerce in
the Baltick, the Sound, the Northern, Weftern, and Britifh feas, and in the Channel; as alfo the privileges and
prerogatives lawfully belonging to either of the confederates, as well by compacts and received cuftoms, as by the
law of nations and hereditary right, againft all manner of
invaders, aggreffors, and difturbers, whether by land or
fea in Europe, as is more particularly declared hereafter.

V. If it happen therefore that her royal majefty, and
her heirs and fucceffors, the kings and kingdom of Sweden, be invaded, infefted or difturbed in their kingdoms,
dominions and provinces, iflands, and jurifdictions, either
within their kingdoms, or without, in thofe parts of Germany now belonging to the kings and kingdom of Sweden,
or even in their poffeffions and prerogatives, privileges and
laws thereon depending, or in any other manner whatfoever
hindered and molefted in the freedom of navigation and
commerce in the feas and channels abovementioned, by
any one or more kings, princes, ftates, republicks, or rebels, or by any one or more ill-defigning perfons in Europe, his facred royal majefty of Great-Britain, and his
heirs and fucceffors the kings thereof, fhall after being duly required, conftantly affift the moft ferene Queen, and
her heirs and fucceffors, the kings and kingdoms of Sweden, againft all fuch aggreffors, difturbers, and rebels,
with an army of 6,000 foot, on the terms, and in the manner as hereafter ftipulated.

VI. And thofe auxiliary forces which fhall hereafter be
fo defired, fhall be all fent in four months after they are
required, or fooner if poffible, to fome convenient place
and port to be nominated and appointed by the party who
de-

defires them; and the preparation and fending of fuch fuccours fhall in no wife be retarded, much lefs fhall thofe friendly offices be wholly withdrawn, which by virtue of this alliance, the confedrate who is fent to is firft of all to make trial of for obtaining an amicable compofition: and when the forces are fent and arrived, they fhall be maintained and fubfifted at the expence of the ally who fends them, till peace be obtained, or as long as the confederate who requires them thinks them neceffary; provided however, that while the fuccours are in his dominions, they may be furnifhed with all neceffaries for food and raiment, at as reafonable a price as his own.

VII. It fhall be free for the confederate who requires the fuccours, to chufe whether he will have the whole number of forces abovementioned, or only a part thereof, and the reft in military ftores ammunition, provifion, fhips, and the neceffary equipage, reckoning each thoufand foot per month, as long as the war lafts, at the rate of 4,000 imperial dollors; which matter the commiffioners on both fides fhall agree on bona fide without delay.

VIII. But if there be danger, that the auxiliary forces may be hindred in coming to the place where they fhall be neceffary for him that requires them, the confedrates fhall be obliged to join their endeavours that their paffage may be made more fafe and eafy; and it fhall be lawful for the confedrate of whom they are required, to appoint his own general to command his forces, and the fame fhall be kept as clofe together in one body, as the ftate of the war will admit of; which is to be underftood in fuch a fenfe, that they may not be difperfed in parties, to places remote from each other. And he who is appointed General of the auxiliary forces, fhall be fubject to the command of the ally who requires them, or to his general in millitary opperations; and all things which relate to action, and all other military events, fhall be fo ordered as is the ufual cuftom in war, and in cafe of furnifhing fuccours; and the fame rule fhall take place if fhips fhoulld happen to be fent inftead of land forces, which, as auxiliaries, fhall be obliged to carry the flag of the ally who requires them.

X. If it happen that the determined number of forces be not fufficient for the greatnefs of the danger, as in cafe the aggreffors be fuccoured by the auxliaries of any of his
con-

confederates, and be fo ftrong as to over-power and defeat either of the allies, then the other ally fhall be obliged as foon as poffible to affift the party injured and oppreffed, with as many forces as he can both by fea and land, and by pecuniary fubfidies; provided neverthelefs, that in fuch cafe, the manner, nature and time of giving fuch aid may be fettled according to the exigencey of the affair. And whereas the kidgdom of Sweden has long ere now been infefted by ferveral neighbouring powers even while the treaty which was concluded in the year 1700 ftill fubfifts, and as the war continues hitherto, for this reafon his facred royal majefty of Great Britain thinks himfelf obliged, as well by the treaty abovementioned, as by virtue of thefe prefents, to give thofe farther fuccours to her facred royal majefty and the kingdom of Sweden, as are hereafter ftipulated.

XI. And whereas every amicable method has been hitherto attempted, but without fuccefs, for putting an end to this Northern war, according to the defire of her royal Swedifh Majefty, his facred royal majefty of Great Britain doth declare, and bind himfelf by thefe prefents, that he will not fuffer any more time to be wafted in vainly attempting fuch a reconciliation, but will next fpring fend a ftrong fquadron of men of war to the kingdom of Sweden, as fuccours to act in conjunction with the men of war of her facred royal majefty of Sewden, under her command, and at her difpofal, for repelling the invafions of Sweden by the Czar of Mufcovy, and for fpeedily obtaining a juft peace from him; and all operations that are to be performed by their joint forces, fhall be ordered and difpofed in a previous council of war, held with the commanders of the fquadrons of both crowns: but for the future, before the auxiliary forces are fent, the party that fuffers any force or injury fhall give notice to the other ally, and then both of the allies fhall ufe their endeavours, that the invaders or difturbers may be induced by fair means to abftain from fuch violence and injury, that there may not be a neceffity of having recourfe to arms; and if the offender fhould be fo obftinate, that he will not condefcend to do juftice by amicable meafures, and confequently the party injured and offended be compelled to repel the violence done to him, and any farther dif-

turbance

turbance by force of arms, then the faid forces fhall be
fent without delay, and fuch fupply fhall be continued till
the party injured has obtained full fatisfaction. He fhall
be accounted an aggreffor, who extorts a juft defence by
injuries.

XII. It fhall likewife be lawful for both of the confederates and their fubjects, to enter the ports of either
with their men of war, and other fhips of force, there to
winter and ftay, and to poffefs and enjoy the immunities
and privileges of thofe ports; provided that they who
are not the common enemies be not infefted in fuch ports
or at their entrance, nor that the traffick to the faid ports,
be interrupted, much lefs wholly cut off. It is alfo determined by the mutual confent of their royal confederate
majefties, that a particular negociation for navigation
and commerce be immediately fet on foot at Stockholm,
for the mutual advantage and emolument of both nations; and in the mean while, and till the fame has its
effect, it is covenanted and agreed between both the allies,
that there fhall be a reciprocal and entire freedom of navigation and commerce in all forts of goods and marchan-
dize, through all and fingular their dominions, jurifdictions and territories fituate in Europe: fo that it fhall be
lawful for one another's fubjects freely and fafely to enter
by land or fea into either's kingdoms, provinces, iflands,
cities, towns, and villages, and there to refide and exercife commerce in all forts of goods and merchandize,
the importation and exportation of which are not particularly prohibited and reftrained by the laws and ftatutes of both kingdoms, provided neverthelefs that fuch
freedom of commerce be not extended to any other
places than to thofe fea ports which have hitherto been
opened for the trade of any foreign nation: in which faid
ports, towns, cities, and places, it fhall always be free and
lawful for the fubjects of both the confederates, not only
to ftay, refide, and inhabit there as long as they pleafe,
without any moleftation, oppreffion, reftraint, or limitation of time, but alfo to tranfport themfelves from thence,
with their goods, merchandize, and effects elfewhere,
whenfoever and wherefoever they think fit, without any
detriment, delay, or impediment, under any pretence, unlefs they have borrowed money, and contracted any juft

and

and lawful debts; nor ſhall the ſaid ſubjeċts be obliged to pay any tributes or taxes of any kind, under any pretence, during their ſtay in the dominions or territories of either of the confederates, which the nations in the moſt entire friendſhip are not obliged to pay. And to the end that the mercantile affairs of the ſaid ſubjeċts may be confirmed and increaſed as much as poſſible, and that commerce may be reciprocally promoted between both kingdoms, the ſaid allies bind one another, and ſeverally engage that the merchandize and manufaċtures of both nations ſhall hereafter pay no other tribute nor taxes, than what are already eſtabliſhed; and ſhall enjoy ſuch immunity, till all points relating to their mutual commerce be more clearly and firmly decided by a ſpecial convention or treaty to be forthwith concluded, and always to be obſerved for the uſe and profit of both nations: nor ſhall it be lawful for the ſubjeċts of both the allies reſpeċtively, to claim and demand greater rates for the weight and menſuration of the goods and merchandize by them imported and exported than what are demanded and paid by the cities, inhabitants, and ſubjeċts of both kingdioms. It is moreover agreed and eſtabliſhed, for a general rule between the ſaid confederates, that all and ſingular their ſubjeċts ſhall enjoy equal favour, at leaſt in all things, and on every occaſion, in the dominions and territories ſubjeċt on both ſides to their obedience: and that they ſhall uſe and poſſeſs the ſame privileges, liberties and immunities which the ſubjeċts of any other prince or ſtate, even in the ſtriċteſt amity, do or may hereafter uſe, enjoy and poſſeſs.

XIII. Whereas by virtue of the fourth and fifth articles of the treaty of 1700, both crowns were obliged reciprocally to furniſh the ſuccours therein ſtipulated; on the conditions nevertheleſs, which are ſpecified in the XVIth of the ſaid treaty, viz. that if the confederate applied to for ſuccours ſhould himſelf be involved in a war, either againſt his own ſubjeċts, or againſt a foreign enemy, he ſhould not only be obliged, during ſuch war, to furniſh ſuccours to the other confederate demanding them, but might alſo after three months previous notice recall the auxiliary forces, ſent in aid of his confederate, by virtue of the league: and whereas it happened that her late ſacred royal majeſty of Great Britain was herſelf engaged

in

in a war againft the crown of France, till the year 1713, when the war was concluded by the treaty of peace at Utrecht, and therefore neither could nor ought to be bound to furnifh the fubfidies promifed to the crown of Sweden; yet forafmuch as the kingdom of Sweden has been in war from that time to this, and for that reafon demands the Swedifh fubfidies which are in arrear; and whereas the fubjects of his facred royal majefty of Great Britain demanded juft fatisfaction for their fhips and merchandize intercepted by the Swedifh men of war and privateers, and afterwards confifcated; and whereas in like manner the fubjects of her facred royal majefty of Sweden require juft fatisfaction for their fhips and goods intercepted by the men of war and privateers of Great Britain; for this reafon it is agreed by the contracting parties, that commiffioners fhall forthwith be elected on both fides, to examine and liquidate the complaints relating to the fhips and goods fo intercepted and taken, that it may appear what part the one owes to the other, and that what is accordingly due, after a calculation made on both fides, may be punctually paid within the term fixed by the commiffioners for fettling thofe pretenfions.

XIV. But the prerogatives mentioned in the beginning of the twelfth article, as granted by either of the confederates to the fhips of the other in his harbours, fhall in no wife be indulged to the enemies of the other, Nor fhall it be lawful for the fubjects of either of the confederates, to affift the enemies of the other confedrate to his inconvenience and detriment, or to ferve them either as foldiers or mariners by fea or land, and therefore they fhall be laid under the fevereft prohibition.

XV. The prefent treaty made between the moft ferene monarchs of Sweden and Great Britain, fhall not derogate in the leaft from the regalities, rights and dominion of her facred royal majefty of Sweden in the Baltick, nor from thofe of his facred royal majefty of Great Britain in thofe commonly called the Britifh Seas; but both of the confederates fhall hereafter preferve and enjoy all the prerogatives and privileges above mentioned, with all things depending thereon, as they have poffeffed them hitherto, freely and without any cavil. Which enjoyment of all
things

things as aforefaid muft be underftood on both fides, faving this prefent treaty.

XVI. After the confederate required as aforefaid, hath
fent his auxiliaries, or difcharged his obligation according
to the laws of treaties, it is neceffary that provifion be made
in like manner for him and his fecurity ; and therefore it is
agreed on both fides, that the confederate who fends forces
to the other confederate at his requeft, fhall always be reputed as an auxiliary, and not be involved in the war for
fending fuch affiftance ; nor fhall any treaty of peace or
truce be entered into, nor any fufpenfion of arms concluded
for a confiderable time, which may be hurtful to the other
confederate, without including and fecuring him that fent
fuch affiftance. But if he fhould be involved in open war
with the aggreffor, or any other whomfoever, by reafon
of his fending fuccours, then neither fhall condefcend to
agree to any preliminaries, or to any general treaty with
the enemy or enemies, without the confent and council of
the other, but all things fhall be acted and treated with
mutual help, communication and counfel, till moft ample
provifion is made with common confent, for the fufficient
fecurity and due fatisfaction of both confederates. Above
all, it fhall be by no means lawful for that ally who is firft
engaged in the war, to make peace, before the other ally,
who by virtue of this treaty has fent help to his ally, fhall
have ample fatisfaction made him for any damage from
the enemy, and be fully reftored at leaft to his former
ftate, which he was in poffeffion of, or had a juft title to
before the war began, in cafe that his ftate and condition
fhall have fuffered any diminution in the progrefs of
war.

XVII. This condition is expreffely added to the former,
concerning fending help at the requeft of his ally. ' That
' if it happens that either of the confederate kings, ei-
' ther he of whom help is required, or he who re-
' quires it, fhould be engaged in war againft a common
' enemy, or be molefted by any other neighbouring king,
' prince or ftate, in his own kingdoms or provinces, (fo
' that he of whom it is required may juftly account fuch
' moleftation for a real war) to the averting of which he
' that requires help might otherwife by virtue of this treaty
                                                    ' be

‘ be obliged himſelf to ſend auxiliaries, then the other
‘ ally ſo moleſted, if any auxiliary forces were ſent at the
‘ requeſt of the other ally before the invaſion, may after
‘ three months notification recall them to his own and his
‘ kingdom’s defence, and while he is preſſed with ſuch in-
‘ vaſion, he ſhall not be obliged to ſend the promiſed ſuc-
‘ cours, as happened heretofore during the war which
‘ continued ſo many years betwixt the Crown of Great
‘ Britain and the moſt Chriſtian King. And although
‘ that treaty of 1700, which ſhall be reckoned as the baſis
‘ of this, was entered into upon this condition, and this
‘ which is concluded even now, ought to be explained in
‘ that manner hereafter, nevertheleſs his ſacred royal ma-
‘ jeſty of Great Britain, in order to give the moſt ſignal
‘ tokens of his friendſhip to the crown of Sweden, engages,
‘ *pro hac vice*, that the preſent war between the crowns of
‘ Great Britain and Spain, ſhall by no means hinder her
‘ royal majeſty of Sweden from obtaining the aids actually
‘ ſtipulated by this treaty, or from enjoying and being
‘ ſupported by the ſame, till the peace is happily reſtored,
‘ viz. the ſubſidies and ſquadron of men of war, pro-
‘ miſed in the VIIIth and IXth articles, till a peace was
‘ reſtored with the Czar of Muſcovy : but if the war with
‘ Denmark ſhould, contrary to expectation, laſt longer
‘ than that with the Czar, then only the ſubſidies ſhall be
‘ continued. On the contrary, her ſacred royal majeſt-
‘ of Sweden obliges herſelf not to admit of any terms
‘ which may be propoſed or offered to her directly or in-
‘ directly by the king of Spain, if thoſe terms are capable
‘ of doing any prejudice or damage to the cauſe for which
‘ a war has been carried on for ſeveral years againſt Spain.
‘ Moreover, her ſacred majeſty of Sweden obliges herſelf,
‘ her heirs and ſucceſſors, to maintain and guarantee
‘ the ſucceſſion to the crown of Great Britain, as it is
‘ eſtabliſhed by the laws of the realm, in the family of his
‘ Britannick Majeſty now upon the throne, and likewiſe
‘ to defend all the dominions and provinces poſſeſſed by
‘ his majeſty ; and that ſhe will not give or grant any
‘ ſhelter or refuge in any part of her dominions to the per-
‘ ſon or his deſcendents, if he ſhould have any, who in
‘ the life-time of James II. took the title of Prince of
‘ Wales,

‘ Wales, and after his death the royal title of King of
‘ Great Britain : promifing likewife for herfelf, her heirs
‘ and succeffors, that fhe will not directly or indirectly
‘ give the faid perfon or his defcendents, any aid, counfel,
‘ or affiftance whatfoever; either in money, arms, military
‘ equipage, fhips, foldiers, mariners, or in any other man-
‘ ner whatfoever; and that fhe will obferve the fame pre-
‘ caution with regard to thofe perfons who may be com-
‘ manded or commiffioned to difturb his Britannick Ma-
‘ jefty’s government, or the tranquillity of his kingdom,
‘ either by open war, or clandeftine confpiraces, or in
‘ exciting feditions and rebellions, or in committing pira-
‘ cies upon his Britannick Majefty’s fubjects; in which
‘ laft cafe, her facred royal majefty of Sweden promifes
‘ that fhe will by no means permit any refuge to be given
‘ to fuch pirates in the harbours of her kingdom. Laftly,
‘ her royal majefty of Sweden obliges herfelf, not to give
‘ any protection or fhelter to any part of her dominions
‘ to thofe fubjects of his royal majefty of Great Britain,
‘ who are now, or fhall hereafter be declared rebels; and
‘ that in cafe there happen to be fuch in her kingdoms,
‘ provinces, and dominions, fhe will command them to
‘ depart her territories in eight days after the warning
‘ given them from court. And if his facred royal majefty
‘ of Great Britain fhall happen to be invaded in a hoftile
‘ manner, fhe obliges herfelf to fend the fuccours above-
‘ mentioned, and to do the fame to his defcendents, if
‘ they fhall happen to be difturbed in the fucceffion to the
‘ crown of Great Britain. And forafmuch as it is of the
‘ greateft importance to the Proteftant Religion, to the
‘ commerce of the kingdoms of Sweden and Great Bri-
‘ tain, and to all Chriftendom, that the Baltick may not
‘ be in the power of the Czar of Mofcovy; if therefore
‘ the faid Czar refufe to make a peace with Sweden, and
‘ to reftore thofe things which are required for the fecurity
‘ of the kingdom of Sweden, and to re-eftablifh the fame
‘ freedom of Commerce in the Baltick, as both enjoyed
‘ before the prefent war, in this cafe his facred royal ma-
‘ jefty of Great Britain obliges himfelf not only to furnifh
‘ thofe aids which are expreffed in this treaty, for obtain-
‘ ing the fame by force of arms, but he promifes to ufe all

‘ his

' his endeavours, and to employ all his offices with his
' confederates, that they may help Sweden with fubfidies,
' and confequently furnifh the crown of Sweden with the
' means for keeping the Czar within bounds.'

XVIII. And although the allies fhall be obliged to
fend auxiliaries to one another, according to the articles
above, yet that obligation fhall not be fo far extended, as
that all friendfhip and mutual correfpondence fhall be taken
away and prohibited with the enemies of the other confederate : for fuppofing that one of the confederates fhould
when required fend his auxiliaries, and not be engaged in
the war himfelf, it fhall then be free for his fubjects and
inhabitants to have trade and navigation with the enemies
of that ally who is engaged in the war ; and it fhall be
lawful for them to carry any goods whatfoever to them,
thofe only excepted which are exprefsly forbid, and commonly called contraband, and declared fuch by the common agreement of all nations..

XIX. Forafmuch as both their royal majefties above-
mentioned do hereby declare that they are ftill bound by
certain conventions and treaties formerly entered into with
other powers, and that they are willing to obferve the fame
duly, according to the ftipulations of the faid articles,
but that neverthelefs they are not at this time bound by any
articles and claufes therein contained, which may or ought
to weaken and obftruct this prefent treaty in any manner,
or under any pretence :. to the end therefore, that the faith
of the confederates, and their perfeverance in this alliance,
may appear the more reciprocal, and that the minds of
their fubjects and friends may be the more confirmed,
both their royal majefties abovementioned do oblige themfelves and declare, that they will fincerely and *bona fide,*
ftand to all and every one of the articles of this treaty, and
that they will not depart a tittle from the genuine and
plain fenfe of the faid articles, under any pretexts of
profit, friendfhip, former treaty, contract and promife,
or for any other colour whatfoever ; but that they will
give effectual orders that all the things which they have
promifed in this treaty, as the ftate of affairs fhall require, be fpeedily and fully put in execution by themfelves, or their minifters and fubjects, according as they

are

are expreſsly ſtipulated, and this without any limitation, exception or excuſe, thoſe excepted which are expreſſed in the preceding articles of this treaty.

XX. This defenſive treaty ſhall laſt 18 years, before the end of which the confederate ſovereigns may again treat concerning its farther continuance, if it ſhall ſeem good to both of them.

XXI. Whereas this treaty has been concluded purſuant to powers and orders received on both ſides, ſo the ſame ought to be approved and ratified in due and ſolemn form, by both their ſacred royal majeſties of Sweden and Great Britain, and the inſtruments of their ratification be delivered and exchanged at Stockholm within the ſpace of three months, to be reckoned from the time of this ſubſcription, or ſooner if poſſible.

For the greater evidence and confirmation of all things aforeſaid, two copies of this treaty have been made, one of which the aforeſaid ſenators and ſecretary of ſtate of her ſacred royal majeſty and the kingdom of Sweden, have ſigned and confirmed with their ſeals, as the other has been by the aforeſaid ambaſſador extraordinary and plenipotentiary of his ſacred royal majeſty of Great Britain, who were all particularly empowered for that end, and that on one and the ſame day, viz. the 21ſt of January 1720.

---

*The Treaty between* Great Britain *and* Spain, *concluded at* Madrid, June 13, N. S. 1721.

IT having pleaſed the Divine Providence to diſpoſe the hearts of the moſt ſerene and potent princes, George, by the Grace of God King of Great Britain, France, and Ireland, &c. and Philip V. by the Grace of God King of Spain, the Indies, &c, to forget all the grounds of diſſatisfaction and miſunderſtanding that have given occaſion to interrupt, for ſome time, the friendſhip and good correſpondence which before flouriſhed between them; and their Britannick and Catholick Majeſties being now deſirous to renew and re-eſtabliſh them by the ſtrongeſt
ties,

ties, have ſtipulated and agreed by their under-written
miniſters plenipotentiary, named for that purpoſe, the
following articles.

I. That, for the future, there ſhall be, between his Britannick Majeſty, his heirs and Succeſſors, and his Catholic
Majeſty his heirs and ſucceſſors, as alſo between their
kingdoms, dominions, ſovereignties, ſubjects and vaſſals,
a good, firm, and inviolable peace, and a perpetual and
ſincere friendſhip, and a general oblivion of every thing
that has been done, on both ſides, upon occaſion of the
laſt war.

II. The treaties of peace and commerce, concluded at
Utrecht on the 13th of July, and the 9th of December,
in the year 1713, wherein are comprehended, the treaty
made at Madrid in the year 1667, and the cedulas therein mentioned, ſhall remain ratified and confirmed by the
preſent treaty, except the third, fifth, and eighth articles of the ſaid treaty of commerce, commonly called
explanatory; which have been annulled by virtue of
another ſubſequent treaty, made at Madrid the 14th of
the month of December 1715, between the miniſters plenipotentiary, named for that purpoſe, by their Britannick
and Catholic Mjeſlies, which treaty remains likewiſe
confirmed and ratified; as alſo the particular contract,
commonly called The Aſſiento, for the importation of
negroe ſlaves into the Spaniſh Indies, which was made
the 26th of March in the ſaid year 1713, in conſequence
of the 12th article of the treaty of commerce of Utrecht;
and likewiſe the treaty of declaration, concerning that of
the Aſſiento, made the 26th of May 1716: all which
treaties, mentioned in this article, with their declaration,
ſhall remain in their full force, virtue, and vigour, in every
thing wherein they ſhall not be contrary to this; and, to
the end they may have their entire effect and accompliſh-
ment, his Catholic Majeſty will cauſe his circular orders, cedulas, to be diſpatched to his viceroys, governors, and other miniſters, to whom it ſhall belong, of
the ports and towns in America, that the ſhips employed
for the traffick of negroes by the royal company of Great
Britain eſtabliſhed at London, may be admitted, with-

out

out hindrance, to trade freely, and in the fame manner as they did before the laft rupture between the two crowns; and the abovementioned cedulas fhall be delivered as foon as the ratifications of the prefent treaty fhall have been exchanged; and at the fame time his Catholic Majefty will give his orders to the council of the Indies, that the junta, compofed of minifters taken out of that council, and appointed for the cognizance (exclufive of all others) of the caufes that refpect the faid Affiento, may again have its courfe, admit of, and confult upon thofe affairs, according to the rule eftablifhed at the time of its appointment; and as to what regards the obfervation of the treaties of peace and commerce, circular orders fhall be difpatched to all the governors of Spain, to the end that they may, without any of their interpretations, caufe them to be obferved and accomplifhed; as in like manner fhall be given, on the part of his Britannick Majefty, the orders which fhall be demanded, and judged neceffary for the accomplifhment of every thing that has been ftipulated and agreed between the two crowns in the abovementioned treaties of Utrecht; and particularly as to what may not have been put in execution of the points fettled by the eighth, eleventh and fifteenth articles of the treaty of peace, which mention the leaving to the Spaniards the free commerce and navigation to the Weft Indies, and the maintaining the antient limits in America, as they were in the time of King Charles II. the free exercife of the Catholic Religion in the ifland of Minorca, and the cod-fifhing in the feas of Newfoundland; as well as with regard to all the other articles which may not hitherto have been put in execution, on the part of Great Britain.

III. Forafmuch as by the feventh article of the treaty of commerce of Utrecht it was agreed, that all the goods confifcated at the beginning of the former war fhould be reftored, in regard to the confifcation thereof had been made contrary to the tenor of the 36th article of the treaty of 1667, his Catholic Majefty, in like conformity, will order, that all the goods, merchandizes, money, fhips, and other effects, which have been feized, as well in Spain as in the Indies, by virtue of his orders of the month of September 1718, or of any other fubfequent orders, at the

time

time before the war was declared between the two crowns, or after it was declared, be fpeedily reftored in their fame kind, as to thofe which fhall be ftill in being ; or, if they are not, the juft and true value of them, at the time that they were feized ; the valuation whereof, if, by omiffion or neglect, it was not then made ; fhall be adjufted, according to the authentic informations that the owners fhall produce before the ordinary magiftrates of the towns and places where the faid effects fhall have been feized. And it is certain, that the orders of his Catholic Majefty (although they directed, that inventories of thofe goods and effects fhould be made and drawn up, and accounts and declarations fhould be kept) have not, however, been executed in that manner in feveral places, it has been agreed, that if the proprietors make it appear, by legal proofs, informations, and other documents, that any of them have been omitted in the faid inventories, his Catholic Majefty wil give exprefs orders, that the value of thofe things which fhall have been omitted, be paid by the treafurers or other perfons, through whofe neglect fuch omiffions fhall have been made.

IV. It is mutually agreed, that his Britannick Majefty fhall give order to his governors, officers, and other minifters, to whom it fhall belong, to caufe to be reftored all the goods and effects of the fubjects of his Catholic Majefty, which they fhall prove to have been feized and confifcated in the dominions of his Britannick Majefty, upon occafion of the laft war ; in the fame manner as it has been fettled in the foregoing article, in favour of the fubjects of his Britannick Majefty.

V. It is alfo agreed, that his Britannick Majefty fhall caufe to be reftored to his Catholic Majefty all the fhips of the Spanifh fleet, which were taken by that of England, in the naval battle that was fought in the month of Auguft 1718, in the feas of Sicily ; with the guns, fails, rigging, and other equipage, in the condition they are at prefent ; or elfe the value of thofe which may have been fold at the fame price that the purchafers fhall have given, according to the proofs and vouchers : and for the execution of this reftitution, his Britannick Majefty fhall caufe the proper orders to be difpatched, immediately

mediately after the ratification of this treaty. It is alſo declared, that the other pretenſions that there may be, on both ſides, between the two crowns, concerning matters whereof there is no mention made in the preſent treaty, and which are not comprehended in the ſecond article hereof, ſhall be treated of at the approaching congreſs of Cambray.

VI. The preſent treaty ſhall have its effect immediately after it ſhall have been mutually ratified ; and the letters of, ratification ſhall be exchanged in ſix weeks after the ſigning, or ſooner, if poſſible ; deferring its publication till the general peace ſhall have been concluded at the congreſs of Cambray, between all the parties concerned ; or till their Britannick and Catholic Majeſties ſhall have particularly agreed upon it.

In witneſs whereof, we the under-written miniſters plenipotentiaries of his Britannick Majeſty and his Catholic Majeſty, being furniſhed with our full powers, which have been mutually communicated, and copies whereof ſhall be here under tranſcribed, have ſigned the preſent treaty, and affixed thereto the ſeals of our arms. Done at Madrid the 13th of June, 1721.

(L. S.) *William Stanhope.*
(L. S.) *El* Marquiſs *de Grima'do.*

---

*Treaty of Defenſive Alliance, betwixt* France, Spain, *and* Great Britain. *At* Madrid, June 13, 1721.

THE differences that have happened betwixt their Britannick and moſt Chriſtian Mejeſties on the one part, and his Catholic Majeſty on the other, having not a little impaired the friendſhip which they always ſhewed to one another, it has been a long time their ardent wiſh to re-eſtabliſh the good correſpondence and ſincere amity which ought to prevail among them, and which will always be the ſtrongeſt ſupport of the greatneſs to which God has raiſed them, and the ſureſt means to preſerve the public tranquillity, as well as the happineſs and
mutual

mutual advantages of their subjects; and it is with a view to cement and corroborate, if possible, these dispositions, which are as conducive to the mutual glory and security of their crowns, as they are conformable to the welfare and tranquillity of all Europe, that their Britannick, most Christian, and Catholic Majesties have resolved to unite in so strict a manner, that they may act hereafter as if they had only the same view, and the same interest: and for this end the most serene King of Great Britain, &c. having given full powers to treat in his name, to William Stanhope, Esq. colonel of a regiment of dragoons, a member of the parliament of Great Britain, and ambassador extraordinary from his Britannick Majesty to the court of the Catholic King; the most serene the most Christian King having given full powers for the same end, to John Baptist Lewis Andrault de Langeron, Marquifs de Maulevrier, lieutenant-general of his armies, commander and grand croix of the military order of St. Louis, his envoy extraordinary to his Catholic Majesty; and the most serene King of Spain having likewise granted his full powers for the same end to Don Joseph Grimaldo, knight of the order of St. Jago, governor of Rueira and Auzechal, a member of the council of the Indies, and his first secretary of state and the dispatches; they have agreed on the following articles.

I. There shall be hereafter and for ever a strict union and a sincere and lasting friendship between the most serene King of Great Britain, the most serene the most Christian King, and the most serene King of Spain, their kingdoms and their subjects, and inhabitants of the countries under their dominion; so that the injuries or damages suffered during the war, to which an end has been put by the accession of the most serene King of Spain to the treaties of London, dated the 2d of August 1718, shall be buried in eternal oblivion, and that for the future each shall take the same care of one another's safety as of his own, and not only inform his ally of the danger that may threaten him, but also oppose with all his power the injuries that may be done him.

II. In

II. In order to eſtabliſh this union and correſpondence firmly, and to render it yet more advantageous to the crowns of their Britannick, moſt Chriſtian and Catholic Majeſties, they promiſe and engage by the preſent treaty of defenſive alliances mutually to guarantee the kingdoms, provinces, ſtates and countries under each other's dominion, in what part of the world ſoever ſituate ; ſo that if their majeſties are attacked, contrary to what was reſolved on at the treaties of Utrecht and Baden, and contrary to the treaties of London, and the ſtipulations which ſhall be made at Cambray, they ſhall mutually aſſiſt one another till the diſturbance is at an end, or till they are ſatisfied, by the reparation of the damages which they ſhall have ſuffered.

III. In purſuance of the foregoing article, the maintenance and obſervation of the treaties of Utrecht, Baden, London, and of that which is to be made at Cambray, for putting an end to the differences that are to be decided betwixt the moſt ſerene King of Spain and the Emperor, ſhall be the chief aim of the preſent alliance. And to ſtrengthen it the more, the moſt ſerene King of Great Britain, the moſt ſerene the moſt Chriſtian King, and the moſt ſerene King of Spain, ſhall by concert invite ſuch powers as they ſhall think fit to enter into the preſent treaty for the common good, and for the preſervation of the public tranquillity.

IV. If it happen (which God forbid) that, contrary to the ſaid treaties of Utrecht, Baden, London, or the ſtipulations of thoſe which ſhall be made at Cambray, their Britannick, moſt Chriſtian and Catholic Majeſties ſhould be attacked, or in any manner diſturbed in the enjoyment of their kingdoms and countries by any potentate, they promiſe and engage to employ their good offices as ſoon as they ſhall be required, in order to procure for the party attacked ſatisfaction for the wrong done to him, and to hinder the aggreſſor from continuing his hoſtilities; and if it happen that his good offices be not ſufficient to procure ſuch reparation out of hand, their ſaid Majeſties promiſe to furniſh the following ſuccours jointly or ſeparately, viz.

His

His Britannick Majefty 8,000 foot, and 4,000 horfe.
His moft Chriftian Majefty 8,000 foot, and 4,000 horfe.
His Catholic Majefty 8,000 foot, and 4,000 horfe.

If the party that happens to be attacked, defire men of war or tranfports, or even fubfidies in ready money, in the room of troops, in that cafe he fhall be at liberty to make his choice, and they fhall furnifh him with the faid fhips or money in proportion to the expence of troops; and in order to prevent all occafion of doubt in the calculation of the faid expence, their Majefties agree that 1,000 foot fhall be fettled at 10,000 Dutch florins, and 1,000 horfe at 30,000 florins per month, obferving the fame proportion with regard to fhipping: their faid majefties promifing to continue and maintain the faid fuccours as long as the troubles fhall laft; and if the faid fuccours be not fufficient to repel the attacks of the enemy, they fhall agree to augment them; and if it be neceffary, their faid Majefties fhall mutually affift one another with all their forces, and declare war againft the aggreffor.

V. Their Britannick, moft Chriftian and Catholic Majefties, being entirely fatisfied in the fentiments which the Duke of Parma has always manifefted towards them, and being defirous to give him marks of the fingular efteem and affection which they have for him, they promife and engage, by virtue of this prefent treaty, to grant him particular protection for the prefervation of his territories and rights, and for the maintenance of his dignity; fo that if he be difturbed contrary to the treaties of peace already made, and contrary to what fhall be ftipulated in thofe that are to be made at Cambray, they fhall join their good offices and efforts, to obtain juft fatisfaction; and if it be refufed, they fhall agree on meafures to procure it for him by all other methods that fhall be in their power.

VI. His Catholic Majefty being defirous to give his Britannick Majefty, and his moft Chriftian Majefty a particular proof of his friendfhip, confirms as far as there may be occafion, all the advantages and privileges which have been granted by the kings his predeceffors to the

English

Englifh and French nations ; fo that the trading fubjects of the moft ferene king of Great Britain, and the moft ferene the moft Chriftian King, fhall always enjoy in Spain, the fame rights, prerogatives, advantages and privileges for their perfons, commerce, merchandize, eftates and effects, which they have enjoyed, or which they ought to have enjoyed by virtue of treaties or agreements, or by virtue of all thofe which have been or fhall be granted in Spain, to the nation that is moft favoured.

VII. The prefent treaty fhall be ratified by their Britannick, moft Chriftian and Catholic Majefties, and the ratifications fhall be mutually delivered in due form, and exchanged in the fpace of fix weeks, reckoning from the day of figning, or fooner, if poffible.

In witnefs whereof, we the underwritten Minifters, Plenipotentiaries of his Britannick Majefty, his moft Chriftian Majefty, and his moft Catholic Majefty, having mutually communicated our full powers, have figned the prefent treaty, and thereunto fet the feals of our arms.  Done at Madrid the 13th of June 1721.

*Signed,*

(L. S.) *William Stanhope.*
(L. S.) *Langeron Maulevrier.*
(L. S.) Marquifs *de Grimaldo.*

*The feparate Article of the Defenfive Alliance between* Great Britain, France, *and* Spain, *concluded at* Madrid, *the* 13*th of* June, *N. S.* 1721.

THE Minifters Plenipotentiaries of their Britannick, moft Chriftian and Catholic Majefties, have this day figned, by virtue of their refpective full powers, a treaty of defenfive alliance between their faid Majefties : they have further agreed, that the particular treaty, which has likewife been figned, this day, between their Britannick and Catholic Majefties, whereof the tenor follows, fhall make a part of the faid treaty of defenfive alliance, concluded between England, France, and Spain.

*Here*

*Here is inserted,* verbatim, *the Treaty between* Great Britain *and* Spain, *concluded at* Madrid, *the 13th of* June, *N. S.* 1721.

THE abovesaid particular treaty shall have the same force, as if it were inserted word for word in the treaty of defensive alliance, signed this day, between the three crowns; and the letters of ratification shall be exchanged at Madrid, in the usual manner, within the space of six weeks, to be computed from the day of signing, or sooner, if possible.

In witness whereof, we have signed these presents, by virtue of our full powers, and have affixed thereto the seal of our arms. Done at Madrid the 13th of June, 1721.

> (L. S.) *William Stanhope.*
> (L. S.) *Langeron Maulevrier.*
> (L. S.) *El* Marquis *de Grimaldo.*

*Another separate Article of the Defensive Alliance between* Great Britain, France, *and* Spain, *concluded at* Madrid *the 13th of* June, *N. S.* 1721.

THE Ministers Plenipotentiaries of their Britannick and most Christian Majesties, having this day signed, with the Minister Plenipotentiary of the King of Spain, by virtue of their respective full powers, a treaty of defensive alliance; the abovesaid Ministers of their Britannick and most Christian Majesties have also agreed between themselves, by virtue of the same powers, that, as the principal intention and aim of that alliance is to maintain and preserve the peace and tranquillity of Europe, in which it cannot be doubted but the States General of the United Provinces of the Netherlands are disposed to concur, and to give their assistance, the first proper occasion shall be taken, in concert, to invite them thereto; and their said Britannick and most Christian Majesties promise

mife and engage, in the mean time, to maintain the treaty
of defenfive alliance, made at the Hague, between the
King of Great Britain, the moft Chriftian King, and the
States General of the 4th of January 1717, N. S. and
that nothing fhall be done, directly or indirectly, to its
prejudice.

---

*Defenfive Treaty of Alliance between the King of* Great Britain, *the moft Chriftian King, and the King of* Pruffia,
*concluded at* Hanover *the 3d of* September 1725. *With
three feparate Articles relating to* Thorn, *and to the Con-
tingency of a War againft the Emperor and the Empire.*

THEIR Majefties the King of Great Britain, the moft
Chriftian King, and the King of Pruffia, having
with pleafure, obferved how much the ftrict union fubfifting between them has contributed, not only to the
happinefs of their own kingdoms and fubjects, but alfo
to the public good and tranquillity; being likewife perfuaded that there is not a more proper means of fecuring
and ftrengthening the faid advantages againft all events
that may happen, than to cultivate the faid union more
and more, and to make it indiffoluble; and having maturely confidered all the treaties that fubfift between their
faid Majefties, (from which they declare that they do not
intend any way to derogate by this prefent treaty) they
have thought fit to take before hand, new meafures,
in cafe any difturbances fhould arife in Europe, by agreeing among themfelves upon what may be neceffary not
only for the fecurity and the moft effential interefts of their
own kingdom, but alfo with regard to the general good
and tranquillity. Upon thefe confiderations, and with
this view, their faid Britannick, moft Chriftian, and
Pruffian Majefties have given their full powers; that is to
fay, his Britannick Majefty to Charles Vifcount Townfhend,
Baron of Lynn, his lieutenant in the county of Norfolk,
knight of the moft noble order of the garter, and his
fecretary of ftate; his moft Chriftian Majefty, to Francis
count de Broglio, lieutenant general of his armies, director general of his horfe, and of his dragoons, governor

nor of Mont-Dauphin, and his ambaffador to the faid moft ferene king of Great Britain ; and his Pruffian Majefty, to John Chriftopher de Wallenrodt, his minifter of ftate, and his envoy extraordinary to the faid moft ferene king of Great Britain ; who, by virtue of the faid full powers, having with all poffible attention weighed the moft proper meafures to attain the end which their faid majefties propofe to themfelves, have agreed upon the following articles.

I. There fhall be now, and in all time coming, a true, firm, and inviolable peace, the moft fincere and intimate friendfhip, and the moft ftrict alliance and union between the faid three moft ferene kings, their heirs and fucceffors, their dominions, countries, and towns fituate in their refpective territories, and their fubjects and inhabitants, as well in as out of Europe ; and the fame fhall be preferved and cultivated in fuch manner, that the contracting parties may faithfully promote their reciprocal interefts and advantages, and prevent and repel all wrongs and damages, by the moft proper means they can find out.

II. As the true aim and intention of this alliance between the faid kings is mutually to preferve the peace and tranquillity of their refpective kingdoms ; their abovefaid majefties do promife to each other their reciprocal guarantee for the protecting and maintaining generally all the dominions, countries and towns both in and out of Europe, whereof each of the allies fhall be actually in poffeffion at the time of the figning of this alliance ; as alfo the rights, immunities, and advantages, particularly thofe relating to trade, which the faid allies enjoy or ought to enjoy refpectively. And to this end the faid kings have agreed, that if out of refentment on account of this alliance, or upon any other pretext, any one of the faid allies fhould be attacked in hoftile manner by, or fhould fuffer any wrong from, any prince or ftate whatfoever, the other allies fhall employ their good offices to procure fatisfaction to be given to the injured party, and to engage the aggreffor to forbear any further hoftility or wrong.

III. And

III. And if any of the contracting parties should be openly attacked, or molested in the above cases, and that the good offices abovementioned should not be effectual, so as to procure a just satisfaction for the wrongs and damages done to the injured party, then the other parties within two months after application shall be made to them, shall furnish the following succours; that is to say,

His majesty the king of Great Britain shall furnish 8,000 foot, and 4,000 horse.

His most Christian Majesty shall, in the like case, furnish 8,000 foot, and 4,000 horse.

And his majesty the king of Prussia, shall furnish 3,000 foot, and 2,000 horse.

But if the party-attacked should rather desire to have men of war, or transport ships, or even subsidies in money, which shall always be left to his choice; then the other parties shall supply him with ships or money, in proportion to the expence of the troops to be furnished as above. And to remove all manner of doubt with regard to this expence, the contracting parties do agree, that 1,000 foot shall be valued at 10,000 Dutch guilders by the month; and 1,000 horse, at 30,000 guilders of the same money also by the month: and the computation shall be made in proportion as to the men of war and transport ships. If the succours above specified do not prove sufficient to cause satisfaction to be made to the injured party, then the contracting parties shall agree together upon further forces to be furnished; and finally, in case of need, the said allies shall assist the injured party with all their forces, and shall even declare war against the aggressor.

IV. And as the said three most serene kings are resolved to bind more and more closely the strict union that subsists among them, by all possible tokens of good faith and mutual confidence, they have reciprocally agreed, not only to enter into no treaty, alliance, or engagement whatsoever, which may, in any manner whatever, be contrary to the interests of each other; but even faithfully to

communicate to each other the propofal that may be made to them, and not to take, upon what may be propofed, any refolution, otherwife than in concert together, and after a joint examination of what may conduce to their common interefts, and be proper for maintaining the ballance of Europe, which is fo neceffary to be preferved for the good of the general peace.

V. His moft Chriftian Majefty being particularly interefted as gaurantee of the treaties of Weftphalia, in the maintaining of the privileges and liberties of the Germanick Body; and their Britannick and Pruffian Majefties as members of that body, obferving with equal concern feeds of divifion and of complaint that may at length break out, and bring on a war, which, by fatal confequences refulting from it, might fet all Europe on fire; their faid majefties being ever attentive to what may one day difturb the tranquility of the empire in particular, and that of Europe in general, do engage and promife to help each other mutally in maintaining and caufing to be obferved the above faid treaties, and the other acts, which having fettled the affairs of the empire, are looked upon as the bafis and foundation of the tranquility of the Germanick Body, and the fupport of its rights, privileges and immunities, which their above faid Majefties are truly defirous to fecure in a folid manner.

VI.. The prefent alliance fhall fubfift during the fpace of 15 years to be computed from the day of the figning of thefe prefents.

VII. Their Britannick, moft Chriftian, and Pruffian Majefties will invite the princes and ftates which fhall by them be agreed upon, to accede to the prefent treaty; and they have now agreed to invite particularly the Lords the States General of the United Provinces.

VIII. This prefent treaty fhall be approved and ratified by their Majefties the King of Great Britain, the moft Chriftian King, and the King of Pruffia, and the ratification fhall be delivered in the fpace of two months from the figning of thefe prefents, or fooner, if poffible.

In

In witnefs whereof, we have figned this prefent treaty and caufed the feals of our arms to be affixed thereto. Done at Hanover, the 3d of September, 1725.

(L. S.) *Townfhend.*
(L. S.) *Broglio.*
(L. S.) *Wallendrodt.*

SEPARATE ARTICLE. No. 1.

WHEREAS the affair that lately happened in the city of Thorn, and what has enfued thereupon, have alarmed many princes and ftates, who apprenend that, to the prejudice of the treaty of Oliva, difturbances may on this occafion arife, not only in Poland, but alfo in the neighbouring countries, their Britannick, moft Chriftian, and Pruffian Majefties, who, as gaurantees of the faid treaty of Oliva, are obliged to fee it maintained and obferved to all intents and purpofes, do engage to employ their offices the moft effectually they can, to caufe reparation to be made for what may have been done contrary to the faid treaty of Oliva; and in order thereunto, their faid Majefties will, in concert together, inform themfelves by their Minifters in Poland, of the infractions that may have been made of the faid treaty of Oliva, and of the means by which the fame may be redreffed, in fuch way as may entirely fecure the public tranquility againft the dangers to which it might be expofed, fhould fo folemn a treaty as that of Oliva be infringed.

SEPARATE ARTICLE. No. 2.

IF out of refentment, on account of fuccours which his moft Chriftian Majefty may furnifh to his Britannick Majefty and to his Pruffian Majefty, to fecure them from the difturbance which they might fuffer in the territories they poffefs, the empire fhould declare war againft his faid moft Chriftian Majefty; as in this cafe fuch a declaration would as well affect the moft ferene King of Great Britain, and the moft ferene King of Pruffia, whofe interefts would be the occafion of fuch a

war,

war, as his moſt Chriſtian Majeſty; they not only will
fórdear to furniſh their quota in troops, or in any other
kind of ſuccours whatever, even though their ſaid Britannick and Pruſſian Majeſties ſhould not be comprehended
and named in the declaration of war which the empire
ſhould make againſt France, but they will even act in
concert with his moſt Chriſtian Majeſty, until the peace
diſturbed on that occaſion be reſtored; his ſaid Britannick
Majeſty expreſſly promiſing, moreover, to execute in ſuch
caſe the treaties he has concluded with his moſt Chriſtian Majeſty, who on his part promiſes faithfully to obſerve
the ſame.

### SEPARATE ARTICLE. No. 3.

IF it ſhould happen, that, notwithſtanding his moſt
Chriſtian Majeſty's firm reſolution to obſerve exactly
all his treaties with regard to the empire, in thoſe things
in which there has been no derogation therefrom by the
preſent treaty, it ſhould be attempted on the part of the
empire to take any reſolution againſt France, to the prejudice of the general guarantee of poſſeſſions, as it is ſtipulated by the treaty ſigned this day; his Britannick Majeſty and his Pruſſian Majeſty promiſe in ſuch caſe to employ their good offices, credit, and authority, the moſt
effectually they ſhall be able, either by their own votes,
and thoſe of the princes in friendſhip with them at the
diet, or by all other proper means, to prevent any thing
being done contrary thereto: and if againſt all expectation
and notwithſtanding all their endeavours, war ſhould be
declared againſt France, on the part of the empire, although in this caſe the ſame being no longer a defenſive
one, they might not by its conſtitutions be obliged to
furniſh any quota; yet to remove all doubt between their
ſaid Majeſties, if they ſhould think they could not be diſ-
penſed with from performing their duty as members of
that body, their ſaid Britannick and Pruſſian Majeſties do
reſerve to themſelves the liberties of furniſhing their quotas
of foot or horſe, of their own troops, or of ſuch as they
ſhall take into their pay from any other prince, at their
own choice; and their Britannick and Pruſſian Majeſties
ſhall

shall not, on account of such furnishing their quotas, be deemed to have acted contrary to the treaty signed this day, which shall contine in all its force: their Britannick and Prussian Majesties promising not to furnish in such case any other or greater number of troops against his most Christian Majesty, than what they are obliged to find for their quota; and that they will in other respects perform, in the cases foreseen, their engagements to his said most Christian Majesty, who on his part shall not on account of the said quota exercise any hostility against the territories and subjects of the said most serene King of Great Britain, or the said most serene King of Prussia, in the empire, or elsewhere; nor demand, or pretend to any contributions, forage, quarters, passage or other things at the charge of the said countries and territories, on any pretence whatsoever. In like manner, it shall also not be lawful for the said territories, places, countries, and subjects, to furnish any of the said things to the enemies of his most Christian Majesty; who does also oblige himself and promise on his part, that if in the empire resolutions should come to be taken, like to those that are mentioned in this article, to the prejudice of the Kings of Great Britain and Prussia, his most Christian Majesty will openly take their part, and will not fail to assist them with all necessary vigour, in pursuance of this treaty, until the disturbances, wrongs, and infractions, shall entirely cease.

These separate articles shall be of the same force, as if they had been inserted word for word in the treaty this day concluded and signed: they shall be ratified in the same manner, and the ratifications therefore shall be exchanged at the same time as the treaty. In witness whereof, we have signed these articles, and have set thereto the seals of our arms. Done at Hanover the third of September 1725.

(L. S.) *Townshend.*
(L. S.) *Broglio.*
(L. S.) *Wallendrodt.*

*Act of the Acceſſion of the* United Provinces *to the Treaty of Defenſive Alliance, ſigned at* Hanover *on the 3d of* September 1725. *Made at the* Hague *the 9th day of* Auguſt 1726.

### *In the Name of the Moſt Holy and Undivided Trinity.*

WHEREAS their Majeſties, the moſt Chriſtian King, the King of Great Britain, and the King of Pruſſia, as well for cementing the ſtrict union which ſubſiſts betwixt them, as for the ſafety of their own kingdoms and dominions, and alſo for the preſervation of the peace and of the public tranquility, thought fit to enter into an alliance with one another; the treaty for which purpoſe was concluded at Hanover the 3d of September 1725, together with three ſeparate articles, which were communicated to their High Mightineſſes the Lords the States General of the United Provinces of the Netherlands, by the Marquis de Fenelon, ambaſſador of France; by Mr. Finch, envoy extraordinary of Great Britain; and by the Sieur Meynhertſhagen, envoy extraordinary from the King of Pruſſia; who in the name of the Kings their maſters jointly invited the ſaid Lords the States General to accede to the ſaid treaty, and the ſeparate articles, conformably to the agreement in the ſeventh article of the ſaid treaty, which with the ſeparate articles are here inſerted *verbatim.*

### *Fiat Inſertio.*

And whereas the ſaid Lords the States General, after having ſeen and examined the ſaid treaty and its ſeparate articles, have declared that they are fully ſenſible of the honour which their majeſties did them by ſo ready and obliging an invitation to accede to the ſaid treaty; and as at the ſame time they acknowledge the care they took in the making of this treaty, as well for the preſervation of the public tranquility in general (without which the peace of their republic cannot be ſecure) as in particular for the maintenance of its commerce, without which

it

it cannot fubfift; and as they are fully convinced moreover, that the aim of this alliance does not at all tend to
give the leaft infringement to any former treaty or alliance,
contracted either by them, or by any one of them; with
other princes or ftates, but that their intention is rather to
corroborate them; and that the grand view of this alliance
only tends to the uniting of themfelves the more clofely
together, without giving offence to any perfon whatfoever, for the gaurantee, protection, and maintenance of
all the dominions, countries, and towns, in or out of
Europe, which each of the allies fhall be actually in poffeffion of at the time of the figning the faid treaty, as well
as of the rights, immunities, and advantages, particularly
thofe relating to commerce, either in Europe or out of it,
which each of the allies enjoyed at the time of the figning
of the faid acceffion.

Moreover, the faid Lords the States General being firmly
perfuaded, that by their acceffion to the faid treaty of
Hanover, it is not required of them that they fhall undertake the general guarantee of the treaties of Weftphalia
and Oliva, mentioned in the fifth article of the treaty of
Hanover, and in the firft of the feparate aritcles, to which
general guarantee they were never engaged : but that their
guarantee in this refpect extends only to the rights and
poffeffions, which the high allies, or any one of them, have
acquired by thofe treaties, and which they enjoy at the
time of the figning.

And as to the affair of Thorn, mentioned in the firft
of the feparate articles of the treaty of Hanover, as they
only engage to employ their amicable offices jointly with
the high contracting powers, to obtain a reafonable fatisfaction and reparation for the infraction of the treaty of Oliva;
and in cafe thofe amicable offices be employed without
effect, and it fhould be thought neceffary to do any thing
further, then their High Mightineffes fhall be at full
liberty of giving their thoughts, without being obliged to
any thing more than good offices, unlefs they renew
their agreement.

Finally, fince this alliance has a particular view to the
eftablifhment of an intire confidence between the con
tracting parties, and the Lords the States General, fup-
posing

poſing that the allies will with all confidence mutually communicate their thoughts to each other about the ways and means which ſhall be thought moſt effectual in caſe of need, for preſerving and maintaining the poſſeſſions and rights abovementioned, as well thoſe relating to commerce as others, in Europe or out of Europe.

And whereas in full perſuaſion and firm confidence, that ſuch is the real aim and intention of their ſaid majeſties, the ſaid Lords the States General, to give a mark of their deſire to unite cloſely with them, and of their high eſteem for their friendſhip and alliance, have reſolved to accede to the treaty, and the ſeparate articles above inſerted: and have for this end appointed the Sieurs Chriſtian Charles, Baron de Lintelo, Lord of Eſſe, bailiff of Lochum, and droſſart of Bedovors; Arnold de Zuylen de Nievelt, late burgomaſter and ſenator of the city of Rotterdam, ruart of the territory of Putten, bailiff and dykegrave of Scieland; Iſaac van Hoornbeeck, penſionary counſellor of the ſtates of the province of Holland and Weſtfrieſland, keeper of the great ſeal, and ſuperintendant of the fiefs of the ſaid province; Nicholas Henry Noey, late burgomaſter of the town of Tholen; Gerrard Godard Tats van Ameronge, knight of the Teutonick order, and a commander of the ſaid order at Doeſburg, great huntſman of the province of Utrecht; John Abraham van Schurman, burgomaſter and ſenator of the town of Slot; Everard Rouſe burgomaſter of the town of Deventer; and Lambert Henry Emmer, ſecretary of Groningen, all deputies in the aſſembly of the ſaid Lords the States General, on the part of the ſtates of Guelderland, Holland, and Weſtfrieſland, Zealand, Utrecht, Frieſland, Overyſſel, Groningen, and Ommelands: and have furniſhed them with full powers to agree about that acceſſion with the Marquis de Fenelon, plenipotentiary of his moſt Chriſtian Majeſty; Mr. Finch plenipotentiary of his Majeſty the King of Great Britain; and M. Meynertſhagen, plenipotentiary of His Majeſty the King of Pruſſia, likewiſe veſted with full powers.

Who after having had a conference together, came to the following agreement; that the ſaid Lords the States General ſhall accede (as the ſaid deputies and plenipotentiaries have declared that they do accede, in their name, and on their behalf) to the faid treaty and feparate articles, engaging themfelves to their faid Majefties in every thing that is therein contained, in the fame manner as if they had contracted with them from the beginning. And their High Mightineffes acknowledging their end and intention to be fuch as is expreffed above, their faid Majefties will accept of their High Mightineffes acceffion, as the faid ambaffadors, minifters, and plenipotentiaries have declared, that they do accept of the faid acceffion, in the name, and on the behalf of their faid Majefties, engaging themfelves to their High Mightineffes in every thing that is contained in the faid treaty and feparate articles, in the very fame manner as if they had contracted with their Majefties from the beginning.

The fuccours which their High Mightineffes are to furnifh in cafe of need, not having been regulated by the treaty, it is agreed that the fame fhall be four thoufand foot, and one thoufand horfe. For clearing up of the 6th article of the treaty, it is declared, that after the expiration of the fifteen years therein mentioned, the whole fhall fall in with the terms of preceding treaties, as they fubfift between the high contracting powers, and efpecially with the terms of the alliance ftipulated in the year 1717.

This prefent treaty for the acceffion of the States General fhall be approved and ratified by their Majefties the moft Chriftan King, the King of Great Britain, and the King of Pruffia, and by the Lords the States General of the United Provinces of the Netherlands, and the ratifications fhall be produced here at the Hague, within the fpace of two months from the day of figning thefe prefents, or fooner, if poffible. In witnefs whereof, we the underwritten plenipotentiaries conftituted for the purpofe aforefaid, and vefted with the full powers of their Majefties the moft Chriftian King, the King of Great Britain, the King of Pruffia, and the faid Lords the States General, have figned the prefent treaty, and caufed the feals of our arms

to

to be thereto affixed. Done at the Hague, the 9th day of Auguſt 1726. *Signed.*

(L. S.) The Marquiſs *de Fenelon.*
(L. S.) *W. Finch.*
(L. S.) *C. C. de Lintelo.*
(L. S.) *A. v. Zuylen van Nievelt.*
(L. S.) *Iſ. Van Hoornbeck.*
(L. S.) *N. J. H. Noey.*
(L. S.) *A. v. Schurman.*
(L. S.) *Everard Rouſe.*
(L. S.) *L. H. Emmer.*

SEPARATE *and* SECRET ARTICLE.

THE Lords the States General having repreſented that it may happen, that in revenge for their acceſſion ſigned this day, they may be attacked or diſturbed, in ſuch manner that they may be obliged to have recourſe to arms for their defence, and that then the time neceſſary to wait for the ſucceſs of the offices which ſhall be employed, when, and not before, their allies are obliged to furniſh them with the ſuccours ſtipulated by the third article of the treaty of Hanover, may be a conſiderable prejudice to them, and leave them expoſed to the moſt vigorous attacks, without being ſuccoured by the princes their allies; their moſt Chriſtian, Britannick, and Pruſſian Majeſties, in order to give the Lords the States General a freſh proof of their concern for the preſervation of their republic, have been pleaſed to engage and promiſe, that in the caſes aforeſaid, which may put the ſaid republic in evident danger, they will furniſh the ſuccours ſtipulated by the third article abovementioned, even without waiting for the iſſue of the offices and inſtances which they ſhall ſet on foot with the agreſſor, to procure the ſatisfaction or reparation required.

This article ſhall remain ſecret, and have the ſame force as if it were inſerted *verbatim* in the treaty this day concluded and ſigned: It ſhall be ratified in the ſame manner, and the ratifications ſhall be exchanged at the ſame time as the treaty. In witneſs whereof, we the underwritten, being appointed plenipotentiaries by virtue

of

of the full powers of their Majesties the most Christian King, the King of Great Britain, the King of Prussia, and of the Lords the States General of the United Provinces, have signed the present article, and caused the seal of our arms to be thereto affixed. Done at the Hague, the 9th of August 1726.

*Signed,*

(L. S.) The Marquis *de Fenelon.*
(L. S.) *W. Finch.*
    (And by the same deputies who signed the act of the accession.)

## DECLARATION.

WHEREAS in the first article of the treaty signed at Hanover on the 3d of September 1725, betwixt their Majesties the most Christian King, the King of Great Britain, and the King of Prussia, among other cases there is mention of the examination to be made of what is proper for maintaining the balance of power, necessary to be preserved in Europe for the sake of peace in general; the deputies of the States General of the United Provinces, with the consent of the Ministers of the three contracting powers, have reserved it to themselves, that when their Majesties think it necessary to concert together, and to advertise the said States General concerning such points as relate to the maintenance of a balance of power in Europe, the Lords the States General shall in every particular proposed for their concert, retain the same liberty they had before their accession to the said treaty, without being obliged by their accession to engage in any measures which they shall not agree to.

This declaration shall be ratified in the same manner, and the ratifications thereof shall be exchanged at the same time as those of the treaty, of which we the underwritten who are constituted plenipotentiaries, by virtue of the full powers of their Majesties, the most Christian King, the King of Great Britain, the King of Prussia, and the Lords the States General of the United Provinces, have signed the present declaration, and have

caused

caufed the feals of our arms to be thereto affixed. Done at the Hague, the 9th of Auguft 1726.

*Signed,*

(L. S.) The Marquis *de Fenelon.*

(L. S.) *W. Finch.*

(And by the fame deputies who have figned the act of acceffion.)

## SEPARATE ARTICLE.

THOUGH it is clear and indifputable, that their High Mightineffes the Lords the States General of the United Provinces of the Netherlands, by the fifth and fixth articles of the treaty of Munfter, in the year 1648, made between Spain and the repubick of the United Provinces, have acquired a right which excludes the fubjects of the Auftrian Netherlands, as well as the fubjects of all other countries, which at that time conftituted a part of the Spanifh monarchy, from navigation and commerce to the Indies within the limits of the privileges or charter granted by the faid Lords the States General to their Eaft and Weft-India companies; and that this right by confequence falls evidently under the guarantee of the rights to which the allies are mutually engaged by virtue of the 2d article of the treaty, concluded at Hanover the 3d of September 1725: neverthelefs, in order to remove all manner of doubt and fcruple upon that head, the underwritten ambaffadors, envoys extraordinary, and plenipotentiaries of their moft Chriftian and Britannick Majefties, at the requeft of the underwritten deputies, plenipotentiaries of their High Mightineffes, have been pleafed to declare, as they do by thefe prefents declare, in the name and on the part of their majefties, that the faid right refulting from the 5th and 6th articles of the treaty of Munfter, is included in the rights which the allies guarantee by the fecond article of the treaty of Hanover; and that if by reafon of the exercife of fuch right, or in revenge for this alliance, any mifunderftanding fhould happen, and his Imperial Majefty, contrary to expectation, fhould fufpend or ftop the payment of the fubfidies due to the republic for the maintenance

*of*

of their troops in the barrier places, or the payment of the interests and the principal sums borrowed upon divers funds assigned by his Imperial Majesty for the security of the said payment, or if he should make use of any sort of reprisal or violence, that then it is their said majesties intention, that the allies shall protect and maintain the said Lords the States General, comformably to the alliance to which they have this day acceded, and shall without delay concert the most effectual and proper means for maintaining the said Lords the States General in this right, and in the exercise thereof, and shall guarantee them against all consequences resulting from the same; but so as not to proceed to violence against the Ostend company, in the Indies or elsewhere, before the contracting powers of this alliance have concerted what to do thereupon. This separate article shall be of the same force as if it had been inserted word for word in the treaty concluded and signed this day: it shall be ratified in the same manner, and the ratifications shall be exchanged within the same time as the treaty. In witness whereof, we the underwritten, constituted plenipotentiaries, by virtue of full powers from their majesties, the most Christian King, the King of Great Britain, and the Lords the States General, have signed the present article, and thereto caused the seals of our arms to be affixed. Done at the Hague, the 9th of August 1726.

(Signed by the two ministers of France and England, and also by the deputies, as above.)

## DECLARATION.

THE deputies of the Lords the States General of the United Provinces, having communicated to the ministers of their majesties the most Christian King, the King of Great Britain, and the King of Prussia, the resolution taken by their High Mightinesses to accede to the treaty of Hanover, according to the invitation made to them by the said ministers on the part of their majesties; and having added, that they the said deputies were vested with a full power, and that they were ready to proceed to the conclusion and signing of the treaty

treaty and feparate articles drawn up upon their acceffion.

The Marquis de Fenelon, plenipotentiary of his moft
Chriftian Majefty, and Mr. Finch, plenipotentiary of his
Britannick Majefty, have declared, that they alfo were
vefted with full powers, and that they were ready to conclude and fign; but the Sieur de Meynhertfhagen, minifter of his Pruffian Majefty declaring, that he had not
yet received orders for the full powers to the fame end
from the king his mafter, the plenipotentiaries of their
moft Chriftian and Britannick Majefties, as alfo the deputies and plenipotentiaries of the Lords the States General, confidering that there was no more time to be loft,
and that every farther delay in completing the acceffion of
the republic to the treaty of Hanover, could not but
be difadvantageous to the end propofed by the faid treaty; and at the fame time there being no reafon to doubt,
that his majefty the king of Pruffia will likewife authorize his minifter to fign the treaty of acceffion, and
feparate articles: in confideration, and in firm confidence hereof, they have proceeded to the figning of the
prefent treaty and feparate articles, leaving a fpace
for the minifter of his majefty the King of Pruffia to
fign in like manner, as foon as he has received his full
power.

Neverthelefs it is agreed and ftipulated, by this feparate
article, that if, contrary to expectation, his majefty the
King of Pruffia doth not come to fuch refolution, the
faid treaty and feparate articles fhall, however, be of
force, and put in execution by the contracting powers,
in all their claufes, in the manner which has been ftipulated, and that the ratifications thereof fhall be exchanged
in the time fpecified.

In witnefs whereof, we the underwritten, who are appointed plenipotentiaries, by virtue of the full powers
of their majefties the moft Chriftian King, and the King
of Great Britain, and the Lords the States General, have
figned the prefent article, and caufed the feal of our arms
to be thereunto affixed. Done at the Hague, the 9th of
Auguft 1726.

(Signed by the minifter and deputies as above.)

Ac-

*Accession of the King and Kingdom of* Sweden *to the Treaty of* Hanover. *Dated at* Stockholm *the* 14th *of* March 172⁶₇.

## *In the Name of the most Holy Trinity.*

BE it known unto all and every one to whom it doth or may appertain, that his majesty the most serene King of Sweden, having been amicably invited, on the part of their majesties the most serene kings, the King of Great Britain, the most Christian King, and the King of Prussia, by their ministers, to accede to the defensive alliance which their majesties concluded at Hanover the 3d of September 1725, and to the three separate articles annexed thereunto; which, as well as the said alliance, have the maintaining and preserving of the publick tranquility, and particularly that of the North for their only object, the tenor whereof is as follows.

### *Fiat Insertio.*

And his majesty the most serene King of Sweden being always disposed to concur in so salutary a view, and being desirous to show how agreeable this invitation was to him, has authorized, by his full power, in due form his commissaries, the underwritten senators of the kingdom of Sweden, and members of the chancery, to enter into conference with the underwritten ministers plenipotentiaries, from their majesties the King of Great Britain and the most Christian King, provided with like full powers, for negotiating and agreeing upon the accession of his majesty the king, and the crown of Sweden, to the said treaty of alliance concluded at Hanover, and to draw up and sign an act in form for that purpose; the said ministers plenipotentiary and commissaries having been in conference several times upon that subject, and having produced their full powers on each side, agreed upon what follows.

His majesty the most serene king, and the crown of Sweden, declare and promise, that his said majesty, his heirs and successors, do full accede to the defensive alliance concluded at Hanover, and here above inserted;

as

as likewife to the three feparate articles that are there-unto annexed; and that his majefty and the crown of Sweden, by virtue of th's folemn acceffion, do join and affociate themfelves as a principal contracting party to their majefties the moft ferene kings, the King of Great Britain and the moft Chriftian King, obliging and en-gaging themfelves towards their faid majefties, their heirs and fucceffors, jointly and feparately, to obferve and fulfil faithfully and effectually all the conditions and claufes comprehended in the faid treaty of a defenfive alliance, and the three feparate articles thereof, and to furnifh, when the cafe of the alliance fhall happen, a fuccour of three thoufand foot, and two thoufand horfe, according to the obligations of the treaty: the whole in fuch manner, and as faithfully, as if his majefty and the crown of Sweden had been a principal contracting party from the beginning, with the abovefaid moft fe-rene confederate kings, and had concluded with their faid majefties jointly or feparately the articles and con-ditions expreffed in this defenfive alliance, and the fe-parate articles thereof.

Their majefti s the moft ferene kings, the King of Great Britain and the moft Chriftian King, do admit and affociate his majefty and the crown of Sweden to the abovefaid treaty of Honover; as likewife to the three feparate articles which are thereunto annexed, as a principal contracting party; declaring and promifing, on their part, that their majefties, their hiers and fuc-ceffors, will obferve and fulfil jointly and feparately, faithfully and effectually, with refpect to his majefty the moft ferene king and the crown of Sweden, all the con-ditions and claufes contained in the faid defenfive al-liance and the feparate article thereof.

This act of acceffion fhall be approved and ratified, on the part of their majefties the King of Great Britain, and the moft Chriftian King, and of his majefty and the crown of Sweden; and the ratifications thereof fhall be exchanged in the fpace of two months, to be reckoned from the day of the figning this prefent act, or fooner, if poffible.

In

In witnefs whereof, we, by virtue of our refpective full powers, have figned this prefent act, and have fet our feals thereunto. Done at Stockholm, the 14th day of March 1727. O. S.

(L. S.) *S. Poyntz.*
(L. S.) *M. J. de Garde.*
(L. S.) *A. Baneer.*
(L. S.) *Clas Ekeblad.*
(L. S.) *J. V. Duben.*
(L. S.) *D. N. Von Hopken.*
(L. S.) *J. H. Von Kochen.*

## SEPARATE ARTICLE.

ALTHOUGH by the act of acceffion and admiffion figned this day, his Majefty and the crown of Sweden accede purely and fimply to the treaty of Hanover, the minifters plenipotentiary of their Britannick and moft Chriftian Majefties have however agreed with the commiffaries of his faid majefty, to the exceptions and articles which follow.

I. As the defenfive alliance concluded at Hanover the 3d of September 1725, has no other view but the peace and tranquility of Europe, and particularly that of the North, their majefties the king of Great Britain, and the moft Chriftian King, as likewife his majefty the king and the crown of Sweden declare, that, being not engaged by any treaties or conventions with other powers that are contrary to this alliance, the faid treaties and conventions fhall not be weakened by this acceffion, but fhall remain in their full force: and their majfties declare, at the fame time, that they are, at prefent, and fhall continue always in a firm refolution to keep and fulfil, inviolably, all that has been ftipulated by the abovefaid alliance of Hanover; obliging themfelves, on each fide, to obferve faithfully all the engagements entered into by the prefent treaty of acceffion, and the feparate articles and fecret one thereof, without neglecting or violating the fame in any wife, under the pretence of former treaties and engagements, or under any other pretence whatfoever.

II. His

II. His majefty and the crown of Sweden having no poffeffions at prefent out of Europe, referve to themfelves that their guarantee fhall not be extended beyond the bounds of Europe.

III. The king and the crown of Sweden having fhewn that they defire not to be under the obligation of fending the troops ftipulated on their part in the act of acceffion to the treaty of Hanover, and by the fecret article of the prefent treaty of acceffion, into countries too far off, it is agreed, among the contracting parties, that, when the cafe of this prefent treaty fhall happen, the faid troops fhall not be employed in Italy, or in Spain, but they may any where elfe; their Britannick and moft Chriftian Majefties preferving always the right of demanding the contingent five thoufand men, ftipulated on the part of the king and of the crown of Sweden, in the act of their acceffion to the treaty of Hanover, in money or in fhips, purfuant to what is fettled in the faid treaty of Hanover.

IV. His majefty and the crown of Sweden, in order to remove all poffibility of doubt, with refpect to the acts mentioned in the fifth article of the treaty of Honover, as having determined concerning the affairs of the empire, declare, that, by the faid acts, they underftand no other than thofe which have been received and approved by the ftates of the empire in the ufual manner.

V. His majefty and the crown of Sweden declare, that they accede to the two laft feparate articles of the treaty of Hanover, as finding nothing therein contrary to the obligations wherewith his faid majefty is bound to the Emperor and the empire, as a prince of the empire.

VI. As by this acceffion his majefty the king and the crown of Sweden, enter into no engagements with any other power whatfoever, except thofe that are comprehended by name in the treaty of Hanover, and whofe minifters fign thefe prefents, their majefty the King of Great Britain, and moft Chriftian King, as likewife his faid majefty and crown, do promife each reciprocally, not to enter, without the knowledge of each other, and without mutual concurrence, into any engagments with any other power, that may be contrary to this treaty and thefe

fepa-

feparate articles and fecret one, or invalidate the fame in any wife.

Their Britannick, moft Chriftian and Swedifh majefties have agreed, and do promife each other reciprocally, that if, in hatred of this prefent treaty, or under any other pretext equally unjuft, they fhould be attacked, infefted or troubled, jointly or feparately, by any power whatfoever, they will make it a common caufe againft the aggreffor; and they will mutually fuccour and affift each other faithfully, and in the moft ready and effectual way, according to the exigency of the danger, and according to the fituation of their affairs, refpectively, without excufing themfelves, under pretence of being in war themfelves, or under any other pretence whatfoever.

### SECRET ARTICLE.

THEIR Britannick and moft Chriftian Majefties, to fhew their friendfhip towards the king and crown of Sweden, promife and engage, by virtue of this prefent fecret article, to pay at Hamburg, Amfterdam, or London, as Sweden fhall chufe each, for three years fucceffively, the fum of 50,000 l. fterling a year, or the value thereof, according to the exchange, to be paid in two payments each year, from fix months to fix months, by way of advance; and whereof the firft payment for the prefent year fhall be made immediately after the exchange of the ratifications; and the fecond payment, for the fame year, a little while afterwards, and as foon as the neceffary difpofitions can be made for that purpofe; the third payment to begin a year after the exchange of the ratifications; and fo the reft from fix months to fix months.

His majefty and the crown of Sweden oblige themfelves, and promife, on their fide, by this article, to hold in readinefs, befides the fuccour agreed upon by the act of this prefent acceffion, a further body of 7,000 foot, and 3,000 horfe, to be emyloyed where the cafes of the alliance fhall render it neceffary.

Provided, that when their Britannick and moft Chriftian Majefties fhall require the fervice of thefe 10,000 men, they fhall be in their pay, and not in that of the King of Sweden; which pay, as well as what concerns the recruits

and

and other matters depending thereon, ſhall be then ſettled by a particular convention ; his majeſty and the crown of Sweden reſerving to themſelves the right of recalling this body of troops, or of not ſending it out of the kingdom, at ſuch times when any real and imminent danger ſhall render it neceſſary for the defence of their own dominions and provinces.

Theſe ſeparate articles, and the ſecret one, ſhall have the ſame force as if they had been inſerted word for word in the act of acceſſion, concluded and ſigned this day ; they ſhall be ratified in the ſame manner, and the ratification thereof ſhall be exchanged at the ſame time with thoſe of the act of acceſſion.

In witneſs whereof, we, by virtue of our reſpective full powers, have ſigned the preſent ſeparate articles, and the ſecret one, and have ſet our ſeals thereunto. Done at Stockholm, the 14th of March, O. S. 1727.

    (L. S.) *S. Poyntz.*
    (L. S.) *M. J. de la Garde.*
    (L. S.) *A. Barneer.*
    (L. S.) *Clas Ekeblad.*
    (L. S.) *J. V. Dubend.*
    (L. S.) *D. N. Von Hopken.*
    (L. S.) *J. H. Von Kochen.*

---

*Treaty of Alliance between* Great Britain, France, *and* Denmark, April 16, 1727.

WHEREAS their majeſties the King of Great Britain and the moſt Chriſtian King are always attentive to fulfil their engagements, and to watch over the quiet and ſecurity of their friends and allies; and as their ſaid Majeſties have really cauſe to believe, that the Muſcovites and their adherents may ſoon concert means, and make diſpoſitions to come and attack the dominions of his majeſty the King of Denmark, either to take away by force from his Daniſh Majeſty the duchy of Sleſwick ; or to prepare the means for executing other projects contrary to the tranquillity of the North, and of the Lower Saxony, and of the countries which are of concern to the contracting

tracting parties in the circle of Weftphalia; and as their Britannick and moft Chriftian Majefties are fo much concerned in intereft to take due precautions againft every thing that by troubling the peace of the faid countries, may, at the fame time, give a blow to the treaty of Hanover, as it efpecially confirms the treaties of Weftphalia; and to put themfelves in a condition to execute faithfully the guarantees given againft any invafion or hoftility on the part of the Czarina, or of any other power whatfoever, which fhould come and attack the duchy of Slefwick: their Britannick, moft Chriftian and Danifh Majefties have thought fit to give their full powers, that is to fay, his Britannick Majefty to John Lord Glenorchy, knight of the order of the Bath, and envoy extraordinary from his majefty the King of Great Britain to his majefty the King of Denmark; his moft Chriftian Majefty to Peter Blouet, Count of Camilly, knight of the grand crofs of the order of St. John of Jerufalem, captain of the fhips of his moft Chriftian Majefty, and his ambaffador plenipotentiary to his majefty the King of Denmark; as likewife his Danifh Majefty to his minifters, viz. Ulrick Adolph of Holftein, Count of Holftenburg, knight of the order of the Elephant, great chancellor, privy counfellor of the council, and chamberlain to his majefty the King of Denmark; John George of Holftein, Lord of Mollenhagen, knight of the order of the Elephant, privy counfellor of the council, and governor of the bailywick of Tondern, for his majefty the King of Denmark; and Chriftian Lewis of Pleffeu, Lord of Tufingoe, Silfoe and Glorup, knight of the order of Dunnebrog, and privy counfellor of the council of his Majefty the King of Denmark; who, having maturely weighed the circumftances of the times, and the dangers which threaten the dominions of his Danifh Majefty, and which may trouble the quiet of Lower Saxony, and of the countries abovementioned, have agreed upon the following articles.

I. His Danifh Majefty being wholly perfuaded, that their Britannick and moft Chriftian Majefties will fulfil the engagments and guarantees given, with refpect to the dutchy of Slefwick, and that they will ufe all the efforts

efforts imaginable to maintain the quiet of the Lower Saxony; his Danish Majesty to concur in the same end, promises to keep on foot a body of troops of 24,000 men, their officers, equipages, and artillery, which shall assemble without any delay, in the place that shall be the most proper; and shall march every where, as it shall be needful, upon the first certain advices which shall be received of the motion of the Muscovite troops, or of any other power whatsoever which shall come to attack Sleswick, and to trouble the quiet and tranqillity of the Lower Saxony, and of the provinces belonging to the high contractors in the circle of Westphalia.

II. His Danish Majesty further obliges himself, when the said body of troops of 24,000 men comes to march, to have on foot at the same time another body of 6,000 men, designed to re-inforce the former body, if there be need.

III. And, towards helping, at present, his Danish Majesty to support the expence he will be obliged to make for fulfilling the engagements specified in the precedent articles, his most Christian Majesty promises to cause to be paid to his Danish Majesty an annual subsidy of 350,000 rixdollars, current money of Denmark: which shall be continued for the space of four years, to be reckoned from the day of the ratification of this present treaty, and shall be paid exactly every three months, by way of advance, at Hamburg.

IV. His most Christian Majesty promises further, in order to ease his Danish Majesty of part of the charge he will be at, in case the said 24,000 men should be put in march towards the place of rendezvous, to take 12,000 men into his pay, in such manner that, as the defence of the King of Denmark is their first concern, his most Christian Majesty shall not pay them but on the foot of 9,000, in the same proportion as his Danish Majesty gives to his troops when they are in the field, as well for the pay of each reigment of foot and horse, as for that of the staff-officers of each regiment, of the general field officers, and of the artillery, in proportion to the number of 12,000 men of

his

his troops, officers, and other perfons neceffary for his fervice.

V. The pay in the manner it is juft now expreffed, fhall not begin to be on the account of his moft Chriftian Majefty, but from the day of the firft review which fhall be made before his majefty's commiffary general, when the troops fhall be drawn together in a body, as an army in order to take the field; the firft month fhall be paid by way of advance, and fo from month to month, as long as the faid troops fhall be in the pay of his moft Chriftian Majefty.

VI. And although his moft Chriftian Majefty might with juftice, pretend, that the fubfidy fhould ceafe on the day that the pay commences; however, as it may happen that the payment of thefe troops might begin before the King of Denmark could receive any effectual fuccour from the faid fubfidy, his moft Chriftian Majefty is willing to confent, that, if the faid pay of the troops fhould commence before the King of Denmark fhould have received two years of the fubfidy, then he will continue the fubfidy as long as is neceffary, to the end that the King of Denmark may always have two years of the fubfidy, what was paffed, and what was to come, being reckoned; and if, after the faid two years, the faid troops fhould remain no longer in the pay of his moft Chriftian Majefty, then the fubfidy ftipulated in the third article fhall continue to be paid to his Danifh Majefty to the end of the four years, which is the term of the prefent treaty.

VII. His moft Chriftian Majefty will, when he fhall be required to do it, fend a commiffary upon the place to affift at the review which fhall be made of the faid troops in order to march; the faid commiffary fhall likewife take the names of the regiments which fhall then go into the pay of his moft Chriftain Majefty; he fhall examine whether they are duly equipped, mounted and armed; the giving of the vacant commiffions, and the adminiftration of juftice, fhall as before, be done by his Danifh Majefty: the commiffary general from his majefty fhall affift at all the confultations for the military

litary operations; and, although it is not poffible to determine beforehand as to any cafe of war, which doth not yet, exift, it is however agreed in genereal, that the twelve thoufand men of the troops in the pay of his moft Chriftian Majefty, on the foot of nine thoufand men, fhall be treated in all things with a perfect equality, as the twelve thoufand men entirely in the pay of the King of Denmark.

VIII. If it happens that his faid moft Chriftian Majefty fhould not think that he has any more need for the fuccour of his allies, to continue the payment of the faid troops, he fhall be obliged to give his Danifh Majefty notice thereof two months before.

IX. His Britannick Majefty on his fide, fhall hold in readinefs to march a body of twelve thoufand men, to be joined to the twenty-four thoufand men of the Danifh troops abovementioned, upon the firft certain advice which fhall be received of the motion of the Mufcovite troops, or of thofe of any other power whatfoever, that fhall come to attack Slefwick, and trouble the quiet and tranquillity of the Lower Saxony.

XI. His Danifh Majefty having given his Britannick Majefty to underftand, that, being engaged by this prefent treaty to march a confiderable body of troops into the Lower Saxony, his maritime provinces will lie expofed to the enterprizes of his enemies; his Britannick Majefty being always difpofed to provide, according to his engagments, as a good and faithful ally, for the fecurity of the dominions of his Danifh Majefty, promifes and engages to fend to the fuccour of his Danifh Majefty upon the firft advices of the motions of the Mufcovite fleet, which fhall give juft occafion for fear, a fufficient fquadron of good fhips of war, to help to cover the fea coafts of his Danifh Majefty, and to hinder the Mufcovites from attacking the fame.

XI. And although their Britannick and moft Chriftian Majefties are not obliged to any fixed fuccour for the King of Denmark; however, as they defire to keep at a diftance from the dominions of that prince all invafion, the confequence whereof would be doubtlefs to kindle the fire of a war in violation of the treaty of Hanover, as
like-

likewife of the treaties of Weftphalia; which would oblige them to come to the fupport of their guarantees, and to the fuccour of their allies, who might be attacked, or in danger of being fo; to this end his moft Chriftian Majefty engages to hold always in readinefs a body, at leaft, of thirty thoufand men; which body fhall be deftined, whenever his faid majefty fhall be required, to march to every place where it fhall be needful, and as it fhall be agreed; or to make diverfions, or other operations neceffary for the common advantage, and for the fecurity of his allies in the empire or in the North; and at the fame time, his Britannick Majefty engages to hold likewife in readinefs another body of troops, which muft not be lefs than twelve thoufand men, to be deftined, in the fame manner, for marching every where, as it fhall be needful, and as it fhall be agreed, either to make diverfions or other operations neceffary for the fecurity of his allies in the empire or in the North, as the cafe fhall require.

XII. As the Mufcovites or other troops that may join them to come and attack the dominions of the King of Denmark, in order to take from him the duchy of Slefwick, may endeavour to pafs through the countries fubject to the King of Pruffia, which the allies perfuade themfelves that this prince will not fail to refufe; in cafe therefore, that the Czarina, or any other power whatfoever, fhould endeavour to force the paffes through the territories of the King of Pruffia, or attack him, or occafion any injury or damage to him, by reafon of the refufal which his majefty might give to the letting the Mufcovites, or other adherents as abovefaid, pafs through his countres; then the contracting Kings fhall caufe their joint army to march to the fuccour of the King of Pruffia, and fhall make war upon thofe who fhall have invaded or troubled him, until the attack and danger fhall ceafe, and the injury and damage be repaired.

XIII. The ratifications of the prefent treaty fhall be exchanged at Copenhagen in fix weeks, to be reckoned from the day of the figning of this treaty, or fooner, if poffible.

In

In witnefs whereof, we have figned this treaty, and have fet the feal of our arms thereunto. Done at Copenhagen, this 16th day of April, in the year 1727.

(L. S.) *Glenorchy.*

*Seperate and facred Articles belonging to the Treaty with* Denmark, April 16, 1727.

ALTHOUGH his moft Chriftian Majefty might juftly pretend, that the troops which he takes into his pay ought to take an oath to him; however, his Danifh Majefty having refolved to command in perfon the confederate army, it is agreed, in confideration of his Danifh Majefty, to rely in that matter on his royal word, for acting purfuant to the engagements which he has entered into by the treaty figned this day; but if it fhould happen, that his Danifh Majefty fhould change his refolution abovefaid, and that the contracting kings fhould find it requifite to feparate the body of troops, for the advantage of the common caufe, then the faid troops, in the pay of his moft Chriftian Majefty, fhall take the oath to him in the ufual form.

2. As their Britannick and moft Chriftian Majefties have made extraordinary efforts for the interefts of the King of Denmark, his Danifh Majefty promifes not to difpofe of any part of his troops, either directly or indirectly, contrary to the interefts of their Britannick and moft Chriftian Majefties; and it is agreed, that, as long as this treaty lafts, his Danifh Majefty fhall not give or fell any part of his troops to any power whatfoever, till after the fame has been concerted with their Britannick and moft Chriftian Majefties, againft whofe interefts he promifes to do nothing; engaging himfelf likewife to oppofe, every where, where it fhall be needful, every thing that may be done or projected contrary thereto, by any power whatfoever; which their Britannick and moft Chriftian Majefties promife reciprocally.

3. It is agreed, that if his moft Chriftian Majefty fhould defire to employ the twelve thoufand men which he pays on the foot of nine thoufand, for affairs which having no refpect to the fecurity of the King of Denmark fhould only

concern

concern the good of the fervice of his moſt Chriſtian Majeſty, or that of the alliance of Hanover, in ſuch caſe
the King of Denmark ſhall not make any difficulty to
give them for the ſervice of his moſt Chriſtian Majeſty ;
and a convention ſhall be made, for that purpoſe, ſix weeks
after the demand ſhall have been made by his moſt Chriſtian Majeſty.

4. And conſidering, that if the Muſcovites ſhould come
by land to penetrate into the North, and trouble the peace
of the empire, they could not have any other paſſage than
through the territories of Poland ; and, as it cannot be
doubted, but that this kingdom remembers ſtill the diſor-
ders which the Muſcovites committed there a few years ago,
it is agreed, by this preſent article, to communicate to the
king, and to the republic of Poland, the concert which
has been formed to hinder their entering into the empire,
and to invite them to take likewiſe on their part the moſt
effectual meaſures to ſtop the paſſes which the Muſcovites
would be deſirous of taking in the territories of the republick of Poland. Done at Copenhagen, this 16th day
of April, in the year 1727.

(L. S.) Glenorchy.

---

*Articles of Peace and Commerce between His Majeſty* George
II. *by the Grace of God, King of* Great Britain, &c. *and
the moſt Noble Prince* Muly Hamet Dahebby, Ben Muley
Iſmael, Ben Muley Zeriph, Ben Muley Aley, *King and
Emperor of the Kingdoms of* Fez *and* Morocco, &c. *Con-
cluded* Jan. 14, 1727-8.

I. THAT all Moors or Jews, ſubject to the Emperor of Morocco, ſhall be allowed a free traffic,
viz. to buy or ſell for 30 days in the city of Gibraltar, or
iſland of Minorca ; and not to reſide in either place, but
to depart with their effects, without let or moleſtation, to
any part of the ſaid Emperor of Morocco's dominions.

II. That the king of Great Britain's ſubjects reſiding in
Barbary, ſhall not be obliged to appear before the Cadi or
Juſtices of the country ; but only the governor of the
place,

place, and his Britannick Majefty's conful, are to take cognizance of and adjuft the differences they may have with the natives of the country.

III. That the menial fervants of his Britannick Majefty's fubjects, though natives of the country, either Moors or Jews, be exempt from taxes of all kinds.

IV. That all his Britannick Majefty's fubjects, as well paffengers as others, taken by any of the Emperor of Fez and Morocco's cruifers, on board any foreign fhip or veffel whatever, fhall immediately be fet at liberty and fent to the city of Gibralter.

V. That there be permiffion for buying provifions, and all other neceffaries for his Britannick Majefty's fleet, or city of Cibraltar, at any of the Emperor of Fez and Morocco's fea-ports, at the market prices; and the fame to be fhipped off without paying cuftom, as has been extorted lately contrary to the treaty of peace fubfifting.

VI. All the other articles being fifteen in number, concluded, agreed and adjufted by the Honourable Charles Steward, Efq; on the behalf of his Britannick Majefty, and by his Excellency Bafhaw Hamet, Ben Aly, Ben Abdalla, and his Imperial Majefty's Treafurer, Mr. Mofes Ben Hatter, a Jew, on the behalf of the faid King of Fez and Morocco, fhall ftand good, and be of the fame force as in the reigns of the moft high and moft renowned Prince George I. King of Great Britain, France and Ireland, &c. of glorious memory, and the high and glorious, mighty and right noble Prince Albumazar Muley Ifmael, late Emperor of Morocco. And it is farther agreed that all the articles aforementioned, as well the fifteen as thefe additional ones, fhall in twenty days after the date hereof, be publifhed in the Arabick language, and affixed on the gates of all the fea-port towns in his Imperial Majefty's dominions.

Signed and dated at the court of Mequinez, Jan. 14, 1727-8.

*Convention*

*Convention between* Spain *and* Great Britain, *relating to the Execution of the Preliminaries; signed at the* Pardo, *the 6th of* March, 1728. *N. S.*

WHEREAS certain difficulties have arifen upon the execution of the articles which are called preliminaries, and which were figned at Paris the laft day of May, and after at Vienna the 13th of June, 1727, by the minifters refpectively furnifhed with fufficient full powers; and whereas, by a certain declaration made by the Count de Rothemburg, with the confent of all the parties, and approved, the aforefaid difficulties have been happily adjufted; of which declaration, and of the acceptation thereof by his Catholic Majefty, as the fame was exhibited and fubfcribed by the Marquis de la Paz, in his name, and by his command, the tenor hereof follows.

Whereas, fince the figning of the preliminaries, certain difficulties have arifen between the contracting parties, in relation to the reftitution of prizes that have been taken on either fide; and namely, that the Prince Frederick and its cargo, belonging to the South-fea company, has been feized and detained by the Spaniards at La Vera Cruz; which difficulties have delayed the execution of the preliminaries, the exchanging the ratification with Spain, and the opening the congrefs: his Britannick Majefty, to facilitate matters as much as lies in his power, and to remove all obftacles that obftruct a general pacification, has declared, and given his royal word to the moft Chriftian King, that he will, without delay, fend orders to his admirals, Wager and Hofier, or the chief commander in his ftead, or withdraw from the feas of the Indies and of Spain; and that he confents that the contraband trade, and other caufes of complaint, which the Spaniards may have in relation to the fhip Prince Frederick, fhall be difcuffed and decided in the congrefs; that all the refpective pretenfion, on each fide, fhall be produced, debated and decided, whether the prizes taken at fea, on each fide, fhall be reftored; and that his Britannick Majefty will abide by what fhall on all this be regulated.

On

On my part, I promife, in the name of the King my mafter, by virtue of the orders and full powers which I have received for that purpofe, that this difcuffion, to be made at the congrefs, fhall be faithfully executed ; that the exchange of the ratifications fhall be performed without delay, and that the congrefs fhall meet, infallibly, and the fooneft that fhall be poffible, according to what fhall be agreed by the minifters of the contracting parties who fhall happen to be at Paris ; provided his Catholic Majefty will give his royal word.

I. To raife, immediately, the blockade of Gibraltar, by fending back the troops to their quarters, by caufing the cannon to be drawn off, the trenches to be filled up, and the works made on the occafion of this fiege to be demolifhed, by re-eftablifhing every thing on each fide, conformable to the treaty of Utrecht.

II. to fend, without delay, his order, clear and exprefs, for delivering up forthwith the fhip Prince Frederick, and her cargo, to the agents of the South-fea company, who are at Vera Cruz, that, when they think fit, they may fend her to Europe ; and to reftore the commerce of the Englifh nation in the Indies, according to what is ftipulated by the Affiento treaty, and agreed by the fecond and third articles of the preliminaries.

III. To caufe the effects of the Flotilla to be immediately delivered to thofe to whom they belong ; and thofe of the Galleons, when they return, as in time of freedom and of full peace, according to the fifth article of the preliminaries.

IV. That his Catholic Majefty does engage, in the fame manner as his Britannick Majefty has engaged above, to abide by all that fhall be regulated by the abovefaid difcuffion and decifion of the congrefs.

*Given at the* Pardo, March 4, 1728.

(L. S.) *Rothemburg.*

I, the under-written Marquies de la Paz declare, by an exprefs order in the royal name of the Catholic King my mafter, in confequence of his full power, that his Majefty, out of his conftant defire to facilitate the negociations for an univerfal lafting peace, is come into an acceptation of, and

do.s

does effectually admit, the proposals lately made by the Count de Rothemburg, Minister and Plenipotentiary of his most Christian Majesty, according to what is here next above inserted.

In witness whereof, I sign this present declaration, and put thereto the seal of my arms, at the Pardo, March 5, 1728.

E. C. Marquis de la Paz.

We the under-written Ministers Plenipotentiary, duly authorised, to the end the above-written declaration and acceptation may obtain the most full force and vigour have signed this special instrument of consent and approbation, in the name, and by the consent of our respective Masters, and have affixed our Seals thereunto, March 6, 1729.

(L. S.) *S. S. Co Konigsegg.*
(L. S.) *B. Keen.*
(L. S.) *Rothemburg.*
(L. S.) *E. C.* Marquis *de la Paz.*
(L. S.) *F. Vander Meer.*

---

*The Treaty of Peace, Union, Friendship, and mutual Defence, between the Crowns of* Great Britain, France *and* Spain, *concluded at* Seville *on the* 9th *of* November, N. S. 1729.

In the Name of the most Holy Trinity, Father, Son, and Holy Ghost, three distinct Persons, and one only true God.

THEIR most Serene Majesties the King of Great Britain, the most Christian King, and the Catholic King, desiring, with equal earnestness, not only to renew and bind more closely their antient friendship, but likewise to remove whatever might hereafter disturb it, to the end that being united in sentiments and inclination, they may for the future act in every thing as having but one and the same view and interest; and for this purpose, the most Serene King of Great Britain having given full power for treating in his name to M. William Stanhope, Vice-Chamberlain

berlain of his Britannick Majefty's houfhold, one of his
Privy-Council, Member of the Parliament of Great Britain, colonel of a regiment of dragoons, and his faid Majefty's ambaffador extraordinary to his Catholic Majefty;
as alfo to M. Benjamin Keene, his faid Britannick Majefty's
Minifter Plenipotentiary to his Catholic Majefty: the
moft Serene moft Chriftian King having given full power
for treating in his name to the Marquis de Brancas,
lieutenant-general of his armies, knight of his orders,
and of that of the golden-fleece, his lieutenant-general
in the government of Provence, and his ambaffador extraordinary to his Catholic Majefty: and the moft ferene
Catholic King having likewife given full power for treating in his name to M. John Babtift D'Orendayn Marquis
de la Paz, his counfellor of ftate and firft fecretary of ftate
and of the difpatches; and to M. Jofeph Patino, commander of Alcuefca in the order of St. James, governor
of the council of the Treafury, and of the tribunals depending thereon, fuperintendant-general of the general revenues, and his fecretary of ftate and of the difpatches
for affairs of the Marine, the Indies, and the treafury:
the above-mentioned minifters have agreed between them
on the following articles.

I. There fhall be from this time and for ever a folid
peace, a ftrict union, and a fincere and conftant friendfhip
between the moft ferene King of Great Britain, the moft
ferene moft Chriftian King, and the moft ferene King of
Spain, their heirs and fucceffors, as alfo between their
kingdoms and fubjects, for the mutual affiftance and defence of their dominions and interefts; there fhall likewife
be an oblivion of all that is paft; and all the former treaties
and conventions of peace, of friendfhip, and of commerce,
concluded between the contracting powers refpectively,
fhall be, as they hereby are, effectually renewed and confirmed, in all thofe points which are not derogated from
by the prefent treaty, in as full and ample a manner, as if
the faid treaties were here inferted word for word, their faid
Majefties promifing not to do any thing, nor fuffer any
thing to be done, that may be contrary thereto directly or
indirectly.

II. In

II. In confequence of which treaties, and in order to eſtabliſh firmly this union and correſpondence, their Britannick, moſt Chriſtian, and Catholic Majeſtis, promiſe and engage by the preſent defenſive treaty of alliance, to guarantee reciprocally their kingdoms, ſtates, and dominions under their obedience, in what parts of the world ſoever ſituate, as alſo the rights and privileges of their com merce, the whole according to the treaties; ſo that the ſaid powers, or any one of them, being attacked or moleſted by any power and under any pretext whatever, they promiſe and oblige themſelves reciprocally to employ their offices, as ſoon as they ſhall be thereto required, for obtaining ſatisfaction to the party injured, and for hindering the continuance of hoſtilities; and if it happen that the ſaid offices be not ſufficient for procuring ſatisfaction without delay, their ſaid Majeſties promiſe to furniſh the following ſuccours, jointly, or ſeparately, that is to ſay, his Britannick Majeſty eight thouſand foot, and four thouſand horſe; his moſt Chriſtian Majeſty eight thouſand foot and four thouſand horſe; and his Catholic Majeſty eight thouſand foot and four thouſand horſe: If the party attacked, inſtead of troops, ſhould demand ſhips of war or tranſports, or even ſubſidies in money, he ſhall be free to chuſe, and the other parties ſhall furniſh the ſaid ſhips or money, in proportion to the expence of troops; and for taking away all doubt touching the valuation of the ſuccours, their aboveſaid Majeſties agree, that a thouſand foot ſhall be computed at ten thouſand florins Dutch money, and a thouſand horſe at thirty thouſand florins Dutch money, by the month; and the ſame proportion ſhall be obſerved with reſpect to the ſhips that ought to be furniſhed; their ſaid Majeſties promiſing to continue and keep up the ſaid ſuccours as long as the trouble ſhall ſubſiſt; and in caſe it ſhould be found neceſſary, their ſaid Majeſties ſhall mutually ſuccour each other with all their forces, and ſhall even declare war againſt the aggreſſor.

III. The miniſters of his Britannick Majeſty and of his moſt Chriſtian Majeſty, having alledged that in the treaties concluded at Vienna between the Emperor and the King of Spain, in the year one thouſand ſeven hundred twenty five, there were divers clauſes that infringed the articles of
the

the feveral treaties of commerce, or of the treaties of peace
in which commerce may be concerned, antecedent to the
year one thoufand feven hundred twenty five, his Catholick Majefty has declared, as he declares by the prefent article, That he never meant to grant, nor will fuffer to fubfift by virtue of the faid treaties of Vienna, any privilege
contrary to the treaties here-above confirmed.

IV. It have been agreed by the preliminary articles,
that the commerce of the Englifh and French nations, as
well in Europe as in the Indies, fhould be re-eftablifhed
on the foot of the treaties and conventions antecedent to
the year one thoufand feven hundred twent-five, and particularly that the commerce of the Englifh nation in America fhould be exercifed as heretofore ; it is agreed by the
prefent article, that all neceffary orders fhall be difpatched
on both fides without any delay, if they have not been
fent already, as well for the execution of the faid treaties
of commerce, as for fupplying what may be wanting for
the entire re-eftablifhment of commerce on the foot of the
faid treaties and conventions.

V. Although it was ftipulated by the preliminaries that
all hoftilities fhould ceafe on both fides, and that if any
trouble or hoftilities fhould happen between the fubjects
of the contracting parties, either in Europe, or in the
Indies, the contracting powers fhould concur for the reparation of damages fuftained by their refpective fubjects ;
and notwithftanding this it is alledged, that on the part of
the fubjects of his Catholic Majefty acts of diftubance
and hoftilities have been continued ; it is agreed by this
prefent article, that as to what relates to Europe, his Catholic Majefty fhall forthwith caufe reparation to be made
for the damages which have been fuffered there fince the
time prefcribed by the preliminaries for the ceffation of
hoftilities : and as to what relates to America, he will
likewife forthwith caufe reparation to be made for the damages which fhall have been fuffered there fince the arrival
of his orders at Carthagena on the $\frac{1}{2}\frac{1}{2}$ day of June one
thoufand feven hundred twent-eight. And his faid Ca-
tholic Majefty fhall publifh the moft rigorous prohibitions for preventing the like violances on the part of
his fubjects; their Britannick and moft Chriftian Majefties

jefties promifing on their part, if there be like cafes, to caufe reparation to be made for what fhall have been fo done, and to give like orders for the prefervation of the peace, tranquility, and good intelligence.

VI. Commiffaries fhall be nominated, with fufficient powers, on the part of their Britannick and Catholic Majefties, who fhall affemble at the court of Spain within the fpace of four months after the exchange of the ratifications of the prefent treaty, or fooner if it can be done, to examine and decide what concerns the fhips and effects taken at fea on either fide to the times fpecified in the preceding article. The faid commiffaries fhall likewife examine, and decide, according to the treaties, the refpective pretenfions which relate to the abufes that are fuppofed to have been committed in commerce, as well in the Indies as in Europe, and all the other refpective pretenfions in America, founded on treaties, whether with refpect to the limits or otherwife. The faid commiffarias fhall likewife difcufs and decide the pretenfions which his Catholic Majefty may have, by virtue of the treaty of one thoufand feven hundred twenty-one, for the reftitution of the fhips taken by the Englifh fleet in the year one thoufand feven hundred eighteen. And the faid commiffaries after having examined, difcuffed, and decided the above faid points and pretenfions, fhall make a report of their proceedings to their Britannick and Catholic Majefties, who promife that within the fpace of fix months after the making of the faid report, they will caufe to be executed punctually and exactly what fhall have been fo decided by the faid commiffaries.

VII. Commiffaries fhall likewife be nominated on the part of his moft Chriftian Majefty, and of his Catholic Majefty, who fhall examine all grievances generally whatfoever, which the faid parties therein interefted may form refpectively, whether for the reftitution of veffels feized or taken, or with refpect to commerce, limits, or otherwife.

VIII. The faid commiffaries fhall finifh punctually their commiffion within the fpace of three years, or fooner if it can be done, to be computed from the day of the figning
of

of the prefent treaty, and this without any further delay, on any motive or pretext whatever.

IX. The introducing of garrifons into the places of Leghorn, Porto-ferraio, Parma, and Placentia, to the number of fix thoufand men of his Catholic Majefty's troops, and in his pay, fhall be effectuated without lofs of time; which troops fhall ferve for the better fecuring and preferving of the immediate fucceffion of the faid ftates in favour of the moft ferene Infante Don Carlos, and to be ready to withftand any enterprife and oppofition which might be formed to the prejudice of what has been regulated touching the faid fucceffion.

X. The contracting powers fhall forthwith ufe all the applications which they fhall judge to be confiftent with the dignity and quiet of the moft ferene Great Duke of Tufcany, and the Duke of Parma, to the end the garrifons may be received with the greateft tranquillity and without oppofition, as foon as they fhall prefent themfelves before the places into which they are to be introduced.

The faid garrifons fhall take an oath to the prefent poffeffors to defend their perfons, fovereignty, poffeffions and ftates, and fubjects, in every thing that fhall not be contrary to the right of fucceffion referved to the moft ferene Infante Don Carlos, and prefent poffeffors fhall not demand or exact any thing that is contrary thereto.

The faid garrifons fhall not meddle directly or indirectly under any pretence whatfoever, in affairs of the political, oeconomical or civil government; and fhall have moft exprefs orders to render to the moft ferene Great Duke of Tufcany and the Duke of Parma, all the refpects and military honours that are due to fovereigns in their own dominions.

XI. The intent of introducing the faid fix thoufand men of his Catholic Majefty's troops and in his pay, being to fecure to the moft ferene Infante Don Carlos the immediate fucceffion of the ftates of Tufcany, Parma, and Placentia, his Catholic Majefty promifes, as well for himfelf as his fucceffors, that as foon as the moft ferene Infante Don Carlos his fon, or fuch other who fhall fucceed to his rights, fhall be the quiet poffeffor of thofe ftates, and in fafety from all invafion and other juft grounds

of

of fear, he will cauſe to be withdrawn from the places in
thoſe ſtates the troops which ſhall be his own, and not belonging to the Infante Don Carlos, or to him who ſhall
ſucceed to his rights, in ſuch manner that thereby the ſaid
ſucceſſion or poſſeſſion may reſt ſecure and cexempt from
all events.

XII. The contracting powers engage to eſtabliſh, according to the rights of ſucceſſion which have been ſtipulated, and to maintain the moſt ſerene Infante Don Carlos,
or him to whom his rights ſhall devolve, in the poſſeſſion
and enjoyment of the States of Tuſcany, Parma, and
Placentia, when he ſhall once be ſettled there; to defend
him from all inſult, againſt any power whatſoever, that
might intend to diſturb him; declaring themſelves by this
treaty, guarantees for ever of the right, poſſeſſion,
tranquillity, and quiet of the moſt ſerene Infante, and of
his ſucceſſors to the ſaid ſtates.

XIII. As to other particulars or regulations concerning
the keeping up of the ſaid garriſons once eſtabliſhed in
the ſtates of Tuſcany, Parma, and Placentia, as it is to
be preſumed that his Catholic Majeſty and the moſt ſerene Great Duke, and Duke of Parma, will ſetile the ſame
by an agreement between themſelves, their Britannick and
moſt Chriſtian Majeſties promiſe, that as ſoon as that
agreement ſhall be made, they will ratify and guarantee
it, as well as to his Catholic Majeſty, as to the moſt ſerene Great Duke and Duke of Parma, as if it were inſerted
word for word in the preſent treaty.

XIV. The States General of the United Provinces ſhall
be invited to come into the preſent treaty and articles.
Such other powers as ſhall be agreed on, ſhall likewiſe
be invited and admitted by concert into the ſame treaty and
articles.

The ratifications of the preſent treaty ſhall be diſpatched within the ſpace of ſix weeks, or ſooner, if it
can be done, to be reckoned frcm the day of the ſigning.

In witneſs whereof, We the underwritten miniſters
plenipotentiaries, of his Britannick Majeſty, of his moſt
Chriſtian Majeſty, and of his Catholic Majeſty, by virtue of our full powers, which have been communicated

ed to each other, tranfcripts of which fhall be hereto annexed, have figned the prefent treaty, and caufed the feals of our arms to be affixed thereto. Done at Seville, the ninth day of November, one thoufand feven hundred twenty-nine.

| | | |
|---|---|---|
| *W. Stanhope.* | *Brancas.* | *El. Marq. de la Paz,* |
| (L. S.) | (L. S.) | (L. S.) |
| *B. Keene.* | | *D. Jofeph Patino,* |
| (L. S.) | | (L. S.) |

*Separate Articles.*

I. ALTHOUGH, conformably to the preliminary articles, it is faid in the fourth article of the treaty figned this day, that the commerce of the Englifh nation in America fhould be re-eftablifhed on the foot of the treaties and conventions anteoedent to the year one thoufand feven hundred twenty-five ; however, for the greater exactnefs, it is further declared by the prefent article between their Britannick and Catholic Majefties, which fhall have the fame force, and be under the fame guaranty as the treaty figned this day, that under that general denomination are comprehended the treaties of peace and of commerce, concluded at Utrecht the thirteenth of July and ninth of December, in the year one thoufand feven hundred thirteen, in which are comprifed the treaty of one thoufand fix hundred fixty-feven, made at Madrid, and the cedulas therein mentioned ; the latter treaty made at Madrid the fourteenth of December, one thoufand feven hundred fifteen ; as alfo the particular contract, commonly called the Affiento, for bringing negro flaves into the Spanifh Indies, which was made the twenty-fixth day of March, in the faid year one thoufand feven hundred thirteen, in confequence of the twelfth article of the treaty of Utrecht ; and likewife the treaty of declaration. touching that of the Affiento, made the twenty-fixth of May, one thoufand feven hundred fixteen : all which treaties mentioned in this article, with their declarations, fhall from this day (even during the examination by the commiffaries) be and remain in their force, virtue and full

vigour ;

vigour; for the obfervation of which his Catholic Majefty fhall caufe to be difpatched forthwith, if they have not been difpatched, the neceffary orders and cedulas to his vice-roys, governors, and other minifters, to whom it fhall appertain, as well in Europe as in the Indies, to the end that without any delay or interpretation they may caufe them to be obferved and fulfilled.

In like manner his Britannick Majefty promifes and engages to publifh the neceffary orders, if any be wanting, for re-eftablifhing the commerce of the fubjects of Spain in all the countries under his dominion, on the footing fpecified by the faid treaties, and for caufing them to be exactly obferved and fulfilled.

II. Confequently, all fhips, merchandife and effects, which fhall not have been taken or feized on account of unlawful commerce, and which fhall now be proved by authentic proofs and documents, to have been detained, feized, or confifcated in the ports of Spain, either in Europe or in the Indies, and namely the fhip Prince Frederic and her cargo, if they have not been reftored already, fhall be immediately reftored, in the fame kind as to thofe things which fhall be found ftill remaining in that condition; or in default thereof, the juft and ttue value of them, according to their valuation, which, if it was not made at the time, fhall be regulated by the authentic informations which the proprietors fhall exhibit to the magiftrates of the places and town where the feizures were made; his Britannick Majefty promifing the like on his part, as to all feizures, confifcations, or detentions, which may have been made contrary to the tenor of the faid treaties: their faid Britannick and Catholic Majefties agreeing, that with refpect to the like feizures, confifcations, or detenfions on either fide, the validity of which may not yet have been fufficiently made out, the difcuffion and decifion of them fhall be referred to the examination of the commiffaries, to do therein according to right upon the foot of the treaties here above-mentioned.

The prefent feperate articles fhall have the fame force as if they were inferted word for word in the treaty, concluded and figned this day. They fhall be ratified in the fame

fame manner, and the ratifications of them fhall be exchanged at the fame time as thofe of the faid treaty.

In witnefs whereof we the underwritten minifters plenipotentiaries of his Britannick Majefty, of his moft Chriftian Majefty, and of his Catholic Majefty, by virtue of
our full powers, have figned the prefent feparate articles,
and caufed the feals of our arms to be put thereto. Done
at Seville the ninth day of November, one thoufand feven
hundred twenty-nine.

*W. Stanhope.*     *Brancas.*     *El Marq. de la Paz.*
(L. S.)       (L. S )       (L. S )
*B. Keene.*                  *D. Jofeph Patino.*
(L. S.)                     (L. S.)

---

*Treaty of Alliance and Commerce between* Great Britain *and
the Nation of the* Cherrokees *in* America. *Sept.* 20,
1730.

I. FORASMUCH as you Scayagufta Oukah, chief
of the city of Teftetfa, you Scalilofken Keta-
guftah, you Tathtowe, you Clogittah, you Kolkannah,
and you Ukwanequa, were fent by Moytoy de Telliquo,
with approbation of the whole nation of the Cherrokees,
in an affembly held at Nikoffen the 14th of April, 1730,
to Sir Alexander Cuming, Bart. in Great Britain, where
you have feen the great King George, at whofe feet the
faid Sir Alexander Cuming, by the exprefs order of Moytoy, and the whole nation of the Cherrokees, has laid the
crown of your nation, the fkulls of your enemies, and the
plumes of honour, as a mark of your fubmiffion : the
King of Great Britain, who has a tendernefs for the
powerful and great nation of the Cherrokees, his good
children and fubjects, has authorifed us to treat with you ;
and in this character we confer with you, as if the whole
nation of the Charrokees, its old men, its young men,
its women and children were here prefent : and you ought
to look upon the words which we fay to you, as if pronounced from the lips of the Great King your mafter,
whom you have feen ; and we will confider the words

which

which you shall speak to us, as the words of your whole nation, delivered frankly and sincerely to the Great King. Whereupon we give you four pieces of striped serge.

II. Hear therefore the words of the Great King, whom you have seen, and who has commanded us to tell you, that the English in all places, and on both sides the great mountains, and great lakes, are his people and children whom he dearly loves; that their friends are his friends, and their enemies his enemies; that he is pleased that the great nation of the Cherrokees has sent you hither, to polish the chain of friendship which is betwixt him and them, betwixt your people and his people; that the chain of friendship betwixt him and the Indians of the Cherrokees, is like the sun which gives light, both here and upon the high mountains that they inhabit, and which warms the hearts both of the Indians and the English. And as we see no spots in the sun, so there is no rust nor dirt on this chain: and as the Great King holds one end of it fastened to his breast, 'tis his intention that you should take up the other end of the chain, and fix it to the breast of Moytoy Telliquo, and to those of your wise old men, your captains and your people, in such manner that it may never be broke nor loosed. And hereupon we give you two pieces of blue cloth.

III. The Great King and the Indians of the Cherrokees, being thus united by the chain of friendship, he has ordered his children, the Indians of Carolina, to traffic with the Indians, and to furnish them with whatever commodities they want, and to build houses, and sow corn with speed, all the way from Charles-Town to the Cherrokees-Town, on the other side of the great mountains; for he would have the Indians and the English live together like children of one and the same family, whose Great King is their dear father: and forasmuch as the Great King has given his lands on both sides the great mountains to the English his children, he grants the Indians of the Cherrokees the privilege to live where they please. And upon this we give you a piece of red cloth.

IV. The great nation of the Cherrokees being at present the children of the Great King of Great Britain, and he being their father, the Indians ought to consider the

English

English as brothers, of one and the same family, and ought always to be ready at the governor's orders to fight against any nation whatsoever, either Whites or Indians, that shall molest or attack the English. And hereupon we give you twenty muskets.

V. The Cherrokees nation shall take care to keep the way of commerce clean, and that there be no blood in the road where the English white men travel, even though they happen to be accompanied by any other nation at war with the Cherrokees. Whereupon we give you two hundred weight of gunpowder.

VI. That the Cherrokees nation shall not suffer any of its people to traffic with any other white men besides the English, and shall grant leave to no other nation to build any fort or habitation, or to sow corn in their country, either near any towns of the Indians, or on the lands belonging to the Great King; and if any thing like it be undertaken, you must give advice of it to the English governor, and act as he shall order you, for maintaining the rights of the Great King over the lands of Carolina. Whereupon we give you five hundred weight of musket bullets, and the same quantity of cannon ball.

VII. That in case any negro slave runs away from his English master into the woods, the Indians of the Cherrokees shall do what they can to apprehend him, and bring him back to the plantation from whence he fled, or to the governor's house; and for every negro which the Indians shall thus retake, they shall have a musket, and a sentinel's suit of cloaths. Whereupon we give you a box full of vermilion, with 10,000 flints, and 6 dozen of hatchets.

VIII. That if an Englishman has the misfortune to kill an Indian, the king or chief of the Cherrokees shall first of all make his complaint to the English governor, and the person who committed the murder shall be punished according to the laws, as much as if he had killed an Englishman; and in like manner if an Indian kill an Englishman; the guilty Indian shall be delivered up to the governor, who shall punish him according to the English laws, and as if he was an Englishman. Whereupon

upon we give you twelve dozen of clafp-knives, four dozen of kettles, and ten dozen of bells.

IX. You are to know, that every thing we have faid to you are the words of the Great King whom you have feen; and to fhew that his heart is open and fincere to his children and friends the Cherrokees, and their whole nation, he puts his hand into this Bandelier, which he demands may be received and fhewn to your whole nation, to their children and Grand-chidlren, to confirm what has been faid to you, and to perpetuate this treaty of peace and friendfhip between the Englifh and the Cherrokees, as long as the mountains and rivers are in being, and as long as the fun fhall fhine. Whereupon we give you this Bandelier.

Signed,

| | |
|---|---|
| *Oukah Ulah,* | *Clogoittah,* |
| *Scalilofken Ketaguftah,* | *Kollannah,* |
| *Tathtowe,* | *Ukwancqua.* |

By order of the Commiffioners at Whitehall, the 30th of September, 1730.

ALLURED POPPLE.

And underneath,

'Tis for the fecurity of Moytoy de Telliquo, that I have feen, examined, and approved of all the articles contained in the above agreement, to which the faid Indians have by my advice given their confent.

Signed,

ALEX. CUMING.

*Treaty of Peace and Alliance, between the Emperor* Charles VI. *and* George II. *King of* Great Britain, *in which the States of the* United Provinces *of the* Netherlands *are included. Made at* Vienna, *the* 16th *of* March, 1731.

In the Name of the moft Holy and Undivided Trinity, Amen.

TO all to whom it does or may any way appertain. Be it known, that the moft ferene and moft potent Prince and Lord, Charles VI. Emperor of the Romans, &c. and

and the moſt ſerene and moſt potent Prince and Lord, George II. King of Great Britain, France and Ireland, together with the High and Mighty Lords the States General of the United Provinces of the Netherlands, having taken into conſideration the preſent unſettled and perplexed ſtate of affairs in Europe, ſeriouſly bethought themſelves of finding proper methods, not only to prevent thoſe evils which muſt naturally ariſe from the cavils and diviſions that were da ly increaſing, but alſo to eſtabliſh the public tranquillity upon a ſure and laſting foundation, and in as eaſy and ſpeedy a manner as it was poſſible : For this end their ſaid Majeſties and the ſaid States General, being fully animated with a ſincere deſire to promote ſo wholeſome a work, and to bring it to perfection, judged it expedient to agree among theſelves upon certain general conditions, which might ſerve as the baſis for reconciling the animoſities, and ſettling the differences of the chief Princes of Europe, which as they are heightened among themſelves, do greatly endanger the public tranquillity.

For which purpoſe, the moſt high Prince and Lord, Eugene Prince of Savoy and Piedmont, &c. and alſo the moſt illuſtrious Lord, Philip Lewis, Hereditary Treaſurer of the Holy Roman Empire, count of Zinzendorf, &c. and alſo the moſt illuſtrious Lord, Gundacker Thomas, count of the holy Roman Empire, &c. on the part of his Sacred Imperial and Catholic Majeſty ; and Thomas Robinſon, Eſq; miniſter of his Majeſty of Great Britain to his ſaid Imperial and Catholic Majeſty, on the part of his Majeſty of Great Britain; and on the part of the High and Mighty States of the United Provinces of the Netherlands; being all furniſhed with full powers, after they had held conferences together, and exchanged their credential letter and full powers, agreed upon the following articles and conditions.

I. That there ſhall be from this time forward, between his ſacred Imperial Catholic Majeſty, his ſacred royal Majeſty of Great Britain, the heirs and ſucceſſors of both, and the High and Mighty Lords the States General of the United Provinces of the Netherland, a firm, ſincere, and inviolable friendſhip, for the mutual advantage of the Provinces and ſubjects belonging to each of the contracting powers ;

powers: and that this peace be fo eftablifhed, that each of the contractors fhall be obliged to defend the territories and fubjects of the others; to maintain the peace, and promote the advantages of the other contractors as much as their own; and to prevent and avert all damages and injuries of every kind whatfoever, which might be done to them. For this end, all the former treaties or conventions of peace, friendfhip and alliance, fhall have their full effect, and fhall preferve in all and every part their full force and virtue, and fhall even be looked upon as renewed and confirmed by virtue of the prefent treaty, except only fuch articles, claufes, and conditions, from which it has been thought fit to derogate by the prefent Treaty. And moreover, the faid contracting parties have exprefsly obliged themfelves, by virtue of this prefent article, to a mutual defence, or as it is called guaranty of all the kingdoms, ftates, and territorries which each of them poffeffes, and even of the rights and immunities each of them enjoys, or ought to enjoy, in fuch manner, that they have mutually declared and promifed to one another, that they will, with all their forces oppofe the enterprifes of all and every one who fhall (perhaps contrary to expectation) undertake to difturb any of the contractors, or their heirs and fucceffors, in the peaceable poffeffion of their kingdoms, ftates, provinces, lands, rights, and immunities, which each of the contracting parties doth or ought to enjoy, at the time of the conclufion of the prefent treaty.

II. Moreover, as it has been frequently remonftrated on the part of his Imperial and Catholic Majefty, that the public tranquillity could not reign and laft long, and that no other fure way could be found out for maintaining the balance of Europe, than a general defence, engagement, and eviction, or as they call it, a guaranty for the order of his fucceffion, as it is, fettled by the imperial declaration of 1713, and received in the moft ferene Houfe of Auftria; his facred Royal Majefty of Great Britain and the High and Mighty Lords the States of the United Provinces of the Netherlands, moved thereto by their ardent defire to fecure the public tranquillity, and to preferve the balance of Europe, as alfo by a view of the

terms agreed upon in the following articles, which are ex-
ceedingly well adapted to anfwer both purpofes, do, by
virtue of the prefent article, take upon them the general
guaranty of the faid order of fucceffion, and oblige themfelves to maintain it as often as there fhall be occafion,
againft all perfons whatfoever; and confequently they promife, in the moft authentic and ftrongeft manner that can
be, to defend, maintain, and (as it is called) to guaranty, with all their forces, that order of fucceffion which
his Imperial Majefty has declared and eftablifhed by a
folemn act of the 19th of April, 1713, in manner of a
perpetual, indivifible, and infeparable feoffment of truft,
in favour of primogeniture, for all his Majefty's heirs of
both fexs; of which act there is a copy annexed at the
end of this treaty: which faid act was readily and unanimoufly received by the orders and eftates of all the kingdoms, archduchies, principalities, provinces and domains,
belonging by right of inheritance to the moft ferene Houfe
of Auftria; all which have humbly and thankfully acknowledged it, and tranfcribed it into their public regifters, as having the force of a law and pragmatic fanction, which is to fubfift for ever in full force. And whereas according to this rule and order of fucceffion, if it
fhould pleafe God of his mercy to give his Imperial and
Catholic Majefty iffue male, then the eldeft of his fons,
or, he being dead before, the eldeft fon's eldeft fon; and
in cafe there be no male iffue, on his Imperial and Catholic Majefty's demife, the eldeft of his daughters, the
moft ferene Archducheffes of Auftria, by the order and
right of feniority, which has always been indivifibly preferved, is to fucceed his Imperial Majefty in all his kingdoms, provinces, and domains, in the fame manner as he
now poffeffes them; nor fhall they at any time, upon any
account, or for any reafon whatever, be divided or feparated in favour of him, or her, or them, who may be of
the fecond, the third, or more diftant branch. And this
fame order and indivifible right of feniority is to be preferved in all events, and to be obferved in all ages; as
well in his Imperial Majefty's male iffue, if God grants
him any, as in his Imperial Majefty's female iffue, after
the extinction of the male heirs; or, in fhort, in all cafes
wherein

wherein the fucceffion of the kingdoms, provinces, and hereditary dominions of the moft ferene Houfe of Auftria fhall be called in queftion. For this purpofe, his Majefty of Great Britain, and the High and Mighty Lords the States Ceneral of the United Provinces of the Netherlands, promife and engage to maintain him, or her, who ought to fucceed according to the rule and order above fet forth in the kingdoms, provinces, or domains of which his Imperial Majefty is now actually in poffeffion; and they engage to defend the fame for ever againft all fuch as fhall perhaps prefume to difturb that poffeffion in any manner whatfoever.

III. And forafmuch as it hath been often reprefented to his Imperial and Catholic Majefty, in terms full of friendfhip, on the part of his facred royal Majefty of Great Britain, and the High and Might Lords the States General of the United Provinces, that there was no furer nor more fpeedy method for eftablifhing the public tranquillity fo long defired, than by rendering the fucceffion of the Duchies of Tufcany, Parma, and Piacentia, defigned for the moft ferene the Infante Don Carlos, yet more fecure by the immediate introduction of 6000 Spanifh foldiers into the ftrong places of thofe duchies, his faid facred Imperial and Catholic Majefty, defiring to promote the pacific views and intentions of his Britannick Majefty and the High and Mighty States General of the United Netherlands, will by no means oppofe the peaceable introduction of the faid 6000 Spaniards into the ftong places of the Duchies of Tufcany, Parma, and Placentia, in purfuance of the abovementioned engagements entered into by his faid Britannick Majefty, and by the States General. And whereas to this end, his imperial and Catholic Majefty judges the confent of the empire neceffary, he promifes at the fame that he will ufe his utmoft endeavours to obtain the faid confent, within the fpace of two months, or fooner, if poffible. And to obviate as readily as may be the evils which threaten the public peace, his Imperial and Catholic Majefty moreover promifes, that immediately after the mutual exchange of the ratifications, he will notify the confent which he, as Head of the empire, has given to the faid peaceable introduction, to the
minifter

minifter of the Great Duke of Tufcany, and to the minifter of Parma refiding at his court, or wherever elfe it
fhall be thought proper.  His faid Imperial and Catholic
Majefty likewife promifes and affirms, that he is fo far
from any thought of raifing, or caufing any hinderance, directly or indirectly, to the Spanifh garrifons being admitted
into the places aforefaid, that on the contrary he will interpofe his good offices and authority, for removing any unexpected obftruction or difficulty that may oppofe the faid
introduction and confequently that the 6000 Spainfh foldiers may be introduced quietly, and without any delay
in the manner aforefaid, into the ftrong places as well of
the Great Duchy of Tufcany, as of the Duchies of Parma
and Placentia.

IV. That therefore all the articles thus agreed to, with
the irrevocable confent of the contracting parties, be fo
firmly and reciprocally eftablifhed, and fo entirely decided,
that it fhall not be lawful for the contracting parties to de-
viate from them in any wife; meaning as well thofe which
are to be put in execution without delay, and immediately after the exchange of the ratifications, as thofe which
ought to remain for ever inviolable.

V. Whereas for attaining to the end which the contracting parties in this treaty propofe to themfelves, it has
been found neceffary to pluck up every root of divifion and
diffention, and therefore that the antient friendfhip which
united the faid contracting parties, may not only be renewed, but knit clofer and clofer every day, his Imperial
Catholic Majefty promifes, and, by virtue of the prefent article, binds himfelf to caufe all commerce and navigation to the Eaft-Indies to ceafe immediately and for
ever in the Auftrian Netherlands, and in all the other
countries which in the time of Charles II. Catholic King
of Spain, were under the dominion of Spain; and that he
will, *bona fide*, act in fuch manner, that neither the Oftend
Company, nor any other, either in the Auftrian Netherlands, or in the countries which, as is abovefaid, were
under the dominion of Spain in the time of the late Catholic King Charles II. fhall at any time directly or indirectly contravene this rule eftablifhed forever.  Excepting
that the Oftend Company may fend, for once only, two
ships,

fhips, which fhall fail from the faid port to the Eaft Indies, and from thence return to Oftend, where the faid Company may, when they think fit, expofe the merchandizes fo brought from the Indies to fale. And his facred royal Majefty of Great Britain, and the High and Mighty States General of the United Provinces, do likewife promife on their part, and oblige themfeves, to make a new treaty with his Imperial Majefty without delay, concerning commerce and the rule of impofts, commonly call'd a Tariff, as far as relates to the Auftrian Netherlands, and agreeable to the intention of the 26th article of the treaty, commonly called (by reafon of the limits therein fettled) the Barrier. And for this purpofe the contracting parties fhall immediately name commiffioners, who fhall meet at Antwerp within the fpace of two months, to be computed from the day of figning the prefent treaty, to agree together upon every thing that regards the entire enxecution of the faid Barrier treaty, which was concluded at Antwerp the $\frac{17}{7}$th day of November, Anno 1715, and of the convention fince figned at the Hague the $\frac{11}{22}$ day of December, 1718; and particularly to conclude a new treaty there, as has been faid, concerning commerce, and the rate of impofts, as far as relates to the Auftrian Netherlands, and according to the intention of the aforefaid 26th article. 'Tis moreover agreed, and folemnly ftipulated, that every thing which it hath been thought fit to leave to the commiffioners who are to meet at Antwerp, fhall be brought to a final iffue, with all the juftice and integrity, as foon as poffible, and in fuch manner that the laft hand may be put to that work, at leaft within the fpace of two years.

VI. As the exmaniation and difcuffion of the other points which remain to be difcuffed, either between the contracting parties, or any of their confedrates, require much more time than can be fpared in this critical fituation of affairs, therefore to avoid all delays which might be too prejudicial to the common welfare, 'tis covenanted and agreed to declare mutually, that all the treaties and conventions which any of the faid contracting powers have made with other princes and ftates, fhall fubfift as they now are, excepting only fo far as they may be contrary to

any

any the points regulated by the prefent treaty; and more-over, that all the difputes which are actually between the faid contracting parties, or any of their allies, fhall be amicably adjufted as foon as poffible; and in the mean time the contracting parties fhall mutually endeavour to prevent any of thofe who have differences, from having refource to arms to fupport their preteufions.

VII. To take away all manner of doubt from the fub-jects of the King of Great Britain, and the Lords the States General, touching their commerce in the kingdom of Sicily, his Imperial and Catholic Majefty has been pleafed to declare, that from this time forward, they fhall be treated in the fame manner, and upon the fame foot as they were or ought to have been treated in the time of Charles II. King of Spain of glorious memory, and as any nation in the ftricteft friendfhip has been ufually treated.

VIII. There fhall be included in this treaty of peace, all thofe who within the fpace of fix months, after its ra-tifications are exchanged, fhall be propofed by either party, and by common confent.

IX. This prefent treaty fhall be approved and ratified by his Imperial and Catholic Majefty, by his facred royal Majefty of Great Britain, and by the High and Mighty Lords the States General of the United Nether-lands, and the ratifications fhall be given and exchanged at Vienna, within fix weeks, to be computed from the day of figning.

In witnefs and confirmation whereof, as well the Im-perial commiffioners, in quality of ambaffadors extratordi-nary and plenipontentiaries, as the Minifter of the King of Great Britain, equally furnifhed with full powers have figned this treaty with their own hands, and fealed it with their feals. Done at Vinnea in Auftria, the 16th day of March, in the year of our Lord, 1731.

(L. S.) *Eugene* of *Savoy*.
(L. S.) *Philip Lewis* of *Zinzendorf*.
(L. S.) *Gundacker Thomas* of *Staremberg*.
(L. S.) *Thomas Robinfon*.

Sepa-

*Separate Article.*

THOUGH by the firſt article of the treaty concluded this day between h's Imperial and Catholic
Majeſty, his ſacred royal Majeſt of Great Britain, and
the Lords the States General of the United Provinces and
the Netherlands, the contracting parties did mutually
promiſe, among other things, that they would with all
their forces oppoſe the enterprizes of any perſon or perſons
who ſhould (perhaps contrary to expectation) offer to give
diſturbance to any of the contracting parties, their heirs
or ſucceſſors, in the peaceable poſſeſſion of their kingdoms, dominions, provinces, countries, rights or immunities, which each of the contractors doth or ought to
enjoy at the time of the concluſion of the preſent treaty;
the ſaid contracting parties have neverthelefs agreed among
themſelves, by virtue of the preſent ſeparate article, That
if it ſhould happen, perhaps in proceſs of time, that the
Turks ſhould offer to diſturb his ſacred Imperial and Catholic Majeſty, his heirs and ſucceſſors, in the quiet poſſeſſion of the kingdoms, dominions, provinces, countries,
right or immunitis, which his Imperial Majeſty actually
doth, or ought to enjoy, the guaranties ſtipulated in the
ſaid firſt article, are not to be exteneded to this caſe now
mentioned.

*This Separate Article ſhall have the ſame Force, &c.*

DECLARATION *concerning the* Spaniſh *Garriſons,
which are to be introduced into the ſtrong Places of* Tuſcany,
Parma, *and* Placentia.

FOraſmuch as his ſacred Imperial Catholic Majeſty
was deſirous to have all manner of ſecurity, before he
would conſent on his part to the third article of the treaty
concluded this day, which regulates the immediate introduction of the Spaniſh garriſons into the ſtrong places of
Tuſcany, Parma and Placentia, agreeably to the real views
and intentions contained in the promiſes made and ſigned
in the treaty of Seville, partly on the 9th, and partly on
the 21ſt day of November, Anno 1729; his ſacred royal
Majeſty of Great Britain and the High and Mighty Lords
the States General of the United Netherlands, have not
only

only exhibited thofe promifes, *bona fide*, as they are here fubjoined to his facred, Imperial, and Catholic Majefty, but moreover they have not hefitated to affirm in the ftrongeft manner, that when they agreed to introduce the Spanifh garrifons into the ftrong places of Tufcany, Parma and Placentia, they had no intention to depart in the leaft from thofe things which had been fettled by the fifth article of the quadruple alliance, concluded at London $\frac{\text{Aug. 2}}{\text{July 22}}$ 1718, either with regard to the rights of his Imperial Majefty, and the Empire, or to the fecurity of the kingdoms and ftates, which his Imperial Majefty actually poffeffeth in Italy, or laftly to the prefervation of the quiet and dignity of thofe who were then the lawful poffeffors of thofe Duchies. For this purpofe his royal Majefty of Great Britain and the High and Mighty Lords the States General of the United Netherlands have declared, and do declare, that they are entirely difpofed, and ready to give his Imperial and Catholic Majefty, as they do by thefe prefents, all the ftrong and folemn promifes, evictions, or, as they are called, guaranties that can be defired, as well in relation to the points above-mentioned, as in relation to all the other points ftill contained in the faid fifth article of the treaty called quadruple.

*This prefent Declaration fhall have the fame Force, &c.*

## DECLARATION *concerning the Succeffion of* Parma.

IT being apprehended that the unexpected death of the late moft ferene prince, Anthony Farnefe, in his lifetime Duke of Parma and Placentia, might in fome fort retard or obftruct the conclufion of this treaty, it having happened at the very time when it was upon the point of being concluded; his Imperial and Catholic Majefty doth by virtue of this prefent act, declare and engage, that in cafe the hopes of the pregnancy of the moft ferene Duchefs Dowager, wife of the faid moft ferene Duke Anthony whilft he lived, do not prove abortive, and the faid Duchefs Dowager fhould bring a man-child into the world, all that has been regulated, as well by the third article of the treaty concluded this day, as by the act of declaration above recited

cited, shall take place, as much as if the unforeseen death of the duke had not happened: but that if the hopes conceived of the pregnancy of the said Duchess Dowager should vanish, or she should bring a posthumous daughter into the world, then his said Imperial Majesty declares, and binds himself, that instead of introducing the Spanish soldiers into the strong places of Parma and Placentia, the most serene Infante of Spain, Don Carlos, shall be put into the possession of the said duchies, in the same manner as was agreed upon with the court of Spain, by consent of the empire, and pursuant to the letters of eventual investiture, the tenor of which shall be looked upon as repeated and confirmed in all its articles, clauses and conditions; in such manner notwithstanding, that the said Infante of Spain, as also the Court of Spain shall first of all fulfil the former treaties, wherein the Emperor is a contracting party with the consent of the empire. And whereas upon the decease of the said Duke Anthony Farnese, the Imperial troops were not put into the strong places of Parma and Placentia, with a view to hinder the eventual succession, as it was secured to the most serene Infante Don Carlos by the treaty of London, commonly called the Quadruple Alliance, but only to prevent any enterprize which might have disturbed the tranquillity of Italy ; his sacred Imperial and Catholic Majesty perceiving, that by the treaty concluded this day, the public tranquillity is restored and confirmed as far as possible, he doth again declare, that in putting his troops into the strong places of Parma and Placentia, he had no other intention than to support as far as lay in his power, the succession, of the most serene Infante Don Carlos, as it is secured to the said Infante by the said treaty of London: and that very far from opposing the said succession, in case the male branch of the House of Farnese should be utterly extinct; or from opposing the introduction of the Spanish garrisons, if the Duchess Dowager should happen to bring a posthumous son into the world, his Imperial Majesty doth on the contrary declare and promise, that the said forces shall by his express orders be withdrawn, either that the said Infante Don Carlos may be put into possession of the said Duchies, according to the tenor of the letters of eventual

in-

inveftiture, or that the Spanifh garrifons may be introduced
peaceably, and without any refiftance whatever; which faid
garrifons are to ferve for no other ufe than to fecure the execution of the promife made to him, in cafe the male
branch of the Houfe of Farnefe fhould be utterly extinct.

*The prefent Declaration fhall have the fame Force, &c.*

DECLARATION *finged by the Minifters of the King
of Great Britain, and the Lords the States General, by
Virtue of their full Powers.*

WHEREAS among feveral articles agreed upon
in the treaty of Seville, on the 9th and 21ft day of
November 1729, in favour of the Great Duke of Tufcany, as well as of the duchies of Parma and Placentia,
it was likewife provided, that as foon as the moft ferene
Infante of Spain, Don Carlos, or the Prince to whom
his rights may devolve, fhould be in peaceable poffeffion
of the fucceffion defigned for him, and fecure from any
infults of enemies, and againft any juft caufe of fear, then
his Royol Catholic Majefty fhould prefently give orders
for withdrawing his own troops out of the faid duchies,
but not thofe belonging to the Infante Don Carlos, or
to the prince upon whom, as abovementioned, his right
may devolve.

The under written minifters of the King of Great Britain, and the Lords States General, do, by virtue of this
prefent inftrument, declare, that as his faid royal Majefty
of Great Britain, and the High and Mighty Lords the
States General of the United Netherlands, are always
accuftomed to fulfil what they have promifed, fo 'tis ftill
their meaning and intention, that in the cafes aforefaid,
the Spanifh troops fhall be immediately withdrawn from
the Duchies of Tufcany, Parma and Placentia.

*This Declaration is to be kept Secret, but is neverthelefs to be
of the fame Force, &c.*

*Separate Atricle.*

WHEREAS the treaty concluded this day between
his Imperial Catholic Majefty, his Britannick
Majefty, and the High and Mighty Lords the States General

**neral** of the United Provinces of the Netherlands, could not be fubfcribed or figned by the Minifter of the faid States General refiding at the Imperial Court; becaufe according to the cuftom of the Republic, and the form of its government, the full powers could not be difpatched to the faid Minifter fo foon as was neceffary ; it is agreed between his Imperial Majefty and his royal Majefty of Great-Britain, that the faid States General (there being feveral conditions in the faid treaty, wherein they are particularly concerned) fhall be held and reputed as a principal contracting party, according as they are alfo named in the faid treaty, in firm hope and confidence that they would accede to it, as foon as the ufual form of their govenment would admit of it. And becaufe the zeal which that republic manifefts for eftablifhing and fecuring the public tranquillity, leaves their faid Majefties no room to doubt, that the faid Republic is defirous of becoming, as foon as may be, a principal contracting party in the faid treaty, to the end fhe may partake of the advantages therein ftipulated for her; both their Majefties will therefore unite their endeavours, that this treaty may be figned at the Hague on the part of the faid States General, within the fpace of three months, to be computed from the day of the figning of the prefent treaty, or fooner if poffible; for it appeared neceffary both to his Imperial, and his royal Britannick Majefty, in order to obtain the end propofed by the prefent treaty, and for completing the public tranquillity, that the faid States General fhould enter into a part and partnerfhip of the faid conventions.

*This feparate Article fhall have the fame Force,* &c.

### A *Declaration concerning* Eaft Friefland.

THE States General of the United Provinces of the Netherlands, having upon feveral occafions affured his Imperial and Catholic Majefty, that how much foever they are interefted in the re-eftablifhment and prefervation of the peace in their neighbourhood, and by confequence that of the province of Eaft Friefland, it was never their intention to prejudice in the leaft the dependence of the faid province of Eaft Friefland, upon the Emperor and the Empire ; his faid Imperial and Catholic Majefty,

to

to give the States a frefh proof of his defire to oblige them
as far as is confiftent with juftice, has been pleafed to ex-
plain to them his true fentiments on that affair, and by that
means to recover them from the fears they feem to have received. In order to this, no hefitation has been made to
declare to them on his part by the prefent act, that his intention always was and ftill is.

I. That an amnefty which he has moft gracioufly granted to thofe of Embden and their adherents, fhall have its
entire effect; and therefore that the feveral pains and penalties pronounced againft thofe of Embden and their adherents, upon the fcore of their renitency (refiftance)
fhall not be put in execution. And as for thofe of them
which have actually been executed fince the moft gracious acceptance of the fubmiffion made by the people
of Embden and their adherents, the whole fhall be reftored upon the foot it ftood before the faid fubmiffion was
accepted, that is to fay before the third of May, 1729,
faving what is hereafter mentioned of an agreement to
indemnify thofe for their loffes, who were plundered during the late troubles.

II. His Imperial and Catholic Majefty, having by his
refolution of the 12th of Sept. 1729, moft gracioufly permitted thofe of the town of Embden, and their adherents, to draw up a frefh account of their grievances, or
matters wherein they thought themfelves aggrieved by the
decrees of 1721, and the years following, concerning the
ground of the affairs upon which they differed with the
prince; and the faid grievances having been afterwards
exhibited to the Imperial Aulick council, with all fubmiffion, the          of November the fame year, his faid
Majefty has already ordered by his moft gracious refolution of the 31ft of Auguft, that thofe grievances fhould
be examined as foon as poffible. And as it has been often
declared, it has been and ftill is his conftant defire, that
they fhould be determined and decided with all the juftice
and difpatch that is poffible, according to the agreements,
conventions and decifions, which make the particular law
of the province of Eaft Friefland, and which are referred
to in the Prince's reverfal letters, paffed and fworn to at
his acceffion to the regency: provided neverthlefs, that
under

under the denomination of thofe agreements, conventions and decifions, none be comprehended which were abro‑ gated and annulled by his Imperial Majefty's auguft pre‑ deceffors in the empire, or which ftrike at the fupreme rights of the Emperor and Empire over the province of Eaft Friefland. And his Imperial and Catholic Majefty, as a farther proof of his moft gracious intention to cut as fhort as juftice will admit him, the examination of the grievances of the people of Embden, and their adherents, has already ordained by his refolutions of the 31ft of Auguft laft year, that as foon as the account thereof is delivered to thofe who are properly to take cognizance of the fame, according to the tenor of the refolution above-mentioned, they fhall anfwer it very foon, and once for all; after which his Imperial Majefty, with the advice of his Imperial Aulick council, will redrefs every complaint, article by article, which fhall appear to be grounded on the agreements above-mentioned.

III. It having been already ordained, purfuant to his Imperial and Catholic Majefty's laft refolution of the 31ft of Auguft, 1730, that the people of the town of Embden, and their adherents, ought to be admitted into the af‑ fembly of the States, which is to be called together to deliberate freely upon the affairs that lie before them; his Imperial and Catholic Majefty, will take care, that this refolution fhall have its entire effect, and that none of thofe who have a right to affift therein be excluded, contrary to the tenor of it.

IV. As to the indemnification, his Imperial Majefty thinks it proper, that an account be taken of the da‑ mages, which according to the tenour of the amnefty pub‑ lifhed the        in the year 1728, and of the refolution of the 12th of September, 1729, ought to be made good by the Renitents; and that the faid account be commu‑ nicated to them, that they may make their objections: after which his Imperial and Catholic Majefty will caufe the difference to be amicably adjufted, or on failure of an accommodation, will, with the utmoft equity, fix the fum which fhall be required to make good the damages fuftained.

V. His

V. His Imperial and Catholic Majefty perfifts in the intention he always had to take particular care of the payment of the intereft of the fums which the States of Eaft Friefland, and of the town of Embden, have borrowed of the fubjeḉts of the United Provinces, as alfo of the reimburfement of the capital, according to the engagements entered into on that account.

---

*Another Treaty concluded at* Vienna *the 22d of* July, 1731, *betwee t h e Emperor of* Great-Britain, *and* Spain.

In the Name of the moft Holy and Undivided Trinity. Amen.

TO all and every one whom it doth or may concern, Be it known, That different troubles having arifen, which feemed even to threaten the public tranquillity, about the introduḉtion of the Spanifh garrifon into the ftrong places of Tufcany, Parma and Placentia, which his Catholic Majefty thinks it proper to guard with his own troops inftead of Neutral, which were to have been there, purfuant to what had been agreed upon in the treaty of the Quadruple Alliance: in confequence whereof, his Imperial and Catholic Majefty, and his Majefty the King of Great-Britain, to prevent the evils which might refult therefrom, did formerly come to an agreement by the third article of the treaty, concluded and figned at Vienna the 16th of March this prefent year, and by two declarations thereunto annexed.

Now the faid article, and the declarations thereon depending, having been communicated to his Majefty the Catholic King, according to his defire, and he having likewife feen that the faid article and declarations tended only to render more fecure to the ferene Infante Don Carlos his Son, the eventual fucceffion to the Duchies of Tufcany, Parma and Placentia: in fhort, his faid Catholic Majefty perceiving that the engagements entered into between him and his Majefty the King of Great-Britain, as they had been communicated to his Imperial and Catholic Majefty,

Majefty, and explained in the aforefaid declarations were entirely performed, he would not be wanting on his part, to do every thing in his power to eftablifh the public tranquillity on a furer foot.

To this end, on the part of his Sacred Imperial and Catholic Majefty, the moft High Prince and Lord, Eugene, Prince of Piedmont and Savoy, actual privy counfellor to his faid Imperial and Catholic Majefty, prefident of the Aulic council of the Netherlands, and his Lieutenant General, Major General of the Holy Roman Empire, and his Vicar General in all the kingdoms and ftates of Italy, colonel of a regement of dragoons, and Knight of the Golden Fleece : and alfo the moft illuftrious and moft excellent Lord, Philip Lewis, Hereditary Treafurer of the Holy Roman Empire, Count of Zinzendorf, Free Baron of Ernftbrunn, Lord of the lands of Gfol, the upper Selowitz, Porliz, Sabor, Mulzig, Lots, Zaan and Drofkan, Burgrave of Reinec, Hereditary Mafter of the Horfe, Great Cupbearer in Upper and Lower Auftria on this fide Ens, Knight of the Golden Fleece, Chamberlain to his Imperial and Catholic Majefty, actual Privy Counfellor, and firft Cancellor of the Court; together with the moft illuftrious and moft excellent Lord Thomas Gundacker, Count of the Holy Empire, of Staremberg, Schaumburg and Wevemburg, Lord of the lands of Echelber, Lichtehneg, Rottenegg, Freyftat, Haus, Ober-Walfee, Senftenberg, Bodendorff, Hatwan, Knight of the Golden Fleece, actually Privy Counfellor to his Imperial and Catholic Majefty, and Hereditary Marfhal of the archduchy of Upper and Lower Auftria: and laftly, the moft illuftrious and moft excellent Lord, Jofeph Lothaire, Count of the Holy Empire, of Konigfegg and Rothenfels, Lord of Aulenderff and Stauffen, actualy Privy Counfellor to his Imperial and Catholic Majefty, Vice-Prefident of the Aulic Council of the Netherlands, General Field Marfhal, Governor General of ———, Colonel of foot, and Knight of the order of the White Eagle in Poland. And on the part of his Majefty the Catholic King, the moft illuftrious and moft excellent Lord James Francis Fitz-James, Duke of Liria and Xerica, Grandee of Spain of

the

the firſt claſs, Knight of the Golden Fleece, of St. Andrew and St. Alexander of Ruſſia, Alcalde-Major, firſt and perpetual Governor of the town of St. Philip, Chamberlain to his Majeſty the Catholic King, Colonel, and his Miniſter Plenipotentiary to his ſaid Imperial and Catholic Majeſty. Laſtly, on the part of his Majeſty the King of Great-Britain, Thomas Robinſon, Eſq; member of the parliament of Great-Britain, and h s Miniſter to the ſaid Imperial and Catholic Majeſty. All which miniſters furniſhed with full power, after having conferred among themſelves, and exchanged their ſaid full powers, have agreed upon the articles and conditions following.

I. His ſacred Majeſty the Catholic King having maturely examined the third article of the treaty concluded the 6th of March the preſent year, having likewiſe maturely examined the declarations mentioned above, which article and two declarations are on the point of being executed, he has declared that he not only deſires nothing more, but that he entirely acquieſces therewith. And in order to remove all occaſion of doubt or diſput-, his ſaid Majeſty has given aſſurances, that he conſents and is ready to do his part, immediately towards renewing and confirming, in all their articles, clauſes, and conditions, as well the treaty of London, commonly called the Quadruple Alliance, concluded the ſecond of Auguſt, 1718, as the peace of Vienna in Auſtria, ſigned the ſeventh of June, 1725, between his ſacred Imperial and Catholic Majeſty, and the holy Roman empire on t e one part, and his ſaid ſacred Majeſty the Catholic King on the other part, excepting only with regard to what is mentioned in the above-mentioned article and declarations, concerning the change of the neutral garriſons into Spaniſh garriſons; which article, and declarations, have been approved by their ſaid Majeſties, and again corroborated by the preſent treaty. For this end his ſacred Majeſty the Catholic King has declared, as he does declare by virtue of this preſent article, that the treaties above-named ſhall be deemed to be fully renewed and confirmed again, in the ſame manner as they are by the preſent article renewed, and again

confirmed :

confirmed: and his Majesty the Catholic King promises, as well for himself as for his heirs and successors, and in particular for him of his male-heirs who is to enter into the possession of the aforesaid Duchies of Tuscany, Parma and Placentia, by right of succession, by virtue of the said treaties, and according to the tenor of the letters of eventual investiture, expedited the 9th of December 1723, in case the male line of the families of Medicis and Farnese should happen to be entirely extinct; or lastly, for him to whom that succession shall devolve hereafter, that as well his said Majesty as his heirs and successors, and in particular, he of his male descendents to whom the said succession shall devolve, shall engage, and be obliged to do and perform every thing in general contained in the two treaties abovementioned.

II. His sacred Imperial and Catholic Majesty, and his sacred Majesty the King of Great-Britain, do likewise promise on their side, and bind themselves to his sacred Majesty the Catholic King, his heirs and successors, that in favour to the male line of the present Queen of Spain, the said male line having been called to the succession of the Duchies of Tuscany, Parma and Placentia, by virtue of the treaties above-named, and according to the tenor of the letters of eventual investiture, they will entirely accomplish all that is settled in the said third article of the treaty, concluded the 16th of March the present year, and in the two declarations mentioned as above; all in like manner, as his sacred Imperial and Catholic Majesty, and his sacred Majesty the King of Great-Britain, consenting to renew the said treaty of Quadruple Alliance; and his sacred Imperial and Catholic Majesty consenting also to renew the peace of the 7th of June 1725, concluded between his said Majesty, and the Holy Roman Empire on the one part, and his sacred Majesty the Catholic King on the other part. Their said majesties promise and engage for themselves, their heirs and successors, faithfully to perform in favour of his Majesty the Catholic King, his heirs and successors, all that they have engaged to do by virtue of their consent to renew, viz. his sacred Imperial and Catholic Majesty every thing contained, as well in the

Quadruple

Quadruple Alliance, as in the said treaty of peace concluded the seventh of June, 1725, and his sacred Majesty
the King of Great-Britain, every thing which he is engaged to do by the treaty of Quadruple Alliance.

III. Every thing which has hitherto been settled by
the common and unalterable consent of the contracting
parties, whether in relation only to the introduction of the
Spanish troops, or to the introduction of the serene Infante of Spain Don Carlos, into the Duchies of Parma and
Placentia, according to the tenor of the treaty of Quadruple
Alliance, is to serve as a rule in case the vacancy remain;
in such manner, however, that in this last case, the said
serene Infante of Spain Don Carlos, or he who according
to the fifth article of the Quadruple Alliance, shall be called
to that eventual succession after him, may and ought to
enter into possession of those Duchies, precisely in the manner expressed in the leters of eventual investiture, dispatched the 9th of December, 1723.

IV. Forasmuch as care has been taken to communicate
long since, and at different times, to the serene Princes
the Great Duke of Tuscany, and the Duke of Parma
and Placentia, who were then both living, every thing
that had been regulated by the 5th article of the Quadruple
Alliance, in favour of the serene Infante of Spain, Don-
Carlos, or in favour of those who succeed to his rights,
pursuant to the treaties above-mentioned, together with
the fore mentioned engagements between his sacred Majesty the Catholic King and his sacred Majesty the King
of Great Britain: moreover, the above-mentioned third
article of the treaty concluded at Vienna the 16th of March
this year, and the two declarations thereto annexed, having likewise been communicated to the Great Duke of
Tuscany's minister, and to the minister of Parma, both
residing at the Imperial Court; and because there is nothing more capable of securing the public tranquillity, than
to remove at once all the obstacles and all the difficulties
which might be started, and retard the execution of what
has been agreed upon between the contracting parties: for
these reasons, his sacred Imperial and Catholic Majesty,
and his sacred Majesty the King of Great-Britain, have
promised

promiſed and obliged themſelves, each for himſelf, bona fide, to try all manner of ways, as ſoon as the preſent treaty ſhall be ſigned, to engage alſo the ſerene Duke of Tuſcany to conſent forthwith, not only to the introduction of Spaniſh troops ſo often mentioned, but alſo to whatever has been formerly regulated in favour of the male line of the preſent Queen of Spain, by the treaties, conventions, and declarations above cited ; in ſuch manner, however, that all that is above-mentioned ſhall not take place till after the mutual exchange of the ratifications, even though the Great Duke of Tuſcany ſhould give his conſent to it ſooner.

V. Furthermore, his ſacred Imperial and Catholic Majeſty, and his ſacred Majeſty the King of Great-Britain declare, that they deſire nothing more than to ſee the ſerene Great Duke of Tuſcany acquieſce with every thing that has been ſettled in the treaties above-mentioned, for the preſervation of his dignity and repoſe, as well as for his own ſafety and that of the ſtates which he governs. Wherefore the ſaid contracting powers promiſe and engage, not only to one another, but alſo to his Royal Highneſs, to look upon all and every point ſettled in the treaties abovementioned to be renewed and confirmed, as well with regard to his dignity, as with regard to his ſafety, and that of the ſtates which are under him : and they undertake to maintain, fullfil, or, as it is called, to guaranty them.

VI. And becauſe for attaining to this end, and to finiſh the wholeſome work which the contracting parties have undertaken, viz. the entire eſtabliſhment of the public tranquillity, nothing has been thought of more importance than the acceſſion of the ſerene Great Duke to the preſent treaty; therefore the ſaid contracting parties have judged it proper to invite his Royal Highneſs to the ſaid acceſſion, in the moſt friendly manner that can be, as they do expreſsly invite him by the preſent article ; to the end that his Royal Highneſs concurring on his part to ſo advantageous a work, the public tranquillity of Europe may be better ſecured.

VII. The

VII. The prefent treaty fhall be ratified and approved by his facred Imperial and Catholic Majefty, by his facred Majefty the Catholic King, and by his facred Majefty the King of Great-Britain; and the letters of ratification fhall be communicated and exchanged at Vienna in Auftria, in the fpace of two months, to be reckoned from the day of figning the prefent treaty, or fooner if it can be done.

In witnefs whereof, the commiffioners of his Imperial Majefty, in the quality of ambaffadors Plenipotentiaries extraordinary, and the minifters of their Catholic and Britannick Majefties furnifhed in like manner with full powers, to give the neceffary force to the prefent treaty, have figned it with their own hands, and fealed it with their feals. Done at Vienna in Auftria, the 22d day of July, A. D. 1731.

(L. S.) *Eugene* of *Savoy.*
(L. S.) *P. L.* Count of *Zinzendorf.*
(L. S.) *G.* Count of *Starembreg.*
(L. S.) *J. L.* Count of *Konigfegg.*
(L. S.) *J.* Duke of *Liria.*
(L. S.) *Thomas Robinfon.*

---

*Convention between the Crowns of* Great-Britain *and* Spain, *Concluded at the* Pardo *on the* 14th *of* January, 1739, N. S.

WHEREAS differences have arifen, of late years, between the two crowns of Great-Britain and Spain, on account of the vifiting, fearching, and taking of veffels, the feizing of effects, the regulating of limits, and other grievances alledged on each fide, as well in the Weft-Indies, as elfewhere; which differences are fo ferious, and of fuch a nature, that if care not be taken to put an entire ftop to them for the prefent, and to prevent them for the future, they might occafion an open rupture between the faid crowns; for this reafon his Majefty

jesty the King of Great-Britain, and his Majesty the King
of Spain, having nothing so much at heart as to preserve
and corroborate the good correspondence, which has so
happily subsisted, have thought proper to grant their full
powers, viz. his Britannick Majesty to Benjamin Keene,
Esq; his minister plenipotentiary to his Catholic Majesty,
and his Catholic Majesty to Don Sabastian de la Quadra,
Knight of the order of St. James, counsellor of state,
and first secretary of state and of the dispatches; who
after previously producing their full powers, having conferred together, have agreed upon the following articles,

## Article I.

Whereas the ancient friendship, so desirable and so
necessary for the reciprocal interest of both nations, and
particularly with regard to their commerce, cannot be
established upon a lasting foundation, unless care be taken,
not only to adjust and regulate the pretensions for reciprocal reparation of the damages already sustained, but above
all to find out means to prevent the like causes of complaint for the future, and to remove absolutely, and for
ever, every thing which might give occasion thereto ; it
is agreed to labour immediately, with all imaginable application and diligence, to attain so desirable an end ; and
for that purpose there shall be named, on the part of their
Britannick and Catholic Majesties respectively, immediately
after the signing of the present convention, two ministers
plenipotentiaries, who shall meet at Madrid within the
space of six weeks, to be reckoned from the day of the
exchange of the ratifications, there to confer, and finally
regulate the respective pretensions of the two crowns, as
well with relation to the trade and navigation in America
and Europe, and to the limits of Florida and of Carolina,
as concerning other points, which remain likewise to be
adjusted ; the whole according to the treaties of the years
1667, 1670, 1713, 1715, 1721, 1728, and 1729, including that of the assiento of negroes, and the convention
of 1716 ; and it is also agreed, that the plenipotentiaries,
so named, shall begin their conferences six weeks after the
exchange

exchange of the ratifications, and fhall finifh them within the fpace of eight months.

## Article II.

The regulation of the limits of Florida and of Carolina, which, according to what has been lately agreed, was to be decided by commiffaries on each fide, fhall likewife be committed to the faid plenipotentiaries, to procure a more folid and effectual agreement; and during the time that the difcuffion of that affair fhall laft, things fhall remain in the aforefaid territories of Florida and of Carolina in the fituation they are in at prefent, without increafing the fortifications there, or taking any new pofts; and for this purpofe, his Britannick Majefty and his Catholic Majefty fhall caufe the neceffary orders to be difpatched immediately after the figning of this convention.

## Article III.

After having duly confidered the demands and pretenfions of the two crowns, and of their refpective fubjects, for reparation of the damages fuftained on each fide, and all circumftances which relate to this important affair; it is agreed, that his Catholic Majefty fhall caufe to be paid to his Britannick Majefty the fum of ninety-five thoufand pounds fterling for a balance, which has been admitted as due to the crown and the fubjects of Great-Britain, after deduction made of the demands of the crown and fubjects of Spain; to the above-mentioned fum, together with the amount of what has been acknowledged on the part of Great-Britain to be due to Spain on her demands, may be employed by his Britannick Majefty for the fatisfaction, difcharge and payment of the demands of his fubjects upon the crown of Spain; it being underftood, neverthelefs, that it fhall not be pretended that this reciprocal difcharge extends, or relates to the accounts and differences, which fubfift, or are to be fettled between the crown of Spain and the company of the Affiento of negroes, nor to any particular or private contracts that may fubfift between

tween either of the two crowns, or their minifters with the fubjects of the other, or between the fubjects and fubjects of each nation refpectively; with exception however of all pretenfions of this clafs mentioned in the plan prefented at Seville by the commiffaries of Great Britain, and included in the account lately made out at London, of damages fuf-tained by the fubjects of the faid crown, and efpecially the three particulars inferted in the faid plan, and making but one article in the account, amounting to one hundred nine-teen thoufand five hundred twelve piaftres, three reals and three quartils of plate; and the fubjects on each fide fhall be entitled, and fhall have liberty to have recourfe to the laws, or to take other proper meafures, for caufing the abovefaid engagements to be fulfilled, in the fame manner as if this convention did not exift.

### Article IV.

The value of the fhip called the Woolball, which was taken and carried to the port of Campechy in the year 1732, the Loyal Charles, the Difpatch, the George and the Prince William, which were carred to the Havana in the year 1737, and the St. James to Porto Rico in the fame year, having been included in the valuation that has been made of the demands of the fubjects of Great Britain, as alfo feveral others that were taken before; if it happens, that in confequnce of the orders that have been difpatch-ed by the Court of Spain for the reftitution of them, part, or the whole of them have been reftored, the fums fo receiv-ed fhall be deducted from the 95,000l. fterling which is to be paid by the Court of Spain according to what is above ftipulated : it being however underftood, that the payment of the 95,000l. fterling fhall not be, for that rea-fon, in any manner delayed; faving that what may have been previoufly received fhall be reftored.

### Article V.

The prefent convention fhall be aproved and ratified by his Britannick Majefty and by his Catholic Majefty; and the ratifications thereof fhall be delivered and ex-
**exchanged**

changed at London within the space of six weeks, or sooner if it can be done, to be reckoned from the day of the signing.

In witness whereof, We the underwritten ministers plenipotentiaries of his Britannick Majesty and of his Catholic Majesty, by virtue of our full powers, have signed the present convention, and caused the seal of our arms to be affixed thereto. Done at the Pardo the 14th day of January, 1739.

B. *Keene,*          *Sebastian de la Quadra,*
(L. S.)                  (L. S.)

His Britannick Majesty's Full Power.

*G E O R G E* R.

GEORGE the Second, by the Grace of God, of Great-Britain, France, and Ireland, King, Defender of the Faith, Duke of Brunswick and Lunenburg, Arch-Treasurer of the Holy Roman Empire, and Prince Elector, &c. To all and singular to whom these presents shall come greeting. Whereas certain differences have arisen of late years, between us, and our good brother the King of Spain, concerning the visiting and searching of merchant ships, and the seizing of them and of their goods and merchandizes, the regulation of limits, and other grievances alledged on each side, as well in the West-Indies, as elsewhere, which, if care be not taken to put an end to them at present, and provision made that the like may not happen for the future, might at length occasion an open rupture. And whereas we have nothing so much at heart, as to take care, by settling the rights, on each side, according to the tenor of the treaties, and by removing, as much as can be done, all cause of complaint for the future, to establish and preserve, for ever, the friendship that has subsisted between us and the King of Spain; and whereas the aforesaid King of Spain has declared, that he will willingly concert with us the proper

mea-

meafures for obtaining fo defirable an end: know ye therefore, that we repofing fpecial truft, in the fidelity, prudence, integrity and diligence of our trufty and well-beloved Benjamin Keene, Efq; our minifter plenipotentiary at the court of the aforefaid Catholic King, have nominated, made, and appointed the faid Benjamin Keene, as We do, by thefe prefents, nominate, make and appoint him our true, certain and undoubted commiffioner, procurator and plenipotentiary, giving and granting to him, all, and all manner of faculty, power and authority, together with general as well as fpecial order, (fo as the general do not derogate from the fpecial, and fo on the contrary) to meet, treat, confer and conclude for us, and in our name, with the minifter or minifters furnifhed with fufficient power on the part of our good brother the Catholic King, of and upon fuch treaty or treaties, convention or conventions, as may moft conduce to the above mentioned purpofes, as alfo upon articles, whether fecret or feparate; and laftly, upon all things which fhall feem moft proper for promoting and perfecting the faid work; and in our name to fign, and mutually to deliver, and receive, what fhall be fo concluded and agreed, and to do and perform all other things neceffary to be done, in as ample manner and form, as we ourfelves, were we prefent, would do and perform; engaging and promifing on our royal word, that whatever fhall be concluded by our faid commiffioner, procurator, and plenipotentiary, we will ratify, approve, and accept it all in the beft manner; and that we will never fuffer any perfon to violate the fame in the whole, or in part, or to act contrary thereto. In witnefs and confirmation of all which, we have caufed our great feal of Great Britain to be affixed to thefe prefents, figned with our royal hand. Given at our palace at St. James's, the ninth day of the month of November, in the year of our Lord, one thoufand feven hundred and thirty-eight, and of our reign the twelfth.

His

### His Catholic Majesty's Full Power.

DON Philip, by the Grace of God, King of Castile, of Leon, of Arragon, of the two Sicilies, of Jerusalem, of Navarre, of Granada, of Toledo, of Valencia, of Galica, of Mayorca, of Seville, of Sardinia, of Cordova, of Corsica, of Murcia, of Jaen, of the Algarves, of Algezira, of Gibraltar, of the Canary Islands, of the East and West Indies, Islands and Terra Firma, of the Ocean Sea, Archduke of Austria, Duke of Burgundy, of Brabant, and Milan, Count of Abspurg, of Flanders, Tirol and Barcelona, Lord of Biscay, and of Molina, &c. Whereas the differences arisen between this crown and that of England, by reason of the captures made by our guarda costas in America, visits, and other proceedings, of the limits of the dominions of both in those regions, and of other points equally worthy of examination and remedy, no less there than in Europe, did require a speedy, secure disposition to settle them all amicably. And whereas the King of Great Britain, our good brother, has manifested to us his desire to concur to so salutary an end as that of quieting the two nations, by the means of a reciprocal agreement, to be preceded by a convention, wherein some difficulties, which might without this step obstruct it, should be removed: now there concurring in you Don Sebastian de la Quadra, Knight of the order of St. James, of our council of state, and our first secretary of state, and of the dispatch, the good qualties that are known to our experience and confidence, we do authorize and give you our whole full power, as it is justly requisite, in the best and most ample manner, to the end that you may, according to the rule of the treaties, discuss, dispose, determine and sign the said convention, with the separate or secret articles that shall seem to you to be necessary for the rendering of them more clearly solid, and for the common utility of our kingdoms; and to the end that you may exchange and receive the instrument, or instruments, that shall be stipulated and made, by virtue of the abovementioned convention, the which and all others besides that
you

you fhall treat, debate, determine and fign, we promife
to fulfill and keep on the faith of our royal word, and to
command to be fulfilled and kept in the fame manner, and
with the fame religious integrity; in purfuance whereof, I
have ordered the prefent full power to be difpatched, figned with our hand, fealed with our fecret feal, and counter-figned by our fecretary of ftate and of the difpatch of
favour and juftice; at the Pardo, the 10th of January,
1739.

*I THE KING*

*Don Jofeph Rodrigo.*

---

Firft feparate Article.

WHEREAS it has been agreed by the firft article of
the convention, figned this day, between the minifters plenipotentiaries of Great Britain and Spain, that
there fhall be named on the part of their Britannick and
Catholic Majefties refpectively, immediately after the
figning the abovefaid convention, two minifters plenipotentiaries, who fhall meet at Madrid within the fpace of
fix weeks, to be reckoned from the day of the exchange
of the ratifications; their faid Majefties, to the end that
no time may be loft in removing, by a folemn treaty,
which is to be concluded for that purpofe, all caufe of
complaint for the future, and in eftablifhing, thereby, a
perfect good underftanding, and a lafting friendfhip, between the two crowns, have named, and do by thefe prefents name, viz. His Britannick Majefty, Benjamin Keene,
Efq; his faid Majefty's minifter plenipotentiary to his Catholic Majefty, and Abraham Caftres, Efq; his faid
Britannick Majefty's conful general at the Court of his
Catholic Majefty, his plenipotentiaries for that purpofe;
and his Catholic Majefty, Don Jofeph de la Quintana, his
counfellor in the fupreme council of the Indies, and Don
Stephen Jofeph de Abaria, Knight of the order of Calatrava, counfellor in the fame council, and fuperintendant
of the Chamber of Accounts, who fhall be immediately inftructed

ftructed to begin the conferences : and whereas it has been agreed by the 3d article of the convention figned this day, that the fum of ninety-five thoufand pounds fterling, is due on the part of Spain, as a balance to the crown and fubjects of Great Britain, after deduction made of the demands of the crown and fubjects of Spain : his Catholic Majefty fhall caufe to be paid at London, within the term of four months, to be reckoned from the day of the exchange of the ratifications, or fooner if it be poffible, in money, the above-mentioned fum of ninety five thoufand pounds fterling, to fuch perfons as fhall be authorized, on the part of his Britannick Majefty, to receive it.

This feparate article fhall have the fame force, as if it was inferted word for word in the convention figned this day; it fhall be ratified in the fame manner, and the ratifications thereof fhall be exchanged at the fame time as thofe of the faid convention.

In witnefs whereof, we the underwritten minifters, plenipotentiaries of his Britannick Majefty, and of his Catholic Majefty, by virtue of our full powers, have figned this feparate article, and have caufed the feals of our arms to be affixed thereto. Done at the Pardo, the 14th day of January, 1739.

B. *Keene*,  *Don Sebaftian de la Quadra*,
(L. S.)     (L. S.)

Second feparate Article.

WHEREAS the under-written minifters plenipotentiaries of their Britannick and Catholic Majefties have this day figned, by virtue of full powers from the Kings their mafters for that purpofe, a convention for fettling and adjufting all the demands, on each fide, of the crowns of Great Britain and Spain, on account of feizures made, fhips taken, &c. and for the payment of a balance that is thereby due to the crown of Great-Britain; it is declared that the fhip called the Succefs, which was taken

on

on the 14th dad of April 1738, as fhe was coming out from the Ifland of Antigua, by a Spanifh guarda cofta, and carried to Porto Rico, is not comprehended in the aforefaid convention ; and his Catholic Majefties promifes, that the faid fhip and its cargo fhall be forthwith reftored, or the juft value thereof, to the lawful owners ; provided that, previous to the reftitution of the faid fhip the Succefs, the perfon or perfons interefted therein do give fecurity at London to the fatisfaction of Don Thomas Geraldino, his Catholic Majefty's minifter plenipotentiary, to abide by what fhall be decided thereupon by the minifter plenipotentiaries of their faid Majefties, that have been named for finally fettling, according to the treaties, the difputes which remain to be adjufted between the two crowns; and his Catholic Majefty agrees, as far as fhall depend upon him, that the abovementioned fhip the Succefs fhall be referred to the examination and decifion of the plenipotentiaries ; his Britannick Majefty promifes likewife to refer, as far as fhall depend upon him, to the decifion of the plenipotentiaries, the brigantine Santa Therefa, feized in the port of Dublin in Ireland, in the year 1735. And the faid under-written minifters plenipotentiaries declare by thefe prefents, that the 3d article of the convention, figned this day, does not extend, nor fhall be conftrued to extend to any fhips or effects that may have been taken or feized fince the 10th day of December, 1737, or may be hereafter taken or feized ; in which cafes juftice fhall be done according to the treaties, as if the aforefaid convention had not been made; it being however underftood, that this relates only to the indemnification and fatisfaction to be made for the effects feized, or prizes taken, but that the decifion of the cafes, which may happen, in order to remove all pretext for difpute, is to be referred to the plenipotentiaries, to be determined by them according to the treaties.

This feparate article fhall have the fame force, as if it was inferted word for word in the convention figned this day : it fhall be ratified in the fame manner, and the ratifications thereof fhall be exchanged at the fame time as thofe of the faid convention.

In

In witnefs whereof, we the underwritten minifters plenipotentiaries of his Britannick Majefty, and of his Catholic
Majefty, by virtue of our full power, have figned the
prefent feparate article, and have caufed the feals of our
arms to be affixed thereto. Done at the Pardo, January
the 14th, 1739.

*B. Keene,*                    *Sebaftian de la Quadra,*
(L. S.)                            (L. S.)

---

### His Britannick Majefty's Ratification of the Convention.

GEORGE the Second, by the Grace of God, of
Great Britain, France and Ireland, King, Defender
of the Faith, Duke of Brunfwick and Lunenburg, Arch-
Treafurer of the Holy Roman Empire, and Prince Elector, &c. To all and fingular to whom thefe prefents fhall
come, greeting. Whereas a certain convention between
us, and our good brother Philip the Fifth, Catholic King
of Spain, was concluded and figned by our minifter plenipotentiary Benjamin Keene, Efq; and by the minifter
plenipotentiary of our good brother, the aforefaid Catholic King, Don Sebaftian de la Quadra, Kinght of the
order of St. James, counfellor of ftate of his faid Catholic
Majefty, and his firft fecretary of ftate and of the difpatch,
at the palace called the Pardo, on the fourteenth day of
this prefent month of January N. S. The tenor whereof
follows.

*Fiat Infertio.*

We having feen and confidered the convention above-
written, have approved, ratified, accepted and confirmed,
as, by thefe prefents, we do, for us, our heirs and fucceffors, approve, ratify, accept, and confirm the fame,
in all and fingular its claufes, engaging and promifing,
upon our royal word, fincerely and faithfully to perform
and obferve all and fingular the things which are contained
in the aforefaid convention, and never to fuffer any perfon

to

to violate them, or in any manner to act contrary thereto. In witnefs and confirmation of all which, we have caufed our great feal of Great Britain to be affixed to thefe prefents, figned with our royal hand. Given at our palace at St. James's, the twenty-fourth day of the month of January, in the year of our Lord one thoufand feven hundred thirty $\frac{8}{9}$, and of our reign the twelfth.

*GEORGE* R.

---

His Catholic Majefty's Ratification of the Convention.

DON Philip, by the Grace of God, King of Caftile, of Leon, of Arragon, of the Two Sicilies, of Jerufalem, of Navarre, of Granada, of Toledo, of Valencia, of Gallicia, of Mayorca, of Seville, of Sardinia, of Cordova, of Corfica, of Murcia, of Jaen, of the Algarbes, of Algezira, of Gibraltar, of the Canary iflands, of the Eaft and Weft Indies, iflands and Terra Firma of the Ocean Sea, Arch-Duke of Auftria, Duke of Burgundy of Barbant and Milan, Count of Abfpurg, of Flanders, Tirol and Barcelona, Lord of Bifcay and of Molina, &c. Whereas there has been adjufted, concluded and figned at the royal feat of the Pardo, on the fourteenth of the prefent month and year, between our minifter plenipotentiary Don Sebaftian de la Quadra, Kight of the order of St. James, of our council of ftate, and our firft fecretay of ftate, and of the difpatch, and Mr. Benjamin Keene, minifter plenipotentiary from the King of Creat-Britain, our good brother, a convention, which is of the tenor following.

*Fiat Infertio.*

Now we do approve and ratify all that is compiehended in the convention abovementioned, and being thus approved and ratified in the moft ample manner that we are able, we promife, on the faith and word of a king, to obferve it and keep it, and to command it to be executed and fulfilled in the fame manner, as if we had treated it in
our

our own perfon, without doing, or letting be done, in any manner whatfoever, or permitting to be done any thing to the contrary; and that, if it fhould be done, we will order it to be repaired in effect, without difficulty or delay. In witnefs whereof we give this prefent, figned with our hand, fealed with our fecret feal, and counterfigned by our underwritten counfellor of ftate, and firft fecretary of ftate, and of the difpatch. Given at the Pardo, the 15th of January, one thoufand feven hundred and thirty-nine.

*I THE KING*

*Sebaftian de la Quadra.*

---

His Britannick Majefty's Ratification of the Firft feparate Article.

GEORGE the Second, by the Grace of God, of Great Britain, France and Ireland, King, Defender of the Faith, Duke of Brunfwick and Lunenburg, Arch-Treafurer of the Holy Roman Empire, and Prince Elector, &c. To all and fingular, to whom thefe prefents fhall come, greeting. Whereas a certain feparate article, entitled the firft, belonging to the convention between us and our good brother, Philip the Fifth, Catholic King of Spain, concluded and figned at the palace called the Pardo, on the fourteenth day of this prefent month of January, N. S. by our minifter plenipotentiary Benjamin Keene, Efq; and by the minifter plenipotentiary of our good brother the aforefaid Catholic King, Don Sebaftian de la Quadra, Knight of the order of St. James, counfellor of ftate, of his faid Catholic Majefty and his firft fecretary of ftate, and of the difpatch, was concluded and figned at the fame place, and on the fame day, the tenor whereof follows.

*Fiat Infertio.*

We having feen and confidered the above-written firft feparate article, have approved, ratified, accepted and confirmed,

firmed, as by thefe prefents we do, for us, our heirs and fucceffors, approve, ratify, accept and confirm the fame, engaging and promifing, upon our royal word, to perform and obferve all and fingular the things which are contained in the aforefaid feparate article in like manner as the convention itfelf. In witnefs and confirmation of all which, we have caufed our great feal of Great Britain to be affixed to thefe prefents, figned with our royal hand. Given at our palace at St. James's, the twenty-fourth day of the month of January, in the year of our Lord one thoufand feven hundred thirty $\frac{eight}{nine}$, and of our reign the twelfth.

*GEORGE* R.

His Britannick Majefty's Ratification of the Second feparate Article.

GEORGE the Second, by the Grace of God, of Great Britain, France and Ireland, King Defender of the Faith, Duke of Brunfwick and Lunenburg, Arch-Treafurer of the Holy Roman Empire, and Prince Elector, &c. To all and fingular to whom thefe prefents fhall come, greeting. Whereas a certain feparate article, entitled the Second, belonging to the convention between us, and our good brother Philip the Fifth, Catholic King of Spain, concluded and figned at the palace called the Pardo, on the fourteenth day of this prefent month of January, N. S. by our mininfter plenipotentiary, Benjamin Keene, Efq; and by the minifter plenipotentiary of our good brother, the aforefaid Catholic King, Don Sebaftian de la Quadra, Knight of the order of St. James, counfellor of ftate of his faid Catholic Majefty, and his firft fecretary of ftate, and of the difpatch, was concluded and figned at the fame place, and on the fame day, the tenor whereof follows.

*Fiat Infertio.*

We having feen and confidered the abovewritten Second feparate article, have approved, ratified, accepted and

and confirmed, as, by thefe prefents, we do, for us, our heirs and fucceffors, approve, ratify, accept, and confirm the fame, engaging and promifing, upon our royal word, to perform and obferve all and fingular the things which are contained in the aforefaid feparate article, in like manner as the convention itfelf. In witnefs and confirmation of all which, we have caufed our great feal of Great Britain to be affixed to thefe prefents, figned with our royal hand. Given at our palace at St. James's, the twenty-fourth day of the month of January, in the year of our Lord one thoufand feven hundred thirty $\frac{eight}{nine}$, and of our reign the twelfth.

*G E O R G E* R.

---

His Catholic Majefty's Ratification of the Firft feparate Article.

DON Philip, by the Grace of God, King of Caftile, of Leon, of Arragon, of the Two Scilies, of Jerufalem, of Navarre, of Granada, of Toledo, of Valencia, of Gallicia, of Mayorca, of Seville, of Sardinia, of Cordova, of Corfica, of Murcia, of Jaen, of the Algarbes, of Algezira, of Gibraltar, of the Canary iflands, of the Eaft and Weft Indies, iflands and Terra Firma of the Ocean Sea, Arch-Duke of Auftria, Duke of Burgundy, of Brabant and Milan, Count of Abfpurg, of Flanders, Tirol and Barcelona, Lord of Bifcay and of Molina, &c. Whereas at the fame time, that at the royal feat of the Pardo, on the fourteenth of the prefent month and year, there was a convention concluded and figned, between our minifter plenipotentiary Don Sebaftian de la Quadra, Kight of the order of St. James, our counfellor of ftate, and our firft fecretary of ftate, and of the difpatch, and the minifter plenipotentiary of the King of Great Britain, Mr. Benjamin Keene, there was alfo concluded and figned a feparate article of the tenor following.

*Fiat Infertio.*

Now the fame having been feen and examined, We have thought fit to approve it and ratify it, (as by virtue
of

of this prefent, we do approve and ratify it) in the beft
and moft ample manner that we are able, according, and
as it is mentioned and expreffed therein; promifing on
the faith of our royal word, to fulfill it entirely, and that
it fhall have the fame vigour and force as if it had been
inferted in the faid convention. In witnefs whereof, we
have ordered this prefent to be difpatched, figned with
our hand, fealed with our fecret feal, and counter-figned
by our under-written counfellor of ftate, and firft fecretary
of ftate and of the difpatch. Given at the Pardo, the
15th of January, one thoufand feven hundred and thirty-
nine.

*I THE KING.*

*Sebaftian de la Quadra.*

His Catholic Majefty's Ratification of the Second
feparate Article.

DON Philip, by the Grace of God, King of Caftile,
of Leon, of Arragon, of the Two Sicilies, of Jeru-
falem, of Navarre, of Granada, of Toledo, of Valencia,
of Galicia, of Mayorca, of Seville, of Sardinia of Cordova, of Corfica, of Murcia, of Jaen, of the Algares,
of Algezira, of Gibraltar, of the Canary Iflands, of the
Eaft and Weft Indies, Iflands and Terra Firma of the
Ocean Sea, Archduke of Auftria, Duke of Burgundy, of
Brabant, and Milan, Count of Abfpurg, of Flanders,
Tirol and Barcelona, Lord of Bifcay, and of Molina, &c.
Whereas at the fame time, that at the royal feat of the
Pardo, on the fourteenth of the prefent month and year,
there was a convention concluded and figned between our
minifter plenipotentiary Don Sebaftian de la Quadra,
Knight of the order of St. James, our counfellor of ftate,
and firft fecretary of ftate, and of the difpatch, and the
minifter plenipotentiary of the King of Great Britain, Mr.
Benjamin Keene, there was alfo concluded and figned a
feparate article, of the tenor following.

*Fiat Infertio.*

Now the fame having been feen and examined, we
have thought fit to approve it and ratify it, (as by virtue
of

of this prefent, we do approve and ratify it) in the beft and moft ample manner that we are able, according, and as it is mentioned and expreffed therein; promifing on the faith of our royal word, to fulfill it entirely, and that it fhall have the fame vigour and force as if it had been inferted in the faid convention. In witnefs whereof, we have ordered this prefent to be difpatched, figned with our hand, fealed with our fecret feal, and counter-figned by our under-written counfellor of ftate, and firft fecretary of ftate and of the difpatch. Given at the Pardo, the 15th day of January, one thoufand feven hundred and thirty-nine.

*I THE KING.*

*Sebaftain de la Quadra.*

---

*The definitive Treaty of Peace, Union, Friendfhip, and mutual Defence, between the Crowns of* Great Britain, Hungary, *and* Sardinia, *concluded at* Worms *on the* $\frac{2}{13}$ *of* September, 1743.

GEORGE the Second, by the Grace of God, King of Great Britain, France, and Ireland, Defender of the Faith, Duke of Brunfwick, and Lunenburg, Arch-Treafurer, and Prince Elector of the Holy Roman Empire, &c. To all and fingular to whom thefe prefents fhall come, greeting. Whereas the minifters plenipotentiary, as well on our part, as on the part of our good Brother the King of Sardinia, &c. and of our good fifter the Queen of Hungary and Bohemia, &c. being affembled at Worms, and fufficiently authorized thereto, did conclude, and fign a certain treaty of mutual friendfhip and perpetual alliance, on the $\frac{2}{13}$ day of the prefent month of September, in the form and words following.

In the Name of the moft Holy Trinity.

BE it known to all, and every one, to whom it appertains, or may appertain, in any manner whatfoever.

Foraf-

Forafmuch as the difturbances, which, upon the deceafe of the Emperor Charles the Sixth, of glorious memory, without male iffue, arofe in Germany, notwithftanding the exprefs tenor of the moft folemn and recent treaties of peace and alliance, corroborated by the authentic guaranty of the body of the Empire, which do affure to his eldeft daugther, and to her pofterity, the entire and indivifible fucceffion to his hereditary dominions, do manifeftly tend to the overthrow of all balance in Europe, and do expofe its liberty, and that of its commerce, to the moft evident danger: which danger is ftill increafed by the conqueft which the Kings of Spain and Naples have openly undertaken to make of the dominions poffeffed by the moft ferene Houfe of Auftria in Italy, contrary to the faith of their own engagements ; after which, the reft of Italy would no longer be able to refift them, and all the coafts of the Mediterranean fea would be under fubjection to one and the fame family.

To obviate, as much as in them lies, fuch imminent evils, and an enterprize, whofe confequences would be fo fatal to all the princes and ftates of Italy, to their liberty and commerce, and to that of the maritime powers in the Mediterranean fea, the moft ferne and moft potent Prince George the Second, King of Great Britain, Elector of Brunfwick, Lunenburg, &c. the moft ferene and moft potent Princefs Maria Therefia, Queen of Hungary and Bohemia, Archduchefs of Auftria, &c. and the moft ferene and moft potent Prince Charles Emanuel King of Sardinia, Duke of Savoy, &c. having fuch an effential intereft in the prefervation of a juft balance in Europe, on which depends the liberty of Europe, and in the maintenance of the liberty and fecurity of Italy in particular, on which depends that of its commerce, and of the commerce of the Mediterranean, have refolved to enter into clofer and more infeparate union, in this fixt intention, and to preferve inviolably in joining their forces and counfels in order to obtain the effect defired therefrom, and more efpecially for the fake of repelling, with one accord, the unjuft invafion made by the Kings of Spain and Naples, and for fecuring Italy, if poffible, for the furture, from all attempts of the fame kind.

In

In this view, and in order to prevent the said invasion, without loss of time, his Majesty the King of Sardinia did enter, from the 1st day of February, 1742, into a provisional convention with her Majesty the Queen of Hungary, the tenor whereof is as follows.

As it is sufficiently evident, that the motions of the Spanish troops, which having landed in the States of the Præfidii, are advancing in the dominions of the Pope, in order to join those of Naples, and from thence to pursue their march as far as Imola, are bent according to certain intelligence, towards Lombardy, and must necessarily very much affect his Majesty the King of Sardina, as well as her Majesty the Queen of Hungary and Bohemia, their Majesties have thought by the means of the Marquis d'Ormea and of the Count de Schulenbourg (they being respectively provided with the necessary full powers) of concerting and agreeing upon the following articles, under the hopes of their being ratified and accepted.

### Article I.

The forces of her Majesty the Queen of Hungary alone, which are now in Italy, appearing sufficient to make head against the aggressors, they shall be brought together, in order to march towards them, and to give an immediate check to their progress, and particularly in order to cover the States of Modena, and Mirandola, which are as it were, a bulwark to the dominions of the Queen of Hungary in Italy.

### Article II.

The said King of Sardinia shall, in the mean while, have a considerable body of his troops upon the frontiers of his dominions towards the borders of the Milanese, and of the Duchy of Placentia, which shall be disposed in such a manner, as that they may be brought together in a short time; and in case the forces of the aggressors should come to be augmented, and that there should be cause to fear a new invasion on any other side, as is probable, according to the advices that have been received, that a second

cond convoy of Spanifh troops has already fet fail at Barcelona, and that they are to land in the harbour of La
Spezia, his Majefty fhall then co-operate with all his forces
for preventing the body of Auftrian troops, which fhall
have marched forward, from being either taken in flank,
or intercepted by that new reinforcement of Spanifh troops;
and to this end, all the paffages in the States above-mentioned, and principally, the places of Parma, Placentia,
and Pavia, fhall remain free and open to the King's
troops for their convenience and fecurity.

### Article III.

As to what relates to further motions, and fuch other
military operations, as might be afterwards undertaken, as
they muft depend upon the circumftances which fall out
from day to day, it is neceffary to refer them to the concert which fhall be entered into, in proportion to the circumftances which fhall happen; and for this purpofe, his
Majefty the King of Sardinia fhall fend one of his general
officers to the army of her Majefty the Queen of Hungary,
and her Majefty the Queen of Hungary fhall fend one of
her's likewife to refide with his Majefty the King of Sardinia: to which general officers fhall be reciprocally communicated, all the advices that fhall be received about the
enemy; and all the refolutions which fhall be taken on
either fide fhall be concerted with them.

### Article IV.

Nothing being fo neceffary towards obtaining the end
defired on each fide, as the reciprocal fecurity of the refpective poffeffions, and rights, and a confidence in the
good faith of the parties, who are to co-operate towards
the fame end, his Majefty the King of Sardinia promifes,
upon the faith and word of a Prince, to her Majefty the
Queen of Hungary; Firft, That, for as long time as
the prefent provifional agreement fhall laft, he will not
avail himfelf of his pretended rights to the ftate of Milan,
which are not entered into in this provifional convention,
forafmuch as the Queen of Hungary cannot admit them,
and

and the King of Sardinia on the contrary thinks them founded; and Secondly, That if it should be necessary that his said Majesty should enter, with his forces, into any one of the states above-mentioned, he will not exercise in the same any act of sovereignty, and will not in any wise hinder the Queen of Hungary from continuing to exercise them in the manner, that that Princefs has done it hitherto; neither will his Majesty exact any contribution, and will content himself in the said case with being furnished with such things as are indifpenfably requifite to an army ; as for inftance, forage, wood, quarters, carts, beds, caferns, and ftraw, the rations where of shall be regulated upon the foot on which they are ufually allowed to his troops; as alfo horfes, mules, and oxen, for the ufe of the artillery, and victuals.

## Article V.

On the other hand, her Majesty the Queen of Hungary declares in the like folemn manner, that it is not her meaning, that the abovefaid promifes of his Majefty the King of Sardinia, nor the execution of them, should prejudice the rights by him pretended to the state of Milan, nor ever to avail herfelf of them, fo as to infer from thence that the faid rights were no longer fubfifting; the intention of the two high contracting parties being to preferve to each of them their refpective rights in their full force, in fuch manner as they may appertain to them, independently of the prefent convention.

## Article VI.

And it is likewife in this view, that his Majefty the King of Sardinia referves to himfelf exprefily the entire liberty of availing himfelf of his faid rights, at whatever time, and by whatever means, either by himfelf fingly, or by fuch alliance as he shall judge to be moft for his convenience.

## Article VII.

But as his Majefty does not mean to acquire any advantage by the faid refervation, and defigns to proceed with
all

all the good faith, which is natural to him, he promifes and engages, in the cafe above-mentioned, not to act himfelf, nor to permit any prince, with whom he might be allied, to act, (which his Majefty will take care to ftipulate as a principal condition, in any treaty whatfoever, which he might conclude) fooner than after the fpace of one month, from the time that he fhall have caufed notice to be given by the means of the general officer, which he fhall have at the Queen of Hungary's army ; to the end that the commanding officer of the Auftrian troops, being thus put upon his guard, may take fuch meafures and refolutions, as he fhall judge moft for his advantage.

### Article VIII.

Moreover the King of Sardinia promifes, in that cafe, to make his troops evacuate all the dominions of the Queen of Hungary, and all the places and pofts, which he fhould have taken poffeffion of during the prefent provifional agreement, without carrying any thing off; to the end that the troops of the abovefaid Queen, may, during the faid month, retake, freely and without any hindrance, the pofts which they fhall think proper.

### Article IX.

The prefent convention fhall be ratified by the King of Sardinia and by the Queen of Hungary, and the acts of ratification fhall be exchanged within the term of twenty days.

### Article X.

During the faid term, the King of Sardinia fhall not underftand himfelf to be obliged to caufe his troops to enter into the ftates poffeffed by the Queen of Hungary ; and if, after the expiration of the faid term, the Queen fhould not have fent her ratification, fo that for want of it, the prefent convention fhould remain without effect, neverthelefs the king fhall not, in that cafe, caufe his troops to enter into the above-mentioned ftates, during the term
of

of other ten days, neither during that term fhall he give any hindrance tô the free return of the Auftrian troops into the fame ftates, and into fuch pofts as the Queen of Hungary's generals fhall judge to be moft convenient.

In witnefs whereof, we the underwritten plenipotentiaries have figned the prefent convention, &c. at Turin, the firft of February, 1742.

In confequence of this convention, his Majefty the King of Sardinia did immediately join a confiderable body of his troops to thofe of the faid Queen, his Majefty the King of Great-Britain having fent a ftrong fquadron to co-operate for the maintenance of the liberties of Italy.

In order not to leave fruitlefs fo great expences, and to fecure ftill further, and to accelerate, for the prefent, the entire execution of fo neceffary and juft a refolution, and in order likewife to perpetuate the effect of it for the times to come, their faid Majefties have authorifed, and do authorife their minifters plenipotentiary to make an immediate regulation of the particulars and of the conditions, viz. His Majefty the King of Great-Britain, his privy-counfellor John Lord Carteret, Baron of Hawnes, one of his principal fecretaries of ftate, &c. His Majefty the King of Sardinia, the Chevalier Offorio, Chevalier Grande Croix, and grand confervator of the religious and military orders of the Saints Maurice and Lazarus, envoy extraordinary and minifter plenipotentiary of his faid Majefty to his Majefty the King of Great-Britain. And her Majefty the Queen of Hungary and Bohemia, the Sieur Ignatius John de Wafner, her minifter plenipotentiary to his faid Britannick Majefty ; who, after having communicated to each other their refpective full powers, and having maturely conferred together, have agreed upon the following articles.

## Article I.

There fhall be, from the prefent time, and for all times to come, between his Majefty the King of Great-Britain, her

her Majefty the Queen of Hungary and Bohemia, and his Majefty the King of Sardinia, a clofe friendfhip, and fincere, perpetual, and inviolable alliance, by virtue of which they fhall be obliged to fupport, defend, and fuccour each other reciprocally and conftantly, to be attentive to the fecurity each of the other, as to their own, to procure all advantages, and to keep off all damage and prejudice from one another to the utmoft of their power.

## Article II.

To this end the allies engage themfelves afrefh to a moft exprefs guaranty of all the kingdoms, ftates, countries, and dominions, which they are now in poffeffion of, or ought to poffefs by virtue of, the treaty of alliance made at Turin in 1703 : of the treaties of peace of Utrecht and Baden : of the treaty of peace and alliance, commonly called the Quadruple alliance: of the treaty of pacification and alliance concluded at Vienna the 16th of March, 1731 : of the act of guaranty given in confequence thereof, and paffed into a law of the empire, the 11th of January, 1732 : of the act of acceffion, figned likewife in confequence of the faid treaty, at the Hague the 20th of February, 1732 : of the treaty of peace figned at Vienna, the 18th of November, 1738 ; and of the acceffion thereto, done and figned at Verfailles the 3d of February, 1793 : all which treaties are fully recalled and confirmed here, forafmuch as they may concern the allies, and as far as they have not derogated from them by the prefent treaty.

## Article III.

In conformity to the guaranty contained in the foregoing article, and to the end that no fubject of difpute may remain between the two moft ferene houfes of Auftria and Savoy, his Majefty the King of Sardinia, for himfelf, his heirs and fucceffors renounces by name, and for ever, but folely in favour of her Majefty the Queen of Hungary and Bohemia, and of her heirs and fucceffors, to his pretended rights upon the ftate of Milan ; which rights, though never admitted on the part of the Queen, he had referved to himfelf,

felf, by the provifional convention, the liberty of availing himfelf of. And befides, his Majefty the King of Sardinia engages himfelf formally and fpecially to the guaranty of the order of fucceffion eftablifhed in the faid moft ferene houfe, by the pragmatic fanction, in the fame manner as it is fet forth in the treaty of pacification and alliance made at Vienna the 16th of March 1731, excepting however, that his faid Majefty fhall never be obliged to fend fuccours out of Italy.

## Article IV.

For this purpofe his Majefty the King of Sardinia, who has already joined his troops to thofe of the Queen of Hungary, and who has already confiderably augmented them, fhall continue to concert and execute, jointly with her and her generals, all the meafures and operations which fhall be judged the moft effectual for keeping off and repelling the invafion now made, or to be hereafter made, againft the dominions of the faid Queen, and for fecuring them from all danger, prefent and future, as much as poffible.

## Article V.

In order to attain this end, and as long as the prefent war fhall laft, her Majefty the Queen of Hungary engages not only to keep in Italy the number of troops which fhe has there now, but to augment them to the number of 30,000 effective men, as foon as the fituation of affairs in Germany will permit it. And his Majefty the King of Sardinia engages to keep and employ the number of 40,000 foot, and 5000 horfe, comprehending in it what will be neceffary for the garrifons, and defence of his own dominions.

## Article VI.

His Majefty the King of Sardinia fhall have the fupreme command of the allied army, when he fhall be there in perfon, and he fhall regulate the military motions and
operations

operations of it, in concert with her Majefty the Queen of Hungary, according as the common interest and occafions fhall require.

## Article VII.

As long as it fhall be neceffary towards favouring and feconding thofe operations, and as long as the danger of the allies, and of Italy, fhall demand it, his Majefty the King of Great-Britain engages to keep in the Mediterranean Sea, a ftrong fquadron of fhips of war, and bomb veffels, and fire-fhips, the admiral and commanders whereof fhall have orders to concert conftantly and regularly with his Majefty the King of Sardinia, or with his generals, and with thofe of her Majefty the Queen of Hungary, who fhall be neareft at hand, the moft proper meafures for the fervice of the common caufe.

## Article VIII.

Moreover, and in order to affift in bearing the extraordinary expence which his Majefty the King of Sardinia is and will be obliged to fupport, for raifing, and caufing to act, a much greater number of troops than his own revenues can maintain, his Majefty the King of Great-Britain engages to furnifh to him, for as long as the war, and the occafion for it fhall continue, a fubfidy of two hundred thoufand pounds fterling per annum, to be paid every three months, and to commence from the 1ft of February, 1742, New Style, being the day upon which the provifional convention was figned between the faid King and her Majefty the Queen of Hungary ; and the faid fubfidy fhall be punctually paid from three months to three months in advance; provided however, that what fhall have been advanced to his Majefty the King of Sardinia, before the fignature of the prefent treaty, fhall be reckoned into it.

## Article IX.

In confideration of the zeal, and generofity, with which his Sardinian Majefty has been willing to expofe his perfon

fon, and his dominions, for the public caufe, and for that of her Majefty the Queen of Hungary and Bohemia, and of the moft ferene houfe of Auftria, in particular, and of the effectual fuccours, which the faid caufe has already received from him; in confideration alfo of the burthen-fome engagements of affiftance, and of the perpetual tye of guaranty, which he contracts with her, by the prefent alliance, her faid Majefty the Queen of Hungary and Bohemia, for herfelf, her heirs and fucceffors, yields, and transfers, from this prefent time and for ever, to his faid Majefty the King of Sardinia, his heirs and fucceffors, to be united to his other dominions, the diftrict of Vige-vano, called the Vigevenafco, the part of the duchy of Pavia, which is between the Po and the Thefin, fo that the Thefin fhall for the future, by the middle of its ftream, form the feparation and limit between the refpective do-minions, from the Lago Maggiore, or greater lake, to the place where it falls into the Po, excepting only the ifland formed by the canal over-againft the city of Pavia, which ifland fhall be referved to her Majefty the Queen, upon thefe conditions, that the King fhall have neverthe-lefs the free communication of the river Thefin for the paffage of barks, without their being either ftopt, vifited, or fubjected to the payment of any duty, and that the faid canal fhall never be filled up, and fhall ferve in this place for a limit. Moreover, that other part of the duchy of Pavia, called the Pavefe, beyond the Po, Bobbio, and its territory being reckoned into it, the city of Plaifance, with that part of the duchy of Placentia, which is between the Pavefan, and as far as the bed of the river Nura, from its fource quite to the Po; in fuch manner that the middle, as well of the Nura as of the Po, do make in this part the limit of the two ftates; and confequently, that which has hitherto belonged to the duchy of Placentia on the other fide of the Po, do remain feparated from it.

Laftly, that part of the county of Anghiera, or of the ftate of Milan, whatfoever particular name may be given to it, which borders upon the Novarefe, the valley of Sefia, the Great Alps, and the country of Vallais, extend-ing to the Swifs prefectures of Val Maggia and Locarno,

and

and along the banks of, and in the Lago Maggiore, to the middle of the said lake, in such manner, that for the future the confines between the dominions of his Majesty the King of Sardinia, and those of her Majesty the Queen of Hungary, shall be continually fixed by a line drawn from the borders of the Swifs, in the middle, and all along the Lago Maggiore to the mouth of the Thesin, which line shall go from thence along the middle of the stream of that river to the place of its falling into the Po, excepting the front of the above-mentioned island before Pavia, and from thence go on along the middle of the course of the Po, to the place where the Nura falls into the Po, and go up by the middle of the bed of the Nura quite to its source, which is opposite to the country of Genoa.

The abovesaid division of the course of the rivers shall not prevent the navigation remaining free, as it is to remain to the subjects of the two sovereigns, in the whole breadth of the said rivers, with liberty to pass upon the banks on either side, for the towing of boats which go up stream, the said banks being nevertheless to appertain, as well with regard to the property, as in all other respects to the sovereigns respectively, on either side of the said rivers, who shall be allowed, each on their own side, to make such reparations as they shall judge necessary towards strengthening of them, provided that those reparations be not prominent, that is to say, that they may not force the stream of the river against the opposite side, and that, on the part of the King of Sardinia, it shall never be lawful, under any pretence whatsoever, to make such works as might prevent the free entry of the waters into the canal or Navilio, which is on the side of her Majesty the Queen of Hungary, and which conducts the said waters to Milan.

To enjoy the same in full property and sovereignty, as her Majesty the Queen and her predecessors have enjoyed them hitherto; which countries her Majesty the Queen dismembers for ever from her hereditary dominions, and from the state of Milan, derogating, for that purpose, as far as there can be occasion for it, from every thing that might in any manner be contrary thereto, saving always the direct jurisdiction of the empire.

Article

## Article X.

Befides, as it is of importance to the public caufe, that his Majefty the King of Sardinia fhould have an immediate communication of his dominions with the fea, and with the martime powers, her Majefty the Queen of Hungary and Bohemia, yields to him all the rights which fhe may have in any manner, and upon any title whatfoever, to the town and marquifate of Final, which rights fhe yields and transfers, without any reftriction, to the faid King, in the fame manner as fhe does the countries defcribed in the foregoing article ; in the juft expectation, that the republic of Genoa will facilitate, as far as fhall be necef-fary, a difpofition fo indifpenfably requifite for the liberty and fecurity of Italy, in confideration of the fum, which fhall be found to be due to the faid republic, without his Majefty the King of Sardinia, nor her Majefty the Queen of Hungary being obliged to contribute to the payment of the faid fum, provided always, that the town of Final be and remain for ever a free port, as is Leghorn ; and that it fhall be allowable for his Majefty the King of Sardinia to re-eftablifh there the forts which have been de-molifhed, or to caufe others to be built according as he fhall judge convenient.

## Article XI.

His Majefty the King of Great-Britain, her Majefty the Queen of Hungary and Bohemia, and his Majefty the King of Sardinia, engage themfelves not to make either peace or truce, without comprehending therein, in exprefs words, all the above-mentioned ceffions, and without fti-pulating alfo a full reftitution to the King of Sardinia of every part of his other dominions, which may have been feized or occupied in hatred of his union with the allies ; provided, that the King of Sardinia fhall hold himfelf to be from this prefent time indemnified for the revenue which might be fo withheld from him, by that of the countries yielded and transferred to him by the prefent treaty.

Article

## Article XII.

In return, his Majefty the King of Sardinia fhall remain firmly and infeparably united and attached to the interefts and to the caufe of the allies, not only for as long as the war may laft in Italy, but to the conclufion of the peace in Germany, and of the peace between Great-Britain and Spain; and this is the principal condition, and fine quâ non, of the ceffions made to him above by the 9th and 10th articles of this treaty, which ceffions fhall not receive their full and irrevocable force, but from its entire accomplifhment, after which the countries yielded to the faid King, fhall be deemed guarantied to him by the allies for ever, as his other dominions are.

## Article XIII.

And as foon as Italy fhall be delivered from enemies, and out of all apparent danger of being a frefh invaded, her Majefty the Queen of Hungary fhall not only be at liberty to withdraw part of her troops, but, if fhe requires it, his Majefty the King of Sardinia, fhall furnifh her fome of his own troops to be employed in the fecurity of her Majefty's dominions in Lombardy, that fo fhe may be able to make ufe of a greater number of her own in Germany, in like manner as, at the requifition of the King of Sardinia, the Queen of Hungary fhould caufe fome of her troops to pafs into the dominions of the faid King, if it were neceffary, for defending the paffages thereof, which an enemy's army fhould undertake to force, and for delivering from enemies all the dominions of his majefty the King of Sardinia, and freeing them from any danger of a frefh invafion.

## Article XIV.

In any cafe, the allies fhall not make either peace, or truce, or accommodation whatfoever, with the common enemy, but in concert, and with the participation and advice one of the other, nor without the guaranty of fuch
power

powers as should have a share in the pacification, for the possessions and acquisitions of the allies, as set forth in this treaty ; and after the conclusion of the peace, the present alliance shall equally and unalterably subsist, as well for the security of its execution, as, in general, for the mutual and constant security of the allies.

## Article XV.

His Majesty the King of Sardinia, and her Majesty the Queen of Hungary and Bohemia, in gratitude for the generous concern of his Britannick Majesty for the public security, and for theirs, and for that of Italy in particular, do not only confirm to the British subjects the advantages of commerce and navigation, which they enjoy in their respective dominions, but promise to secure them still farther to them, and as far as it shall be found reasonable and practicable, by a specific treaty of commerce and navigation, whenever his Britannick Majesty shall require it of them.

## Article XVI.

The Lords the States-General of the United Provinces being already under the same engagements towards the most serene House of Austria, and having the same interest with his Britannick Majesty in all the objects of the present treaty, the allies will jointly invite them to enter into this alliance, as a principal contracting party.

## Article XVII.

The other princes and states, who have at heart the peace, the liberty, and the security of Europe, of the Empire, and of Italy, and who will be willing to enter into the present alliance, shall be admitted into it.

## Article XVIII.

This treaty of alliance shall be ratified by all the allies, and the ratifications of it shall be exchanged within the space of six weeks, or sooner if possible.

In

In witnefs whereof, we the plenipotentiaries above-named have figned the prefent treaty with our own hands, and have fet our feals with our coats of arms thereunto. Done at Worms, this ₁²₃ day of September, one thoufand feven hundred and forty-three.

(L. S.) *Carteret.*    (L. S.) *Offorio.*    (L. S.) *De Wafner.*

We having feen and confidered the treaty above-written, have approved and ratified it in all and fingular its articles and claufes, as we do by thefe prefents approve and ratify the fame for ourfelves, our heirs and fucceffors, under-taking and promifing, upon our royal word, that we will religioufly and inviolably perform and obferve all the fingular the things which are contained in it; and that we will never fuffer, as much as in us lies, that they be violated by any body, or that any thing be done, in any manner whatfoever, to the contrary thereof. For the greater faith and corroboration of all which, we have commanded our great feal of Great-Britain to be fet to thefe prefents, figned by the hands of our guardians and juftices of our king-dom of Great-Britain, and our lieutenants in the fame. Given at Weftminfter the 20th day of September, in the year of our Lord, 1743, and of our reign the feventeenth.

| | |
|---|---|
| *Hardwicke,* C. | *Holles Newcaftle.* |
| *Harrington,* P. | *Tweeddale.* |
| *Dorfet.* | *Winchelfea.* |
| *Grafton.* | *Ilay.* |
| *Bolton.* | H. *Pelham.* |
| *Montagu.* | |

*The Definitive Treaty of Peace and Friendfhip, between his* Britannick Majefty, *the moft* Chriftian King, *and the* States General *of the United Provinces. Concluded at* Aix la Chapelle *the* 18th *Day of* October N. S. 1748.

In the Name of the moft holy and undivided Trinity, the Father, Son, and Holy Ghoft.

BE it known to all thofe, whom it fhall or may con-cern, in any manner whatfoever. Europe fees the day, which Divine Providence had pointed out for the
re-

re-eftablifhment of its repofe. A general peace fucceeds to
the long and bloody war, which had arofe between the moft
ferene and moft potent Prince George II. by the Grace of
God, King of Great-Britain, France, and Ireland, Duke of
Brunfwick and Lunenbourg, Arch-Treafurer and Elector
of the Holy Roman Empire, &c. and the moft ferene
and moft potent Princefs Mary Therefia, by the Grace
of God, Queen of Hungary and Bohemia, &c. Emprefs of the Romans, on the one part, and the moft ferene and moft potent Prince Lewis XV. by the Grace of
God, the moft Chriftian King, on the other ; as alfo between the King of Great-Britain, the Emprefs Queen
of Hungary and Bohemia, and the moft ferene and moft
potent Prince Charles Emanuel III. by the Grace of God,
King of Sardinia, on the one part, and the moft ferene
and moft potent Prince Philip V. by the Grace of God,
King of Spain and the Indies, (of glorious memory) and
after his deceafe, the moft ferene and moft potent Prince
Ferdinand VI. by the Grace of God, King of Spain and
the Indies, on the other; in which war the high and
mighty Lords the States General of the United Provinces
of the Low Countries had taken part, as auxiliaries to
the King of Great-Britain ; and the Emprefs Queen of
Hungary and Bohemia : and the moft ferene Duke of
Modena, and the moft ferene republic of Genoa, as
auxiliaries to the King of Spain. God, in his mercy,
made known to all thefe powers, at the fame time, the
way which he had decreed for their reconciliation, and for
the reftoration of tranquility to the people, whom he had
fubjected to their government. They fent their minifters
to Aix la Chapelle, where thofe of the King of Great-
Britain, his moft Chriftian Majefty, and of the States General of the United Provinces, having agreed upon preliminary conditions for a general pacification ; and thofe of
the Emprefs Queen of Hungary and Bohemia, of his Catholic Majefty, of the King of Sardinia, of the Duke
of Modena, and of the republic of Genoa, having acceded thereunto, a general ceffation of hoftilities, by fea
and land, hapily enfued. In order to compleat, at Aix
la Chapelle, the great work of a peace, equally ftable and
convenient

convenient for all parties, the high contracting powers have nominated, appointed, and provided with their full powers, the moft illuftrious and moft excellent Lords their ambaffadors extraordinary, and minifters plenipotentiary, viz. His facred Majefty the King of Great-Britain, John Earl of Sandwich, Vifcount Hinchinbrook, Baron Montague of St. Neots, Peer of England, firft Lord Commiffioner of the Admiralty, one of the Lords regents of the kingdom, his minifter plenipotentiary to the States General of the United Provinces, and Sir Thomas Robinfon, Knight of the moft honourable order of the Bath, and his minifter plenipotentiary to his Majefty the Emperor of the Romans, and her Majefty the Emprefs Queen of Hungary and Bohemia.

His facred moft Chriftian Majefty, Alphonfo Maria Lewis Count de St. Severin of Arragon, Knight of his orders, and John Gabriel de la Porte du Theil, Knight of the order of our Lady of mount Carmel, and of St. Lazarus of Jerufalem, Counfellor of the King in his councils, fecretary of the chamber, and of the cabinet of his Majefty, of the orders of the Dauphin, and of Mefdames of France.

Her facred Majefty the Emprefs Queen of Hungary and Bohemia, Wenceflaus Anthony Count of Kaunitz Rittberg, Lord of Effens, Sedefdorff, Wittmund, Aufterlitz, Hungrifchbrod, Wite, &c. actual intimate counfellor of ftate to their Imperial Majefties.

His facred Catholic Majefty, the Lord Don James Maffone de Lima and Sotto Major, gentleman of the bedchamber to his Catholic Majefty, and Major General of his forces.

His facred Majefty the King of Sardinia, Don Jofeph Offorio, Knight, Grand Croix and Grand Confervator of the military order of the Saints Maurice and Lazarus, and envoy extraordinary of his Majefty the King of Sardinia to his Majefty the King of Great-Britain; and Jofeph Borre, Count Chavanne, his counfellor of ftate, and his minifter to the Lords the ftates General of the United Provinces.

The High and Mighty Lords the States General of the United Provinces, William Count Bentinck, Lord of Rhoon and

and Pendrecht, one of the nobles of the Province of Holland and Weſt Frieſland, curator of the univerſity of Leyden, &c. &c. &c. Frederic Henry Baron of Waſſenaer, Lord of Catwyck and Zand, one of the nobles of the Province of Holland and Weſt Frieſland, Hoog-Heemrade of Rhynland, &c. Gerard Arnout Haſſelaer, burgomaſter and counſellor of the city of Amſterdam, director of the Eaſt-India company ; John Baron of Borſele, firſt noble and repreſentative of the nobility in the ſtates, in the council and admiralty of Zealand, director of the Eaſt-India company; Onno Zwier Van Haren, Grietman of Weſt-Sterlingwerf, deputy-counſellor of the Province of Frieſland, and Commiſſary General of all the Swiſs and Grifon troops in the ſervice of the aforeſaid States General, and reſpectful deputies in the aſſembly of the ſtates General, and in the council of ſtate, on the part of the Provinces of Holland and Weſt Frieſland, Zealand, and Frieſland.

The moſt ſerene Duke of Modena, the Sieur Count de Monzone, his Counſellor of State, and colonel in his ſervice, and his miniſter plenipotentiary to his moſt Chriſtian Majeſty.

The moſt ſerene republic of Genoa, the Sieur Francis Marquis Doria.

Who, after having communicated their full powers to each other, in due form, copies whereof are annexed at the end of this preſent treaty ; and having conferred on the ſeveral objects, which their ſovereigns have judged proper to be inſerted, in this inſtrument of general pacification, have agreed to the ſeveral articles, which are as follows.

### Article I.

There ſhall be a Chriſtian, univerſal and perpetual peace, as well by ſea as land, and a ſincere and laſting friendſhip between the eight powers above-mentioned, and between their heirs and ſucceſſors, kingdoms, ſtates, provinces, countries, ſubjects and vaſſals, of what rank and condition ſoever they may be, without exception of places or perſons. So that the high contracting powers may have the greateſt attention to maintain between them and their ſaid ſtates and ſubjects, this reciprocal friendſhip and correſpondence, not permitting any ſort of hoſtilities to be committed, on one ſide or the other, on any cauſe, or under any pretence whatſoever; and avoiding every thing that may, for the future, diſturb the union happily re-eſtabliſhed between them; and, on the contrary, endeavouring to procure, on all occaſions, whatever may contribute to their mutual glory, intereſts and advantage, without giving any aſſiſtance or protection, directly or indirectly, to thoſe who would injure or prejud ce any of the contracting parties.

II. There ſhall be a general oblivion of whatever may have been done or committed during the war, now ended. And all perſons, upon the day of the exchange of the ratifications of all the parties, ſhall be maintained or re-eſtabliſhed in the poſſeſſion of all the effects, dignities, eccleſiaſtical benefices, honours, revenues, which they enjoyed, or ought to have enjoyed, at the commencement of the war, notwithſtanding all diſpoſſeſſions, ſeizures, or confiſcations, occaſioned by the ſaid war.

III. The treaties of Weſtphalia of 1648; thoſe of Madrid between the crowns of England and Spain, of 1667, and 1670; the treaties of peace of Nimegen of 1678, and 1679; of Ryſwick of 1697; of Utrecht of 1713; of Baden of 1714; the treaty of the Triple Alliance of the Hague of 1717; that of the Quadruple alliance of London of 1718; and the treaty of peace of Vienna of 1738, ſerve as a baſis and foundation to the general peace, and to the preſent treaty; and, for this purpoſe, they are renewed and confirmed in the beſt form, and as if they were herein inſerted, word for word; ſo that they ſhall be punctually obſerved for the future in all their tenor, and religiouſly executed on the one ſide and the other; ſuch points however, as have been derogated from in the preſent treaty, excepted.

IV. All the priſoners made on the one ſide and the other, as well by ſea as by land, and the hoſtages required or given during the war, and to this day, ſhall be reſtored, without ranſom, in ſix weeks at lateſt, to be reckoned from the exchange of the ratification of the preſent treaty; and it ſhall

ſhall be immediately proceeded upon after that exchange : and all the ſhips of war, as well as merchant veſſels, that ſhall have been taken ſince the expiration of the terms agreed upon for the ceſſation of hoſtilities at ſea, ſhall be, in like manner, faithfully reſtored, with all their equipages and cargoes ; and ſureties ſhall be given on all ſides for payment of the debts, which the priſoners or hoſtages may have contracted in the ſtates, where they had been detained, until their full diſcharge.

V. All the conqueſts, that have been made ſince the commencement of the war, or which, ſince the concluſion of the preliminary articles, ſigned the 30th of April laſt, may have been or ſhall be made, either in Europe, or the Eaſt or Weſt Indies, or in any other part of the world whatſoever, being to be reſtored without exception, in conformity to what was ſtipulated by the ſaid preliminary articles, and by the declarations ſince ſigned ; the high contracting parties engage to give orders immediately for proceeding to that reſtitution, as well as to the putting the moſt ſerene Infant Don Philip in poſſeſſion of the ſtates, which are to be yielded to him by virtue of the ſaid preliminaries, the ſaid parties ſolemnly renouncing, as well for themſelves as for their heirs and ſucceſſors, all rights and claims, by what title or pretence ſoever, to all the ſtates, countries and places, that they reſpectively engage to reſtore or yield; ſaving, however, the reverſion ſtipulated of the ſtates yielded to the moſt ſerene Infant Don Philip.

VI. It is ſettled and agreed, that all the reſpective reſtitutions and ceſſions in Europe ſhall be entirely made and executed on all ſides in the ſpace of ſix weeks, or ſooner if poſſible, to be reckoned from the day of the exchange of the ratifications of the preſent treaty of all the eight parties above mentioned ; ſo that, within the ſame term of ſix weeks, the moſt Chriſtian King ſhall reſtore, as well to the Empreſs Queen of Hungary and Bohemia, as to the States General of the United Provinces, all the conqueſts which he has made upon them during this war.

The Empreſs Queen of Hungary and Bohemia ſhall be put, in conſequence hereof, in full and peaceable poſſeſſion of all that ſhe poſſeſſed before the preſent war in the

Low

Low Countries, and elſewhere, except what is otherwiſe regulated by the preſent treaty.

In the ſame time the Lords the States General of the United Provinces ſhall be put in full and peaceable poſ-ſeſſion, and ſuch as they had before the preſent war, of the places of Bergen-op-Zoom and Maeſtricht, and of all they poſſeſſed before the ſaid preſent war in Dutch Flan-ders, Dutch Brabant, and elſewhere :

And the towns and places in the Low Countries, the ſo-vereignty of which belongs to the Empreſs Queen of Hungary and Bohemia, in which their High Mightineſſes have the right of garriſon, ſhall be evacuated to the troops of the republic, within the ſame ſpace of time.

The King of Sardinia ſhall be in like manner, and within the ſame time, entirely re-eſtabliſhed and maintained in the Duchy of Savoy, and in the county of Nice, as ſhell as in all the ſtates, countries, places and forts con-quered, and taken from him on occaſion of the preſent war.

The moſt ſerene Duke of Modena, and the moſt ſerene republic of Genoa, ſhall be alſo, within the ſame time, entirely re-eſtabliſhed and maintained in the ſtates, coun-tries, places, and forts conquered and taken from them du-ring the preſent war, conformably to the tenor of the 13th and 14th articles of this treaty, which relate to them.

All the reſtitutions and ceſſions of the ſaid towns, forts and places, ſhall be made, with all the arillery and war-like ſtores, that were found there on the day of their ſurrender, during the courſe of the war, by the powers who are to make the ſaid ceſſions and reſtitutions, and this according to the inventories which have been made of them, or which ſhall be delivered bona fide, on each ſide. Pro-vided that, as to the pieces of artillery, that have been re-moved elſewhere to be new caſt, or for other uſes, they ſhall be replaced by the ſame number of the ſame bore, or weight in metal. Provided alſo, that the places of Char-leroy, Mons, Athe, Oudenarde, and Menin, the out-works of which have been demoliſhed, ſhall be reſtored without artillery. Nothing ſhall be demanded for the charges and expences employed in the fortifications of all

the

the other places ; nor for other public or private works,
which have been done in the countries that are to be reftored.

VII. In confideration of the reftitutions that his moft
Chriftian Majefty, and his Catholic Majefty make, by the
prefent treaty, either to her Majefty the Queen of Hungary
and Bohemia, or to his Majefty the King of Sardinia, the
duchies of Parma, Placentia, and Guaftalla fhall, for the
future, belong to the moft ferene Infante Don Philip, to
be poffeffed by him and his male defcendants, born in
lawful marriage, in the fame manner, and in the fame
extent, as they have been, or ought to be, poffeffed by
the prefent poffeffors ; and the faid moft ferene Infante, or
his male defcendants, fhall enjoy the faid three duchies,
conformably and under the conditions expreffed in the
acts of ceffion of the Emprefs Queen of Hungary and
Bohemia, and of the King of Sardinia.

Thefe acts of ceffion of the Emprefs Queen of Hungary and Bohemia, and of the King of Sardinia, fhall be
delivered, together with their ratifications of the prefent
treaty, to the ambaffador extraordinary and plenipotentiary
of the Catholic King, in like manner as the ambaffadors
extraordinary and plenipotentiaries of the moft Chriftian
King and Catholic King, fhall deliver, with the ratifications of their Majeflies, to the ambaffador extraordinary and
plenipotentiary of the King of Sardinia, the orders to the
generals of the French and Spanifh troops to reftore Savoy
and the county of Nice to the perfons appointed by that
Prince to receive them ; fo that the reftitution of the faid
flates, and the taking poffeffion of the duchies of Parma,
Placentia, and Guaftalla, by or in the name of the moft
ferene Infante Don Philip, may be effected within the fame
time, conformably to the acts of ceffion, the tenor whereof
follows.

WE Mary Therefia, &c. make known by thefe prefents : Whereas, in order to put an end to the fatal
war, certain preliminary articles were agreed upon the 30th
of April of this year, between the minifters plenipotentiaries
of the moft ferene and moft potent Prince George II. King
of Great-Britain, and the moft ferene and moft potent
Prince

Prince Lewis XV. the moſt Chriſtian King, and their high Mightineſſes the States General of the United Provinces, which have been ſince ratified by all the powers concerned. The tenor of the 4th article whereof is conceived in the following manner.

The duchies of Parma, Placentia, and Guaſtalla ſhall be yielded to the moſt ſerene Infante Don Philip to ſerve him, as an eſtabliſhment, with the right of reverſion to the preſent poſſeſſors, after that his Majeſty the King of the two Sicilies ſhall have ſucceeded to the crown of Spain ; as alſo in caſe the ſaid moſt ſerene Infante Don Philip ſhould happen to die without children.

And whereas a definitive treaty of peace having ſince been concluded, the ſeveral points relating to this affair, have been, by virtue of the articles thereof, explained by the common conſent of the parties concerned, in the following manner.

In conſideration of the reſtitutions, that his moſt Chriſtian Majeſty and his Catholic Majeſty make, by the preſent treaty, either to her Majeſty the Queen of Hungary and Bohemia, or to his Majeſty the King of Sardinia, the duchies of Parma, Placentia, and Guaſtalla ſhall, for the future, belonging to the moſt ſerene Infante Don Philip, to be poſſeſſed by him, and his male deſcendants born in lawful marriage, in the ſame manner, and in the ſame extent, as they have been or ought to be poſſeſſed by the preſent poſſeſſors ; and the ſaid moſt ſerene Infante, or his male deſcendents, ſhall enjoy the ſaid three duchies, conformably and under the conditions expreſſed in the acts of ceſſion of the Empreſs Queen of Hungary and Bohemia, and of the King of Sardinia.

Theſe acts of ceſſion of the Empreſs Queen of Hungary and Bohemia, and of the King of Sardinia, ſhall be delivered, together with their ratifications of the preſent treaty, to the ambaſſador extraordinary and plenipotentiary of the Catholic King, in like manner as the ambaſſadors extraordinary, and plenipotentiaries of the moſt Chriſtian King and Catholic King ſhall deliver, with the ratifications of their Majeſties, to the ambaſſadors extraordinary and plenipotentiaries of the King of Sardinia, the orders to the General of the French and Spaniſh troops to reſtore

Savoy

Savoy and the county of Nice, to the perfons appointed by that Prince to receive them ; fo that the reftitution of the faid ftates, and the taking poffeffion of the duchies of Parma, Placentia, and Guaftalla, by or in the name of the moft ferene Infante Don Philip, may be effected in the fame time, conformably to the faid acts of ceffion.

Wherefore, in order to fulfil thofe things, to which we have bound ourfelves by the articles before inferted, and in the firm hope, that the moft Chriftian and Catholic Kings, and the future poffeffor of the aforefaid three duchies, and his male defcendants will, on their part, *bona fide*, and punctually, fulfill the tenor of the articles abovementioned, and will likewife reftore to us, within the fame time, the ftates and places which are to be reftored to us, in confe-quence of the fecond and eighteenth articles of the fame preliminaries, we do yield and renounce, for us and our fucceffors, under the conditions expreffed in the above mentioned articles, all rights, claims, and pretenfions to us under any title or caufe whatfoever belonging, upon the aforefaid three duchies of Parma, Placentia, and Guaf-talla, formerly poffeffed by us; and to transfer the fame rights, claims and pretenfions, in the beft and moft folemn manner poffible, to the moft ferene Don Philip Infante of Spain, and his defcendents, to be born in law-ful marriage, abfolving all the inhabitants of the faid duchies from the allegiance and oath, which they have ta-ken to us, who fhall be obliged, for the future, to pay the fame allegiance to thofe to whom we have yielded our rights; all which however is to be underftood only for that fpace of time, that either the faid moft ferene Infante Don Philip, or one of his defcendents, fhall not have afcended either throne of the Two Sicilies, or of Spain; for at that time, and in cafe the aforefaid Infante fhould die with-out male defcendents, we exprefsly referve to ourfelves, our heirs and fucceffors, all rights, claims and pretenfions, which have heretofore belonged to us, and confequently the right of reverfion to the faid duchies. In witnefs whereof, &c.

CHARLES

CHARLES EMANUEL, &c. The defire we have to contribute, on our part, to the moft fpeedy re-eftablifhment of the public tranquillity, which lately induced us to accede to the preliminary articles, figned the 30th of April laft between the minifter of his Britannick Majefty, his moft Chriftian Majefty, and the Lords the States General of the United Provinces, which we did, on the 31ft of May laft, by our plenipotentiary, accordingly accede to, inducing us now to accomplifh as much as is to be performed, on our part, in purfuance of them; and particularly for the execution of what is contained in the fourth article of the faid preliminaries, by virtue whereof the duchies of Parma, Placentia, and Guaftalla, are to be yielded to the moft ferene Prince Don Philip, Infante of Spain, to hold, as an eftablifhment, with the right of reverfion to the prefent poffeffors, as foon as his Majefty the King of the two Sicilies fhall have fucceeded to the crown of Spain, or that the faid Infante fhould happen to die without iffue male; we, in conformity thereto, do, by the prefent act, renounce, yield, and transfer, for ourfelves and our fucceffors, to the aforefaid moft ferene Infante Don Philip, and to his male iffue, and their defcendents born in lawful marriage, the town of Placentia, and the Plaifantine, (whereof we were poffeffed) to be held and poffeffed by him as Duke of Placentia, renouncing to this end all rights, claims, and pretenfions, which we have upon them; referving, however, exprefly to us, and our fucceffors, the right of revefion, in the cafes above-mentioned.

In witnefs whereof, &c.

VIII. In order to fecure and effectuate the faid reftitutions and ceffions, it is agreed, that they fhall be entirely executed and accomplifhed on all fides, in Europe, within the term of fix weeks, or fooner, if poffible, to be reckoned from the day of the exchange of the ratifications of all the eight powers; it being provided, that in fifteen days after the figning of the prefent treaty, the Generals, or other perfons, whom the high contracting parties fhall think proper to appoint for that purpofe, fhall meet at

Bruffels

Bruffels and at Nice, to concert and agree on the method of proceeding to the reftitutions, and of putting the parties in poffeffion, in a manner equally convenient for the good of the troops, the inhabitants, and the refpective countries; but fo that all and each of the high contracting powers may be agreeable to their intentions, and to the engage-ments contracted by the prefent treaty, in full and peace-able poffeffion, without any exception, of all that is to be acquired to them, either by reftitution, or ceffion, within the faid term of fix weeks, or fooner if poffible, after the exchange of the ratifications of the prefent treaty by all the faid eight powers.

IX. In confideration that, notwithftanding the recipro-cal engagement taken by the 18th article of the prelimi-naries, importing, that all the reftitutions and ceffions fhould be carried on equally, and fhould be executed at the fame time, his moft Chriftian Majefty engages, by the 6th article of the prefent treaty, to reftore, within the fpace of fix weeks, or fooner if poffible, to be reckoned from the day of exchange of the ratifications of the prefent treaty, all the conquefts which he has made in the Low Countries; whereas it is not poffible, confidering the dif-tance of the countries, that what relates to America fhould be effected within the fame time, or even to fix the time of its entire execution; his Britannick Majefty likewife engages on his part to fend to his moft Chriftian Majefty immediately after the exchange of the ratifications of the prefent treaty, two perfons of rank and confidera-tion, who fhall remain there as hoftages, till there fhall be received a certain and authentic account of the re-ftitution of Ifle Royal, called Cape Breton, and of all the conquefts which the arms or fubjects of his Britannick Majefty may have made before, or after the figning of the preliminaries, in the Eaft and Weft Indies.

Their Britannick and moft Chriftian Majefties oblige themfelves likewife to caufe to be delivered, upon the ex-change of the ratifications of the prefent treaty, the dupli-cates of the orders addreffed to the commiffaries appointed to reftore, and recieve, refpectively whatever may have been conquered, on either fide, in the faid Eaft and Weft Indies,

Indies, agreeably to the 2d article of the preliminaries, and to the declarations of the 21ft and 31ft of May, and the 8th of July laft, in regard to what concerns the faid conquefts in the Eaft and Weft Indies. Provided nevertheless, that Ifle Royal, called Cape Breton, fhall be reftored with all the artillery and warlike ftores, which fhall have been found therein on the day of its furrender, conformably to the inventories, which have been made thereof, and in the condition that the faid place was in, on the faid day of its furrender. As to the other reftitutions, they fhall take place conformably to the meaning of the fecond article of the preliminaries, and of the declarations and convention cf the 21ft and 31ft of May, and the 8th of July laft, in the condition in which things were on the 11th of June, N. S. in the Weft Indies, and on the 31ft of October, alfo N. S. in the Eaft Indies. And every thing befides fhall be re-eftablifhed on the foot that they were or ought to be before the prefent war,

The faid refpective commiffaries, as well thofe for the Weft, as thofe for the Eaft Indies, fhall be ready to fet out on the firft advice that their Britannick and moft Chriftian Majefties fhall receive of the exchange of the ratifications, furnifhed with all the neceffary inftructions, commiffions, powers, and orders, for the moft expeditious accomplifhment of their faid Majefties intentions, and of the engagments taken by the prefent treaty.

X. The ordinary revenues of the countries that are to be refpectively reftord or yielded, and the impofitions laid upon thofe countries for the entertainment and winter quarters of the troops, fhall belong to the powers that are in poffeffion of them, till the day of the exchange of the ratifications of the prefent treaty, without, however, its being permitted to proceed to any kind of execution, provided fufficient fecurity has been given for the payment; it being always to be underftood, that the forage and utenfils for the troops fhall be furnifhed till the evacautions; in confequence of which, all the powers promife and engage not to demand or exact impofitions and contribut ons which they may have laid upon the countries, towns, and places that they have poffeffed during the courfe of the war, and which had not been paid at the time that the events of the faid war had obliged them to abandon the
faid

faid countries, towns, and places; all pretenfions of this nature being made void by the prefent treaty.

XI. All the papers, letters, documents, and archives, which were in the countries, eftates, towns and places which are reftored, and thofe belonging to the countries yielded, fhall be refpectively, and *bona fide*, delivered or given up at the fame time, if poffible, as poffeffion fhall be taken, or at fartherft two months after the exchange of the ratifications of the prefent treaty of all the eight parties, in whatever places the faid papers or documents may be, namely, thofe which may have been removed from the archive of the great council of Mechlin.

XII. His Majefty the King of Sardinia fhall remain in poffeffion of all that he antiently and newly enjoyed, and particularly of the acquifition which he made in the year 1743, of the Vigevanafque, a part of the Pavefan, and the county of Anghiera, in the manner as this prince now poffeffes them, by virtue of the ceffions that have been made of them to him.

XIII. The moft ferene Duke of Modena, by virtue as well of the prefent treaty, as of his rights, prerogatives, and dignities, fhall take poffeffion fix weeks, or fooner if poffible, after the exchange of the ratifications of the faid treaty, of all his ftates, places, forts, countries, effects, and revenues, and, in general of all that he enjoyed before the war.

At the fame time fhall be likewife reftored to him, his archives, documents, writings, and moveables of what nature foever they may be, as alfo the artillery, and war-like ftores, which fhall have been found in his countries, at the time of their being feized. As to what fhall be wanting, or fhall have been converted into another form, the juft value of the things fo taken away, and which are to be reftored, fhall be paid in ready money; which money, as well as the equivalent for the fiefs, which the moft ferene Duke of Modena poffeffed in Hungary, if they are not reftored to him, fhall be fettled and adjufted by the refpective generals or commiffaries, who, according to the 8th article of the prefent treaty, are to af-femble at Nice in fifteen days after the fignature, in order to agree upon the means for executing the reciprocal

reftitu-

reftitutions and putting in poffeffion, fo that at the fame time, and on the fame day as the moft ferene Duke of Modena fhall take poffeffion of all his ftates, he may likewife enter into the enjoyment either of his fiefs in Hungary, or of the faid equivalent, and receive the value of fuch things as cannot be reftored to him. Juftice fhall alfo be done him, within the fame time of fix weeks after the exchange of the ratifications, with refpect to the allodial effects of the Houfe Guaftalla

XIV. The moft ferene Republic of Genoa, as well by virtue of the prefent treaty, as of its rights, preroga-tives, and dignities, fhall re-enter into the poffeffion, fix weeks, or fooner if poffible, after the exchange of the ratifications of the faid treaty, of all the ftates, forts, places, countries, effects, of what nature foever they be, rents and revenues, that it enjoyed before the war; par-ticularly, all and every one of the members and fubjects of the faid republic fhall, within the aforefaid term, after the exchange of the ratifications of the prefent treaty, re-enter into the poffeffion, enjoyment, and liberty of difpofing of all the funds, which they had in the bank of Vienna in Auftria, in Bohemia, or in any other part whatfoever of the ftates of the Emprefs Queen of Hun-gary and Bohemia, and of thofe of the King of Sardinia ; and the intereft fhall be exactly and regularly paid them, to be reckoned from the faid day of the exchange of the ratifications of the prefent treaty.

XV. It has been fettled and agreed upon between the eight high contracting parties, that for the advantage and maintenance of the peace in general, and for the tranquil-lity of Italy in particular, all things fhall remain there in the condition they were in before the war; faving, and after, the execution of the difpofions made by the prefent treaty.

XVI The treaty of the Affiento for the trade of ne-groes, figned at Madrid on the 26th of March, 1713, and the article of the annual fhip making part of the faid treaty, are particularly confirmed by the prefent treaty, for the four years during which the enjoyment thereof has been interrupted, fince the commencement of the pre-fent war, and fhall be executed on the fame footing, and

and under the fame conditions, as they have or ought to have been executed before the faid war.

XVII. Dunkirk fhall remain fortified on the fide of the land, in the fame condition as it is at prefent; and as to the fide of the fea, it fhall remain on the footing of former treaties.

XVIII. The demands of money that his Britannick Majefty has, as Elector of Hanover, upon the crown of Spain; the differences relating to the Abby of St. Hubert; the enclaves of Hainault, and the bureaux newly eftablifh-ed in the Low Countries; the pretenfions of the Elector Palatine; and the other articles, which could not be regulated, fo as to enter into the prefent treaty, fhall be amicably adjufted immediately by the commiffaries appointed for that purpofe, on both fides, or otherwife, as fhall be agreed on by the powers concerned.

XIX. The 5th article of the treaty of the Quadruple Alliance, concluded at London the 2d of Auguft, 1718; containing the guaranty of the fucceffion to the kingdom of Great Britain in the houfe of his Britannick Majefty now reigning, and by which every thing has been provid-ed for, that can relate to the perfon who has taken the title of King of Great Britain, and to his defcendents of both fexes, is exprefsly confirmed and renewed by the prefent article, as if it were here inferted in its full extent.

XX. His Britannick Majefty, as Elector of Brunfwick Lunenbourg, as well for himfelf, as for his heirs and fuc-ceffors, and all the ftates and poffeffions of his faid Ma-jefty in Germany, are included and guarantied by the prefent treaty of peace.

XXI. All the powers interefted in the prefent treaty, who have guarantied the Pragmatick Sanction of the 19th of April 1713, for the whole inheritance of the late Em-peror Charles VI. in favour of his daughter the Emprefs Queen of Hungary and Bohemia, now reigning, and of her defcendents for ever, according to the order eftablifh-ed by the faid Pragmatick Sanction, renew it in the beft manner poffible; except, however, the ceffions already made, either by the faid Emperor, or the faid Princefs, and thofe ftipulated by the prefent treaty.

XXII. The

XXII. The dutchy of Silefia, and the county of Glatz, as his Pruffian Majefty now poffeffes them, are guarantied to that Prince by all the powers, parties and contractors, of the prefent treaty.

XXIII. All the powers contracting and interefted in the prefent treaty, reciprocally and refpectively guarantee the execution thereof.

XXIV. The folemn ratifications of the prefent treaty, expedited in good and due form, fhall be exchanged in this city of Aix la Chapelle, between all the eight parties, within the fpace of one month, or fooner if poffible, to be reckoned from the day of its fignature.

In witnefs whereof, we the underwritten their Ambaffadors Extraordinary and Minifters Plenipotentiaries, have figned with our hands, in their name, and by virtue of our full powers, the prefent treaty of peace, and have caufed the feals of our arms to be put thereto.

Done at Aix la Chapelle, the 18th of October, 1748.

*(Signed)*

(L. S.) *Sandwich.*  (L. S.) *St. Severin d'Aragon.*
(L S.) *T. Robinfon*  (L. S.) *La Porte du Theil.*
(L. S.) *W. Bentinck.*
(L. S.) *G. A. Haffalaer.*
(L. S.) *J. V. Borffele.*
(L. S.) *O. Z. Van Haren.*

*Separate Articles.*

I. SOME of the titles made ufe of by the contracting powers, either in the full powers, and other acts during the courfe of the negociation, or in the preamble of the prefent treaty, not being generally acknowledged, it has been agreed, that no prejudice fhall at any time refult therefrom to any of the faid contracting parties; and that the titles taken or omitted on either fide, on account of the faid negotiation and of the prefent treaty, fhall not be cited, or any confequence drawn therefrom.

II. It has been agreed and determined, that the French language made ufe of in all the copies of the prefent treaty,
and

and which may be used in the acts of accession, shall not be made a precedent that may be alledged, or drawn into consequence, or in any manner prejudice any of the contracting powers; and that they conform themselves for the future to what has been and ought to be observed with regard to, and on the part of powers, who are used and have a right to give and receive copies of like treaties and acts in another language than the French.

The present treaty, and the accessions, which shall intervene, having still the same force and effect, as if the aforesaid practice had been therein observed : and the present separate articles shall have likewise the same force, as if they were inserted in the treaty.

In witness whereof, we the under-written ambassadors extraordinary and ministers plenipotentiaries of his Britannick Majesty, of his most Christian Majesty, and of the Lords the States General of the United Provinces, have signed the present separate articles, and caused the seals of our arms to be put thereto.

Done at Aix la Chapelle, the 18th of October, 1748.

(Signed)

(L. S.) *Sandwich.*        (L. S.) *St. Severin d'Aragon.*
(L. S.) *T. Robinson.*      (L. S.) *La Porte du Theil.*
                            (L. S.) *W. Bentinck.*
                            (L. S.) *G. A. Haffalaer.*
                            (L. S.) *J. V. Borffelle.*
                            (L. S.) *O. Z. Van Haren.*

---

His Britannick Majesty's Full Power.

*GEORGE* R.

GEORGE the Second, by the Grace of God, of Great-Britain, France and Ireland, King, Defender of the Faith, Duke of Brunswick and Lunenburg, Arch Treasurer of the Holy Roman Empire, and Prince Elector, &c. To all to whom these presents shall come, greeting. Whereas, in order to perfect the work of a general

neral peace, fo happily begun, and to bring it, as foon as
poffible, to the defired conclufion, we have thought pro
per to inveft two fit perfons with the title and character of
our ambaffadors extraordinary, and plenipotentiaries at the
prefent congrefs ; know ye therefore, that we, having en
tire confidence in the zeal, judgment, fkill and abilities in
managing great affairs, of our right trufty and well-be
loved coufin, John Earl of Sandwich, as alfo our trufty
and well-beloved Thomas Robinfon, Knight of the moft
honourable order of the Bath, and our minifter plenipo
tentiary to our good fifter the Emprefs of Germany, Queen
of Hungary and Bohemia, have named, made, conftituted
and appointed, as we by thefe prefents name, make
coftitute and appoint, them our true and undoubted am
baffadors extraordinary, minifters, commiffioners, depu
ties, procurators and plenipotentiaries, giving unto them
or each of them, jointly or feparately, all and all manne
of power and authority, as well as our general and fpecia
command, (yet fo, that the general do not derogate from
the fpecial, or otherwife) to repair to Aix la Chapelle, or
to any other place where the treaty and negotiations for the
above-mentioned peace and tranquillity may be to be car
ried on ; and there, for us, and in our name, together
with the ambaffadors, commiffioners, deputies, and pleni
potentiaries of the princes and ftates, whom it may con
cern, properly vefted with the fame power and authority
to meet, in congrefs and conference, either fingly and fe
parately, or jointly and in a body ; and with them to agree
upon, treat, confult and conclude what may be neceffary
for making a firm and ftable peace, and re-eftablifhing a
fincere friendfhip and good harmony ; and to fign, for us
and in our name, every thing fo agreed upon, and con
cluded ; and to make a treaty or treaties upon what
fhall have been fo agreed and concluded, and to do and
tranfact all other matters, which may appertain to the fi
nifhing the abovefaid work, in as ample manner and form
and with equal force and efficacy, as we ourfelves could
do, if perfonally prefent, engaging, and on our roya
word promifing, that whatever things fhall be tranfacted
and concluded by our faid ambaffadors extraording, and
plenipotentiaries, or by either of them, fhall be agreed to
acknowledged

acknowledged and accepted by us, in the fulleft manner; and that we will never fuffer, either in the whole, or in part, any perfon whatfoever to infringe or act contrary to the fame. In witnefs whereof we have figned thefe prefents with our royal hand, and have caufed to be affixed thereto our great feal of Great-Britain. Given at our palace at Herenhaufen the $\frac{\text{thirtieth}}{\text{tenth}}$ day of $\frac{\text{July}}{\text{Auguft}}$ in the year of our Lord 1748, and in the twenty-fecond year of our reign.

The moft Chriftian King's full power.

LEWIS, by the Grace of God, King of France and Navarre. To all thofe, to whom thefe prefents fhall come, greeting. Whereas we are defirous of omitting nothing in our power, in order to accelerate the conclufion of the great and falutary work of peace, and the re-efta-blifhment of the public tranquillity, trufting entirely to the capacity and experience, zeal and fidelity for our fer-vice of our dear and well-beloved the Count de St. Se-verin d'Aragon, Knight of our orders, and the Sieur de la Porte du Theil, counfellor in our councils, fecretary of our chamber and cabinet, and of the commands of our moft dear and moft beloved fon the Dauphin. For thefe caufes, and other good confiderations us thereto moving, we have commiffioned and ordained them, and by thefe prefents figned with our hand, do commiffion and ordain, and have given them, and do give to the one and to the other jointly, as well as to either of them feparately, in cafe of abfence or indifpofition of the other, full power, commiffion, and fpecial order, in our name, and in the quality of our ambaffadors extraordiny and plenipoten-tiaries, to agree with the ambaffadors and minifters actually affembled at Aix la Chapelle for the conclufion of a peace, provided with full powers in good form on the part of their mafters, to fettle, conclude, and fign fuch treaties, ar-ticles, and conventions, as the one and the other together, or either of them, in the aforefaid cafe of abfence or in-difpofition of the other, fhall think good, and chiefly the definitive treaty, which fhall re-eftablifh a folid peace and perfect union between us and the princes and ftates for-

merly

merly at war, or auxiliaries of the powers at war; promising on the faith and the word of a king, to accept, keep firm and stable for ever, accomplish and execute punctually, all that the said Count de St. Severin d'Aragon, and the said Sieur de la Porte du Theil or either of them, in the said cases of absence or indisposition of the other, shall have stipulated, promised and signed by virtue of this present power, without ever contravening the same, or suffering it to be contravened, for what cause, or under what pretext soever; as also to cause our letters of ratification thereof to be dispatched in good form, and exchanged in the time that shall be agreed upon : for such is our pleasure. In witness whereof, we have caused our seal to be put to these presents. Given at Fontainebleau the seventh day of October, in the year of Grace 1748, and of our reign the thirty-fourth.

(Signed) LEWIS,

(And lower) By the King,

(Signed) Brulart.
And sealed with the great seal in yellow wax.

---

### The States General's Full Power.

THE States General of the United Provinces of the Netherlands. To all those, who shall see these presents, greeting. Whereas we desire nothing more ardently, than to see the war, with which Christendom is at present afflicted, terminated by a good peace, and the city of Aix la Chapelle has been agreed upon for the place of the conferences; we, by the same desire of putting a stop, as far as shall be in us, to the desolation of so many provinces, and to the effusion of so much Christian blood, having been willing to contribute thereto all that depends upon us; and, to this end, to depute to the said assembly some persons out of our own body, who have given several proofs of the knowledge and experience which they have of public affairs, as well as of the affection which they have for the good of our state.

And whereas the Sieurs William Count Bentinck, Lord of Rhood and Pendrecht, of the body of nobles of the

province

province of Holland and Weft-Frizeland, curator of the
Univerfity of Leyden, &c. Frederic Henry Baron Waffenaer, Lord of Catwyck and Zand, of the body of nobles
of the province of Holland and Weft-Frizeland, Hoog,
Heemrade of Rhynland, &c. Gerard Arnold Haffeiaer,
Schepen and Senator of the city of Amfterdam, and director of the Eaft-India Company; and Onno Zwier van
Haren, Grietman of Weft Stellingwerf, deputed counfellor of the province of Frizeland, and Commiffary-Ge-
neral of all the Swifs and Grifon troops in our fervice;
refpective deputies in our affembly, and in the council of
ftate, on the part of the provinces of Holland and Weft-
Frizeland, and Frizeland, have diftinguifhed themfelves in
feveral employments of importance for our fervice, in which
they have given marks of their fidelity, application and
addrefs in the management of affairs; for thefe caufes, and
other good confiderations us thereunto moving, we have
commiffioned, ordained and deputed the faid Sieurs Bentinck, Waffenaer, Haffelaer, and Van Haren, do commiffion, ordain and depute them, by thefe prefents, and
have given and do give unto them full power, commiffion,
and fpecial order, to go to Aix la Chapelle, in quality of
our ambaffadors extraordinary and plenipotentiaries for
the peace, and there to confer with the ambaffadors
extraordinary and plenipotentiaries of his Moft Chriftian
Majeft, and his allies, provided with fufficient powers,
and there to treat of the means of terminating and
pacifying the differences which at prefent occafion the
war; and our faid ambaffadors extraordinary and plenipotentiaries, all together, or any of them, or any one
among them, in cafe of abfence of the others, by ficknefs or other impediment, fhall have power to agree about
the fame, and thereupon to conclude and fign a good and
fure peace, and, in general, to tranfact, negociate, promife,
and grant whatever they fhall think neceffary to the faid
effect of the peace, and generally to do every thing that
we could do, if we were there prefent, even though a
more fpecial power, and order, not contained in thefe
prefents, fhould be neceffary for that purpofe; promifing
fincerely and bona fide, to accept and keep firm and ftable
whatever by the faid ambaffadors extraordinary and pleni-

potentiaries,

potentiaries, or by any, or any one of them, in cafe of ſickneſs, abſence, or other impediment of the others, ſhall have been ſtipulated, promiſed and granted, and thereof to cauſe our letters of ratification to be diſpatched, in the time that they ſhall have promiſed in our name to furniſh them. Given at the Hague in our aſſembly, under our great ſeal, the paraphe of the preſident of our aſſembly, and the ſignature of our Firſt Greffier, the eighth day of March, 1748.

(Signed)

H. van Iſſelmuden, Vt.

(Lower)

By order of the ſaid Lords the States-General, (Signed)

H. Fagel.

## The States General's Full Power.

THE States General of the United Provinces of the Netherlands. To all thoſe, who ſhall ſee theſe preſents, greeting. Whereas we deſire nothing more ardently, than to ſee the war, with which Chriſtendom is at preſent afflicted, terminated by a good peace; and the city of Aix la Chapelle has been agreed upon for the place of the conferences; we, by the ſame deſire of putting a ſtop, as far as ſhall be in us, to the deſolation of ſo many provinces, and to the effuſion of ſo much Chriſtian blood, have been willing to contribute thereto all that depends upon us; and, to this end, have already deputed ſome perſons heretofore to the ſaid aſſembly out of our own body, who have given ſeveral proofs of the knowledge and experience, which they have of public affairs, as well as of the affection, which they have for the good of our ſtate; to wit, the Seurs William Bentinck, Lord of Rhoon and Pendrecht, of the body of nobles of the province of Holland and Weſt-Frizeland, curator of the univerſity of Leyden, &c. Frederic Henry Baron Waſſenaer, Lord of Catwyck and Zann, of the body of nobles of the province of Holland and Weſt-Frizeland, Hoog-Heemrade of Rhynland, &c. Gerard Arnold Haſſelaer, Schepen and Senator of the city of Amſterdam, and director of the Eaſt-India company; and Onno Zwier Van Haren, Grietman

of

of Weſt-Stellingwerff, deputed counſellor of the province of Frizeland, and commiſſary-general of all the Swiſs and Griſon troops in our ſervice; reſpective deputies in our aſſembly, and in the council of ſtate, on the part of the provinces of Holland and Weſt-Frizeland, and Frizeland. And whereas we have at preſent thought proper to join a fifth perſon to the four above-mentioned, for this ſame purpoſe; and the Sieur John Baron Van Borſſele, firſt noble, and repreſenting the nobility, in the ſtates, in the council, and in the admiralty of Zeeland, director of the Eaſt-India company, and deputy in our aſſembly on the part of the ſaid province of Zeeland, has diſtinguiſhed himſelf in ſeveral employments of importance for our ſervice, in which he has given marks of his fidelty, application and addreſs in the management of affairs: for theſe cauſes, and other good conſiderations, us thereunto moving, we have commiſſioned, ordained, and deputed the ſaid Sieur Van Borſſele, do commiſſion, ordain, and depute him, by theſe preſents, and have given, and do give unto him full power, commiſſion, and ſpecial order, to go to Aix la Chapelle, in quality of our ambaſſador extraordinary and plenipotentiary for the peace, and there to confer with the ambaſſadors extraordinary and plenipotentiaries of his Moſt Chriſtian Majeſty and his allies, provided with ſufficient full powers, and there to treat of the means of terminating and pacifying the differences, which at preſent occaſion the war, and our ſaid ambaſſador extraordinary and plenipotentiary, together with the ſaid Sieurs Bentinck, Waſſenaer, Haſſelaer, and Van Haren, our other four ambaſſadors extraordinary and plenipotentiaries, or with any, or any one of them, or even alone, in caſe of abſence of the others, by ſickneſs or other impediment, ſhall have power to agree about the ſame, and thereupon to conclude and ſign a good and ſure peace, and in general to tranſact, negociate, promiſe, and grant, whatever he ſhall think neceſſary for the ſaid effect of the peace, and generally do every thing that we could do, if we were there preſent, even tho' a more ſpecial power and order, not contained in theſe preſents, ſhould be neceſſary for that purpoſe; promiſing ſincerely, and bona fide, to accept and keep firm and ſtable, whatever by the ſaid Sieur Van

Borſſele,

Borffele, together with our other four ambaffadors extraordinary and plenipotentiaries, or any, or any one of them,
or by him alone, in cafe of ficknefs, abfence, or other impediment of the others, fhall have been ftipulated, promifed, and granted, and thereof to caufe our letters of ratification to be difpatched, in the time that they fhall have
promifed in our name to furnifh them. Given at the
Hague, in our affembly, under our great feal, the paraphe
of the prefident of our affembly, and the fignature of our
Firft Greffier, the 25th day of April, 1748.

(Signed) *H. V. Hamerfler*, Vt.
(Lower) By order of the faid Lords the States General,
(Signed) *H. Fagel*.

---

The Acceffion of the Emprefs Queen of Hungary.

In the Name of the moft Holy and Undivided Trinity,
Father, Son, and Holy Ghoft.

BE it known to all, whom it fhall or may concern.
The Ambaffadors extraordinary and plenipotentiaries of his Britannick Majefty, of his moft Chriftian Majefty, and of the High and Mighty Lords the States General of the United Provinces, having concluded and figned, in this city of Aix la Chapelle, on the 18th day of
this prefent month of October, upon the bafis of the preliminaries which were agreed upon and concluded between
them the 30th day of April of the prefent year, a general
and definitive treaty of peace, and two feparate articles,
the tenor of which treaty and feparate articles follows.

*Fiat Infertio.*

And the faid ambaffadors extraordinary and plenipotentiaries having, in a friendly manner, invited the ambaffador extraordinary and plenipotentiary of her Majefty
the Emprefs Queen of Hungary and Bohemia, to accede
thereto, in the name of her faid Majefty.

The

The ambaſſadors under-written, that is to ſay, on the part of the moſt ſerene and moſt potent Prince, George the Second, by the grace of God, King of Great-Britain, John Earl of Sandwich, Viſcount Hinchinbrooke, Baron Montagu of St. Neots, Peer of England, firſt Lord com-miſſioner of the Admiralty, one of the Lords of the Re-gency of the kingdom, his miniſter plenipotentiary to the Lords the States General of the United Provinces; and Sir Thomas Robinſon, knight of the moſt honourable order of the Bath, and his miniſter plenipotentiary to his Majeſty the Emperor of the Romans, and to her Majeſty the Em-preſs Queen of Hungary and Bohemia; and on the part of the moſt ſerene and moſt potent Princeſs Maria Thereſia, by the grace of God, Queen of Hungary and Bohemia, Empreſs, the Lord Wenceſlas Anthony Count de Kaunitz Rittber, Lord of Eſſens, Steteſdorff, Wittmund, Auſter-litz, Hungriſchbrod, Wieſe, &c. actual privy counſellor to their Imperial Majeſties, by virtue of their full powers, which they have communicated to each other, and copies whereof are annexed to the end of this preſent act, have agreed on what follows.

That her Majeſty the Empreſs Queen of Hungary and Bohemia, being deſirous of contributing to re-eſtabliſh and confirm, as ſoon as poſſible, the repoſe of Europe, accedes, by virtue of the preſent act, to the ſaid treaty and two ſe-parate articles, without any reſerve or exception, in the firm confidence that every thing, which is therein promiſed to her ſaid Majeſty, ſhall be bona fide fulfilled; declaring, at the ſame time, and promiſing, that ſhe will, in like manner, moſt faithfully perform all the articles, clauſes and conditions, which relate to her.

His Britannick Majeſty likewiſe accepts the preſent ac-ceſſion of the Empreſs Queen of Hungary and Bohemia, and promiſes, in like manner, to perform, without any reſerve or exception, all the articles, clauſes, and condi-tions, contained in the ſaid treaty and the two ſeparate ar-ticles before inſerted.

The ratifications of the preſent act ſhall be exchanged, in this city of Aix la Chapelle, within the ſpace of three weeks, to be computed from this day.

In

In witnefs whereof, we the ambaffadors extraordinary and plenipotentiaries of his Britannick Majefty, and her Majefty the Emprefs Queen of Hungary and Bohemia, have figned the prefent act, and have thereunto affixed the feal of our arms.

Done at Aix la Chapelle, the 23d day of October, 1748.

(L. S.) *Sandwich*.      (L. S.) *Le Comte V. A.*
(L S.) *T. Robinfon*.      *de Kaunitz Rittberg.*

The Emprefs Queen of Hungary's Full Power.

WE Maria Therefia, by the grace of God, Emprefs of the Romans, and of Germany, of Hungary, Bohemia, Dalmatia, Croatia, Sclavonia, &c. Queen, Arch-Dutchefs of Auftria, Dutchefs of Burgundy, Brabant, Milan, Styria, Carinthia, Carniolia, Mantua, Parma and Placentia, Limburgh, Luxemburgh, Gueldre, Wurtemberg, of the Upper and Lower Silefia, Princefs of Suabia, and Tranfilvania, Marchionefs of the holy Roman Empire, Burgovia, Moravia, and the Upper and Lower Lufatia ; Countefs of Habfpurg, Flanders, Tirol, Ferrete, Kybourg, Goritia, Gradifca, and Artois, Countefs of Namur, Lady of the Marches of Sclaonia, the Port of Naon, Saline, and Mechlin, &c. Duchefs of Lorraine and Barr, Great Duchefs of Tufcany, &c. Do make known, and certify, by virtue of thefe prefents. Whereas we are informed, that the congrefs which had been opened at Breda is diffolved ; and that conferences are to be held at Aix la Chapelle, between the minifters of the feveral princes engaged in the prefent war, authorifed to agree upon the means of terminating the differences that have arifen between them, and reftoring peace : and as we have nothing more at heart, than to do every thing, that depends upon us, towards obtaining, as foon as poffible, fo defirable an end, in the moft fecure and effectual manner ; we lofe no time in doing our part towards the promoting fo falutary a work, by fending thither our minifters Plenipotentiaries, whom we have, moreover invefted with the character of our ambaffadors. Confiding therefore entirely in the often tried fidelity, experience in bufinefs, and

and great prudence of our actual privy counsellor, Wenceslaus Anthony de Kauntiz & Rittberg, Count of the Holy Roman Empire, as also of Thaddaeus, Free Baron of Reifchach, our Lord of the bed-chamber, counsellor of the government of Anterior Auſtria, and our miniſter to the High and Mighty the States General of the United Provinces; both of whom, and each of them, we have inveſted with the character of our ambaſſadors, as well as with full powers, as we do accordingly, by theſe preſents, inveſt them both, and each of them, in caſe of the abſence or hindrance of the other, in the moſt ample manner poſſible; to the end, that both, or either of them, in caſe of the abſence or hindrance of the other, may join their endeavours with our allies, and their miniſters, hold friendly conferences with thoſe of other princes engaged in the preſent war againſt us or our allies, and with any one or more of them, furniſhed with the like full powers, and agree upon any matters and things relating thereto, and whatever ſhall have been ſo agreed upon, whether jointly, or ſeparately, to ſign and ſeal; and, in a word, to do all thoſe things, in our name, which we ourſelves could do, if perſonally preſent: promiſing, on our Imperial, Royal, and Archiducal word, that we will agree to, accept of, and faithfully fulfill, all and ſingular ſuch acts, as our aforeſaid miniſters plenipotentiaries, inveſted over and above with the characters of our ambaſſadors, ſhall have ſo done, concluded, and ſigned. In witneſs whereof, and for its greater force, we have ſigned the preſent full powers with our own hand, and ordered our Imperial, Royal, and Archiducal ſeal to be affixed thereto. Given in our city of Vienna, the 19th day of December, in the year 1747, the 8th year of our reign.

(Signed)
MARIA THERESIA.
*C. Count Ulfeld.*
By command of her Sacred, Imperial Royal Majeſty,
*John Chriſtopher Bartenſtein.*

His

## His Catholic Majesty's Accession.

In the name of the most Holy and Undivided Trinity, Father, Son, and Holy Ghost.

BE it known to all those, to whom it shall belong or can belong. The ambassadors and plenipotentiaries of his Britannick Majesty, of his most Christian Majesty, and of the High and Mighty Lords the States General of the United Provinces, having concluded and signed at Aix la Chapelle, the 18th of October of this year, a definitive treaty of peace, and two separate articles; the tenor of which treaty and separate articles is as follows:

*Fiat Insertio.*

And the said ambassador and plenipotentiaries having amicably invited the ambassador extraordinary and plenipotentiary of his Catholic Majesty to accede thereto in the name of his said Majesty. The under-written ambassadors; to wit, on the part of the most serene and most potent Prince, George the Second, by the grace of God, King of Great-Britain, France, and Ireland, Duke of Brunswick and Lunenburg, Arch-Treasurer and Elector of the Holy Roman Empire, &c. the Lords, John Earl of Sandwich, Viscount of Hinchinbrooke, Baron Montagu of St. Neots, Peer of England, first Lord commissioner of the Admiralty, one of the Lords regents of the kingdom, his minister plenipotentiary to the Lords the States General of the United Provinces; and Thomas Robinson, knight of the most honourable order of the Bath, and his minister plenipotentiary to his Majesty the Emperor of the Romans, and her Majesty the Empress Queen of Hungary and Bohemia. And on the part of the most serene and most potent Prince, Ferdinand the Sixth, by the grace of God, King of Spain and of the Indies, the Lord Don James Massone de Lima y Soto Mayor, Lord of the Bed-chamber of his said Catholic Majesty, and Major General of his armies. By virtue of their full powers, which they have communicated, and copies whereof are

added

added at the end of the prefent act, have agreed upon what follows.

That his Catholic Majefty, defiring to contribute and concur to re-eftablifh and fettle, as foon as poffible, the peace of Europe, accedes, by virtue of the prefent act, to the faid treaty, and two feparate articles, without any re- ferve or exception, in a firm confidence, that whatfoever is promifed therein to his faid Majefty, fhall be faithfully fulfilled ; declaring at the fame time, and promifing, that he will alfo perform moft faithfully all the articles, claufes and conditions, which concern him.

In like manner his Britannick Majefty accepts the pre- fent acceffion of his Catholic Majefty ; and likewife pro- mifes to perform, without any referve or exception, all the articles, claufes, and conditions, contained in the faid treaty, and two feparate articles, inferted above.

The ratifications of the prefent act fhall be exchanged in this city of Aix la Chapelle in the fpace of a month, to be computed from this day.

In teftimony whereof, we the ambaffadors extraordiny and plenipotentiaries of his Britannick Majefty, and of his Catholick Majefty, have figned the prefent act, and have caufed the feal of our arms to be fet thereto.

Done at Aix la Chapelle the 20th of October, 1728.

(L. S.) *Sandwich.*    (L. S.) *Don James Maffone de Lima*
(L. S.) *T. Robinfon.*        *y Soto Major.*

## His Catholic Majefty's Full Power.

FERDINAND, by the Grace of God, King of Caftile, of Leon, of Arragon, of the two Sicilies, of Jeru- falem, of Navarre, of Grenada, of Toledo, of Valencia, of Gallicia, of Mayorca, of Seville, of Sardinia, of Cor- dova, of Corfica, of Murcia, of Jaen, of the Algarbes, of Algezira, of Gibraltar, the Canary iflands, of the Eaft and Weft Indies, Iflands and Terra Firma of the Ocean Sea, Arch-Duke of Auftria, Duke of Burgundy, of Brabant and Milan, Count of Habfpurg, of Flanders, Tirol and Barcelona, Lord of Bifcay and of Molina, &c. Whereas it had been my moft and earneft defire, ever fince Divine Providence has trufted me with the government
of

of the vaſt dominions annexed to my crown, to put an honourable end to the troubles in which I found my arms involved, and to concur in giving peace to Europe, by all the juſt means that ſhould appear moſt conducive to that end : and whereas I knowing that ſeveral miniſters, particularly thoſe of the powers now at war, are meeting at Aix la Chapelle with the ſame view to a general pacification ; and it being therefore neceſſary that I ſhould appoint one to aſſiſt on my part, endowed with that fidelity, zeal, and underſtanding, requiſite for ſuch a purpoſe, and finding in you, Don James Maſone de Lima, Lord of my Bed-chamber, and Major-General of my armies, theſe ſpecial and diſtinguiſhed qualifications ; I do chuſe and nominate you, to the end that, inveſted with the character of my ambaſſador extraordinary and plenipotentiary, you do repair, in my name, to Aix la Chapelle, and repreſenting, at that place, my own perſon, you do treat and confer with the miniſter or miniſters of the powers now at war, who do already, or ſhall hereafter, reſide there, or in any other place where it ſhall be thought convenient to treat ; and to the end that you may, in the ſame manner, conclude and ſign with the ſaid miniſters, the treaty or treaties which ſhall tend to the ſole view of producing a ſolid and honourable peace ; and whatever you may thus treat of, conclude, and ſign, I do from this time acknowledge as accepted and ratified, and promiſe, upon my royal word, to obſerve and fulfill, and to cauſe the ſame to be obſerved and fulfilled in the ſame manner, as if I myſelf had treated and conferred upon, concluded and ſigned the ſame. To which end, I do hereby give you all my authority and full power, in the moſt ample manner as by law required. In witneſs whereof, I have cauſed theſe preſents to be diſpatched, ſigned with my hand, ſealed with my ſecret ſeal, and counterſigned by my underwritten counſellor, and ſecretary of ſtate, and of the general diſpatch of war, the revenues, Indies and Marine. Given at Aranjués the 12th of May, 1748.

I THE KING.

*Cenon de Some de Villa.*

His

### His Sardinian Majefty's Acceffion.

In the name of the moft Moly and Undivided Trinity, Father, Son, and Holy Ghoft.

BE it known to all thofe, to whom it fhall or may belong.

The ambaffadors extraordinary and plenipotentiaries of his Britannick Majefty, of his moft Chriftian Majefty, and of the High and Mighty Lords the States General of the United Provinces, having concluded and figned in this city of Aix la Chapelle, the 18th of the month of October laft, upon the foundation of the preliminaries at firft agreed to and fettled among them the thirtieth of April of this year, a general and definitive treaty of peace, and two feparate articles, the tenor of which treaty and feparate articles are as follows :

*Fiat Infertio.*

And the faid ambaffadors extraordinary and plenipotentiaries having amicably invited the ambaffadors extraordinary and plenipotentiaries of his Majefty the King of Sardinia to accede thereto in the name of his faid Majefty.

The under-written ambaffadors, to wit, on the part of the moft ferene and moft powerful Prince George the Second, by the Grace of God, King of Great-Britain, France, and Ireland, the Lords, John Earl of Sandwich, Vifcount of Hinchinbrooke, Baron Montagu of Saint Neots, Peer of England, firft Lord Commiffioner of the Admiralty, one of the Lords Regents of the kingdom, his minifter plenipotentiary to the Lords the States General of the United Provinces; and Thomas Robinfon, knight of the moft honourable order of the Bath, and his minifter plenipotentiary to his Majefty the Emperor of the Romans, and her Majefty the Emprefs Queen of Hungary and Bohemia ; and on the part of the moft ferene and moft potent Prince, Charles Emanuel the Third, by the grace of God, King of Sardina, the Lords Don Jofeph Offorio, Chevalier Grand Croix, and Grand Confervator of the military order

of

of the Saints Maurice and Lazarus, and envoy extraordinary of his Majesty the King of Sardinia to his Majesty the King of Great-Britain; and Joseph Borre Count de la Chavanne, his counsellor of state, and his minister to the Lords the States General of the United Provinces, by virtue of their full powers, which they have communicated to each other, and copies whereof are added at the end of the present act, have agreed upon what follows.

That his Majesty the King of Sardinia, desiring to contribute and concur to re-establish and settle, as soon as possible, the peace of Europe, accedes, by virtue of the present act, to the said treaty and two separate articles, in a firm confidence, that whatsoever is promised therein to his said Majesty, shall be faithfully fulfilled; declaring at the same time, and promising, that he will also perform, most faithfully, all the articles, clauses, and conditions, which regard him.

In like manner, his Britannick Majesty accepts the present accession of his Majesty the King of Sardinia; and likewise promises to perform, without reserve or exception, all the articles, clauses, and conditions, contained in the said treaty and the two separate articles, inserted above.

The ratifications of the present act shall be exchanged in this city of Aix la Chapelle, in the space of twenty-five days, to be computed from this day.

In testimony whereof, we the ambassadors extraordinary and plenipotentiaries of his Britannick Majesty, and of his Majesty the King of Sardinia, have signed the present act, and have caused the seal of our arms to be set thereto.

Done at Aix la Chapelle, the seventh of November, one thousand seven hundred forty-eight.

(L. S ) *T. Robinson.*　　(L. S.) *Ossorio.*
　　　　　　　　　　　　　(L. S.) *De la Chavanne.*

The King of Sardinia's Full power.

CHARLES EMANUEL, by the Grace of God, King of Sardinia, of Cyprus, and of Jerusalem; Duke of Savoy, of Mountferrat, of Aoste, of Chablais, of Genevois and of Plaisance; Prince of Piedmont and of Onielle;

Onielle ; Marquis of Italy, of Saluces, of Sufa, of Ivree, of Ceve, of Maro, of Oriftan, and of Sefane ; Count of Maurienne, of Geneva, of Nice, of Tende, of Romont, of Aft, of Alexandria, of Gocean, of Novara, of Tortona, of Vigevano and of Bobbio ; Baron of Vaud and of Faucigny : Lord of Verciel, of Pignerol, of Tarantaife, of the Lumelline and of the Valley of Sefia ; Prince and perpetual Vicar, of the Holy Empire in Italy, &c. To all, who fhall fee thefe prefents, greeting : whereas, after having acceded to the preliminary articles of peace, figned the 30th of April laft at Aix la Chapelle, we are fincerely defirous of concurring in the perfect re eftablifh-ment of the general peace in Europe, to which all the powers, that have figned and acceded, as we have done, to the aforefaid preliminary articles, are difpofed to give their affiftance, by reducing thofe faid preliminary articles, and other acts depending theron, in one definitive treaty of general peace. For thefe reafons, and other confiderations us thereunto moving, we, trufting in the capacity, experience, zeal and fidelity for our fervice, of our dear, well-beloved and trufty, the Chevalier Offo-rio, knight grand croix and grand confervator of our military order of the faints Maurice and Lazarus, and our envoy extraordinary to the King of Great-Britain ; and the Count Borre de la Chavanne, our counfellor of ftate, our minifters to the Lords the States General of the United Provinces, and our minifter plenipotentiary to the confe-rences of Aix la Chapelle, have named and deputed them, as by thefe prefents we do name and depute them our am-baffadors extraordinary and plenipotentiaries ; and have given them, and do give them, power, commiffion, and fpecial order, in our name, and in the faid quality of our ambaffadors extraordiny and plenipotentiaries, to make, conclude and fign, both jointly, or one of them alone, in cafe of abfence, ficknefs, or other hindrance of the other, with the refpective ambaffadors extraordinary and pleni-potentiaries of the above-mentioned powers, jointly or fe-parately, provided with powers for that purpofe, fuch de-finitive treaty of peace, articles, conventions, or acts, as they fhall think fit, for re-eftablifhing, in a folid manner,

the

the general peace in Europe, or to accede to thofe, which
fhall have been already concluded and figned for the fame
end ; willing, that they fhould, upon thofe occafions, act
with the fame anthority, as we would do, if we were prefent in perfon, and even if any thing fhould occur, which
might require a more fpecial order, not contained in thefe
prients : promifing, upon the faith and word of a King,
to obferve and caufe to be obferved, inviolably, all that
fhall be done, agreed, regulated and figned by the above-
mentioned Chevalier Offorio, and Count de la Chavanne,
our ambaffadors extraordinary and plenipotentiaries, without contravening, or fuffering any controvention thereto,
directly or indirectly, for that caufe, or under what pretext foever it fhall or may be ; as alfo to caufe to be difpatched, our letters of ratification thereof in due form, to
be exchanged within the term which fhall de agreed on.
In witnefs whereof, we have figned thefe prefents with our
hand, and caufed them to be counterfigned dy the Marquis
D. Leopold de Carret de Gorzegne, our firft fecretary of
ftate for foreign affairs, and caufed the fecret feal of our
arms to be affixed thereto. Given at Turin, the twenty-
fourth of the month of Auguft, in the year of our Lord
one thoufand feven hundred and forty-eight, and of our
reign the nineteenth.

(L. S.)  C. E M A N U E L.
(Lower)
Carret de Gorzegne.

---

The Acceffion of the Duke of Modena.

In the name of the moft Holy and Undivided Trinity,
Father, Son, and Holy Ghoft.

BE it known to all thofe, to whom it fhall or may
belong. The ambaffadora extraordinary and plenipotentiaries of his Britannick Majefty, or his moft Chriftian
Majefty, and of the High and Mighty Lords the States General

neral of the United Provinces, having concluded and signed, in this city of Aix la Chapelle, the 18th of the prefent month of October, upon the foundation of the preliminaries, at firſt agreed upon and concluded amongſt them the 30th day of April of this year, a general and definitive treaty of peace, and two ſeparate articles ; the tenor of which treaty and ſeparate articles follows.

*Fiat Inſertio.*

And the ſaid ambaſſadors extraordinary and plenipotentiaries having amicably invited the miniſter plenipotentiary of his moſt ſerene Highneſs, Francis the Third, by the Grace of God, Duke of Modena, Reggio, Mirandola, &c. to accede thereto in the name of his moſt ſerene Highneſs.

The under-written ambaſſadors and miniſter plenipotentiary ; to wit, on the part of the moſt ſerene and moſt potent Prince, George the Second, by the Grace of God, King of Great-Britain, France, and Ireland, the Lords, John Earl of Sandwich, Viſcount of Hinchinbrooke, Baron Montagu of St. Neots, Peer of England, firſt Lord Commiſſioner of the Admiralty, one of the Lords regents of the kingdom, his miniſter plenipotentiary to the Lords the States General of the United Provinces; and Thomas Robinſon, knight of the moſt honourable order of the Bath, and his miniſter plenipotentiary to his Majeſty the Emperor of the Romans, and her Majeſty the Empreſs Queen of Hungary and Bohemia. And on the part of his moſt ſerene Highneſs the Duke of Modena, the Sieur Count de Montzone, his counſellor of ſtate and colonel in his ſervice, and his miniſter plenipotentiary to his moſt Chriſtian Majeſty, by virtue of their full powers, which they have communicated to each other, and of which copies are added at the end of the preſent act, have agreed on what follows.

That his moſt ſerene Highneſs the Duke of Modena, deſiring to contribute and concur to re-eſtabliſh and ſettle, as ſoon as poſſible, the peace of Europe, accedes, by virtue of the preſent act, to the ſaid treaty, and two ſeparate articles, without any reſerve or exception, in a firm confidence

dence, that what is promiſed to his ſaid moſt ſerene Highneſs therein, ſhall be faithfully fulfilled; declaring and
promiſing at the ſame time, that he will alſo perform
moſt faithfully all the articles, clauſes and conditions,
which concern him.

In like manner his Britannick Majeſty accepts the preſent acceſſion of his moſt ſerene Highneſs the Duke of
Modena, and promiſes likewiſe to fulfill, without any reſerve or exception, all the articles, clauſes, and conditions,
contained in the ſaid treaty, and the two ſeparate articles,
inſerted above.

The ratifications of the preſent act ſhall be exchanged,
in this city of Aix la Chapelle, in the ſpace of three weeks,
to be computed from this day.

In teſtimony whereof, we the ambaſſadors extraordinary
and miniſter plenipotentiary of his Britannick Majeſty,
and of his moſt ſerene Highneſs the Duke of Modena,
have ſigned the preſent act, and have cauſed the ſeal
of our arms to be ſet thereto.

Done at Aix la Chapelle the 25th of October, 1748.

(L. S.) *T. Robinſan*.　(L. S.) *Le Comte de Monzone*.

The Duke of Modena's Full Power.

FRANCIS, Duke of Modena, Reggio Mirandola.

WHEREAS, in the conferences to be held at Aix la
Chapelle, for a general pacification between the
powers concerned in the preſent war, affairs are to be
treated of which regard us; ✴for which it is neceſſary to
have a miniſter there, on whoſe ability, fiedlity and prudence we may ſafely rely, we have not thought that we
could employ and perſon with greater confidence, on this
occaſion, than the Count de Monzone, our counſellor of
ſtate, miniſter plenipotentiary at the court of his moſt
Chriſtian Majeſty, and colonel in our ſervice; for which
reaſon we do chuſe and depute him for our miniſter plenipotentiary at the ſaid congreſs, by giving and granting
to him, faculty, authority, and full power, with general
and ſpecial order, to treat there, in our name, of all matters which concern us, and to promiſe, agree to, conclude,

clude, ftipulate and fign, on our part, whatever he fhall judge moft convenient for our fervice; defiring, for this end, the minifters plenipotentiary of all the courts concerned, which fhall be prefent at the faid congrefs, to accept of, and acknowledge him, as our minifter plenipotentiary; promifiing, on the faith and word of a Prince, to hold as confirmed and ratified, and to approve and obferve all that fhall be concluded, accepted of, and ftipulated by the fame minifter plenipotentiary.

In witnefs whereof, we have figned thefe prefents, which fhall be counter-figned by one of our minifters, and have our feal affixed thereto. Given at Marfeilles this 30th of November, 1748.

(Signed)　　　　　　FRANCESCO
(And underneath counter-figned)
                              De Bondigili.

## The Rupublic of Genoa's Acceffion.

### In the Name of the moft Holy and Undivided Trinity, Father, Son, and Holy Ghoft.

BE it known to all thofe, to whom it fhall, or may belong.

The ambaffadores extraordinary and plenipotentiaries of his Britannick Majefty, of his moft Chriftian Majefty, and of the High and Mighty Lords the States General of the United Provinces, having concluded and figned, in this city of Aix la Chapelle, on the 18th of the prefent month of Octobor, upon the foundation of the preliminaries, at firft agreed upon and fettled amongft them the 30th day of April of this year, a general and definitive treaty of peace, and two feparate articles, of which treaty and feparate articles the tenor is as follows.

### Fiat Infertio.

And the faid ambaffadors extraordinary and plenipotentiaries, having amicably invited the minifters plenipotentiary of the moft ferene Republic of Genoa, to accede thereto, in the name of the faid moft ferene Republic.

The under-written ambaffadors and minifter plenipotentiary; to wit, on the part of the moft ferene and moft

potent

potent Prince, George the Second, by the grace of God, King of Great Britain, France, and Ireland, the Lords, John Earl of Sandwich, Viscount of Hinchinbrooke, Baron Montagu of St. Neots, peer of England, first Lord Commissioner of the Admiralty, one of the Lords Regents of the kingdom, his minister plenipotentiary to the Lords the States General of the United Provinces; and Thomas Robinson, Knight, of the most honourable order of the Bath, and minister plenipotentiary to his Majesty the Emperor of the Romans, and to her Majesty the Empress Queen of Hungary and Bohemia; and on the part of the most serene Republic of Genoa, the Sieur Francis Marquis Doria, by virtue of their full powers, which they have communicated to each other, and copies whereof are added at the end of the present act, have agreed upon what follows.

That the most serene Republick of Genoa, desiring to contribute and concur to re-establish and settle the quiet of Europe, accedes, by virtue of the present act, to the said treaty and two separate articles, without any reserve or exception, in a firm confidence that whatsoever is promised therein to the said most serene Republic, shall be faithfully fulfilled; declaring, at the same time, and promising, that she will also perform, most faithfully, all the articles, clauses and conditions, which regard her.

In like manner his Britannick Majesty accepts the present accession of the most serene Republic of Genoa; and likewise promises to perform, without any reserve or exception, all the articles, clauses, and conditions, contained in the said treaty and the two separate articles inserted above.

The ratifications of the present act shall be exchanged, in this city of Aix la Chapelle, in the space of twenty-five days, to be computed from this day.

In testimony whereof, we the ambassadors extraordinary and minister plenipotentiary of his Britannick Majesty, and of the most serene Republic of Genoa, have signed the present act, and have caused the seal of our arms to be affixed thereto.

Done at Aix la Chapelle, the 28th of October, 1748.

(L.S.) *T. Robinson*  (L.S.) *Fr. M. Marquis D'Oria.*

The

## The Republic of Genoa's Full Power.

### The Doge, Governors, and Procurators of the Republic of Genoa.

CONSCIOUS of the experience, fidelity and zeal of our Patrician Francefco Maria D'Oria, we have chofen and deputed him, as our minifter plenipotentiary at the conferences of peace at Aquifgrano, otherwife Aix la Chapelle, or any other place where the faid conferences of peace may hereafter be held, or transferred to, and we have given and conferred upon him, as we do give and confer upon him, ample faculty and full power, with general and fpecial order, to treat there in our name, upon the affairs which regard us, and to agree to, conclude, ftipulate and fign, on our part, whatever he fhall apprehend to be moft fuitable to our interefts, and that, in the fame manner, as we ourfelves, were prefent, could do, although a more full and fpecial order than the prefent might be requifite, defiring, for this end, the minifters plenipotentiaries of all the courts concerned, which fhall be prefent at the faid conferences, to accept of, and acknowledge him, as our minifter plenipotentiary; promifing, on the faith and word of a Prince, to hold as confirmed and ratified, and to obferve all that fhall be concluded, accepted, ftipulated and figned by the fame, in virtue of the prefent full power; as alfo to difpatch our ratifications in due form, to be exchanged within the time which fhall be agreed upon.

In witnefs whereof, thefe prefents fhall be figned by our underwritten fecretary of ftate, with our ufual feal affixed thereto.

Given at our royal palace, this firft of March, 1748.

C. *Giufeppe Maria Sertorio,*
(L. S)  *Secretary of State.*

*A*

*A Treaty concluded and signed at* Madrid, *on the 5th of* October *N. S.* 1750, *between the Ministers Pelenipoten-tiaries of their* Britannick *and* Catholic *Majesties.*

WHEREAS by the 16th article of the treaty of Aix la Chapelle, it has been agreed between their Britannick and Catholic Majesties, that the treaty of the Assiento for the commerce of negroes, and the article of the annual ship, for the four years of non-enjoyment, should be confirmed to Great Britain, upon the same foot, and upon the conditions, as they ought to have been executed before the late war; and the respective ambassadors of their said Majesties having agreed, by a declaration signed between them on the 11 June, 1748, to regulate, at a proper time and place, by a negociation between ministers named on each side for that purpose, the equivalent which Spain should give in consideration of the non-enjoyment of the years of the said Assiento of negroes, and of the annual ship granted to Great Britain, by the 10th article of the preliminaries signed at Aix la Chapelle, on the 18 April, 1748.

Their Britannick and Catholic Majesties, in order to fulfil the said engagements of their respective ministers, and to strengthen and perfect more and more a solid and lasting harmony between the two crowns, have agreed to make the present particular treaty between themselves, without the intervention or participation of any third power; so that each of the contracting parties acquires by virtue of the cessions which that party makes, a right of compensation from the other reciprocally : and they have named their ministers plenipotentiaries for that purpose, viz. His Britannick Majesty, Benjamin Keene, Esq; his minister plenipotentiary to his Catholic Majesty; and his Catholic Majesty, Don Joseph de Carvajal and Lancaster, minister of state, and Dean of his Council of state; who, after having examined the points in question, have agreed on the following articles.

I. His Britannick Majesty yields to his Catholic Majesty his right to the enjoyment of the Assiento of negroes,

and

and the annual ſhip, during the four years ſtipulated by the 16th article of the treaty of Aix la Chapelle.

II. His Britannick Majeſty, in conſideration of a compenſation of one hundred thouſand pounds ſterling, which his Catholic Majeſty promiſes and engages to cauſe to be paid, either at Madrid or London, to the royal Aſſiento Company, within the term of three months at lateſt, to be reckoned from the day of the ſigning of this treaty, yields to his Catholic Majeſty, all that may be due to the ſaid Company for balance of accounts, or ariſing in any manner whatſoever from the ſaid Aſſiento; ſo that the ſaid compenſation ſhall be eſteemed and looked upon as a full and entire ſatisfaction on the part of his Catholic Majeſty, and ſhall extinguiſh from this preſent time, for the future and for ever, all right, pretenſion, or demand, which might be formed in conſequence of the ſaid Aſſiento, or annual ſhip, directly or indirectly, on the part of his Britannick Majeſty, or on that of the ſaid Company.

III. The Catholic King yields to his Britannick Majeſty all his pretenſions or demands in conſequence of the ſaid Aſſiento and annual ſhip, as well with regard to the articles already liquidated, as to thoſe which may be eaſy or difficult to liquidate; ſo that no mention can ever be made of them hereafter, on either ſide.

IV. His Catholic Majeſty conſents that the Britiſh ſubjects ſhall not be bound to pay higher, or other duties, or upon other evaluations for goods which they ſhall carry into, or out of the different ports of his Catholic Majeſty, than thoſe paid on the ſame goods in the time of Charles the Second, King of Spain, ſettled by the cedulas and ordonances of that King, or thoſe of his predeceſſors. And although the favour or allowance called Pie del Fardo be not founded upon any royal ordonance, nevertherleſs his Catholic Majeſty declares, wills and ordains, that it ſhall be obſerved now, and for the future, as an inviolable law; and all the abovementioned duties ſhall be exacted and levied, now and for the future, with the ſame advantages and favours to the ſaid ſubjects.

V. His Catholic Majeſty allows the ſaid ſubjects to take and gather ſalt in the iſland of Tortudos, without
any

any hindrance whatfoever, as they did in the time of the faid King Charles the Second.

VI. His Catholic Majefty confents, that the faid fubjects fhall not pay any where, higher or other duties than thofe which his Catholic Majefty's fubjects pay in the fame place.

VII. His Catholic Majefty grants, that the faid fubjects fhall enjoy all the rights, privileges, franchifes, exemptions and immunities whatfoever, which they enjoyed before the laft war, by virtue of cedulas or royal ordonances, and by the articles of the treaty of peace and commerce made at Madrid in 1667; and the faid fubjects fhall be treated in Spain, in the fame manner as the moft favoured nation, and confequently, no nation fhall pay lefs duties upon wool, and other merchandifes which they fhall bring into, or carry out of Spain by land, than the faid fubjects fhall pay upon the fame merchandifes, which they fhall bring in or carry out by fea. And all the rights, privileges, franchifes, exemptions and immunities, which fhall be granted or permitted to any nation whatever, fhall alfo be granted and permitted to the faid fubjects; and his Britannick Majefty confents, that the fame be granted and permitted to the fubjects of Spain in his Britannick Majefty's kingdoms.

VIII. His Cahtholic Majefty promifes to ufe all poffible endeavours on his part, to abolifh all innovations which may have been introduced into commerce, and to have them forborn for the future; his Britannick Majefty likewife promifes to ufe all poffible endeavours to abolifh all innovations, and to forbear them for the futrue.

IX. Their Britannick and Catholic Majefties confirm by the prefent treaty, the treaty of Aix la Chapelle, and all the other treaties, therein confirmed, in all their articles and claufes, excepting thofe which have been derogated from by the prefent treaty: as likewife the treaty of commerce concluded at Utrecht in 1713, thofe articles excepted, which are contray to the prefent treaty, which fhall be abolifhed and of no force, and namely, the three articles of the faid treaty of Utrcht, commonly called explanatory.

X. All

X. All the reciprocal differences, rights, demands, and pretensions, which may have subsisted between the two crowns of Great Britain and Spain, in which no other nation whatever has any part, interest, or right of intervention, being thus accommodated and extinguished by this particular treaty; the two said most serene Kings engage themselves mutually to the punctual execution of this treaty of reciprocal compensation, which shall be approved and ratified by their said Majesties, and the ratifications exchanged, in the term of six weeks, to be reckoned from the day of it signing, or sooner if it can be done.

In witness whereof, we the above-mentioned ministers plenipotentiaries, that is to say, Benjamin Keene, Efq; in the name of his Britannick Majesty, and Don Joseph de Caravajal and Lancaster, in the name of his Catholic Majesty, by virtue of our full powers, which we have mutually communicated to each other, have signed these presents, and have caused the seals of our arms to be put thereto. Done at Madrid the fifth of October, 1750, New Stile.

(L. S.) *B. Keene.*          (L. S.) *Joseph de Carvajal y Lancaster.*

END OF VOL. II.